CHINA AND POST-SOCIALIST DEVELOPMENT

Andrzej Bolesta

First published in Great Britain in 2015 by

Policy Press
University of Bristol
1-9 Old Park Hill
Clifton
Bristol
BS2 8BB
UK
UK
t: +44 (0)117 954 5940
pp-info@bristol.ac.uk
www.policypress.co.uk

North America office:
Policy Press
c/o The University of Chicago Press
1427 East 60th Street
Chicago, IL 60637, USA
t: +1 773 702 7700
f: +1 773-702-9756
sales@press.uchicago.edu
www.press.uchicago.edu

© Policy Press 2015

British Library Cataloguing in Publication Data
A catalogue record for this book is available from the British Library

Library of Congress Cataloging-in-Publication Data
A catalog record for this book has been requested

ISBN 978 1 44732 150 7 hardcover

The right of Andrzej Bolesta to be identified as author of this work has been asserted by him in accordance with the Copyright, Designs and Patents Act 1988.

All rights reserved: no part of this publication may be reproduced, stored in a retrieval system, or transmitted in any form or by any means, electronic, mechanical, photocopying, recording, or otherwise without the prior permission of Policy Press.

The statements and opinions contained within this publication are solely those of the author and not of the University of Bristol or Policy Press. The University of Bristol and Policy Press disclaim responsibility for any injury to persons or property resulting from any material published in this publication.

Policy Press works to counter discrimination on grounds of gender, race, disability, age and sexuality.

Cover design by Policy Press
Front cover image: istock
Printed and bound in Great Britain by CPI Group (UK) Ltd,
Croydon, CR0 4YY
Policy Press uses environmentally responsible print partners.

To Drussilla and Zachary
with all my love

Contents

List of tables and figures   vi

About the author   vii

Acknowledgements   viii

Introduction   1

One   The developmental state   7

Two   Post-socialist transformation in China   55

Three   The politics of development   129

Four   The policies of development   167

Five   China as a post-socialist developmental state   227

References   255

Index   289

List of tables and figures

Tables

2.1   Transition Indicators (1989–2012)   109
2.2   The change in the size of an economy at an annual   125
        GDP [gross domestic product] growth rate of 4%

Figures

2.1   GDP [gross domestic product] per capita (in constant   60
        1990 prices) in 1950 and 1990
2.2   GDP [gross domestic product] and HDI [Human   121
        Development Index] change in post-socialist economies
2.3   Average annual change in the HDI [Human Development   122
        Index] (2000–2012) (%)
2.4   2.4. Average annual GDP [gross domestic product] growth   122
        (1989–2012) (%)
2.5   HDI [Human Development Index] change among   124
        post-socialist and developmental states
2.6   The change in the size of national economies (1989–2008;   126
        1989 = 100%)
3.1   Four actors of the developmental state   146

About the author

Andrzej Bolesta was educated at the London School of Economics and Political Science, where he obtained his PhD in the Department of Government, and at the University of Oxford, where he received his Master's degree. For the last eight years he has lived in East Asia, most of this time in Beijing, China, where he was responsible for economic affairs at the Polish embassy. During his term Poland and China established a strategic partnership. Prior to this, he lectured at a university in Poland, was advisor on international affairs to the Speaker of the Parliament and a research assistant to one of the architects of Poland's post-socialist economic transformation. In 2006 he authored the first book on post-Mao China's economy in the Polish language. He currently works in Bangkok, Thailand, where, among other duties, he is involved in the economic transformation of Myanmar.

Acknowledgements

This book would not have been possible were it not for the support, advice and constructive criticism of many people with whom I have had the pleasure and honour to cooperate, and to whom I am very grateful. First and foremost is Dr Chun Lin from the London School of Economics and Political Science, a friend and a mentor, whose guidance and support enabled me to develop my research on China's development into a concrete shape and form. I cherish my friendship with Chun and feel privileged to have worked with her. I am also grateful to Professor Shaun Breslin (the University of Warwick) and Dr Tat Yan Kong (School of Oriental and African Studies, University of London), for their extensive comments and insightful suggestions.

My first trip to China took place shortly after the death of Deng Xiaoping. Soon after, I developed my interest in China's economy and development, working as a research assistant to one of the architects of Poland's post-socialist economic transformation, former Deputy Prime Minister and Minister of Finance Professor Grzegorz W. Kolodko, who encouraged me to delve deeper into this fascinating topic and to question commonly accepted 'truths', for which I am very grateful. While living in China, I had the great fortune to cooperate with Ambassador Krzysztof Szumski, who, as an outstanding diplomat with 40 years of experience, was able to add a new dimension to my research and created conditions for me to study China in greater detail.

I would like to thank Policy Press's editorial team, in particular, Laura Vickers and Emily Watt, and commend them on their courage in taking on board an unknown scholar from Central Europe. I am also grateful to the anonymous referees for their positive reviews and recommendations, which enriched the manuscript.

Last, but not least, I would like to thank my wife Drussilla, a person who has lived in China, who knows China and who understands China. Without her support, this book would literally not have come to fruition. I benefited immensely from her comments, suggestions and help. Dru has read every single word of this manuscript many times over. It is to her and to our son Zachary that I dedicate this book

Introduction

In the course of economic history, various civilisations have risen and fallen and the gravity of mankind's socio-economic development has shifted from one region to another. In the modern era, up until the 19th century, China was the largest economy in the world and Adam Smith would see it more appropriate to compare the Chinese economy with that of the whole of Europe, rather than separate European states. Maddison (2007) claimed that China owed its position to the intensive economic growth between the seventh and the 13th centuries, and that this was attributable to the development of an intensive and sophisticated agrarian production sector, to the creation of an internal market to trade goods, and to the well-organised and effective state[1] supported by a highly qualified state bureaucracy. At least until the end of the 15th century, China's civilisation was considered to be more advanced than that of Europe. Smith pointed out in 1776 that 'no other country has yet arrived at this degree of opulence [and that] China had probably long ago acquired that full complement of riches' (Smith, 2003 [1776], p 132).

Nevertheless, the overall progress of mankind in terms of socio-economic development in the first 18 centuries AD was relatively slow as compared with the subsequent time periods. It is estimated that the aggregated output of the world's economy between year 1 and 1000 did not increase at all, and between 1000 and 1800 increased by a meagre 50%, with an average annual economic growth of 0.05% (Kolodko, 2008, pp 68, 70).

The consequences of the Industrial Revolution of the late 18th and early 19th centuries, preceded by 300 years of pre-capitalist development that had commenced with the Renaissance epoch in Europe, allowed for a significant acceleration of socio-economic development and subsequently firmly established the representatives of the so-called Western world as the leaders of developmental advancements, first, the UK, then the US, Germany and other European countries. The Industrial Revolution marks perhaps the establishment of the first effective developmental model of the modern era. This model was characterised by capital-driven economic expansion. The

---

[1] The state, defined by Max Weber as a compulsory association claiming control over a territory and the people therein (cited in Evans, 1995, p 5), is considered here to be the structure of governance institutions (Wade, 2003, p 8). In keeping with Wade (2003), the term 'state' is often used interchangeably with the term 'government'.

capital was generated through an increase in production, enabled by technological advancements. At the same time, economic expansion was facilitated by military means. China seemed not to be affected by the Industrial Revolution and, as a consequence, the developmental rift between Europe and the 'Middle Kingdom' continued to increase. It is believed that the initial waves of Industrial Revolution failed to have an effect on China,[2] otherwise a relatively well-developed state with well-educated elites and efficient bureaucracy, because of its 300-year policy of isolationism, which limited the diffusion of foreign technologies, domestic incentives for modernisation and the effective exchange of ideas related to economic policies. The militarist model of capitalist development of Western Europe was soon to affect the political situation in China, which, as a result of several wars and domestic rebellions, became a semi-colonial state with 92 'treaty ports' with extraterritorial rights. For example, 19 foreign nationalities residing in the treaty ports were granted effective diplomatic immunity from Chinese legal jurisdiction (Maddison, 2007; see also Brinkley, 1904).

The beginning of the Industrial Revolution prompted a critique of mercantilism, until then broadly considered to be the world's main economic doctrine, which advocated state-controlled foreign trade monopolies as paramount for developmental advancements (Skousen, 2007). Adam Smith and then David Ricardo, among others, supported the idea of trade liberalisation leading towards international production specialisation and utilisation of comparative advantage (Haakonssen, 2006). However, their classical economy theory of 'natural liberty' met opposition among the representatives of less developed countries. For example, a German economist, Friedrich List, believed that Smith's ideas would bring benefits to more affluent countries and leave the less developed vulnerable. His perception was influenced by Alexander Hamilton's (2008) American School, developed by the President of the United States John Quincy Adams and Senator Henry Clay into the American system – an economic plan to support US domestic industrial development by providing the necessary physical and financial infrastructure, as well as by protecting the industrial sector from foreign competitors through tariff barriers. Hamilton, the first US Secretary of Treasury, believed that state interventions and protectionist measures are necessary for overall socio-economic development. As a result, List saw politics and economics as inseparable. He argued that:

---

[2] For this, see Lin (2012).

> economies need to be seen in their political context, if their relative successes and failures are to be understood.... It is only when a polity gains the status of a geographically substantial nation-state that it can become and remain a successful manufacturing and commercial entity. (Winch, 1998, p 302)

The model of capitalist development brought enormous wealth to the industrial elite, whereas the labour force employed in the newly established factories suffered the problems of low wages and difficult working conditions. Social marginalisation and exclusion, as well as widespread industrial exploitation, as opposed to the earlier agrarian exploitation related to the feudal system, became urgent issues, with the long-term potential capacity to politically destabilise many countries. This prompted considerations for a new economic model, based on Marxist critiques of capitalism, labelled as socialism or – due to the fact that the proposals for new systemic arrangements were presented in the document called *The Manifesto of the Communist Party* (Marx and Engels, 1969 [1848]) – communism. In its socio-economic form, the model advocated the abolition of private property and, therefore, elimination of the capitalist elite. It eventually evolved into advocating the abolishment of market mechanisms in economic affairs and the establishment of a state-command mechanism in which the decision on the quantity and assortment of production, goods allocation and price would be met by the state (see Schumpeter, 1942). This model had a significant impact on China's development trajectory, since the state ideology of Mao Zedong – the founder of the People's Republic of China (PRC) – drew significantly from Marxism. Without subsequent extensive acceleration of socio-economic development, the implementation of the new model nevertheless reversed the trend of economic decline, as a result of which, 'Chinese GDP [gross domestic product] per capita was lower in 1952 than in 1820 [and] China's share of world GDP fell from a third to one-twentieth' (Maddison, 2007, p 43).

However, the second half of the 19th century was also marked by the enforcement of Listian political economy into the systemic arrangements in continental Western Europe and thus by the creation of what can perhaps be seen as initial institutional fundamentals for what would later become a developmental state – a model believed to be largely responsible for the effective developmental catching up of some countries from the so-called group of late developers. This model denied the capitalist class the dominant role in development, entrusting the guiding of the process of socio-economic development to the state. Its origins can be traced from the institutional arrangements of Bismarck's Prussia and the Meiji restoration in Japan,[3] influenced by the ideas presented by List (1909 [1841]) in his study entitled *The National System of Political Economy* and by the 'American system' of the early 19th century. In this model, the state elite, supported by effective state bureaucracy, would guide the process of the industrialisation of national economies. It was consistent, to some extent, with the perception prevalent after the Great Depression until the late 1970s and motivated by Keynes' theory that the role of the state or the public sector is crucial in the developmental endeavour, especially among underdeveloped countries.

In the mid-20th century, Western countries, predominantly comprising Western Europe and North America, outstripped the rest of the world in terms of the level of development and continued to rely on what evolved from the model of capitalist development and the Prussian interventionist state. At the same time, Eastern Europe was coerced into adopting the state-command economic system. This left the so-called developing countries, many of which were emerging from colonialism, in desperate need of a developmental model to enable significantly better developmental dynamics in order to establish a sound trajectory of 'catching up'.

By the end of the 20th century, among the most successful late developers were those countries who became developmental states, that is, South Korea, Taiwan and Singapore, as well as Japan – considered a prime example of the developmental state model, despite a rather 'early' start to 'late development'.

However, this did not secure the developmental state model's position as a feasible developmental option for less developed countries worldwide. In fact, the political competition between the Western world and the communist-controlled Eastern bloc, especially between the superpowers of both structures, that is, the US and the Soviet Union, extensively affected the popularity of developmental models and subsequently the readiness to draw conclusions from certain developmentally effective systemic and policy solutions. Through a simple comparison of the medium-term effects of the two very different economic systems, that of the US and the Soviet Union, without in-depth historical considerations, one arrived at

---

[3] The Meiji restoration (1868–1912) was the process of significant changes in Japan's political, social and economic structures, which accelerated the country's industrialisation.

an oversimplified conclusion that the liberal model was an adequate solution to developmental shortcomings. With support and pressure from influential financial centres in Washington, it was agreed among many policymakers that the extensive retreat of the state from the economy would unleash market forces and human entrepreneurship and would translate into better developmental dynamics. Although economic neoliberalism – as the doctrine would come to be called – advocating extensive economic liberalisation and strict fiscal discipline, later proved not to be an effective developmental model, its rise to the position of an alleged global remedy for underdevelopment significantly affected the coinciding process of post-socialist transformation (PST) characterised by extensive systemic reformulation. The implementation of the provisions of the neoliberal economic model into state policies is often blamed for the economic decline that most of the post-socialist countries have experienced during the process of systemic reformulation. More peculiar is the case of China, which has been undergoing a similar institutional transformation from state-command economy to a market economy, but which has not experienced any economic contraction during the process. On the contrary, it has made significant developmental advancements.

During the period of post-socialist transformation, China has managed to avoid economic recession and has been growing rapidly at an almost two-digit speed for over 30 years, prompting a plethora of scholarly publications on its development and systemic reforms. This book is intended to contribute to the discussion on China's development trajectory. It does so by examining it in the context of the historical developmental state model and of the post-socialist transformation process, fusing those two intellectual streams. It is argued here that China's development trajectory during the process of post-socialist transformation has been determined by the provisions of the developmental state (DS) model.

China's certain degree of affinity to historical developmental states, such as Japan, Korea and Taiwan, comes to many scholars as hardly a surprise (see White, 1988; Baek, 2005; Gallagher, 2005; Breslin, 2007). Post-socialist China is believed to have adopted at least some DS solutions. However, it is often emphasised that only a handful of policy and institutional choices are consistent with DS solutions, as China is considerably different from the historical DS cases (see Howell, 1998, 2006). Against this perception, it will be argued here that Chinese state development policies, state ideological background and institutional solutions in terms of politics and economics draw extensively from DS experiences, despite the fact that the process is taking place in a different international environment (ie more advanced globalisation) and China's institutional experiences (ie the systemic transformation from socialism) are different from those of historical developmental states. Moreover, the argument that it is not surprising that China's development trajectory has been determined by DS experiences is, to some extent, misplaced. This perception seems to ignore other experiences of post-socialist transformations. If we see China's development trajectory in a broader context of the PST process, then we notice how unordinary China's behaviour has been. Most of the post-socialist countries have chosen different modes of political and economic transformation to facilitate development. Naturally, one may claim that China is unique in its size and its capacity and that its transformation preceded similar processes in Central and Eastern Europe and the former Soviet Union (CEEFSU). However, once all the Eastern bloc countries were in transition, China's mode of reforms changed, but never emulated the paths of CEEFSU states. Despite this, China's policy and institutional selections determined by the DS model are believed here to be the natural choice in the process of post-socialist transformation, that is, not merely preferred, but also more logical and obvious, even though it is rather a deviation from the standard behaviour of countries in systemic transition. Were it not for certain ideological pressure, it would be possible for other post-socialist countries to become types of developmental state in order to more effectively satisfy their post-socialist economic prerogative.

This is why this book goes further than the examination of China's post-socialist development trajectory in the context of the DS model and the PST process. It is argued here that due to the incorporation of DS solutions into the Chinese post-socialist development trajectory, China has become a genus of post-socialist developmental state (PSDS) model – PSDS being a viable, normative, post-socialist option.

CHAPTER ONE

The developmental state

The concept of the developmental state is widely believed to be the conceptual background of state policies and state institutional arrangements leading to the unprecedented developmental achievements among the so-called late developers of the Asian continent. Countries such as Japan, Korea and Taiwan became developed nations within a short period of time in the second half of the 20th century. Especially remarkable is the case of Korea, whose gross domestic product (GDP) per capita in the 1950s was comparable to some impoverished post-colonial states in sub-Saharan Africa. Nonetheless, the concept is often portrayed as only a historically justifiable phenomenon that cannot relate to contemporary conditions, mostly due to the accelerating pace of the process of globalisation, which, in effect, is believed to render the significance of state policies minimal.

Nevertheless, the 'relatively fresh' significant developmental achievements of Japan, Korea and Taiwan, broadly considered to have been developmental states, should make us wonder about the applicability of the developmental state model contemporarily, especially in view of their neighbour, China's, recent developmental achievements, as well as in view of the necessities of those countries whose recent efforts at systemic changes are aimed at the acceleration of socio-economic development. Such a group may well constitute post-socialist countries, as the increase in developmental dynamics seemed to be one of the main reasons behind the commencement of their transformation. Moreover, as it will be argued in this study, post-socialist states are a natural selection group for potentially developmental states due to various systemic and institutional legacies. First, however, one needs to discuss the features of the DS concept and its contemporary applicability. The world has changed since the peak hour of East Asian successes. Did this change lead to an effective demise of the model, or are we perhaps in desperate need to resurrect it and yet again draw some conclusions for contemporary circumstances?

The overview

The concept of the developmental state in scholarly literature seems to be examined from various angles; addressed through its historical and ideological background and necessary preconditions, as well as through social, political and economic features, state policies, external conditionality, and institutional arrangements. For example, Weiss (2000, p 23) distinguishes three main criteria for developmental states: their priorities to eventually close the technological gap between themselves and highly industrialised nations; their organisational arrangements with an insulated state bureaucracy and a pilot state agency in charge of development; and their institutional links with organised economic actors as the locus of policy input, negotiations and implementation. Stubbs (2009, pp 5–6) distinguishes three key ingredients of the developmental state: first, one that is 'essentially institutional', having 'a cohesive set of institutions with a relatively autonomous capacity to implement a planned strategy for capitalist economic growth'; second, relational aspects that emphasise the interaction among DS actors in political, economic and social dimensions as a 'seamless web of influences';[4] and, third, an 'ideational aspect with particular attention being paid to nationalism, (neo) mercantilism, economic transformation, rapid industrialisation, performance legitimacy or some amalgam of a number of these ideas'. For Howell (2006, p 275):

> the ideal-typical developmental state has the following key features: first it has a political and policy elite committed to economic growth and transformation, with a power, authority and legitimacy to promote a developmental agenda. Often motivated by strong nationalist sentiments, such elites strive to modernise their countries, raise economic living standards and bridge the developmental gap. Second, complementing such a development-focused elite is a competent, authoritative state administration, particularly in the economic sphere, with the technical and managerial capacity to guide and steer economic and social development.

Many of the DS analyses are country-specific – see, for example, Johnson (1982) in reference to Japan, Amsden (1989) in reference to Korea and Wade (1990) in reference to Taiwan – or comparative.[5] They are also often positioned within a broader theoretical discourse on various developmental trajectories. For example, Gereffi and Fonda

---

[4]   See Woo-Cumings (1999).
[5]   See Chapters Three and Four for more details.

(1992) examine the concept within the discussion on regional paths of development.

In order to illustrate the main components of the DS model, as portrayed in scholarly analyses and examinations, several points need to be addressed: first, the broad and narrow perception of developmental states; second, 'the relational aspects', that is, state–society relations and the concept of state–business alliance; third, the general DS policies; and, fourth, the main ideological background. The analysis is continued in the political and economic conditionality sections, with the comparative examination following in Chapters Three and Four.

The limitations

It is believed that, historically, the roots of the developmental state can be traced not only to Bismarck's Prussia and to Japan's Meiji restoration, but also to Hamilton's American School and the American system, and Listian political economy. Therefore, some scholars would like to see the definition of the developmental state being applied to a broad group of countries who possess a historically proven track of fast development, in addition to certain institutional arrangements and policies examined later. As a consequence, Woo-Cumings (ed., 1999) and colleagues analyse the applicability of the concept to European countries such as Austria and Finland. Furthermore, France and Germany, as well as Scandinavian countries, are sometimes portrayed as genera of the developmental state. Schneider (1999) describes the *desarrollista* states of Mexico and Brazil as being examples of certain types of developmental states. In Africa, Botswana was in the past sometimes seen as the African example of the DS model. In Asia, a number of countries are analysed in the context of the developmental state, namely, Japan, Korea, Taiwan, Singapore and Malaysia, as well as, on occasions, Thailand, Indonesia and the Philippines. This poses the question as to the geographical limits of the applicability of the developmental state concept.

The origins of the concept are believed to be connected with Chalmers Johnson's institutional analysis of Japan's industrialisation in the book entitled *MITI and the Japanese Miracle: The Growth of Industrial Policy, 1925–1975* (Johnson, 1982). In his work, Johnson shows the existence of a certain correlation between institutional arrangements and developmental successes. Japan, a predominantly rural and relatively poor country, became an affluent, developed nation in a shorter period of time than Western European and North American states. Johnson's analysis was followed by the examination of former developing nations – Korea and Taiwan (see Cumings, 1984; Amsden, 1989; Wade, 1990). Consequently, the question of a DS transformation concerns 'relatively poorer' countries, also called late developers, and their ability to accelerate socio-economic development to achieve an effective catching-up trajectory. This leads us to a somewhat geographically narrower applicability of the developmental state, excluding Western European and North American countries.

A relatively extensive share of the development-related literature concerned with the concept of the developmental state deals with comparisons between two regions – Latin America and East Asia – since Latin America, as pointed by Gereffi and Fonda (1992) and others, is often considered to be the first 'third world' region to industrialise. Gereffi and Fonda (1992) argue that developmental experiences of Latin America, such as bureaucratic-authoritarian approaches and dependency theory, have been used by experts on East Asia to frame the discussion on regional developmental changes (see also Cumings, 1984). Haggard (1990), focusing on their respective developmental strategies, examines, among others, society-related conditions, including the legacy of the countryside, the position of the labour force and the interest of capital, paying special attention to Mexico and Brazil. He underlines that the general DS development policies were, in their regional variation, very much an element of the Latin American developmental experience. For instance, import-substitution industrialisation was a characteristic feature of development in Mexico and Brazil, which eventually resulted in the expansion of manufactured export, although not to the extent observed in East Asia. On a country-to-country comparative basis, Cummings (1984) considers Mexico the best analogy to Taiwan, and Argentina to Korea, in terms of political arrangements (authoritarian system, strength of the state) and industrialisation.

Unsurprisingly, the discussion eventually focuses mostly on the East Asian region. Akamatsu (1962), in his wild-geese-flying pattern, employs Western European and Asian states to illustrate the development of 'advanced and less advanced countries'. Cumings (1984) and Bernard and Ravenhill (1995) would later use the pattern to explain the interdependencies within the East Asian region. This, however, does not seem to solve the issue of the geographical limitation entirely, as Weiss (2000, p 23) complains that 'the term developmental state is [so] loosely applied that it has become virtually synonymous with the state in East Asia'. Indeed, some DS analyses venture outside of the Northeast Asia realm, as does, for example, Hayashi's (2010). He sees some of the Southeast Asian (SEA) countries as developmental states, which for

Stubbs (2009), seems to create an important area of disagreement in terms of categorisation.

The DS model is often perceived as being limited to the Northeast Asian late-developer group of countries and Singapore, which, in addition to having achieved impressive long-term developmental dynamics to allow for successfully catching up with the developed world, share, to some extent, similar cultural values. The scholarly literature sometimes focuses on the 'Asian Three', that is, Japan, Korea and Taiwan, and deals with their interdependencies (see, among many others, Cumings, 1984; Kohli, 1994; Bernard and Ravenhill, 1995). Naturally, there are unavoidable differences among the successful Northeast Asian developmental states in terms of their state policies and institutional arrangements. For example, Jeon (1995) divides the Northeast Asian (plus Singaporean) DS pattern of economic growth into three categories: South Korea's 'growth-obsessed'; Singapore's 'growth-with-stability'; and Taiwan's 'equity-and-stability-based growth'. Moreover, as a first developmental state, Japan is usually seen as an unordinary and peculiar example of the DS model.

The developmental achievements of developmental states are usually time-framed within the course of the 20th century, as opposed to so-called Western countries, whose roots of developmental achievements can be traced as far back as the great geographical discoveries of the 15th century, or at least to the Industrial Revolution and its aftermaths. More accurately, the period between the 1950s and 1980s is considered the fast growth time of developmental states.

However, the narrow–broad discourse also applies to the time frame in which states cease (or not) to be developmental states, due: first, to their reorganisation of the DS-like institutional environment and termination of the DS-related policies; second, to their de-acceleration of developmental dynamics or, in extreme cases, their developmental regress (as was the case of Botswana in the 1990s[6]); and, third, through achieving a developmental level comparable with Western nations (as was the case of Japan). Those three conditions refer to endogenous factors for the demise of developmental states, as opposed to possible exogenous factors examined later in this chapter and usually more extensively featured in the scholarly literature. They relate to the changing external conditionality of the DS functioning.

It can be plausibly argued that the first endogenous condition effectively terminates the existence of a developmental state as such,

---

[6]   Between 1990 and 2004, Botswana's Human Development Index (HDI) fell by 0.11 points.

and Wade (2000) claims that it was, indeed, the case of Korea prior to the 1997 Asian financial crisis. The second condition seems also likely to do so. The third, however, is indeed an issue to be resolved in terms of whether a developmental state remains a developmental state after it reaches the developmental level of developed nations. This seems especially important in the comparative analysis of China with historically successful DS cases such as Japan and Korea, as it defines the time limits of the examination. The main purpose of DS policies and institutional arrangements is believed to be the effective catching up with the highly developed nations in terms of standards of living and technological advancements. Weiss (2000) describes it as the 'catch-up thesis'. In other words, the DS is often portrayed as the means to become a developed country. Once a state becomes a developed country, it can be perceived as no longer being a DS case. However, Weiss (2000) believes that the purpose of the developmental state falls beyond this description. What she describes as a 'transformative project aimed at maximising national goals' is a long-term DS-style policy tailored to create a transformative state capable of continuously upgrading its industrial economy to allow a gradual increase in wealth. Weiss (2000, p 29) thus believes that 'catching-up does not bring automatic retirement for the developmental state', as there is a new task of 'keeping up'. She ushers in a compromise by reconceptualising the term as 'the transformative state'. Moreover, Stubbs (2009, p 12) claims that the DS has never been entirely dismantled in the East Asian countries from the time when they became developed nations, despite the institutional changes worldwide, as it became deeply embedded in formal institutions and informal governmental practices. It proved durable, as it became central to the East Asian political economy by bringing prosperity and stability to the region (Stubbs, 2009).

Nevertheless, although some DS institutional features continue to be a part of the systemic arrangements after a developmental state becomes a developed country, it can be argued that the core activity of the developmental state is related to the period in which the country is pursuing the goal of becoming a developed nation. Lee and Mathews (2010) argue that the institutional arrangements need to be transformed once 'imitation' becomes largely irrelevant in the process of elevating the economy's level of sophistication and needs to be replaced by 'innovation', which happens when a state reaches a technological frontier associated with a high level of development. If we disregard Weiss's (2000) concept of a 'transformative state' and accept that the purpose of the developmental state is a successful catching up, then the completion of this process should imply a termination of the developmental state. On the other hand, this DS purpose seems only implicitly indicated in the literature, which is dominated by the perception of the developmental state as an overall state philosophy without limits defined by the extent of developmental achievements. Additionally, a developmental level indicating the completion of a successful catching-up process seems, to some extent, arbitrary. Without fully resolving the issue of the alleged time frame of the existence of the developmental state, for comparative purposes, the term 'developmental state' will refer to the 'DS core activity' period of the historically proven successful DS cases, during which the three sets of endogenous conditions described earlier did not occur extensively, that is, there was no broad departure from the DS institutional environment and policies, the pace of development continued to be relatively high, and the states in question would retain a status of not being as developed as so-called Western countries. These somewhat elusive limitations are necessary for the comparative examination of China's contemporary development trajectory, which possesses similar features to those characteristic of the states in 'DS core activity' periods, namely, underdevelopment, high growth and, as it will be argued, limited economic liberalisation, with the state at the centre of the process of socio-economic development.

The relational aspects

'Developmental state is a shorthand for the seamless web of political, bureaucratic, and moneyed influences that structures economic life in capitalist Northeast Asia' (Woo-Cumings, 1999, p 1). Therefore, one of the main elements characterising the concept of the developmental state is what Stubbs (2009) calls 'relational aspects'. They are defined by the interrelation of effectively four actors of the developmental state; the state political elite; the state bureaucracy; the society; and business (as analysed in reference to particular examples in Chapter Three).

In his analysis on states and industrial transformation, Evans (1995) distinguished two ideal types characterising state structure and state–society relations, namely, predatory states and developmental states: 'Predatory states extract at the expense of society, undercutting development even in the narrow sense of capital accumulation' (Evans, 1995, p 12). Pareto (1966, p 114) underlines that they are characterised by the process of 'the appropriation of the goods of others by legal or illegal means'. Nozick (1974, p 2, cited in Leftwich, 2000, p 101) states that it is the political elite's 'degree of control over coercive, economic and political resources [that] determines the state predatory capacity'. Mobutu's Zaire is often seen as a prime example of a predatory state.

Zimbabwe under the Mugabe regime seems to be one of the most distinctive recent cases:

> There are clear structural differences between predatory and developmental states. Predatory states lack the ability to prevent individual incumbents from pursuing their own goals. Personal ties are the only source of cohesion; and individual maximization takes precedence over the pursuit of collective goals. Ties to society are ties to individual incumbents, not connections between constituencies and the state as an organisation. (Evans, 1995, p 12)

Consequently, there seem to be two opposite patterns of interrelation between the state and society, as reflected in the two models. In predatory states, the ruling elite thrive on the dwindling resources of society, whereas in developmental states, those resources are multiplied partly by cohabitation and cooperation between the state and society for the benefit of both. This is what seems to initially constitute a concept of 'embedded autonomy'. According to Evans (1995), developmental states possess such 'embedded autonomy', an autonomy of the state administration that allows it to impartially fulfil its duties, as:

> the elites and state institutions ... [are] able to achieve relative independence (or insulation) from the demanding clamour of special interests (whether class, regional or sectoral, where they exist) and that [they] can and [do] override these interests in the putative national interest. (Nordlinger, 1987, cited in Leftwich, 2000, p 161)

At the same time, embedded autonomy is 'embedded in a concrete set of social ties that binds the state to society and provides institutionalised channels for the continual negotiation and renegotiation of goals and policies' (Evans, 1995, p 12). This conceptual system seems to provide the autonomy necessary to rule the state effectively (which allows for composing and implementing unbiased long-term development policies), as well as to maintain the dialogue between the state and society, as the people are believed to participate in policy formulation through established channels that connect the state and society. These channels are necessary to form coalitions (see Waldner, 1999; Doner et al, 2005) between the state and various social groups, including entrepreneurs, in order to minimise opposition to the formulated developmental trajectories. Waldner (1999) and Doner et al (2005) present somehow conflicting views as to the coalitions in developmental states. Waldner (1999, pp 137–8) gives the examples of the Taiwanese and the Korean DS as characterised by conservative or narrow coalitions, as opposed to cross-class coalitions, which support collaboration between the state and large businesses and exclude significant sectors of the population to minimise so-called side payments (understood as concessions to certain social groups in order to gain their support for the overall development trajectory) extensively present in broad coalitions. In contrast to Waldner (1999), Doner et al (2005) claim that broad coalitions contributed to the creation of developmental institutions, as the side payments, necessary in the conditions of broad coalitions and unaffordable in the conditions of scarce resources and security threats (both the scarcity of resources and security threats characterised the economic and political environment of historical DS cases), would not be possible without the continuous 'upgrading' of the economic structure. According to Doner et al (2005), broad coalitions produce stronger institutions.

Leftwich (2000, p 160) seems to offer, to some extent, a different view from that of Evans (1995) on the existence of the interaction between the state and society, as he sees several elements that define a developmental state, namely: a determined developmental elite; relative autonomy of the developmental state; a powerful, competent and insulated economic bureaucracy; a weak and subordinate civil society; the capacity for effective management of private economic interests; and an uneasy mix of repression, poor human rights (especially in the non-democratic developmental states), legitimacy and performance. Leftwich suggests the existence of a certain imbalance. On one hand, there is the powerful state with its powerful bureaucracy, powerful to the extent that it can manage private economic interests effectively. On the other hand, there is a weak society, which, in reality, does not have any effective influence on the ruling elite as it is subordinate to the latter. Stubbs (2009, p 6) supports the idea of an unbalanced relationship between the state and society being critical for the DS, where a 'weak society is unable to offer any concerted resistance to the rise of a relatively strong state'. Amsden (1989) validates, to some extent, Leftwich's opinion on the imbalance by providing an example in the form of the Korean case. She believes that the strength of the Korean state or its consolidation of power was possible to achieve partly due to 'the weaknesses of social classes', as 'workers were a small percentage of the population, capitalists were dependent on state largesse, the aristocracy was dissolved by land reform, and the peasantry was atomised into smallholders' (Amsden, 1989, p 52).

The political weakening of agricultural interests was conducted by the implementation of land reforms (see Cumings, 1984; Haggard, 1990). It usually involved the dismantling of the influential landlord class and the fragmentation of agrarian power centres. Haggard (1990, p 36) points out that rural changes were aimed at achieving two objectives: to eliminate rural elites as potential opposition towards state preference for industry and thus the country's industrialisation; and to gain rural support for state policies by empowering the so far less privileged elements of the rural classes. He concludes that although there might not be a direct link between eliminating rural elites and the ability to industrialise, their absence gave the DS governments more freedom to manoeuvre.

As far as the DS working class is concerned, Cumings (1984, p 27) points out that 'labour was excluded [from participating in the political process of policymaking] in the 1950s and remained excluded in the 1960s' in Korea and in Taiwan. Haggard (1990) underlines that all newly industrialised countries (NICs) were characterised by the political weakness of the industrial working class due to the inherent lack of empowerment (eg Taiwan) or repression (eg Korea). He points out that the DS governments would ensure that labour forces did not possess an extensive influence on policymaking. However, at the same time, they would implement policies that would enable them to gain natural support from the working class, such as the development of import-substitution production, which would generate additional employment. The control of labour would have its political reasons – the proximity of communist states, as discussed in the section on political conditionality, and therefore a somewhat increased possibility of leftist political movement outbursts within the labour force – and economic reasons – keeping wages low, thus increasing the international competitiveness of a domestic production base.

It is important to reiterate the state's dual attitude towards the working and rural classes. Waldner (1999), in his country-specific analyses of Korea and Taiwan, reminds us that the DS rural and labour classes were repressed (a lack of political power to advance their postulates), but, at the same time, empowered (transfer of land, import-substitution production). The DS governments' perception was that, on one hand, the rural and working classes needed to be controlled, but, on the other, it was important to gain their support for the developmental endeavour.

Wade (1990), White (1988) and Robinson and White (eds, 1998) and colleagues, in their respective analyses, pay more attention to the interconnectedness of state and domestic business as the main points defining the developmental state, often described as a state–business alliance. Wade (2003) focuses on the role of the state as the power centre capable of nurturing development via certain policy incentives, realised through the 'government big followership'. The 'big followership', as opposed to 'small followership', describes a situation in which business is ready to realise certain projects only with state assistance, as they would otherwise not be profitable or would be highly risky. Indeed, as Amsden (1989, p 112) states, the government also becomes the entrepreneur by '[usurping] the domain of the traditional private entrepreneur by making milestone decisions about what, when, and how much to produce'. In this way, it creates institutional arrangements close to what Hall and Soskice (2001, p 8) call a coordinated market economy, where 'firms depend more heavily on non-market relationships to coordinate their endeavours with other actors':

> They are market economies in the sense that initiative rests mainly with the enterprise, profit remains the enterprise's main motive, and enterprises which do not make profits will in most cases go out of business. In general, but with many important exceptions, the state tries to get things done by influencing the market, by shifting the composition of what is profitable [by 'getting prices wrong'[7]], rather than by direct regulation or direct production. (White and Wade, 1988, pp 5–6)

According to Doner et al (2005), this state–business relation is not clientelist, as is usually the case in many developing countries. This government–business cooperation takes place on functional industry-based criteria and the transparent environment according to consistent rules and norms.

From an economic perspective, the state–business alliance is a crucial element of the developmental state, 'in which expert and coherent bureaucratic agencies [meaning a competent state] collaborate with organised private sectors [meaning business] to spur national economic transformation' (Doner et al, 2005, p 328), and in which the advantages of the state sector and the business sector are combined for the benefit of the developmental endeavour. The state secures an overall development plan, which is intended to provide improvements for the entire society, whereas the business sector realises the plan, making it in some respects rational, via the effective mechanism of product manufacturing, as well as effective organisational management of the development-related

[7] See Amsden (1989).

projects. Haggard (2004), however, warns that there is no single model of business–government relations in the East Asian region. This is due to the varied extent of business opportunities created by political institutions and the different strengths of national businesses.

The DS state–business alliance is often blamed for extensive corruption, which is believed to be in a way incorporated into the institutional arrangements of the developmental state. Scholars are divided as to the extent and influence of corruption as an inevitable element of DS institutionalisation: 'Corruption is breaking legal and organisational rules to use public goods or power vested in one's public office for private ends.... It is an exchange of power for personal benefits' (Kwong, 1997, p ix). It is one of the manifestations of institution failure (Guo and Hu, 2004). Undoubtedly:

> the developmental states have … not been immune from [corruption]. In rapidly growing economies, sudden wealth (and tidal flows of aid or investment) can generate huge temptations, especially so where … the role of the state in economic life is intense. (Leftwich, 2000, p 161)

However, Bramall (2009a, p 20) suggests that a certain type of corruption may have a positive influence on development.[8]

The development policies and ideology

In an institutional environment where the state intervenes in the market to the extent that it is believed to significantly influence the economic environment, as examined later, state policies are of paramount importance as far as socio-economic development is concerned. The scholarly literature examines in detail the policies present in DS historical cases and responsible for developmental advancements.

The developmental state is often defined as a theory of state-led industrialisation (Hayashi, 2010). Indeed, the notion that dominates the economic aspects of the developmental state is the process of industrialisation. For example, Evans (1995, p 12) states that the embeddedness in the concept of embedded autonomy is believed to provide 'the underlying structural basis for successful state involvement in industrial transformation' and that 'developmental states not only have presided over industrial transformation, but can be plausibly argued to have played a role in making it happen'. Woo-Cumings (1999, p

---

[8]   The issue of corruption is examined in Chapter Three.

1) describes the developmental state as the explanation for East Asian industrialisation. Johnson (1982), in his prominent analysis of Japan, focuses on industrialisation. Industrial policy, examined in Chapter Four, is thus an important element of the DS environment.

This industrialisation starts with import-substitution industrialisation (ISI), where a state gradually replaces imported goods with domestically manufactured products. According to Haggard (1990, p 26):

> ISI may occur 'naturally' as the result of balance-of-payments problems, supply interruptions associated with wars or growth of the domestic market. ISI is advanced, however, by policies to manage balance-of-payments crises, particularly trade and exchange controls, and by explicit industrial policies designed to raise the rate of return to manufacturing.

Haggard (1990, pp 25–6) distinguishes three phases of ISI: 'In the first stage, the state earnings come from primary-product exports and foreign borrowing finance the imports of selected producer goods. These imports provide the foundation for local manufacturing'. In its second stage, the dependency on raw material and food exports, as well as on foreign borrowing, is maintained, 'since investment in new industrial capacity increases the demand for imported capital and intermediate goods' (Haggard, 1990, p 26). The third phase is characterised by the supplementing of import substitution with the expansion of manufactured exports. Thus, ISI gradually moves towards export-oriented industrialisation (EOI) (Jeon, 1995; Stubbs, 2009). EOI is historically believed to be the core state policy among developmental states, as their economic growth and developmental advancements were export-driven and would be difficult to achieve without the export-oriented policies.[9] The EOI would create a structural relation of a developmental state with the world economy (Haggard, 1990) in which the world economy would become the market for national production excessive to domestic consumption capacities. As compared to ISI, the EOI policy would be characterised by greater support for export and some trade liberalisation. It would be accompanied by a number of arrangements within the state trade and financial system policies related to the exchange rate and credit availability. Some scholars see in ISI and EOI the main difference between the Latin

---

[9] Japan is a peculiar DS case here, as export orientation was delayed compared to the institutionalisation of other DS features.

American and East Asian industrialisations. Another important DS policy aspect concerns industrial upgrading, that is, a gradual and continuous change of the assortment of industrial production towards higher sophistication and technological advancement. According to Bernard and Ravenhill (1995), industrial upgrading was the key issue for East Asian developmental states. It would be the result of state support for selected industrial sectors.

The process of industrialisation is believed to have taken place in the conditions of a specific nationalist state. Woo-Cumings (1999), Leftwich (2000) and Johnson (1982, 1999) are all convinced that a developmental state is also a nationalist state, as Johnson (1982, p 24) claimed that 'the very idea of the developmental state originated in the situational nationalism of the late industrialisers'. This perception does not seem to derive exclusively from the fact that East Asian societies seem more homogeneous and less culturally diverse as compared with certain Western nations, but rather from the conditionality of the developmental state. A developmental state requires a certain level of societal mobilisation made possible by adherence to common values and determined by common goals, as exemplified in a somewhat elusive contract between the ruling elite, business elite and society. By analysing East Asian nationalism and its role in the DS concept, one can plausibly argue that what matters is economic nationalism as the main philosophy behind development-related actions.

Economic nationalism is by no means a new phenomenon. Friedrich List is considered to be the founding father of economic nationalism. A fierce critic of Adam Smith, he argued for the extensive role of states in shaping international economic relations and guiding national developmental progress. Levi-Faur (1997, p 360) states that:

> national economic thought ... is best characterised by following three assertions: a nation's citizenry largely shares (or should share) a common economic fate; the state has a crucial positive role in guiding the national economy to better performance; and the imperatives of nationalism should guide the state's economic policies.

He continues by saying that:

> nations matter ... in the shaping of economic policies [and] that national imperatives should direct the course of a nation's economic policy not only in regard to national

security issues but also in regard to the welfare of the nation's citizens. (Levi-Faur, 1997, p 370)

He sees economic nationalism as one of three principal schools of political economy – in addition to economic liberalism and economic socialism. Cohen (1991) distinguishes benign and malign forms of nationalism. In the latter, the government 'seeks national goals relentlessly', whereas in the former, it 'is prepared to compromise national policy priorities where necessary to accommodate the interests of others' (Cohen, 1991, p 47). Using List's arguments, Reich (1991) and Levi-Faur (1997) advocate the positive or benign form of economic nationalism, calling it 'the benevolent version'.

All great economic powers used economic nationalism to advance the realisation of their own targets. This was the case for 19th-century Britain as much as for 20th-century US. In fact, the apparent 'consensus around benign economic nationalism led American society to a prosperity never experienced before in the history of humankind' by 'nourishing American corporations and American products' (Levi-Faur, 1997, pp 368, 365). Consequently, economic nationalism does not always need to be in opposition to economic liberalism, though most of the time it is believed to be.

Akamatsu (1962) saw economic nationalism as an indispensable feature of the emerging East Asian capitalist economies. He believed that what gave birth to the economic nationalism in the region was 'a conflicting relationship between imported consumer goods and native-produced goods' (Akamatsu, 1962, p 8). As a result, the governments would raise import tariffs or directly limit importation. He saw economic nationalism in less developed countries as an effect of the international economic environment shaped by colonialism. He considered it a defence mechanism in the developing economies' conflict with advanced countries in the process of homogenisation of industries of both groups of states. Naturally, this process would be particularly visible in East Asia. Therefore, economic nationalism would become an important, if not the leading, ideology behind state economic policies in the region. However, especially in the East Asian context:

> rather than [being] a coherent and systematic body of economic and political theory, economic nationalism [would] refer to certain measures of public policy and administration in such areas as trade and commerce, investment, finance and welfare that have historically been

seen and characterised as nationalistic. (Cai, 2010b, p 11; see also Chapter Three)

The political conditionality

There are certain controversies concerning the concept of the developmental state, as presented in the scholarly literature. One can address them by establishing certain political and economic conditionalities of the DS model. The first controversy concerns the question as to whether a developmental state can be both democratic and undemocratic, and how it can be applied in the two different systemic arrangements. The second issue surfaces when we take into account Johnson's (1999, p 32) statement that 'one of the main purposes in introducing the idea of the capitalist developmental state ... was to go beyond the contrast between the American and Soviet economies', hence, beyond state command and liberal capitalism. This poses a question centring on the in-between options of economic systems, and where the developmental state should be situated on the map, as far as the genus of economic system is concerned. The political conditionality of the DS model goes beyond the issue of its applicability to various geneses of political regimes. It concerns the general perception of the state positioning. Therefore, the following analysis commences with the discussion on political systems, then continues with the institutional arrangements and the concept of the strong state, and finally addresses the external political conditionality.

Although there does not seem to be a direct link between the concept of the developmental state and the genus of political system, the possibility of such a correlation should not be dismissed. As far as the interdependencies between the type of political system and the dynamics of socio-economic development are concerned, there are three basic theories: first, there is no correlation between authoritarianism/democracy and development; second, authoritarianism supports development more effectively than democracy and the latter may inhibit the pace of developmental advancements; and, third, democracy and development are mutually reinforcing. Robinson and White (1998) underline that authoritarianism was seen as a favourable system for accelerating socio-economic development throughout the 1960s, 1970s and until the early 1980s, based on the assumption that the process required a strong state, and a democratic state in poor societies lacked this strength. Indeed, Hayashi (2010, p 58) claims that, 'at least historically, authoritarianism [seemed] to be a shorter route to development', partially because of democracy's inability to restrain the labour class. Przeworski and Limongi (1993) point out that authoritarianism's developmental superiority would also be argued from the economic policy perspective. Democracy would undermine investment as it would 'generate an explosion of demands for current consumption' (Przeworski and Limongi, 1993, p 54), and thus inhibit capital accumulation; however, '[economic] growth requires capital accumulation, which in turn demands that resources be diverted from consumption to investment' (Haggard, 2004, p 58). From the mid-1980s, democracy and socio-economic development have often been viewed as complementary. The argument has been that:

> greater mass participation and popular pressure, and increased political representation by women and other disadvantaged groups, can help to make democratic regimes more sensitive to issues of poverty, social welfare, and forms of discrimination based on gender, ethnicity, and the like and impel them to take appropriate remedial action through policy commitments. (Robinson and White, 1998, p 5)

Democratisation is seen 'as opening spaces for socio-economically positive forms of popular mobilization' (White, 1998, p 21). This may partly translate into Evans's 'embedded autonomy', in which popular opinions are taken into consideration by ruling elites. In fact, Evans's requirement for embedded autonomy could be seen as a suggestion, not, however, as a requirement, for a fully functional democracy in developmental states. On the other hand, the 'old perception', dubbed by White (1998) as *the pessimistic view*, still prevails to some extent, and is based on the belief of a certain incompatibility between democracy and development, as the former – to quote Leftwich (2000, p 174) – is a conservative system of power, whereas the latter is a rather radical and turbulent process.

In the literature, there are examples of both democratic developmental states and authoritarian developmental states. Naturally, neither democracy nor authoritarianism guarantees extensive developmental achievements. The authoritarian developmental states, however, seem to be a given and little effort is made in terms of questioning their existence.[10] Perhaps the indisputable emergence of authoritarian developmental states such as Korea and Taiwan, as well as developmental

---

[10] It seems all the more odd that the prime example of the developmental state, Japan, is a liberal democracy and not an authoritarian state. The case of Japan is discussed later.

failures of democratic India, prompted an ideologically motivated quest to prove that a democratic environment in developing countries does not need to inhibit developmental efforts. If we apply the broad perception as to which countries are the genera of the DS model, then democratic developmental states are considered to be or to have been Botswana, Malaysia, Mauritius (Robinson and White, 1998) and Japan. In particular, Amartya Sen (1997, 1999) is keen to advocate the positive developmental effects of democracy, based on the cases of Botswana and the Indian state of Kerala. White (1988, 1998) and Leftwich (2000) remain extremely sceptical about the possibility of the emergence of additional democratic developmental states. White (1998, p 42) sees several constraints: historical (historically, all the 'old' developmental states were authoritarian and the developmental breakthrough preceded democratisation), contextual (designing developmentally effective democratic institutions may be utopian because of the political and economic constraints, both domestic and international) and systemic (democracy is ill-equipped to generate the broader form of public interest that is necessary to provide basic collective goods, because it is characterised by regularised conflict between political forces and policy outcomes are the result of competing pressures). Leftwich (2000) supports this view by underlining that a lack of a large number of democratic developmental states is a result of the very features characterising the above-mentioned concept. Moreover, in democracies, the necessary developmental autonomy of the state seems greatly reduced. Again, on the economic policy level, this autonomy is needed to counteract various distributionist pressures. Haggard (1990) believes that authoritarianism can ensure this; however, he is far from assuming that it is exclusively possible in authoritarian conditions (Haggard and Moon, 1986). Consequently, White (1998, p 42) attributes the existence of democratic developmental states to the fact that they are 'authoritarian forms of democratic regimes'.

To further elaborate on the issue of political regimes in developmental states, one needs to refer to the regional context, taking into consideration the cradle of the modern developmental state, namely, East Asia. It is true that a developmental state existed in authoritarian Korea and Taiwan, as well as in reputedly democratic Japan. In fact, Japan was the first East Asian state to be considered a developmental state, one perhaps that bridges the 'old historical' European and the 'modern historical' Asian concepts of the developmental state. One should take into consideration that the fundamentals of the developmental state in Japan can be traced back to the Meiji era, an undemocratic period of time in Japanese history, as well as the fact that, until very recently, the country was the prime example of what Leftwich (2000, p 177) calls a dominant-party developmental democratic state, where development continuity is secured by a lack of political contestation of the ruling elite. Moreover, historically, the DS model was facilitated by Japan's bureaucratic structure, which was believed to manage the country's affairs, with democratically elected politicians having limited influence in the running of the state. As Johnson (1982, cited in Woo-Cumings, 1999, p 14) puts it:

> who governs Japan is Japan's elite state bureaucracy. It is recruited from the top ranks of the best law schools in the country; appointment is made on the basis of legally binding national examinations – the prime minister can appoint only about twenty ministers and agency chiefs – and is unaffected by election results.

This is why Camilleri (2000, p 431) sees Japan as 'a hybrid political system given to recurring oscillations between authoritarian and democratic impulses'.

Consequently, it seems justifiable to claim that a developmental state might be difficult to sustain in a fully democratic system in which people enjoy extensive rights. Nevertheless, as historical examples prove, it is not entirely impossible once the condition of a lack of political contestation is met. Unfortunately, as it seems, in order to follow a strict development path, one needs to limit society's ability to counteract the state's efforts, in favour of particular goals dependent on one's affinity to a certain social group. In the macro-perspective, societies, democratic or not, are mostly interested in increasing their own wealth in a relatively short period of time:

> The developmental state does enable developmental advancements. However, the process of improvements is by no means linear and steady and would probably involve interim recession and undoubtedly geographical and social differentiations in gains. (Bolesta, 2007, pp 107–8)

It requires a set of policies motivated by an overall long-term target and not individualistic micro-goals. In democracies, however, 'political-self-interest, that of both politicians and their parties [not necessarily complicit with the overall developmental objective], is a dominant motivation behind the choice of institutional designs. And these politicians are not just self-interested thinkers but also short-term thinkers' (Lijphart and Waisman, 1996, p 244, cited in White, 1998, p 43).

Johnson, however, stresses the significant differences between traditionally authoritarian states and authoritarian or limited-democracy-type developmental states by drawing from the concept of legitimacy of power. He stresses that:

> the source of authority in the developmental state is not one of Weber's 'holy trinity' of traditional, rational-legal, charismatic sources of authority. It is rather, revolutionary authority; the authority of a people committed to the transformation of the social, political or economic order. Legitimisation occurs from the state achievements, not from the way it came to power. (Johnson, 1999, p 53)

Furthermore, 'In the true developmental state ... the bureaucratic rulers possess a particular kind of legitimacy that allows them to be much more experimental and *undoctrinaire* than in the typical authoritarian regime' (Johnson, 1999, p 52). On the other hand, although Leftwich (2000, p 136) distinguishes geographical, constitutional and political legitimacy as the possible justifications for the societal acceptance of the ruling elites, he stresses that the concept is extremely elusive, hence difficult to measure and define, especially among authoritarian states.

It is important to note that the discussion on the political regimes of developmental states is sometimes seen as unimportant. Leftwich (2000) claims that the debate about the applicability of the concept of the developmental state to various political regimes will not determine the favourable systemic environment for the former, as he seems to believe that, as White (1998, p 25) puts it, 'the nature of the political regime is not a central issue'. According to Leftwich, the primacy of politics (and not of a political system) in development is unquestionable: 'Politics matters because politics shapes states, and states shape development' (Leftwich, 2000, p 191). Consequently, political institutions do matter, but thinking in terms of political regimes does not correctly address the conditionality of economic growth (Przeworski and Limongi, 1993).

Indeed, although DS political conditionality, as featured in the scholarly literature, is examined from the perspective of different political regimes, it is often believed that political systemic arrangements are secondary factors to the institutions – understood as rules of the game and its constraints (North, 1990) – that shape developmental states.[11] Waldner (1999) describes DS institutions as institutional innovations, which feature several elements. First, the arrangements of the political regime that are in opposition to what he calls the precocious Keynesian regime of constituency clientelism allow for relatively depoliticised economic policymaking, partly because of a lack of influence of labour and the agrarian class. Second, because, to quote Johnson (1981, p 12), 'the politicians reign and the bureaucrats rule', the formulation of a long-term development strategy is by competent technocrats. Third:

> fiscal policy is controlled by a state elite that is singularly devoted to economic development and thus uses state resources only for production and capital accumulation. [Fourth,] state intervention is devoted largely to measures that will either guide the economy into targeted sectors or assist firms in given sectors to become internationally competitive (Waldner, 1999, pp 143–4)

For Doner et al (2005), as for many other scholars, the main DS institutional features fall within the relational aspects and partly concern the existence of an autonomous and highly professional bureaucracy with a state 'pilot' agency. This bureaucracy allies with the private business sector, and ideally with labour as well, to 'govern the market' in order to achieve rapid development. This perception mirrors Haggard's (2004) analysis, in which he highlights the role of 'big' institutions and, in the case of East Asia, concentrates on what he calls 'partially representative' and 'delegative' institutions. Partially representative institutions concern the linkage between the public and private sectors; delegative institutions are bureaucratic agencies granted broad developmental mandates. For Haggard (2004), the big institutions of East Asian high-growth countries, such as strong property rights, allow for capital accumulation and subsequent investment. He also argues for small institutions or 'micro-institutions', which address selective intervention and coordination problems and thus make industrial policy effective and efficient.

The institutional positioning of the state at the centre of developmental activities, either via its pilot agency, which is largely responsible for creating and implementing a national development strategy, or as the main actor in forming coalitions via its bureaucracy

---

[11] This is not to say that there is no relation between the genus of political regime and DS institutions (see Waldner, 1999; Haggard, 2004).

with other participants of domestic economic life for the developmental endeavour, directly leads to the issue related to the strength and the capacity of the state. The historical DS cases were in opposition to what Myrdal (1968), in his analysis of India's developmental shortcomings, labelled a 'soft state'. Myrdal's soft state is described by Lankester (2004, p 291) as being 'unable to enforce the discipline [that is] needed to implement [a] development plan'. A state is incapable of coercing other agents of state functioning, such as society and domestic business, into supporting state developmental actions. In effect, it experiences meagre developmental results. The developmental state's 'politics' (as Leftwich puts it) is about the effective mobilisation of various actors behind the development trajectory guided by the state. A strong state (see Katzenstein, 1978; Deyo, 1987; Migdal, 1988, 2001) 'can formulate policy goals independently of particular groups, can change group or class behaviour, and can change the structure of society' (Cumings, 1984, p 7). It 'embodies three dimensions: coercive capacity, comparative independence from particular groups and classes, and an interventionism capable of restructuring society or substituting for other structures, such as the market' (Woo, 1991, p 2). This state does not need to be a hard state (this concept is often positioned against the concept of a soft state), but a strong state capable of exercising its power. Its developmental competence derives partly not from being harsh towards its society, but from having the strength to effectively guide development. Haggard (1990) claims that this capability comes from the degree of insulation from societal pressures, cohesiveness of the decision-making structure and the availability of instruments to pursue political and substantive goals. Stubbs (2009), however, reminds us that a strong state needs to be accompanied by a relatively weak society. Nevertheless, the emergence of strong states is not possible 'unless sufficient resources, in the form of money, skilled manpower, and organisational and technical knowledge [within society,] is available' (Stubbs, 2009, p 5). He quotes Migdal, whose conditions for strong states to emerge are remarkably close to external and internal conditions during which developmental states were formed, namely: exogenous political forces favouring concentrated social control; the existence of a military threat; the presence of skilful top leaders to create the 'grand design'; and 'a social grouping with people sufficiently independent of existing bases of social control and skilful enough to execute the grand designs' (Migdal, 1988, cited in Stubbs, 2009, p 4).

Finally, scholarly publications often present political factors other than domestic ones that contributed to the developmental dynamics of developmental states. The developmental successes of Japan, Korea and Taiwan, and a comparable lack thereof on the part of China and North Korea, are sometimes partly attributed to external political factors associated with their geopolitical location.

The capitalist developmental states of East Asia took their dominant institutions and policy form during the tense political situation of the Cold War. As much as in some other parts of the world, the military conflict between the socialist Eastern bloc and the capitalist states seemed a real possibility in the East Asian region. South Korea and Taiwan seemed in a particular predicament, as they faced military threats from North Korea and China, respectively. Therefore, developmental states were emerging within the political conditions of severe security threats (Doner et al, 2005; Stubbs, 2009; Hayashi, 2010). In view of insufficient military power, the circumstances enabled the governments to implement uncompromising development policies aimed at increasing wealth and consequently military capacity, regardless of their interim social costs. The security threat served as an incentive for societal mobilisation behind the political elites.

Unsurprisingly, it was the US who took the role of containing the communist expansion by supporting the capitalist states of East Asia, especially Japan, as a heavyweight economic power and initially a US semi-periphery, to balance the regional aspirations of China. US financial and technological assistance and the opening of its domestic market for consumer goods from capitalist East Asia created economic conditions for faster development, whereas US military involvement in the region guaranteed relatively stable political conditions for such development. To quote Cumings (1984, p 17), 'security and economic considerations were inextricably mixed'. The capital and technological support of the US and other Western states enabled the effective DS policy of upgrading industrial bases, initially in Japan and later in Korea and Taiwan. Japan subsequently joined ranks with the US in technological and financial support to NICs.

All the Northeast Asian developmental states benefited from US assistance. It is estimated that US post-Second World War assistance to Japan was USD2.2 billion (Serafino et al, 2006), the aid provided to Taiwan between 1951 and 1968 was USD1.5 billion (Otero, 1995) and help to Korea after the Korean war until 1975, excluding military assistance, was around USD6 billion (Otero, 1995). This assistance preceded the periods of high growth associated with the existence of the developmental state. The role of aid, although important in generating the initial impetus for growth, should not be overestimated. It is believed that although Japan and Taiwan spent 40% of the aid on infrastructure expansion, Korea consumed most of the obtained funds. Nevertheless, due to the political circumstances, it remained an important recipient of US funds. From the perspective of the concept of the developmental state, what seemed to matter more was the extensive transfer of technologies from the US, initially to Japan and then to Korea and Taiwan, for the initial industrial upgrading, as well as the opening of the large US market to the products of newly established developmental states. In addition, the Cold War allowed the governments of Japan, Korea and Taiwan to be relatively free in implementing various types of economic policies, as long as they meant strengthening the capacity for containing the communist bloc.

The external political factors that shaped the developmental states of East Asia cannot be limited to the Cold War. Cumings (1984), Kohli (1994) and Bernard and Ravenhill (1995) point to the regional interdependencies that influenced the creation of North East Asian NICs. These interdependencies go beyond the relationship defined by the wild-geese-flying pattern (Akamatsu, 1962). They underline the historical linkage between Japan, Korea and Taiwan, which goes back to the end of the 19th century:

> Industrial development in Japan, Korea and Taiwan, cannot be considered as an individual country phenomenon; instead it is a regional phenomenon in which a tripartite hierarchy of core, semi-periphery, and periphery was created in the first part of the twentieth century and then slowly recreated after World War II. (Cumings, 1984, p 38)

Cumings (1984, pp 8, 10) argues that the 'region's economic dynamism [comes] with the advent of Japanese imperialism' and colonialism, since 'in Korea and Taiwan the [Japanese] colonial power emphasised not only military and police forms of control but also development under strong state auspices'. Kohli (1994) establishes three state/society characteristics, which although seen as core elements of the Korean DS, originated from Japanese colonial rule, namely: transformation of the state into a highly authoritarian, penetrating organisation, capable of controlling and transforming Korean society; evolution of the production-oriented alliance resulting in the increase in manufacturing and export; and control of the lower classes.

The economic conditionality

The developmental state is often conceptually positioned between a free-market capitalist economic system and a centrally planned economic system, and is called a plan-rational capitalist system, 'conjoining private ownership with state guidance' (Woo-Cumings, 1999, p 2), which suggests it being neither purely capitalist nor purely socialist (Bolesta, 2007).

Johnson (1999), however, believes that the developmental state is, in principle, capitalist. He points to the important element of the developmental state from a microeconomic perspective, namely, the cooperation between private business and government or, broadly speaking, the private sector and the public sector. Private business becomes a partner for the government in the developmental endeavour. It is, then, private business – an important element of the landscape of the capitalist system – which is a crucial part of the developmental state. Indeed, although the format of capitalism in the Japanese and the Korean DS seems to be distinctive to some extent, in principle, the existence of a capitalist system in those two states has seldom been questioned.

However, some Chinese experts are convinced that the idea of a socialist state is firmly connected with the idea of the developmental state; hence, a socialist state is, by definition, a developmental state, at least as far as the paramount concept is concerned.[12] White and Wade (1988, p 4) insist that 'the developmental limitations of capitalism are well known, in particular its tendency to enrich propertied classes and privileged groups at the expense of the poor and socially marginalised'; hence, taking into account the historical record, socialist economies cannot be easily excluded from the developmental state group. Indeed, they emphasise that:

> historical experiences suggest … that in certain circumstances, for developmental purposes, direct planning along classical Soviet lines can play a positive role in the initial stages of industrialisation: in raising the rate of investment, generating and focusing scarce resources, defining and directing strategic changes in the industrial structure, regulating international ties, generating overall political support and establishing a social structure favourable to accumulation. (White and Wade, 1988, p 15)

Thus, the idea of a socialist developmental state does not need to be a utopian one. For example, Chun Lin (2006) points to significant

[12] Personal communication with Justin Lin Yifu, a renowned economist and a former chief economist of World Bank, Beijing, 10 September 2007.

developmental achievements in communist China during the Mao era, in spite of large setbacks and ill-formulated policies.

However, some researchers object to the usage of the terms 'capitalism' or 'socialism', as they are often believed to be obscure, and prefer to position the debate against the concept of the market as an economic-institutional arrangement. The discussion on the market is an important part of the conceptualising of the DS model. It also extends to the analysis of China's development trajectory. In general, socialism is believed to be synonymous with central planning, whereas capitalism is synonymous with a market economy.

A market economy is believed to be a system in which the allocation of resources and products is decided according to supply and demand; this is the 'mechanism'-based definition. Moreover, it is an environment where the agents of economic activities can represent private, state and other forms of ownership; this is the 'ownership'-based definition. A market economy is often associated with the capitalist economic system. The capitalist system falls within the definition of market. However, the reverse relation is often seen as not necessarily irrefutable. This results in a growing perception that one must distinguish between the market and capitalism. Arrighi (2007, p 24), following Fernand Braudel (1977), argues that there is a 'world-historical difference between the process of market formation and the process of capitalist development', and that this distinction can be traced to Asian and European economic development in the times preceding and following the Industrial Revolution. As a result of the Industrial Revolution, Europe started the process of capitalist market development, whereas Asian states, and especially China, were characterised by non-capitalist market-based development for centuries. Arrighi (2007) commences the formulation of the set of differences by citing Adam Smith, who considered the Chinese development model as a natural path and the European model as an unnatural path. Furthermore, Arrighi summarises the historical differences between capitalist development and non-capitalist market development as follows:

• The Asian non-capitalist model is labour-intensive and energy-saving, whereas the European capitalist model is capital- and energy-intensive (Siguhara, cited in Arrighi, 2007, p 39).
• The capitalist class are subordinate to the state's interests (non-capitalist); the state is subordinate to the class interests of capitalists and the bourgeoisie (capitalist).
• Wealth comes from agriculture (non-capitalist); wealth comes from trade (capitalist).

- The main economic process is the accumulation of capital (capitalist); no such phenomenon exists in proliferation (non-capitalist).
- Militarist in nature (capitalist); non-militarist in nature (non-capitalist).

Arrighi's historical reference is an important source of information on market formation in Europe and Asia; however, his attempt to clearly detach the market economy and capitalist development is problematic and difficult to be considered fully applicable contemporarily. The capitalist mode of development has evolved and proliferated in genus, so did the institutional conditionality, as discussed later.

An additional question is posed by the interchangeable usage of the terms 'market economy' and 'free-market economy'. To some extent, the term 'free-market economy' seems a pleonasm. The idea behind a market economy is that it is free or at least significantly freer than a non-market economy in the sphere of economic activities, though none of the market economies can be entirely free, and some are freer than others. 'Market economy', on the other hand, indicates that market forces are the paramount principles, without, however, disregarding the regulatory powers and interventionist policies of the state, as the degree of the alleged economic 'freedom' is anticipated but not clearly defined.

Guo (2003, p 555) reminds us that 'there have been many mixed types of political economy ... because states and markets have played various roles in the economy throughout the world'. In particular, they seem to apply to the conditions of East Asia. In his analysis of ownership and state control, he points to the two most important hybrid types of economies: state capitalism – dominant at certain stages of South Korea's and Taiwan's development and distinctively different from a free-market economy model; and market socialism – a concept that differs from state command and is often believed to be crucial for understanding some tenets of China's systemic transformation. He sees the general difference between state capitalism and market socialism as follows: in state capitalism, the state is in control of the market and plays a vital role in economic processes, though the means of production are privately owned; in market socialism, the situation is the opposite – market mechanisms are dominant, but the state owns the means of production. The term 'state capitalism' is often used to describe the systemic arrangement of the developmental state. Hence, White and Wade (1988) see developmental states as guided market economies or governed market economies (Wade, 1990). Wade (2003) perceives developmental states as those who possess a mixture of free market (fm), simulated free market (sm) and governed market (gm) (for details, see Wade, 2003, p 297).

As far as market socialism is concerned, one first needs to address the meaning of a 'socialist economic system'. A socialist economy is defined as lacking, to a considerable degree, the market mechanism of allocation and as limiting options for ownership. Means of production are publicly owned by the state or collectives. Indeed, for Kornai (1992), public ownership of means of production was the defining feature of socialism. Schumpeter (1942, p 415) saw it as an 'organisation of society in which the means of production are controlled, and the decisions on how and what to produce and on who is to get what, are made by public authority instead of by privately-owned and privately-managed firms'. The term 'socialism' is often replaced by the terms 'central planning' and 'state command'. The phrase 'central planning', however, does not seem to fully capture the nature of a socialist economy. Central planning also played an extraordinarily important role among some market, non-socialist, economies. State command, on the other hand, seems to be a broader concept, which implicitly points to the state not only as the central planner, but also as the paramount executor of those plans in an institutional environment where all the economic activities are subject to command and regulation. The state role as the paramount executor of the plans seems to be reserved for non-market conditions, where hardly any other agents are in a position to participate in economic activities.

As mentioned earlier, the terms 'socialism' and 'market' are sometimes put together. The 'socialist calculation debate', commenced by Barone and Pareto, and continued by Lange (mostly against Von Mises), led to the conceptualisation of market socialism, in which a 'rational economic calculation [characteristic of a market system] is equally feasible in the conditions of a centralised [socialist] economy without [extensive] freedom of consumption, freedom of labour force migration and freedom of resources allocation' (Lange, 1973, p 233). 'The key idea … was that a market socialist system could through rational planning eliminate the abuse of monopoly power and the irrational production of capitalism, and yet ensure individual freedom by allowing a free market in consumer goods' (Boettke, 2004, p 8). Lange argued that a benevolent central planner can clear the markets by raising prices in response to shortages and by cutting prices in response to surpluses, as is done in the conditions of a free market. At the same time, the socialist state is able to distribute income more equitably, to solve the problems of externalities and to avoid monopolies from being created (Shleifer and Vishny, 1994, p 166). The concept was heavily criticised by

Hayek, who, like Von Mises (1951), saw rational economic calculation under socialism as impossible (Boettke, 2004, p 4), and recently by Stiglitz (1993), who saw the failure of market socialism as owing to its underestimation of the significance of the incentive problem, the role of innovation in the economy and the difficulty in allocating capital. Shleifer and Vishny (1994), however, point out that despite this criticism, the process of post-socialist transformation revived the debate on market socialism (see, eg, Roemer 1994).

Does it mean that there can be a case of a socialist developmental state? Unlike in most of the states of Central and Eastern Europe (CEE), where central planning was the consequence of totalitarian communist regimes imposed by the Soviet Union after the Yalta Treaty and the developmental prerogative was not an element of the systemic arrangement, in the case of self-imposed socialism in China, the then new systemic doctrine was an alternative to the developmental incompetence of the previous regimes. Hence, it is believed that developmentalism played an important role in moulding the frames of Chinese socialism. Nevertheless, East Asian comparative studies seem to suggest that the developmental achievements of what are believed to be capitalist states have been far greater than those of socialist countries. Moreover, DS systemic arrangements suggest that the private sector, absent to a great extent in socialist economies, plays a crucial role in the strategic business–state partnership. Consequently, socialism could have been about development, but the pace of development in socialist states would seldom match the pace of development in capitalist developmental states due to some systemic and other limitations. Therefore, it would be difficult to speak of the existence of a developmental state in China prior to the reform period, despite the fact that Chinese systemic arrangements at that time may have been aimed at the acceleration of development and, indeed, brought some positive results.

The historical developmental states, despite their guided and governed market status and thus various market-distorting state interventions, were in essence capitalist countries. The degree and genus of capitalist state interventions is the subject of the DS-related analysis below. What constitutes an economically liberal state, perceived as having very little interventionism, and what is the definition of an interventionist state, or, rather, what constitutes less as opposed to more interventionism? It is important to mention that from the perspective of political economy, the interventionist state is understood as one that is characterised by the Keynesian economic model, where the arbitrary and inequitable distribution of wealth and income is corrected by the government, to the extent that it is widely perceived to be interventionist. It is believed that the degree of interventionism can be measured by the size of governmental ownership, specific economic regulations and level of taxes.

As far as the relation between the developmental state and interventionism is concerned, Loriaux (1999, p 24) believes that 'the developmental state is an embodiment of a normative or moral ambition to use the interventionist power of the state to guide investment in a way that promotes a certain solidaristic vision of national economy'. Ha-Joon Chang, one of the most well-known Korea-born scholars to contribute to the literature related to the developmental state, underlines that 'economic development requires a state which can create and regulate the economic and political relationships that can support sustained industrialisation – or in short, a developmental state' (Chang, 1999a, p 183). Consequently, the introduction of the developmental state concept into state ideology means, in real terms, the creation of a certain type of interventionist state. Cumings (1984) points out that a developmental state needs to consider the 'Listian assumption', and, as a late developer, rather than follow laissez-faire ideology, must create a strong state with protectionist barriers. The developmental state is a strong interventionist state in the way in which it shapes and reinforces developmental directions, as opposed to a weak state, or Myrdal's soft state. However, the broadly contested, but nevertheless influential, World Bank report entitled *The East Asian Miracle: Economic Growth and Public Policy* questions the relation between the performance of historical developmental states and state interventionism: 'It is difficult to test whether interventions increased growth rates.... We know that intervention did not significantly inhibit growth' (World Bank, 1993, p 6). The report acknowledges that East Asian high-growth countries are characterised by a certain level of state interventionism; however, it claims that this intervention was 'mild' and 'careful' and, in many cases, such as the Korean heavy and chemical industries, the free market would play an either equally effective or better allocative role (World Bank, 1993).

Following the argument by the authors of the World Bank report, one needs to ask the question as to whether a developmental state can be created in an economy shaped by neo-liberal principles. In theory, it seems hardly possible to achieve extensive developmental goals in a relatively short period of time in an environment where authorities have very limited power in directing investment, regulating its intensity and influencing institutions, companies and communities so that they follow a certain overall development strategy, and where the nation is not sufficiently rich to invest large financial assets for mutual benefit in its own country (Bolesta, 2007). By definition the societies of developmental states are, on average, in the process of accumulating wealth and are believed to be relatively poor. According to Chang (1999a), in this respect, a neo-liberal economic model seems to have a number of shortcomings that hinder fast development in developing countries. He argues that this is due to the fact that the model does not take into consideration that there has to be a limit on the liberalisation and depoliticisation of an economy for developmental purposes. He points out that 'politicising certain "economic" decisions may not only be inevitable, but also desirable, because the world is full of assets with limited mobility and owners who are naturally determined to prevent changes that threaten their current positions' (Chang, 1999a, p 191). He also underlines that 'the most important insight from early development economics was that systemic changes need coordination' (Chang, 1999a, p 192). Successful coordination requires a state that has the necessary tools to deal with the burden, and is not merely the guardian of certain freedoms.

Moreover, the issue of a neo-liberal economy versus an interventionist state can be addressed not necessarily by taking into consideration domestic conditions, as has been the case so far, but by taking into account the global environment. The so-called global economy is by no means liberal; hence, liberalism cannot be held responsible for developmental achievements worldwide. Setting aside Joseph Stiglitz's important argument about the asymmetry of information, and Hamilton's (cited in Woo-Cumings, 1999, p 5) shyness of capital, one needs to remember that there are still many trade barriers, as well as powerful forces, such as governments of large economies and international corporations, with a capacity to distort, for example, the international level of prices by following certain policies.[13] As their economies are, to a large extent, export-driven (as examined later), developmental states must comply with the international conditionality and work out their own position in the global economy. It cannot be achieved without a strong state legally able to influence the direction of development. The international economic conditionality puts poorer countries who would like to accelerate their pace of development in an especially disadvantageous position, as they are forced not only to compete with stronger opponents on the global market, but also to follow the rules created by the developed states for the very benefit of developed states themselves. To navigate this, in a way, 'hostile

---

[13]   See more in Ha-Joon Chang (1999a, p 197).

environment', not only must a relatively poor country be 'strong', but the state also needs to posses certain interventionist powers.

Naturally, interventionism is by no means a remedy for shortages in developmental achievements. Evans (1995, pp 3, 4, 10) rightly emphasises that although 'the state lies at the centre of solutions to the problem of order' and 'fervent calls for the dismantling of the state by late-twentieth-century capitalist free marketeers served to derail the state's ability to act as an instrument of distributive justice', clearly taking the side of some sort of interventionist ideology, 'sterile debates about "how much" states intervene have to be replaced with arguments about different kinds of involvement and their effects'. He continues to state that:

> contrasts between 'dirigiste' and 'lineral' or 'interventionist' and 'noninterventionist' states focus attention on degrees of departure from ideal-typical competitive markets. They confuse the basic issue. In the contemporary world, withdrawal and involvement are not the alternatives. State involvement is a given. The appropriate question is not 'how much' but 'what kind'. (Evans, 1995, p 10)

How, then, is DS interventionism different from the ordinary, somewhat classical, interventionism present in continental Western Europe? In general, the DS type of interventionism takes as its task the guiding of the development trajectory via a mix of regulations, policies and additional incentives. A more detailed description is presented below.

First, the purpose of DS interventionism is different. The main objective of a developmental interventionist state is to realise the original purpose of the developmental state, namely, the acceleration of socio-economic development in the long term, via certain instruments, to catch up with highly developed nations. A classical interventionist state does not require this conditionality. The contemporary Western European interventionist state's target is to secure societal cohesion. In this type of interventionism, overall development is seen as an important but secondary issue. Consequently, an interventionist developmental state is not a social state, as usually is the classical model of the interventionist state present in continental Western Europe. On the contrary, the early developmental states in Japan and Korea resulted in suppressing and exploiting the less affluent rural part of the society, as well as the working class.

Second, ordinary interventionist states do not lack an extensive bureaucratic apparatus, but they do lack economic bureaucracy as the dominant power in the governmental structure, responsible for the 'guiding' of the economy by setting developmental goals and monitoring progress. For Evans (1998), this economic bureaucracy is a result of a 'renovation' of classic bureaucracy, conditioned by: the willingness of the state to invest political and economic resources in the construction of a capable state apparatus; the commitment to target the most critical parts of the bureaucracy from the perspective of economic policies; and the ability to address the challenge of constructing a relationship between the government and private business. This challenge is associated with the issue of bureaucracy's autonomy. Economic bureaucracy is usually materialised in the form of a governmental institution, a pilot agency largely in charge of development, or, as Weiss (2000) puts it, of transformative goals. In the case of Japan, this role was assumed by the Ministry of International Trade and Industry (MITI), in Singapore by the Economic Development Board, in Taiwan by the Council on Economic Planning and Development, and in Korea by the Economic Planning Board (EPB). According to Waldner (1999), the pilot agency is needed due to the manner of DS-style industrial restructuring, which displaces market signals through various mechanisms such as subsidies, the socialisation of risk and administered pricing. These mechanisms are nothing less than the features of DS interventionism.

Third, an important issue relates to the degree of interventionism present in classical interventionist states and developmental interventionist states. It is believed that despite being in opposition to the liberal economic model, developmental state interventionism is more limited in form than common interventionism. Sakoh (1984, p 523) insists that the Japanese DS model, in fact, featured very limited state involvement, as demonstrated by the analyses of capital formation and lending sources. Although one can probably argue that DS interventionism is less extensive than classical interventionism, what matters more is Evans's argument about the type and quality of engagement. DS interventionism is not about the strict regulation of economic processes, but rather about governmental leadership over the facilitation of the development trajectory. This trajectory can only be achieved once the business sector enjoys an adequate free-market environment in which to perform.

Finally, the essence of DS interventionism as opposed to classical interventionism lies chiefly in the state–business alliance, where the state intervenes in the business sector in a less (Korea) and more (Japan) subtle way by distributing the incentives for the realisation of certain projects related to the overall developmental strategy.

Having analysed the overall features and the conditionalities of the developmental state, one needs to address the following two issues: 'Is the DS model still a viable option to follow?'; and 'How does the debate extend to China's development trajectory?' Let us here, however, summarise the features of the 'traditional' developmental state, as they have been agreed in the course of international research on the subject and presented earlier.

The developmental state is an institutional and policy arrangement that is intended to enable some relatively poor economies to effectively catch up developmentally with highly developed nations. Sometimes, the concept is believed to go beyond the catching-up period and is referred to as aiming at creating a transformative state focused on the continuous upgrading of the economic structure.

The developmental state is largely defined by the interrelation of four actors: the political elite; the state economic bureaucracy, or, together, 'the state'; society; and business. Their interaction is defined within the concept of 'embedded autonomy'. Society, including business, is able to influence the state; however, the state remains extensively insulated and independent in the process of decision-making concerning economic and development policies and institutional arrangements. In general, society is perceived as subordinate to the strong and developmentally capable state. The state forms an alliance with the private business sector in which the government designs the plans for industrial development and, by means of various policy incentives and legal solutions, supports business expansion within the targeted areas and aids export-related activities. The close interaction between the public and private sectors is often blamed for corruption in this institutional arrangement.

The main state ideology is nationalism – to gain societal support for the 'transformative' project – and, within this category, economic nationalism as the background of the state economic policy – to assist in developing the domestic business base. In the scholarly literature, the state development policies are framed within the process of industrialisation, and, more precisely, import-substitution industrialisation, which is followed by export-oriented industrialisation.

As far as political conditionality is concerned, the DS model is characterised by various degrees of authoritarianism or authoritarian mechanisms within a democratic system. What matters more for the DS model is a strong state supported by effective development-focused institutions rather than the genus of the purely systemic arrangement. Moreover, the external conditionality of political insecurity and economic and political support also play an important role. As far as economic conditionality is concerned, the developmental state is a capitalist state or a market economy. It is, however, an interventionist state, with the central government having extensive planning capacities and market-distorting instruments that it uses towards the realisation of its preferred development trajectory. The intervention is partly possible due to the existence of a large economic bureaucracy, mostly concentrated in a state pilot agency, to navigate socio-economic development.

The future of the developmental state

What is, however, the future of the developmental state in the contemporary world? Should one expect the final demise or a revival or resurrection of the concept, which is believed to greatly influence the development trajectories of some states? Is the DS model destined to head towards what Weiss (2000, p 25) calls 'normalisation' (abandoning its priorities, dismantling its organisational architecture and steadily disengaging from economic coordination), or does it still remain a viable option in an era of increased economic openness and capital mobility?

Initially described by Johnson (1982), the concept of the developmental state took into account the previous theoretical works on the role of the state in development and framed them into the conditions of late developers' reforms and transformation. The plan-rational governmental ideology was realised by the involvement of the government in the process of development. The state was believed to be at the centre of the solution to the problem of underdevelopment, which was in line with the common opinion that the rapid development of poor countries cannot be sustained without the guiding role of the government. The rapid industrialisation of Japan, which became an affluent developed country by extensively using the carefully designed development plan created and supported by the central government, was an important argument in defending the role of the state as a crucial factor in developmental transformation.

This perception was subsequently verified on the occasion of the emergence of neo-liberal economic thought to be the superior economic ideology, during the Ronald Reagan era. The developmental superiority of the US was obvious to the extent that alternative institutional scenarios aimed at accelerating development were mostly ignored. Without consideration for certain social, economic and historical factors, it was assumed that an extensively liberalised economy was the key solution to underdevelopment. This contradicted state involvement as the developmental remedy advocated in the concept of the developmental state.

Moreover, the positioning of the DS model within very specific geopolitical conditions would produce a claim that once those conditions expired, DS institutional and policy arrangements could not be sustained. Some would argue that developmental states could only have worked in the context of the Cold War (Hayashi, 2010). The threat from the communist bloc, especially to countries such as Korea and Taiwan, generated domestic public support for governmental policies, and the regional political situation encouraged the US to assist by military, financial and technological means, as well as to open its domestic market for goods from DS countries. At the same time, the protectionist national economic policies of developmental states did not cause significant concerns in Washington as long as the political commitment to the common cause of communism containment prevailed. However, once the political conditions changed due to the collapse of the Eastern bloc, the US started 'demanding that the East Asian countries open their economies and implement trade, investment and capital liberalisation' (Hayashi, 2010, p 46). The end of the Cold War meant, on one hand, 'that the United States no longer felt it could ignore the neo-mercantilist protectionist economic policies of its regional allies' (Stubbs, 2009, p 10) and, on the other, an end to 'massive military and economic aid' (Stubbs, 2009, p 11).

The financial crisis in East Asia (1997) was believed to be an additional blow to the perception of the DS applicability to underdeveloped countries. Allegedly strong developmental states appeared to be weak and ineffective in dealing with dramatic regional turbulences in the financial markets. It was believed to be caused by the inability of the developmental states' governments to counteract possible negative effects, due to a high level of corruption generated by the presence of special public–private partnerships, in addition to the slow process of decision-making caused by an over-interventionist system. For some, the East Asian economic system became synonymous with 'crony capitalism' (Beeson, 2004, p 5).

Finally, the phenomenon of increasing the interdependencies of economic processes worldwide, resulting in the creation of the scaffolding for a global economy, was believed to render the concept of the developmental state incompatible with contemporary economic conditions. It is often believed that, as a result of globalisation, the role of the state in national economies is diminishing, as governments are incapable of controlling global economic processes because a situation in one part of the world influences the conditions in another. The gradual liberalisation of economic relations followed by the easing of regulatory regimes and by the process of the sophistication of exchange of information, including technologies and management techniques, is believed to make the so-called global economy less receptive to incentives from national governments.

In view of globalisation processes, changes in the geopolitical situation and certain purported shortcomings of the institutional arrangements in the East Asian countries, as revealed during the 1997 financial crisis, it was concluded that the formula of the developmental state was eventually losing its significance. Beeson (2004) points out that what was initially the strength of the Japanese economy and resulted in significant developmental successes eventually became an obstacle in the reform process necessary as a response to changes in the global market. Allegedly, Evans's embedded autonomy eventually transformed into intensive corruption-prone state–business relations. From the microeconomic perspective, extensive interventionism was believed to have hindered the innovative behaviour of Japanese companies, necessary for survival in the competitive global economy. *Keiretsu* and others, due to the maintenance of a prolonged conservative mechanism of management, were unable to effect an adequate response to the needs generated by the international market.

It became a rather common perception that the DS model was a contemporarily non viable historical phenomenon, as it was not possible to duplicate the conditions during which historical developmental states achieved rapid growth, and thus 'the experiences of the East Asian high achievers [could not] be applied directly to today's developing world' (Hayashi, 2010, p 46). 'Most would agree that the [contemporary] "post-WTO" [World Trade Organization] global context [is] different from the one in which the East Asian countries succeeded in transforming themselves into industrial powers' (Evans, 1998, p 69).

The preceding analysis leads us to the question of possible scenarios as far as the applicability of the concept of the developmental state is concerned. Is there space for it to be applied in the time of globalisation? Can any state benefit from it? These questions are all the more significant as the second-largest economy in the world – China – is facing critical choices as to the direction it develops, which will eventually have a direct impact on global economic relations and on the global economic situation. At the same time, a large number of underdeveloped countries struggle in their quest to accelerate socio-economic development in the long term and are indeed searching for an adequate developmental model.

The gradual disappearance of regulatory barriers in economic interactions between states, regions, economic sectors and so on seems to be aimed at the creation of one global economic organism without borders. Indeed, this may happen in the long term. Observing the contemporary international scene, both political and economic, with its interventionist forces, one must surely arrive at the conclusion of how elusive, at the current stage of mankind's history, this postulate is. Some barriers disappear, but in their place, new mechanisms of protection are created. It is a popular opinion that the new rules favour strong entities within the global economy and marginalise the weak ones, including developing countries. Consequently, the dismissal of a scenario in which the role of the state will still be crucial, upon the conviction that one borderless global economy is rapidly emerging, seems premature. On the contrary, the role of the state will most likely remain extremely important to defend national interests, as the 2008/09 economic crisis clearly illustrates, allowing space for the possible utilisation of the provisions of the DS model. This can be advocated using the following arguments.

First, the argument about the weaknesses of developmental states, as allegedly proved during the 1997 financial crisis, is in many ways misplaced. Certain East Asian countries were affected by the crisis not because they were developmental states, but because they abandoned DS rules and followed certain liberalisation policies. At the time of the crisis, they were already open liberal economies. China, on the other hand, was barely affected, as it was not economically open enough, with its financial system's infrastructure being guarded from the regional economic turmoil. The developmental state concept does not advocate the absolute necessity for opening up, as neo-liberal economic ideology, allegedly more receptive to global market changes, does. At the time of the crisis, Japan, Korea and Taiwan were no longer classical developmental states. In the Korean case, the 'government dismantled a previously effective developmental state during the 1990s' (Wade, 2000, p 8). Thus, the crisis affected Korea not because it was a developmental state, but because it was not. Due to economic liberalisation, global integration processes and changes in the features of the domestic social environment, certain instruments of the DS model were no longer at those countries' disposal (see Chang et al, 1998). Weiss (2000) repeats Wade's argument and stresses that it would be more plausible to argue that the countries' vulnerability to a financial shakedown was due to their neo-liberalism-motivated change in policies and economic liberalisation. She broadens her analysis to address the situation in Southeast Asia and Japan, as she claims that the affected Southeast

Asian states were not developmental states as they did not possess the 'institutional strength' characteristic of Japan, whereas Japan was mostly affected by the self-induced banking crisis pre-dating the 1997 crisis rather than the regional financial crisis (Weiss, 2000).

Second, even if the developmental state produces corruption, as described by Perkins (2001), White (1996) and many others in their examination of East Asian industrialisation, and this corruption is believed to have inhibited innovation and contributed to an economic slowdown and recession in the Japanese economy, has the alleged corruption inhibited the process of socio-economic development in the DS cases to the extent that they have not produced spectacular developmental results? Political corruption is a widespread phenomenon that is believed to inhibit equal and equitable development. Nevertheless, it is present in all institutional arrangements and its reputed character of endemic East Asian crony capitalism is not a strong enough argument to dismiss what are indeed the remarkable developmental achievements of the DS model. Moreover, one can contemplate the thought that in certain circumstances, corruption does not inhibit development. On the contrary, it can be growth-promoting if its result is a resource allocation to growth-generating sectors (see White, 1996; Bramall, 2009a).

Third, the actual process of globalisation has left most of the nations and a plethora of social groups dissatisfied. The development-related disparities are increasing. Although some manage to accumulate significant wealth, the majority remains only marginally better off. This is because 'a more aggressively enforced internationalisation of the global economy, [has been] built around rules that work primarily to the benefit of current holders of financial capital' (Evans, 1998, p 82). In this situation, only states are believed to offer adequate political resources to avert and redirect the process to make it more socially equitable, and the nations seem prone to turn towards interventionist practices to achieve better developmental dynamics.

Fourth, globalisation may not be as demanding of state dismantling as might be believed. Weiss (2000) states that the argument that economic liberalisation caused by globalisation has prompted DS dismantling is flawed. For example, according to her *proposition three*, there is empirical evidence that it was DS dismantling that paved the way for liberalisation in the Korean developmental state and not the other way around (Weiss, 2000, p 33). In other words, domestic politics might be considered a more important factor than the international conditionality in the process of states following the rules of the era of globalisation:

> The new global regulatory environment and the more highly internationalised structure of business organisation do make some of the policies used by the East Asian NICs more difficult to implement, but what puts East Asian practices out of reach is less likely to be external compulsion than anticipatory acquiescence by developing country governments to perceived constraints. (Evans, 1998, p 81)

Moreover, Weiss (2000) believes that financial liberalisation does not need to lead to state disengagement, that is, the neo-liberal path is not the only route to regulatory reform (*proposition two*).

Fifth, the global economy is far from being free from the protectionist attempts and interventionist economic forces of the multinational corporations and governments of affluent states. What have changed are the mechanisms of intervention and protection. Despite the official propaganda, developed nations intensively use protectionist policies in order to protect their own markets from various less or more illusionary threats. They defend their actions on the grounds of national security, as has often been the case in the US, or on the grounds of unfair competition, as is usually the case in the European Union. Moreover, DS-style policies and DS-style interventionism have by no means been cast aside in the US defence and high-tech sectors. Block (2008, pp 174–5) points out that 'governmental funding and infrastructure played a key role in [developing] such technologies as computers, jet planes, civilian nuclear energy, lasers and biotechnology'. Many projects were pioneered by the Pentagon's Advanced Research Projects Agency (ARPA), within the arrangements described by Block as a Development Network State (DNS). He stresses the generally proactive role of ARPA, in particular, in setting the technological goals, and of the National Institutes of Health (NIH) in funding the projects on biotechnology. Both ARPA and NIH can be seen as state agencies contributing to industrial policy by targeting certain sectors. This DS-style state-sponsored targeting has been, according to Block (2008), a common phenomenon in the US. The government has extensively contributed towards research and development (R&D) projects via, for example, funds for early stage technology development.

Sixth, as the emergence of China as an economic superpower provides an important argument in opposition to the recommendations motivated by the neo-liberal economic ideology, as far as economic development and economic transformation are concerned, the final and inevitable discrediting of this ideology, due to the 2008/09 financial crisis, as a result of which criticism of global capitalism has intensified significantly (see Chang, 2010; Stiglitz, 2010; Scott, 2011), seems to leave the pool of effective developmental models for underdeveloped states rather limited. The DS model resurfaces as a historically effective option that elevates development to the ranks of the paramount ideology, above political and other considerations.

Naturally, globalisation, understood as a multi-level integration of national and regional economies and as a growth of interdependence of various socio-economic processes worldwide, will most likely continue in one form or another and the pressure of the external economic environment to influence the processes internally will continue to take place. This is what constitutes the predicament of 'late-late' development, as described by Beeson (2004). Therefore, the state needs to play an important role in poor countries, who require better developmental dynamics, by attempting to benefit from international conditionality (eg from trade liberalisation, from easier technology diffusion) and by resisting external threats (such as attempts by foreign economic agents/actors to take over certain domestic industrial sectors in order to eliminate possible competition). Consequently, the concept of the developmental state has been buried prematurely. In view of relatively recent East Asian economic achievements and the lack thereof in other regions, the necessity of creating developmental states cannot be easily dismissed. In reality, we are clearly observing DS features becoming more prominent in contemporary policymaking. Governments are becoming less shy to speak about interventionism and regulation to nurture development. Even places considered to be the bastions of neo-liberal thought implementation seem to be giving in.[14] International organisations such as the Organisation for Economic Co-operation and Development (OECD) have begun to admit the successes of the developmental state model.[15]

In sum, it can be argued that developmental state failures seem to be exaggerated and the corruption-proneness of the systemic arrangements does not need to dismiss the DS as a valuable option. Globalisation is far from being a socially equitable phenomenon and considering interventionist policies is common among all states, also among those who officially advocate the superiority of the liberal economic model. In turbulent times of the global economy and the rapidly increasing

---

[14] The case of Poland is a good example. The government led by the Civic platform, a party with very strong neo-liberal roots, has dramatically changed its attitude towards regulating economic processes, increasingly relying on state interventionism.

[15] I was personally audience to such statements by OECD officials during a conference in Beijing in 2011.

interconnectedness of national economies, developing nations have no choice but to rely on the state as a defender of their interests internationally, and as a facilitator of socio-economic progress internally. Wherever there is space for the developmental role of the state, there is space for implementation of the DS model in one form or another.

The DS model cannot, however, be seen as a paramount remedy for underdevelopment in the various parts of the world, and its provisions, applied to state policies and institutional arrangements, will not instantly solve existing economic and social problems. Many conditions for East Asian developmental successes are historically specific and perhaps not repeatable. Therefore, each state needs to consider its own set of remedies, which depends on a number of factors. Although one may agree with the opinion that a number of countries from various parts of the world seem to share some political, institutional and social characteristics of the DS model, the realm of truly developmental states is probably limited to some examples of Northeast Asia. This rather conservative perception is usually not only based on the conviction that developmental states have certain important institutional and policy features in common, as well as share a historical geopolitical locality, but also considers the very effects of the long-term development trajectories of such countries like Japan, Korea and Taiwan. Those countries have indeed become highly developed economies, and the latter two could have been considered developing nations at the beginning of their DS-style transformation.

In this respect, the argument for the 'consensus candidates' (Stubbs, 2009) or the 'Asian Three' (Weiss, 2000) as the only real DS cases is rather convincing. So is the claim that the Asian Three had already ceased to be fully developmental states (Wade, 2000), despite the correct assertions of Weiss (2000) and Stubbs (2009) that 'DS residues' feature in Japan's, Korea's and Taiwan's contemporary institutions.

This is, however, not to say that the DS model does not deliver any transferable lessons. On the contrary, Evans's (1998) argument about the 'transferable lessons' from the DS concept and East Asian countries' successes for a broader audience is indeed convincing. He is against a simple replication of policies and institutional arrangements. Instead, he believes that:

> trying to transfer [some] lessons from East Asia makes ... sense. Constructing local counterparts to the proximate institutional prerequisites of East Asian success – bureaucracies with a capable economic core and government–business relations based on scepticism

> combined with communication and support in return for performance delivered – is not an impossible task. (Evans, 1998, p 83)

Some institutional solutions and policy directions of historical developmental states may be employed in contemporary conditions, as will be discussed in the following chapters in the case of China.

China and the developmental state

The DS model, in one form or another, is still a valid developmental option, as the state needs to remain the main actor in the process of socio-economic progress in less developed countries. As the most effective developmental institutional and policy arrangements of the second half of the 20th century, it stands in sharp contrast to the neo-liberal economic doctrine, not merely in systemic terms, but most importantly in developmental results. The discussion on the developmental state concept will probably continue as long as the state's role is seen by some as being of paramount importance to the developmental endeavour. This perception is very unlikely to change unless the process of growing disparities between the poor and the rich is effectively averted.

The recent developmental advancements by China, despite the overall trend of growing inequalities, prompt the question as to the sources of the Chinese development trajectory and the role of its government. The country's geographical proximity and cultural affinity to Japan, Korea and Taiwan makes some scholars wonder about its relation to the historical DS cases. How does China fit into the discussion on the concept of the developmental state? How does this debate extend to China? To quote Baek (2005, p 485), 'does China follow the East Asian development model?'

As illustrated in the following chapters, China's systemic arrangements and institutional environment are characterised by an active developmental role of the state. In this respect, the contemporary Chinese development trajectory can perhaps be perceived as a continuation of a tradition of state-guided development, with its roots in the American system of the early 19th century, Listian political economy and the experiences of developmental states in East Asia. Breslin (1996) believes that the Chinese path of development contains some similarities to capitalist developmental states of East Asia, but he is not convinced that China is actually a developmental state. This is because of what he calls a dysfunctional development, which the Chinese reform period is characterised by. He argues that despite the fact that the DS's political-bureaucratic elite should not acquiesce to political demands that would undermine economic growth, 'political demands have been a major factor in the Chinese economic decision-making process' (Breslin, 1996, p 692). As a result of this and of the decentralisation of fiscal and other powers, which provide the provinces with the ability to design their own development-related activities, 'China's developmental trajectory owes at least as much to the dysfunctional agglomeration of numerous local initiatives, as it does to the plans and strategies of the national level decision-making elites' (Breslin, 1996, p 689). Indeed, for Howell (2006), China's degree of decentralisation and, as a consequence, lack of an effective central state as a prime actor undermines the case for China as a developmental state. She situates the PRC, together with India and Brazil, somewhere between a developmental and predatory state. Howell (2006) further examines the decentralisation issue, claiming that what partly drives the developmental advancements is local and sometimes personal interests, which creates a sort of a 'dual developmental state', as described by Xia (2000, cited in Howell, 2006, p 284), where central and local elites' ambitions influence the overall development trajectory. Therefore, as well as due to other factors, the central government is believed to 'have difficulties ... in asserting its will on subordinate parts of the state and [thus] steering a coherent nationwide trajectory of economic development' (Howell, 2006, p 285). In the environment of a plethora of quasi-developmental decision-making centres, their own survival takes precedence over national development (Howell, 2006, p 287). Therefore, what is created in China is a polymorphous state rather than a developmental state. This results in unbalanced and uneven development. Breslin (1996) discusses several elements that distinguish the developmental process in China from that in historical DS cases. In the case of China, the reforms were motivated by the ruling elite's desire to hold on to power, and the reform policies were designed so that no group within the ruling elite and key social groups, as well as geographical locations, lose too much in the process. The reform process itself was characterised by a conflict within the ruling elite as to the specifics and destination of the reforms. The reformers had no previous experience in and knowledge of utilising and controlling market mechanisms (Breslin, 1996, pp 692–3). Howell (2006) continues her line of argument by questioning the existence of Evans's embedded autonomy in China. She believes that what characterises the ties between government officials and business officials is far from embedded autonomy, due to the 'historically-rooted mutual suspicion between the Party and private entrepreneurship' (Howell, 2006, p 288).

There is a group of scholars, however, who has seen China as a developmental state during the period of state-command economy and/or during the time of market reforms. White (1988) called China a socialist developmental state, as Chinese socialism has often been believed to be driven by developmental ideals (see Lin, 2006): 'The key features of the socialist developmental state are the virtual elimination of private industrial capital, all-pervasive controls over the economy, and a state that, at least initially, represents the interests of a revolutionary coalition' (White, 1984, p 103, cited in Howell, 2006, p 276). Baek (2005), partly contesting Howell's arguments, claims that the contemporary China of market reforms is a genus of the developmental state:

> Chinese aspects of this developmental state include: the high rate of domestic savings, the huge infrastructure of heavy industry, the promotion of industrial policy, the legacy of central planning, labour-intensive industry accompanied by import-substitutive capital-intensive industry, a strong central government with huge bureaucracy, and corporatist control over the society. (Baek, 2005, p 487)

He claims that 'these characteristics seem to fit into Wade's (1990) ten policy advice for "governed market" to promote government-guided development' (Baek, 2005, p 487). Moreover, the Chinese government is believed to control the financial system and channel resources into specific targets, and the national economy is highly dependent on export, as was the case of classical developmental states. He does, however, acknowledge that China's rapid development is taking place in a different international and domestic conditionality. He also admits that the main business actors of the Chinese developmental state are different from those of Japan and Korea, as far as ownership control is concerned. Knight (2012) is convinced that China is a type of developmental state, and – considering the pace of growth and the government policies to cope with various challenges – indeed, a very successful one. Meier (2009) shares that view, citing the automotive industry as proof. Following the scholars of the China Foreign Affairs University, Ping (2011, p 171) describes the Chinese developmental state model as based on 'socialist state directed market capitalism'. Lee and Mathews (2010) underline that China today draws on the entire Northeast Asian developmental experience, including Japan, Korea and Taiwan, as well as Singapore. In fact, the two scholars combine the developmental experiences of Japan, Korea and China, describing them as 'the BeST Consensus for development', where BeST stands for Beijing, Seoul and Tokyo. Cai (2010a, p 5) quotes Wong (2004) that '[al]though there are significant differences between the current path of China's development and that of Japan and South Korea, they should be seen as in different stages traveling along the same route'.

China, as much as Japan, Korea and Taiwan previously, is often perceived as a corporatist state. According to Unger and Chan (1995, p 95):

> in the ideal-type corporatist system, at the national level the state recognises one and only one organisation as the sole representative of the sectoral interests of individuals, enterprises or institutions that comprise that organisation's assigned constituency. The state determines which organisations will be recognised as legitimate and forms an unequal partnership of sorts with such organisations.

All four countries erected strongly authoritarian corporatist structures during periods of intensive development (see also Wade, 2003, pp 8–33). Already in the period of state-command, China possessed two 'ingredients' of the Japanese corporate model: the cultural – a shared belief in the subordination of individual interests to the good of collective; and the institutional legacies of the Maoist era, more precisely, the role of enterprises as multifaceted benefactors (Unger and Chan, 1995, pp 126–7). Oi (1995) further explores Chinese corporatism and links it more directly to the developmental state model. She considers China to be a local corporatist state, where the corporate-like ties characterise every level of state bureaucracy within the state structure, as well as with business actors. She illustrates how, on one hand, the Maoist legacy provided the political capacity for the local corporatist state in China and, on the other, the orientation towards economic growth and development resulted in the state bureaucracy taking a new role as a local developmental agent, often in collision with state-level interests. This has created a decentralised developmental state, which adopted Maoist institutions for a transitional economy (Oi, 1995, p 1139). Indeed, Howell (2006, p 279) reminds us that a number of 'new conceptualizations of the state in the reform period have emerged, such as the "entrepreneurial state" (see Duckett 1998), the "corporatist state", "the regulatory state", "the dual developmental state", "the market-facilitating state" [and] the "rent-seeking state"', and China's arrangements may also at least partly fall within their definitions.

Contemporary China shares some policy, institutional and social characteristics with the developmental states of Japan, Korea and Taiwan. Its affinity with the countries of the 'East Asia miracle' is not without controversies. However, the pool of similarities is believed to be large, as examined later, to the extent that it is argued here that the Chinese development trajectory has been determined by provisions of the DS model and that China has become a genus of the post-socialist developmental state (see Deans, 2004). Consequently, the contemporary discussion on the DS model extends to China, partly in the context of the contemporary applicability of the DS model's variation and the expansion of its applicability to the states of post-socialist transformation.

CHAPTER TWO

Post-socialist transformation in China

Until the early 19th century, China was the largest economy in the world (Maddison, 2007) and was characterised by a market system. The institutional departure from the market towards state command followed over a century of economic stagnation and was the result of the new state ideology introduced by Mao Zedong and the Chinese Communist Party (CCP) after establishing the People's Republic of China (PRC) in 1949. Over the last 30 years, we have been observing the installation of a new market system and China is often believed to have been undergoing an extensive process of post-socialist transformation. This process will be the subject of the examination in this chapter.

Post-socialist transformation – the overview

As it embraces around 25% of the human population, post-socialist transformation is by all means a process of historical significance. It is hardly possible to imagine complex and extensive systemic changes that equal those taking place in parts of Europe and Asia. In simplistic terms, the process is twofold in nature: from the political perspective, authoritarian regimes are being replaced by democracies; and from the socio-economic perspective, the systems are being transformed 'from centrally-planned economies based on state ownership domination and bureaucratic control mechanisms into the free market economies based on private ownership and a deregulated market' (Kolodko, 2004b, p 32). Some scholars also include a third process of the transformation, namely, nation building. Naturally, there are regional variations, and, indeed, each country in transition would have its own personal set of characteristics.

The process of post-socialist transformation is often referred to in the scholarly literature as post-communist transformation, since the term 'communism' was broadly associated with the Eastern bloc's authoritarian political regimes of one-party rule propagating communist principles. The scholarly discussion on what defines socialism and what defines communism is broad and falls beyond the main scope of this book. Nevertheless, in order to establish what constitutes post-socialist and post-communist transformations in very general terms, one needs to attempt to present some general perceptions as to the differences between socialism and communism. A communist country or a communist regime would commonly be defined as a state/regime in which a communist party rules and political mechanisms do not allow for the contestation of its power. The regime would be perceived as severely limiting both political and economic freedoms. This is, however, the common perception from a political point of view of what constituted a communist state. Although Engels (1969 [1847]) suggested that 'Communism is the doctrine of the conditions of the liberation of the proletariat', indicating that it is a type of political system, the subsequently written *Manifesto of the Communist Party* (Marx and Engels, 1969 [1848]) also describes the socio-economic features of communism and its postulates, such as the abolition of private property and the reorganisation of labour relations. In fact, Schumpeter (1942) saw Marx not only as a philosopher, but also as an economist. Marx's *Das Kapital*, as a critique of capitalism, was in its character an analysis of political economy. Indeed, this 'economic perception' was the very interpretation of communism in most of the countries in the Eastern bloc, where the state ideology often propagated that socialism is an interim period between capitalism and communism, that is, a process rather than a system (see Brugger and Kelly, 1990; Dirlik, 2005), or a stage in human development, as the proponents of scientific socialism would claim, leading towards communism – Marx's final social and systemic arrangement upon eliminating capitalism (see Singer, 1980). Consequently, to a great extent, in addition to its necessary political layer, communism was considered a future socio-economic arrangement. The interpretation would be that communism was, thus, in its economic-institutional form, never achieved in the Eastern bloc, while socialism, with its distinctive economic features, was believed to have been firmly installed. It is important to note that what may seem to be an institutional monolith from the outside would be a variety of micro-systemic solutions inside, allowing various degrees of political and economic repression/freedom. In an attempt to reconcile both perceptions, that is, the commonly accepted political perception and the scholarly related economic-institutional perception, it could perhaps be argued that the Eastern bloc states were politically 'communist', as they were ruled by communist parties, and economically 'socialist', as they could have been seen as being in the socialist period of transformation towards communism. This is, however, not to say that post-socialist transformation would refer exclusively to economic liberalisation and post-communist transformation to political reforms.

This statement bears important consequences for our subsequent analysis. In many former members of the Eastern bloc, the terms 'post-communist' and 'post-socialist' in reference to the systemic transformation can be used in a somewhat complementary way, as those countries witnessed the departure of communist parties from power, or at least the change in the political mechanism that would earlier prevent an effective power contestation, and the departure of the socialist economy. However, China, together with a handful of states, seems to be an exception, as the CCP is still in control of the country, and the single-party regime is still present. Socialism, as an economic-institutional system, on the other hand, is subject to reformulation. Following the previous line of argument, one can conclude that China might be undergoing post-socialist transformation but is not necessarily subject to post-communist transformation.

The economic transformation seems better reflected in the term 'post-socialist transformation' than in the phrase 'post-communist transformation', not because the former does not apply to political arrangements, as it does, but because the latter, in its Western-originated common perception, ignores economic arrangements to some extent. More importantly, from the point of view of Marxist theory and of the political elites of the Eastern bloc, communism, as an economic-institutional arrangement, had never been achieved, and thus could not be in the process of transformation. In the analysis of the concept of the developmental state, the examination of a genus of the political system is a rather secondary issue and the economic-institutional arrangements take priority. Therefore, for the purpose of the examination of 'developmental-stateness', one may wish to refer to the post-socialist transformation as the process that, without the exclusion of the political aspects, underlines the economic reforms.

As far as the political perspective is concerned, the last few decades show that the need for democratisation – the desire to elect citizens as representatives to decision-making institutions – is very powerful in most nations.[16] In particular, this desire can be observed in Central and

---

[16] Although seen by Plato as a form of degeneration of the order of the state (Sylwestrzak, 1996), in recent times, democracy has been the dominant political system in the world: 'The 1980s and 1990s saw a huge increase in the global spread of democracy. Some 81 countries – 29 in Sub Saharan Africa, 23 in Europe, 14 in Latin America and 5 in the Arab States – took steps towards democratisation' (HDR, 2003, p 134). However, as pointed out by *The Economist* (2014), its popularity is waning.

Eastern European states, where authoritarian regimes led by communist parties have been replaced by multiparty democracies. In most of these cases, the democratisation processes were indeed extremely fast because: first, after many years of authoritarian regimes, people expected more political power; and, second, the introduction of democracy could take place in a decree-like fast-track legislative procedure. Naturally, one must take into consideration its possible interim failures, caused by the fact that a civic society may not be fully formed and that the new institutions fail to function correctly; however, the installation of the systemic legal frame can be almost immediate. Despite the democratic ambitions of many, some states of post-socialist transformation did not introduce democratic procedures. Consequently, the two main types of political systemic reform among the states of the former Eastern bloc are 'political liberalisation' (eg Poland, Hungary, Czech Republic, among others) and 'political reformulation without liberalisation' (eg Kazakhstan, Uzbekistan, among others), the former resulting in the establishment of a democratic system and the latter in the creation of another form of authoritarianism.

As far as the economic perspective is concerned, years of experience allow for the assumption that at the current level of development of our civilisation, the market seems to prevail over any non-market system. Historically, this does not need to be a paramount truth, nevertheless, contemporarily, it seems to be a general rule. Therefore, post-socialist transformation (PST), in its economic-institutional form, constitutes a departure from state command towards market economy. The process consists of several elements. According to Kolodko (2001a, p 22), they are: liberalisation and macroeconomic stabilisation; institution building; and microeconomic restructuring. In the Chinese context, Guo (2003, pp 562–3) refers to the processes of:

> economic liberalisation – the loosening or elimination of government restrictions on economic transactions, including freeing prices, trade, delegating control rights or decision-making rights from the state to enterprise managers, and allowing the development of various types of new business firms and enterprises, such as joint-ventured, individual-owned, private-owned, and foreign-owned; marketisation – the attempt to develop important elements of a market economy and create market institutions such as legal, financial, and social welfare systems; privatisation – a political process wherein the government, by the use of state power, administers a privatising programme and policy for

the purpose of the dramatic and fundamental transformation of the existing public ownership, with the massive transfer of state-owned or collective-owned enterprises, land, and other public assets to private hands.

The divisions presented in the scholarly literature essentially describe three mutually dependent, interrelated and often not clearly separable processes: economic liberalisation, market institutionalisation and microeconomic restructuring. Economic liberalisation is related to the process of the external and internal opening of closed economies for economic activities. Market institutionalisation is, in real terms, an introduction of market mechanisms into economic conduct by the implementation of certain laws and the creation of certain institutions, which supervise and define the limits of economic activities. Microeconomic restructuring involves sectoral changes in the structure of the national economy. It includes ownership reforms, redefining central–local relations and industrial restructuring. In the developmental state (DS) context, many post-socialist reforms, such as market institutionalisation, economic liberalisation and ownership changes, among others, may contribute to the establishment of a DS-style institutional environment. However, they also may not, as discussed later in this chapter. It depends on the particular micro-solutions within and the extent of state reforms.

For the post-socialist transformation to commence, there were both political and economic factors that contributed to the mounting pressure for changes. Predominantly, however, economic factors should be considered as catalysts of the collapse of state-command economies ruled by communist regimes. In post-Second World War Europe, Western market economies developed faster than socialist states and their societies successfully maintained a more affluent position. A good example is illustrated by the case of Spain, with its Franco-era capitalism, and Poland, with its state-command system. Shortly after the Second World War, the gross domestic product (GDP) per capita of Poland – the country most affected by the war – was still marginally larger than that of Spain. After the collapse of the Eastern bloc, Spain's GDP per capita was over twice as large as that of Poland, as illustrated in Figure 2.1.

In East Asia the story is indeed similar. The market economies of Japan and Korea experienced better developmental dynamics than socialist

Figure 2.1: GDP [gross domestic product] per capita (in constant 1990 prices) in 1950 and 1990

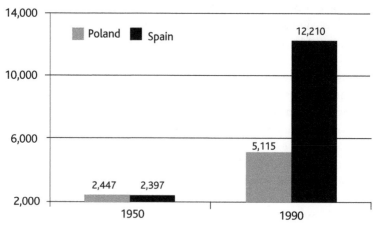

Source: Balcerowicz (2003), after Maddison Database.

China.[17] Consequently, the pressure to achieve better developmental results gradually increased in parts of Europe and Asia. State-command economies, in general, were eventually to collapse or to be transformed, in practice, due to their inherent low effectiveness, bureaucratic management inhibiting growth and lack of sufficient development and modernisation mechanisms as compared with market economies.

There are a number of countries that have participated in the process of post-socialist transformation; however, there is some misunderstanding as to which states actually belong to the group. The confusion may derive from inaccuracy of the definition of socialist states or, even more, from a liberal appliance of the term 'communist state' to those, with a few exceptions, which are now in transition. It is widely accepted that post-socialist transformation has been evident in Europe and Asia. A similar process might take place in America, in the case of Cuba, the only socialist country on the continent. In fact, Raul Castro's reform may put Cuba on the track of economic transformation leading to a market system of some kind. The suggestion that there are any other socialist or post-socialist countries there, using the argument that the states were run by socialist ideologists/driving forces, as was the case of Salvador Allende's Chile (1970–73), Daniel Ortega's Nicaragua

---

[17] A lack of market economic conditions is not the sole reason for communist China's developmental dynamics not being as impressive as that of Korea, Japan and Taiwan in the 1960s and 1970s. Other factors include international conditions, as discussed in Chapter One.

(1979–90) or Hugo Chavez' Venezuela, is very questionable.[18] It is just as questionable to assume that so-called 'African socialism', a term adopted as an ideology by African leaders (Kwame Nkrumah, Kenneth Kaunda, Samora Machel, Robert Mugabe and others) after colonial rule, which was very much a reaction to oppressive capitalist colonial powers and combined elements of traditional indigenous culture with a socially oriented philosophy of state, has much to do with real socialism, despite the fact that Nkrumah referred to himself as the African Lenin and members of ZANU-PF – Robert Mugabe's ruling party in Zimbabwe – address themselves as comrades.

To clarify the matter, post-socialist transformation has taken place in Europe and Asia. Among the European states in transition, there have been 21 countries of Central and Eastern Europe, of South-Eastern Europe and the former Soviet republics: Russia, Belarus, Ukraine, Moldova, Estonia, Latvia, Lithuania, Poland, Czech Republic, Slovakia, Hungary, Romania, Bulgaria, Slovenia, Croatia, Bosnia and Herzegovina, Serbia, Montenegro, Macedonia, Albania, and Kosovo.[19] Naturally, one may also include the former German Democratic Republic. Some argue that many of the European countries completed their PST process upon creating systemic environments, legal conditions, economic mechanisms and institutions similar to that of their neighbours in Western Europe. However, this is not without controversy, as some would see, for example, the developmental disparities between the so-called old European Union (EU) (also known as the EU-15) and the post-socialist EU members, or unresolved property rights issues, as indicators that the PST process has not in actual fact been completed.

It is the inaccurate account of the Asian states in post-socialist transformation that leads to misunderstanding. There seems to be some confusion with the term 'Asian socialism', as has been the case with 'African socialism'. Gyan Chand (1965), a close aide to India's Prime Minister Jawaharlal Nehru (1947–64), wrote in his book entitled *Socialist Transformation of Indian Economy* about the necessity of continuing to build socialism in India. Chand is by no means the only author discussing India as a socialist economy (see Jain, 2000; Shah, 2001). Moreover, the preamble of the 1949 constitution of India declares the state a sovereign, socialist, secular, democratic republic. Indeed, state economic interventionism, as well as good relations with the so-called Eastern bloc, could confuse some that India, if not already,

---

[18]   Since 2007, Daniel Ortega has yet again been the president of Nicaragua.

[19]   The issue of Kosovo is still a controversial one as many countries do not recognise it as an independent state.

would eventually become a socialist state. One should note, however, that Chand pitted 'democratic socialism' in India against 'communist totalitarianism' in the Soviet Union and China. Consequently, his vision of 'Indian socialism' was rather a vision of a state interventionist country with a market economy, closely associated with the ideas of European social democrats. Therefore, even in realising Chand's ideas, India would not have become a socialist country and could not therefore be classified as being in post-socialist transition.

In the post-socialist transformation group, former Asian Soviet republics such as Georgia, Armenia and Azerbaijan (the Caucasus region),[20] and Kazakhstan, Uzbekistan, Tajikistan, Kyrgyzstan and Turkmenistan (Central Asia), can undoubtedly be included. It is widely accepted that Mongolia, China and Vietnam are, indeed, undergoing transformation. Often, Laos and sometimes Cambodia and Myanmar are named among the Asian post-socialist states. In fact, the post-socialist transformation in Myanmar has accelerated significantly since 2011 (Bolesta, 2013a). North Korea, however, is still a state-command economy with marginal reforms having been initiated in the late 1980s.

Post-socialist transformation – the debate

The discussion on paths and methods of post-socialist transformation is chiefly held among scholars and, most importantly, among policymakers. One should remember that, as Kornai (2004) rightly points out, the analysis of transformation, even in the economic dimension, is about politics, as the politicisation of every decision is unavoidable (see also Duckett, 2003). As far as the large and extensive literature on this subject is concerned, most of the well-known experts, such as Dornbush (1994), analyse only certain aspects of post-socialist transformation, focusing, for example, as he did, on financial policy. Some dedicate their research partly to Central and Eastern Europe, like Sachs (1989, 1993), who also examined Latin American economies; some focus predominantly on one individual country, as Aslund (1991, 1995) does on Russia. The literature on post-socialist transformation seldom features the DS concept, as the PST process has taken place in a time of denial of the state's important role in the economy and development. Moreover, the literature on post-socialist transformation seldom targets China, as it is biased towards Central and

[20] There is a growing tendency to perceive the Caucasus states as European due to their historical and political ties, culture and the ambiguity as far as the border between the European and Asian continents is concerned.

Eastern Europe and the former Soviet Union. However, the literature on China is extensively engaged in the PST process, under various conceptualisations of reform, transformation and transition.

Although most scholars tend to accept the superiority of the market system over the state-command system as far as the dynamics of socio-economic development is concerned, the very process of building a market economy in the post-socialist states is controversial. China seems to be at the core of this discussion. On the one hand, there are supporters of rapid and aggressive economic liberalisation without any significant consideration for institutional reforms, the so-called 'shock therapy' doctrine, and, on the other hand, there are advocates of incremental changes who emphasise the need to build systemic institutions and for microeconomic restructuring, and who stress the fact that these types of reforms require time. The very primal debate of 'gradualism versus radicalism' – though not uncontested in its nature – has been present since the beginning of the post-socialist transformation, and both options have had influential proponents. Jeffrey Sachs, a central figure to the PST process at the beginning of transformation, although subsequently easing his tone, spoke in favour of radical changes, pointing to the fact that such reforms would allow faster adjustability to and integration with the increasingly globalised world. Stronger ties with the rest of the world would create conditions for faster development (Sachs, 1994). Such changes were introduced by Poland's Minister of Finance Leszek Balcerowicz between 1989 and 1991, and were broadly known as *Plan Balcerowicza* (Balcerowicz's Plan). Balcerowicz (1998) defends the radical reform path as the only way to eliminate hyperinflation, as well as to unleash human capital, and eventually allow for a constant increase in productivity. He believes that gradualism enabled the consolidation of certain groups of interests capable of sabotaging the course of pivotal economic changes in favour of their sectoral/personal gains. Murrell (1993) points out that the 'shock therapy' in Russia under Yegor Gaidar – Russia's Minister of Finance (1991–93) – was even more intensive than in Poland. However, Gaidar was forced to back down after, as he describes it, populist pressure (Gaidar, 2005). Kolodko, who like Balcerowicz also held the position of Minister of Finance of Poland, seems to be a great opponent of the radical reform path. He sees the gradualism versus radicalism discourse in the economic liberalisation and stabilisation context, underlining that the imposition of drastic discipline in economic policy resulted in the overshooting syndrome (see Kolodko, 1999a, 2001b, 2004a). In other words, the remedy was too strong for the problem; hence, the economic depression was eventually extensively larger and longer-lasting than anticipated. Most of the observers of the Chinese systemic transformation in comparison with other former socialist states support the incremental transformation mode as the means to achieve high developmental dynamics (see Naughton, 1995, 1999; McMillan and Naughton, 1996; Jefferson and Rawski, 1999a; Saich, 2001). This is due to the overwhelmingly better developmental results of China than those of the other countries of the former Eastern bloc. This perception complies with Kornai's (2004) statement that some reforms need time if they are to be implemented correctly. Kornai himself seems to suffer from 'Sachs syndrome', where we observe a steady departure from the support for radical reforms in favour of the differentiation in reform policy and the acceptance that gradual reforms might be a better solution, due, as it seems, to the failure of the former, as far as the anticipated results are concerned. Kornai currently advises against accepting any overall doctrine in pursuing transformation goals and warns against the assumption that 'the faster the reform, the faster the growth': 'There is no universal prescription [for successful transformation]. There are no specific, practical recommendations equally valid for every country' (Kornai, 2004, p 3). Gradual approach supporters also point to well-constructed development policy as an element of post-socialist transformation, which, it is claimed, cannot be sustained during rapid radical changes. The followers of the 'shock therapy' doctrine are convinced that some changes had to be quick and drastic to avoid an economic catastrophe and to create a healthier environment for economic development. Hardly any of the PST countries, however, are believed to have followed exclusively either the gradual or the shock therapy way, if, indeed, such rather elusive concepts can be clearly defined, as far as systemic transformation policies are concerned.

It is often believed that it is the Washington Consensus that can be considered the starting point for the discussion on methodologies of post-socialist transformation, as exemplified in the gradual versus radical discourse, as well as in the entire philosophy as far as the final target of the transition is concerned, namely, the imaginary future state system construction. In the late 1980s, the Washington Consensus, taking its name after the city where the world's most important financial decisions were made, became the very element of a new reigning doctrine of economic policy. Coined by the economist John Williamson (1990), the Consensus itself contains 10 points vital for stabilising the economy and public finances: introducing fiscal discipline; reordering public expenditure priorities by switching to better funding of basic health and education; constructing a tax system that would combine a broad tax base with moderate marginal tax rates; liberalising interest rates;

allowing a competitive exchange rate; trade liberalisation; liberalisation of inward foreign direct investment (FDI); privatisation; deregulation aimed at easing entry and exit barriers; and securing property rights (Williamson, 2002). It is important to note that, in many ways, the Consensus stood in sharp contrast with the developmental state concept, as far as trade liberalisation, interest rate liberalisation, exchange rate liberalisation and economic deregulation are concerned.

The Consensus has had an enormous impact on post-socialist transformation, despite the fact that its intentions have been questioned. In official propaganda the sets of economic policy recommendations were originally intended to guide Latin American countries out of their economic and financial crisis. Indeed, only tough disciplinary measures seemed to be able to reverse the process of these otherwise deteriorating economies. In practice, the recommended policies served as a tool for mainly private and commercial financial organisations based in the developed world to recover the money that they had previously lent to the countries of the region but, because of the debt crisis, had been unable to retrieve. It was the debt crisis and not the economic crisis itself that seems to have prompted a reaction in Washington. In the late 1980s, the total outstanding debt in Latin America approached USD500 billion. Although other countries were affected, in the year 1983, 'sixteen of the nations were from Latin America, and the four largest – Mexico, Brazil, Venezuela and Argentina owed various commercial banks US\$ 176 billion' (FDIC, 1997, p 191).

In the Latin American countries, the success of the Washington Consensus was partial and limited. It brought some positive changes to their economies: 'healthier budgets, lower inflation, lower external debt ratios, and economic growth' (Clift, 2003), to mention the most important advantages. However, there were no positive trends in poverty eradication and there was no decrease in social disparities. At the same time, states became more vulnerable to external shocks. According to Lee and Mathews (2010), the inadequacy of the Consensus as a guide to development arose from its lack of recognition of economic development as a catch-up process, its failure to see development as a dynamic process of sequential stages and its silence on the fundamental role of capability building. Nevertheless, its partial and limited success allowed for the presumption that the model was applicable to other regions. Indeed, a new stable economic environment needed to be created, especially in some countries of Central and Eastern Europe ravaged by stagflation (economic stagnation and inflation) (Kolodko, 1993) and, in some cases, hyperinflation. Jeffrey Sachs (then a professor at Harvard University), acting as an advisor to the Polish government, was among the first to attempt to incorporate Consensus provisions into the packet of economic reforms in the PST world. In reality, most of the Western experts had no idea how to help the transformation process in Central and Eastern Europe (see Greenspan, 2007), so the Consensus-driven provisions related to macroeconomic discipline and economic opening-up amounted to nothing more than a great experiment. Soon after, closer studies (Ahrens, 1999; Kolodko, 1999b) revealed that many countries adopting Consensus principles suffered losses in their economies. In fact, all the former Soviet republics experienced extensive economic recession. The infamous record-holder was Moldova, whose economy decreased by 68% between the years 1989 and 2000 (EBRD, 2001, p 16). The apparent failure in the countries of post-socialist transformation prompted furious attacks on the authors and executors of the Consensus. Additional vehement criticism of the International Monetary Fund's (IMF's) and World Bank's handling of the Asian financial crisis using the Consensus guidelines, voiced in the book *Globalisation and Its Discontents* by Joseph Stiglitz (2002), resulted in a significant increase in opponents of the Consensus. The argument about the failure of the Washington Consensus in the case of states in post-socialist transformation seemed, indeed, valid if one takes into consideration the achievements of those countries that in full or partly rejected its provisions. The prime example is China, which has achieved high economic growth and instantly strongly opposed the Consensus doctrine. This failure was due to the fact that in its recommendations regarding economic policies, the Consensus did not take into account the necessity of extensive institutional reforms needed for restructuring the state system in the process of post-socialist transformation, and that without such time-consuming reforms, tough fiscal discipline and extensive economic liberalisation may harm the vulnerable socio-economic environment in transition. Moreover, regardless of the various arrays of post-socialist predicaments, perhaps the Consensus, inspired by neo-liberal economic thought, presented neither desirable nor feasible solutions to the former socialist states, positioned outside of the sphere of Western liberal capitalism. In other words, the assumption that the reform methodology and desired reform target would be universal was flawed.

The discussion about the wrongs and rights of the Washington Consensus and its applicability is not over; hence, the genus of the best post-socialist transformation trajectory continues to be debated. In fact, Arrighi (2007) managed to engage Adam Smith in the debate, questioning the perception that the latter was a supporter of the liberal economic model and a potential proponent of shock therapy (see also Kolodko, 2011): 'The dogmatic belief in benefits of minimalist governments and self-regulating markets … or the equally dogmatic belief in the curative powers of "shock therapies" advocated by the Washington Consensus … were completely alien to Smith' (Arrighi, 2007, p 43). Very influential policymakers speak in favour of the Consensus, while others strongly oppose it. Stiglitz (2002) reveals the ill-advised policy recommendations based on the Consensus' principles that contributed to the 1997 Asian financial crisis, despite being designed as remedies. Kolodko (2001a) illustrates the inadequacy of the provisions of the Consensus for the post-socialist environment, pointing to a certain lack of institutional background and fragility of the systemic arrangements, citing North's (1997) argument about the importance of institution building. Williamson (2008), however, questions the interpretation that the Consensus equals neo-liberalism or market fundamentalism and thus embodies the culprit of the current maladies of the global economic order, and 'likes to emphasize [that] many policy recommendations that have been attributed to the Washington Consensus cannot be found in his original formulation' (Krugman, 2008, p 34). Perhaps as a result, Sachs and Woo (cf Sachs and Woo, 1994; Woo, 2004) seem undecided about the final outcome, accepting the fact that the uniqueness of post-socialist transformation prohibits the liberal applicability of all the sets of policies created for a different occasion.

The alleged developmental failures caused by the implementation of the Consensus provisions, as envisaged in post-socialist transformation, resulted in the formulations of alternative sets of recommendations. Those recommendations are usually conceptually closer to the DS model, as they reinstate the importance of the state in the developmental endeavour. For example, the initiative of the 2002 Monterey Consensus (ICFD, 2002), which was wider in scope, included not only economic policy, but also governmental and administrative reforms, human rights, and so on. The most commonly used term to describe the initiatives is the 'Post-Washington Consensus' (Stiglitz, 1998; Ahrens, 1999; Jayasuriya, 2001; Kolodko, 2001b; Serra and Stiglitz, 2008). Ramo (2004), however, decided to use the term 'Beijing Consensus'. There does not seem to be one widely accepted definition of what the Beijing Consensus actually means. This is most likely due to the fact that by rehearsing some known concepts, it brings little into the contemporary debate on the general guidelines for effective development. Ramo (2004) underlines the importance of an active role of the government in developmental efforts, which is a mere rediscovery of an already-existing concept that was nevertheless abandoned during, what Arrighi (2007) calls, the neo-liberal counter-revolution of the 1980s, which resulted in the adoption of 'a hyper-liberal model' (Nuti, 2010) in a number of countries. Moreover, acknowledging the positive developmental changes in China, as well as in other states of the Northeast Asia region, Lee and Mathews (2010) coined the term 'BeST Consensus', as mentioned in Chapter One. With capability enhancement and development as the central feature, it is characterised by two principal agents: pilot agencies to guide industrialisation and domestic firms to advance economic development.

Post-socialist transformation in China

The main question of this chapter concerns the process of post-socialist transformation in China, whether it is taking place and, if it is, what its features are, including those related to DS-style institutionalisation. At no stage of the reforms, which already account for half of the time of the PRC's existence, would the Chinese authorities use the term post-socialist transformation. On the contrary, all efforts would be directed at improving socialism.

China during the state-command period

During the Cold War, China was perceived as a member of the Eastern bloc. There were, however, always significant differences among the socialist states, not only as far as the level of development was concerned, but also with reference to political and economic arrangements. Khrushchev's Thaw, as the 1956 limited political liberalisation in the Soviet Union and the CEE was described, was met in China with Mao's articulate opposition. During the socialist times, economic freedom was always greater in countries such as Poland than in China. Unlike in CEE, where the system was in most cases imposed by the Soviet Union and was not related to socio-economic development, Chinese socialism was self-imposed and believed to be developmentalist. Its definition falls beyond the description of the production mode and refers to a certain positioning of the state as the guardian of what Lin (2006) calls a 'public good regime'. She argues that Chinese 'socialist development lay in both its historical origin of revolutionary modernity and its post-revolutionary mission of overcoming backwardness' (Lin,

2006, p 70).[21] The so-called central planning, however, was significantly less 'central' in comparison with CEE and the Soviet Union. As a large and underdeveloped country, whose authorities could not effectively control its territory for decades prior to the establishment of the PRC, it lacked the sophistication necessary to maintain the type of system in which most economic and development-related decisions were met in the capital and most of the economic processes were regulated. Nevertheless, a lack of market institutions, as well as the presence of certain types of macroeconomic policies and regulations concerned with the mechanism of the allocation of production and goods, price control, and origins of the means of production, clearly show that China was a socialist state. Ironically, from the economic-institutional perspective, China could have been seen as more 'advanced' in building the futuristic communism than some of the CEE countries, where private means of production were partially allowed and price control was not complete. Consequently, although lacking executive machinery to some extent, state command was indeed exercised, by ordering the type and volume of production, and its distribution and price. Moreover, the country was governed by a communist party.

At the time of the establishment of the People's Republic of China, the country was considered to be very poor by international standards, with large class- and geographical location-determined inequalities. The national economy was dominated by agricultural production. Politically, the state had emerged from the domestic civil war, preceded by and partly overlapping with the war against the Japanese, and the 19th-century period of semi-colonialism. The new authorities, drawn from the CCP, with Chairman Mao Zedong as the state leader, began to reform the entire country following Marxist ideology. The problems of the revolutionary government included, among others, establishing and consolidating administrative control and reviving and modernising the national economy (Riskin, 1987, p 38). Maddison (2007, p 62) identified four economic reform objectives pursued during the Mao era:

- a change in property rights, with three main targets: landlords, the national bourgeoisie (capitalists, merchants, bankers) and foreign interests (mostly in Manchuria and in the former treaty ports);

---

[21]   Naturally, this perception does not come without controversies. Some analyses question the developmental intentions of Mao's regime or, for that matter, Mao's dedication to socialism. See, for example, Dikotter (2010) and Chang and Halliday (2005), and the criticism of the latter in Benton and Lin (2010).

- a big increase in state revenue to finance expanded administrative mechanisms, maintain a high level of military preparedness and raise the rate of 'accumulation';
- market forces were to be replaced by regulatory devices for allocating investment funds and physical inputs, controlling the movement of labour, and fixing prices and wages; and
- foreign trade was to become a state monopoly.

The acceleration of socialist transformation in the mid–1950s resulted in the official elimination of privately owned companies and in complete rural collectivisation. The State Planning Commission was established in 1952. The first five-year plan – the guidance for short-term state economic planning – was inaugurated in 1953. China became a fully institutionalised centrally planned economy by 1956 (OECD, 2009a).

Despite following the Soviet model of heavy industry development aimed at building up military capacity and expanding general infrastructure, Mao Zedong underlined in 'On the Ten Major Relationship' (see Mao, 1977) that unlike in the Soviet Union, light industry and especially agriculture remained important sectors of China's development policy and could not be neglected (see also Lardy, 1983). By 1958, China's agricultural economy went through several phases of transformation; from confiscating land from privileged landowners, through pulling peasant resources together, creating 'advanced cooperatives', to creating large people's communes containing around 5,000 households each (Maddison, 2007, p 72). Lardy (1983, p 96) points out that the entire Mao period was characterised by informal experimentation as to the organisational structures determining the relative economic freedom of farmers. However, in the mid-1950s, there was a diversion of productive forces from agriculture to producer goods production, such as steel and iron in heavy industry, in order to achieve a new policy objective, namely, the Great Leap Forward. This diversion resulted in an extensive famine, with starvation affecting millions of people (see Dikotter, 2010).

The period between 1963, when the famine effectively ended and Premier Zhou Enlai called for four modernisations, and 1978, when the systemic reforms were ordained, is often referred to as late Maoism. The main socio-economic objectives of that period were creating self-reliance in the economy and improving the degree of egalitarianism in society (Riskin, 1987). It was characterised by the strategies of accelerating rural development, partly by way of infrastructural investment, improving the education base and health care, and defence-centred industrialisation. In 1964, the *dazhai* model was declared a national model of agricultural development, underlying the collective character of rural production, distribution and consumption (Riskin, 1987, p 220). Nevertheless, as discussed by White (1987, p 413), the 'rural political economy [continued to be] dominated by two institutional systems; the state exercised ... direct controls over the rural population ... [and] the three-tiered system of rural collectives was a tightly knit framework for the comprehensive organisation of rural society and economy'. Foremost, however, the period is associated with the Cultural Revolution as the means to abruptly rearrange the governing structure of the country and to reformulate social relations, in response to Mao's weakening political position.

As far as the management of national industry is concerned, Brandt et al (2008) point to the gradual decentralisation of companies' control after the Great Leap Forward. Eventually, a large part 'of industrial output came from smaller collective firms located in both urban and rural areas, most owned and directed by local governments' (Brandt et al, 2008, p 571). In neither large enterprises controlled by the central government nor in smaller firms in the hands of local authorities was the role of the managerial staff more important than that of the party leadership. Simultaneously, the hidden private sector continued to operate (Huang, 2008), for example, in such places as Zhejiang province, where people resisted rural collectivisation, especially in Wenzhou county (Liu, 1992). As far as the financial system during the state-command period is concerned, it consisted of a single bank, namely, the People's Bank of China (PBC):

> a central government-owned and controlled bank under the Ministry of Finance, which served as both the central bank and a commercial bank, [in the late 1970s] controlling [as much as] 93 percent of the total financial assets of the country and handling almost all financial transactions. With its main role to finance the physical production plans, it used both a 'cash plan' and a 'credit plan' to control the cash flows in consumer markets and transfer flows between branches. (Allen et al, 2008, p 509)

China's state-command economy created certain mechanisms, as well as institutional conditions, for the subsequent implementation of a genus of the developmental state model. These will be discussed in more detail further in Chapters Three, Four and Five. However, one can mention here the following factors as positively contributing towards post-socialist developmental state (PSDS) establishment: administrative centralisation, despite business decentralisation; some aspects of the central-planning mechanism implementation and the expansion of state bureaucracy; the improvements in human capital; and the banking system's subordination to the state agenda. Moreover, the process of industrialisation, partly within the frames of four modernisations in terms of overall industry, national defence, science and technology, can be seen as convergent with the historical DS pattern. On the other hand, the elimination of private entrepreneurship as an important economic force created the lack of a private sector partner for the state–business alliance, while the termination of market institutions abolished the market mechanisms necessary for a DS model.

China in the process of post-socialist transformation

As far as the subsequent post-socialist transformation is concerned, the main controversy concerns the issue as to whether China has actually been effectively dismantling the socialist regime, not merely in its political form, but also in being a socio–economic system characterised by a state–command economy. During the reform period, in 1982 (at the 12th CCP Congress), China's leader Deng Xiaoping coined the term 'socialism with Chinese characteristics', whereas in 1987 (at the 13th Congress), Party Secretary Zhao Ziyang declared that China was merely at 'the initial stage of socialism' (Dirlik, 2005, pp 231, 232). The official propaganda continuously affirms that the PRC is building a socialist society and a socialist market economy (the term officially used for the first time in 1992).

'Socialism' and 'market' are, however, mostly seen as mutually exclusive, despite the concept of market socialism. This is our understanding from the previous analysis, backed by a mass of scholarly publications and, as it seems, the general perception. Nevertheless, the concept of market socialism is featured extensively in the analysis of the process of China's transformation. It is sometimes believed that China's reforms initiated in the late 1970s were geared in their first decade towards market socialism (Lin, 2006; Bramall, 2009a), as during that period, the ownership of the means of production remained predominantly in the state or collective hands (despite economic restructuring and the gradual removal of entry barriers for other economic agents), whereas prices became determined predominantly by market forces. For China's political elites, the model was considered sustainable and logical, as economic liberalisation and opening up would be accompanied by maintaining public ownership and a drive to egalitarian prosperity. Guo (2003, p 560) repeated Feng's (1995) argument that the de-collectivisation of China's rural economy in the 1980s led to a new type of collective economy characterised by public ownership of land and individualised operations of production. Because of that, Bowles and Dong (1994) saw China as a successful case of socialist state-led development. However, Greenfield and Leong (1997) argue that it was difficult to envisage China as an example of market socialism due to the state's oppression of the working class, as discussed later in this book. They dub the systemic arrangements 'communist capitalism', with the CCP in power and the marginalisation of the working class.

However, Justin Yifu Lin (2005) points to certain differences in perception of what constitutes a classical model of socialism and socialism with Chinese characteristics. He describes Chinese socialism as, in effect, the creation of a harmonious society (the concept publicised by China's fourth-generation leader Hu Jintao) via extensive developmental efforts. Socialism is, then, closely associated with being a mechanism of development and modernisation, and in the process of systemic transformation, with a social element of the transformational endeavour and not merely with economic-institutional reform. In this respect, the terms 'socialist regime' or 'socialist state' do not need to refer exclusively to the economic-institutional construction of the country and may encompass certain political, historical and philosophical dimensions of the concept. Some Chinese scholars partly adopted Chand's (1965) rhetoric on socialism, in addition to Lin's (2006) historically grounded motives of socialism and Lin's (2005) incarnation of socialism as a harmonious society concept, and perceive socialism as a set of developmental ideals realised by state interventionist policies. It is important to reiterate that many proponents and opponents of socialism alike saw it as an overall state ideology not limited to economic-institutional arrangements, but encompassing various strata of societal existence (see, eg, Schumpeter, 1942; Von Mises, 1951).

The replacement of the term 'socialism' with 'central planning' does not dismiss the argument that China is creating a socialist economy. On the contrary to common opinion, the inability to modernise and develop among the states of the Eastern bloc as efficiently as among market economies did not lie within the actual concept of central planning, but rather within the cross-sectoral extent to which central planning was applied. Among the developmentally successful DS countries, central planning in the form of 'plan-rational', as described by Johnson (1982, 1999) and Woo-Cumings (1999), played a crucial role in the developmental endeavour. In socialism, the shortcomings were in the rationality of planning, and, more importantly, the agents designated to implement the plans. Therefore, in China, which is purportedly undergoing systemic reorganisation, central planning remains an important instrument in the formulation of general developmental objectives, though the actual policies' implementation prerogatives have mostly been transferred from central authorities to provincial and other levels, in the process of post–Mao 'administrative decentralisation' (see Breslin, 1999), and many processes are subject to market scrutiny. Thus, Howell (1998, p 57) probably rightly claims that China went from 'command planning' to 'guidance planning'.

However, to narrow the definition of socialism to its economic-institutional form, one is inclined to arrive at a conclusion that China has been building socialism without socialism, at least since the economic liberalisation of the 1990s. The uninterrupted governing of the CCP and the state's official propaganda, backed by some institutional experiments of an interim nature, cannot sufficiently blur the picture that from an economic perspective, a market system with very little socialist institutionalisation is being created in the PRC, and that the departure from socialism was decided on and is being implemented. Naturally, it still leaves scope for philosophical debate about the distinctiveness in meaning and arrangements of the socialist state in China, hence the definitive abandonment of the system. An assumption that Deng Xiaoping's policies were intended at reforming socialism does not need to be dismissed, as:

> the actual reform trajectory nevertheless followed its own logic, and given the tremendous pressures of ideological and institutional globalisation, it was not 'allowed' to adjust until it would meet the 'standards' of post-socialist transition set up within a framework of global capitalism. (Lin, 2006, p 268)

Indeed, China has been building a new institutional environment for economic activities and a new institutional platform for economic interaction and, hence, creating a new economic order. This capitalist institutionalisation, which emanates from the conformity with World Trade Organization (WTO) guidelines, seems to have driven the systemic reforms in the long run.

The rhetoric of 'building socialism' seems to be used as a certain justification by the CCP, perhaps not to rule, as the developmental legitimacy of its power has been rather firmly established (as shown later), but to remain nominally a communist party, as the change in the official rhetoric could, nevertheless, prompt some questions related to power-holding. In addition to, as Lin (2006) points out, the ideological and historical baggage it brings in developing the country, 'socialism with Chinese characteristics' can perhaps be used as a key to the gateway to some experimental policies in the authorities' constant quest for various options. Such experimentalism often guided the authorities of historical DS cases, as pointed out by Johnson (1999).

By emphasising 'market' in the phrase 'socialist market economy' and by accepting the philosophical perception of what socialism is supposed to constitute in Chinese conditions, the idea of a 'socialist market economy' does not need to be dismissed in its entirety. Perhaps an attempt at creating a harmonious society, on some level, consistent with the continental European welfare state and Chand's option for India, can be seen as building a socialist market economy. Nevertheless, two arguments speak against this idea in the case of China.

First, as a result of the reforms, the process of creating a harmonious society has so far been ineffective. The deterioration of societal ties is accelerating, with large parts of society being marginalised. This is caused by economic conditions such as historical poverty, which generates additional poverty, but also institutional shortcomings – for example, legally based exclusions of certain groups from free education, the health-care service, the employment market, and social security on an unparalleled scale (in European terms). Consequently, the number of citizens of a 'second category', drawn predominantly from the inhabitants of rural areas, who either still reside in villages or have become China's migratory workforce of 250 million or so people, is increasing. This marginalisation, unique in its scale, as it concerns a very large proportion of the country's population, sharply contradicts the idea of a harmonious society. Government efforts to reverse the trend are, for the most part, insufficient. The growing disparities are reflected in the increasing Gini coefficient, which currently positions China among the countries where societal disintegration has for long been a significant problem.

Second, China seems to be characterised by an increasing number of features previously assigned by Arrighi (2007) to historical capitalist development. For example, foreign trade is believed to play a crucial role in China's development. The nation with the largest foreign trade volume in the world dominates certain sectors of world manufacturing. Although efforts are being made for a dramatic increase in domestic consumption, and some argue that, as opposed to common perception, international trade is not the driving force of economic growth in China (see Anderson, 2007), World Bank experts estimate that it will take decades for domestic consumption to replace trade as a dominant engine behind economic growth.[22] Foreign trade is believed to have been one of the main factors enabling the surge in developmental dynamics in the militarist model of capitalist development. Moreover, in contemporary China, capital is extremely important as an instrument of economic expansion and as a tool in stimulating certain sectors of the national economy. This has been the *rationale* behind the state's accumulation of around USD4 trillion worth of currency reserves as a result of China's export-oriented economy. Currently, China's budgetary capacities allow for securing its economic presence in the most remote corners of the world as part of the strategy to strengthen its international position and to secure its long-term access to natural resources necessary for further development. These capacities also enable the channelling of extensive financial assistance to favoured domestic sectors, such as the energy sector, infrastructure building and others. Accumulation of capital and its subsequent utilisation in the developmental endeavour became something more than just an element of Chinese market reality. The abundance of capital now serves broad economic as well as political purposes. Naturally, the state seems to remain in control of the overall development trajectory to a significant degree and does not seem to be subject to capitalist class interests at large, as was the case in the historical European model of capitalist development. However, a lack of institutional transparency and – to borrow a phrase from Johnson (1999) – a 'seamless web' of connections between state officials and business makes it difficult to evaluate how influential entrepreneurs are in their attempts to gear institutional building, regulations and economic policies towards their self-interests.

Breslin (2007) argues that China is indeed a capitalist state, with, however, Chinese characteristics, in which:

> the state creates the space for the private sector to be increasingly important, and regulates the market to ensure that the new bourgeoisie [the emerging business elite] can appropriate surplus value thanks to the bourgeoisie's close relationship with the party state. (Breslin, 2007, p 80)

Nevertheless, Dirlik (2005) suggests that China's departure from socialism should not be perceived as an inevitable drifting towards liberal capitalism. He argues that China's state policies and reforms may be described as 'post-socialism', an arrangement that, in a way,

---

[22] Personal communication with one of the World Bank's representatives to China, Beijing, 10 August 2009.

is a continuation of socialism perceived as the desire to overcome capitalism's deficiencies:

> Postsocialism seeks to avoid a return of capitalism, no matter how much it may draw upon the latter to improve the performance of 'actually existing socialism'. For this reason ... it strives to keep alive a vague vision of future socialism as the common goal of humankind while denying to it any immanent role in the determination of present social policy. (Dirlik, 2005, p 231)

Putting aside the debates on the definitions of socialism and capitalism, one needs to reiterate that there seems to be a consensus that China was a country characterised by the socialist state-command economic system and is now building a type of market economy. This market economy seems far from adhering to socialist principles, even in their Chinese philosophical form. In economic terms, China is undergoing a process of systemic reforms and its development trajectory exhibits features of capitalist development. Both the transformation from socialism to capitalism and the attempt to maintain the central state as the paramount power centre are, from the DS perspective, desired processes, and contribute to the creation of the DS-style institutional environment.

China's systemic transformation is often described as a dual transition. Peculiarly, this refers to at least several different processes. Pei (2006) claims that China's dual track is about transition from a state-socialist economic system and from a quasi-totalitarian political system. Indeed, Hamrin (1990) sees the dual strategy as bold economic reform combined with cautious political change. Focusing on economic affairs, Gallagher (2005) sees this dualism in the state withdrawal from the economy and its embracing of market principles. Lau and Qian (2000) discuss China's dual-track approach to transition as containing simultaneous enforcement of the plan (the plan track) and market liberalisation (the market track). The dual transition can also be seen as economic-systemic reform transforming state institutional arrangements, on one hand, and fast socio-economic development promoting the country into the group of more developed nations, on the other, as China is by all means characterised by these two processes.

Political reforms and the gradual path

As far as political reformulation is concerned, it is clear that, unlike CEE countries and some former Soviet republics, Chinese political elites have not chosen to implement a democratic system. The systemic reforms commenced in 1978 had never been intended at introducing democracy, even less one which is based on Western principles. As a consequence, the dynamics of Chinese political reforms have never caught up with the economic changes. The philosophy of economic liberalisation and the policy of opening up did not – according to Deng Xiaoping, the main ideologist of the reforms – contradict maintaining the ideological platform based on four cardinal principles: the CCP leading role; proletariat dictatorship; socialist way; and Marxist, Leninist and Maoist thought. Zhang (2000, p 154) believes that:

> the excessive caution in political reform may be attributable to the following reasons:
>
> • political reform is much more sensitive in the Chinese political system, and there has been no consensus yet on how to redefine the role of the Party in the Chinese political structure;
> • it entails the reform of the Party cadre system or the nomenclature, which is deeply entrenched and involves many vested interests;
> • it affects many people, as [at the end of the 20th century] the state apparatus employed over 40 million people, and consisted of parallel institutions at all levels of bureaucratic hierarchy. China's citizen–official ratio ... reached an alarming proportion of 30 to 1, unprecedented in China's entire history. Over 60 per cent of the state budget went to pay the wages of officials. Zhu Rongji [former Premier] complained ... that the state revenues had been 'eaten up' (*chīfàn cáizhèng*) by the country's huge bureaucracy;
> • despite massive economic reforms, officials still retain considerable power.... It is not easy for them to give up this power and privileges;
> • there is no other successful experience to refer to in 'decommunizing' a vast and populous country like China.

Breslin (2004), however, indicates that economic reform generated extensive political change, redefining the relationships between state actors.[23] The core elements of the political reforms have been concerned with: restructuring relations between the CCP, the government and the economy; institutionalising local–central relations; and democratising rural governance (Zheng, 1999b). It seems symptomatic that the state has almost exclusively followed political reform to the extent necessary for the facilitation of economic changes, fast development and a more extensive international economic and political presence, as well as in response to social changes, with one main prerogative in mind – to retain and to strengthen the power over and the control of society and the economy in the dynamically changing circumstances. Howell (1998, p 79) emphasises that 'the state has played a crucial role in refashioning the intermediary sphere so as to regain control over the society', as the systemic transformation resulted in an emergence of new socio-economic groups and in an increase of various social activities.

Many scholars discuss the CCP's ability to adapt to changing conditions and, at the same time, to influence the direction of changes in a way favoured by the CCP's apparatus. Dickson (2001) points to the 'inclusion' policies of co-optation and of creating links with other social organisations as the recipe for remaining affluent. The CCP has had a policy of attracting those who could contribute more effectively to the new role of the CCP leadership, defined as presiding over economic modernisation and rapid development – initially, technocrats, better educated and more competent than the old revolutionaries, and finally, economic practitioners, businessmen and also those in possession of very significant wealth, such as Liang Wengen.[24] By forging links with social non-party organisations:

> the state created a dense web … in order to channel interest articulation, regularise the flow of information between the state and key groups of society, replace direct state controls over the economy and society with at least partial social regulation, and screen out unwanted groups (Dickson, 2001, pp 520–1)

---

[23]   The relations between various existing state actors are examined later in the book.

[24]   Liang Wengen is considered to be one of China's richest men. He is the founder and main shareholder of Sany Group, a heavy industry manufacturer based in Changsha, Hunan Province.

From the CCP's perspective, this was absolutely necessary, as the changes enabled by the economic transformation and institutional reforms had a strong impact on society and societal activeness. As a result, the sphere between the CCP and the masses has partly been filled with 'social organisations', some of which are considered illegal (Howell, 1998).

In the absence of democratisation, political reformulation has taken the form of the separation of powers and redefining of the links between the state and other entities, as well as within the state – between the CCP and the government, and between central and local authorities. Goodman (1985) points out that China's leadership intended benign modernisation based on collective leadership and inner-party democracy in decision-making under the banner of socialist democracy. Decentralisation – a gradual process of transferring powers and responsibilities to lower levels of China's state administration – was foremost aimed at increasing the effectiveness of economic policies. This resulted in the fragmentation of authoritarian power in the national space, as opposed to the political space occupied by the CCP (Breslin, 2007, p 72). Nevertheless, by the 1990s, the process of strengthening local political power centres was met with central government efforts of re-centralisation. According to Zheng (1999b), its main element was the 'party management of cadres' system, which seems to prevail until now, as exemplified by the rotation of officials among provinces and the centre on a regular basis. It coincided with the political power being passed from the revolutionary leadership – often participants of the *chángzh ng* (the Long March), who were involved in creating the People's Republic – to the generation of new leaders – the technocrats who were the products of party bureaucracy (Fewsmith, 2001).

Although, as Zheng (1999b, p 1161) points out, the political reform in China has not been about opening of the political process to the general public and should be seen as a process of institutional adjustment, some political liberalisation is believed to be taking place and is visible in media broadcasting, in the increasingly more openly expressed opinions of policymakers and in a growing number of socially motivated protests and demonstrations.[25] The most important example of limited political

[25]   The debate on democratisation of the political scene is persistently present during the conferences of the influential China Reform Forum. It is believed that the Special Administrative Region (SAR) of Hong Kong will serve as a laboratory for the wider introduction of democratic practices in China. Some media, especially the Guangzhou-based Nanfang group, have not been consistent with the authorities for quite some time in respect to economic debates, but also in political themes.

liberalisation is often considered to be the quasi-democratisation of rural governance, where members of local communities gained the power to influence who would be seated in the villagers' committees. Initially self-established in two counties in Guangxi province in the early 1980s, rural elections became institutionalised through a course of laws and regulations (O'Brien and Li, 2000). However, despite it being an obvious gain on the front of political liberalisation, resulting in greater accountability, social acceptance and, usually, competence of local leaderships, Lewis and Xue (2003) argue that rural democracy does not work properly, as it is insufficiently supported by the state. Moreover, due to various local political factors, the system has developed unevenly throughout the country.

A lack of extensive political liberalisation is not uncommon among other PST states, especially former Asian Soviet republics, which makes China, in this respect, hardly an exceptional case. Gallagher (2002) believes that what delayed democratisation in China was the economic reform pattern, as the changes redirected popular attention and weakened social resistance to a lack of political transformation. For Pei (2006, pp 8–9) a lagging behind of the political reforms risks getting trapped in a 'partial reform equilibrium', where partially reformed economic and political institutions support a hybrid neo-authoritarian order that caters mostly to the needs of a small ruling elite. This is, indeed, a valid claim clearly observed on the ground. However, China's political reformulation and the maintaining of an authoritarian system seems to be consistent with the East Asian model and White's *pessimistic view* as to the political necessities for effective developmental advancements, if only the Japanese style soft-authoritarianism is not available, due to historical factors. In fact, the post-socialist separation of powers between the CCP and the government, even if to a large extent elusive, but nevertheless empowering a certain dualism in decision-making mechanism, may be perceived as an obstacle in creating a PSDS. So may administrative decentralisation.

It is a prevailing opinion that China's mode of transformation is a gradual one, thus positioning China among the grand opponents of the Washington Consensus and among proponents of the incremental reform path (see CIRD, 2008). Zheng (1999b, p 1161) states that 'China's political reform can be defined as political incrementalism aimed at continuously adjusting its institutional framework to guarantee economic reforms and political stability on one hand, and accommodate drastic changes resulting from socio-economic development, on the other.' Indeed, gradualism is often named in reference to economic transformation, as China's 'approach to economic reform was experimental and evolutionary' (Nolan, 2004, p 7).

Naturally, it would be a mistake not to consider some of the reforms in the PRC to be radical, as the cases of socially costly widespread redundancies motivated by economic restructuring show, or as the economically motivated demolition of the cooperative health-care system in rural areas proves. Some drastic restructuring efforts, however, cannot disguise the fact that the overall philosophy of step-by-step reforms, inspired by Chen Yun's[26] phrase 'crossing the river by touching the stones' (and partly caused by the indecisiveness of the political elite), is being followed, often with careful evaluation of the reforms' necessity for and influence on the Chinese economy. The 'radical' is conceptually positioned against the 'gradual', meaning 'fast' against 'slow'. What often took a matter of months in the CEE states upon embarking on the transformation seems to take years in the PRC; the examples being price liberalisation, banking system institutionalisation and private property and private means of production legalisation. Even if we accept Huang's (2008) arguments – who advocates against the perception of China being gradualist, giving the alleged reversal in economic liberalisation of rural areas in the 1990s as an example – or even if we acknowledge the ad hoc reformism of China's elite marked by swings in policy – focused at times on short-term gains and being reactive rather than anticipatory, as described by Hamrin (1990), which creates conditions for rapid radical changes in policies – the paramount idea of a gradual approach to systemic reforms in China does not need to be dismissed, as both small retrenchments discussed by Breslin (1992) and the apparent gross reversal illustrated by Huang (2008) may be perceived as the very features of the landscape of gradual change, with its accelerations, slowdowns, standstills and reversals. There are various important reasons why the Chinese leadership prefers the gradual reform path, namely: the developmental failure of radical paths; a necessity to maintain social stability; and, last but not least, the cautiousness needed in order to be able to maintain power by controlling the economy and the development trajectory. This is why economic liberalisation is accompanied by plan-determined compensation activities to create 'reform without losers'[27] (Lau and Qian, 2000).

---

[26] Chen Yun is considered to have been one of the PRC's top communist leaders and an influential economic and development policymaker.

[27] See Shirk (1993) and Lautard (1999).

Chinese gradualism is praised by some and criticised by others. Many scholars support the idea of gradual post-socialist transformation (as indicated earlier). However, many see the disadvantages of this model. Young (2000, p 1092) believes that 'incremental reform releases segments of the economy from centralised control, while maintaining, for a prolonged period, many of the distortions of the central plan'. As a result, 'the freed segments of the economy find it profitable to exploit the rent seeking opportunities implicit in the remaining distortions of the economy. Their attempts to capture and then protect these rents leads to the creation of new distortions' (Young, 2000, p 1092), which inhibit the process of creating a market economy. Lardy (1998) claims that the Chinese strategy of gradualism has been far from optimal, as it distorted resources allocation, did not relieve state-owned enterprises (SOEs) from social burdens and effectively contributed to the non-performable loans (NPL) crisis, among others, making China's reforms an 'unfinished economic revolution'. Again, China risks getting trapped in a 'partial reform equilibrium' (Pei, 2006).

Economic reforms

To reiterate, the process of post-socialist transformation in its economic-institutional dimension consists of economic liberalisation and opening up, market institutionalisation, and microeconomic restructuring. It is extremely difficult, if not impossible, to make clear divisions among these PST components. For example, liberalisation of domestic economic activities in initially semi-closed, state-command economies concerns, among others, the liberalisation of ownership of the means of production and the introduction of market mechanisms and market institutions. The latter is analysed in reference to the entire process of marketisation; the former is a main element of microeconomic restructuring, namely, the ownership rights reform.

As far as economic liberalisation is concerned, the government has introduced a number of policies that gradually allowed an increasingly large palette of various types of companies to participate in business activities. Those policies were believed to be often reactive and not anticipatory (Hamrin, 1990), as the authorities would sanction the type of firms and forms of economic activities already existing in different parts of the country. Initially, economic liberalisation was concerned with rural de-collectivisation. In 1984, some controls on establishing private companies were lifted (Bramall, 2009a, p 411). Following the 13th CCP Congress' acceptance of further deviation from state command, the year 1988 saw legal reform, which established private enterprises as a formal business category (Breslin, 2007). After the reforms were stalled in the late 1980s, internal economic liberalisation picked up after Deng Xiaoping's southern trip (*nánxún*), and effectively accelerated in the mid-1990s in view of an approaching perspective for China to join the WTO. Not only have various forms of ownership and economic activities been sanctioned, but Jiang Zemin (China's third-generation leader) also invited private entrepreneurs to join the CCP.

Deng Xiaoping's decision to end the period of Mao's isolationism is believed to be a clear mark of the beginning of China's opening-up process. Naturally, China's re-engagement with the global economy was not as abrupt as one may think, nor was the Mao regime isolationist to the extent that many perceived. During the state-command period, China was involved in international trade. Its international economic cooperation was often related to projects in other developing countries; however, not on a scale compared to that of today. Taking into account China's gradual re-engagement with the global economy, Breslin (2007) identified four phases of the PRC's opening up to the outside world. Phase one (1978–86) was characterised by the creation of special economic zones for foreign investment. The state's attitude changed from permissive to facilitative during phase two (1986–92), when, as a result of 22 regulations, the regulatory environment became more beneficial for foreign investors, for example, via lower fees and freer capital transfer. The acceleration of opening up took place during phase three (1992–99), resulting in the creation of a dualistic economy with a liberalised internationalised export regime and protected domestic trading regime. Investment in export-processing zones became easier, whereas certain industrial sectors, contained in 'the Catalogue', were prohibited for foreign investors. Phase four is related to the period of joining the WTO, when effective international pressure to liberalise the economy grew due to the ongoing access negotiations. It is often claimed that the state leadership became genuinely more inclined to believe that further economic liberalisation would bring more positive developmental effects. However, some insist that the process of economic liberalisation during the Hu–Wen regime (named after President Hu Jintao and Premier Wen Jiabao) lost its dynamics or was even put on hold. Some foreign investors believe that the process was, in fact, in regression at that time (PP, 2009, 2010), though this may partly reflect the disappointment with the pace of change previously hoped for. The current administration presided over by President Xi Jinping and Premier Li Keqiang is publicly adamant about the necessity to continue economic liberalisation. It remains to be seen, however, how much of this attitude will be transformed into actual policies.

It is believed that the opening up had an enormous effect on China's developmental dynamics. Rightly so, as perhaps many policies could not have been implemented were it not for the technical and managerial knowledge and capital from outside. It is important to note, however, that some scholars question the extent of the positive effects of opening up. Bramall (2009a, pp 389–90), for example, argues that the foreign sector contribution to development has been small, and technological diffusion and other spillover effects have been rather weak. From the perspective of the DS model, this selective liberalisation was important in creating a DS-style economic environment for subsequent extensive engagement in international trade.

Market institutionalisation is about 'creating market institutions and legal norms and mechanisms, as well as market organisations, to enable market based allocation of resources' (Kolodko, 2001a, p 31). In the DS context, it is a desired process, as the DS institutional environment is characterised by a market economy. Naturally, it is impossible to examine in this book the entire process of law changes and institutionalisation that concern the rules of engagement in China's domestic economy. It can be noted, however, that some of the most important regulations were passed in the mid-1990s, that is, the company law, the labour law and the new commercial banking law (OECD, 2009a, p 41). Those regulations were followed by bankruptcy law, pension and social regulations, and property rights. For the Organisation for Economic Co-operation and Development (OECD) experts, the new competition regulations – a set of regulations dealing with monopoly behaviour and abuse of position, which laid the regulatory framework for competition in the national economy – are the most important sign of effective marketisation. The core of it constitutes a new anti-monopoly law adopted in 2008 (OECD, 2009a).

Moreover, it is important to note that post-socialist administrative reforms can be seen as an element of market institutionalisation, despite the fact that they also clearly fall within the microeconomic restructuring category. Up until 2008, there were six rounds of administrative reforms (1982, 1988, 1993, 1998, 2003 and 2008), which Yang (2008) divided into two stages. The first stage (1978–2002) was aimed at fostering the market and removing the planned economy by decentralisation; the second phase (from 2002) aimed to accelerate governance transition by promoting law-based administration. According to Breslin (2007, p 70), the 1998 governmental restructuring was 'designed to make a final move from government control over the economy to macroeconomic supervision and regulation' and included a reduction in state bureaucracy and alterations to the PBC. The 2003 changes put in place further necessary institutions for market development (OECD, 2009a, p 154), partly by deregulating the SOE environment (Yang, 2008) and introducing new state bodies to supervise economic activities and the development process (eg National Development and Reform Commission [NDRC], Ministry of Commerce [MOFCOM], State-Owned Assets Supervision and Administration Commission [SASAC]). The 2008 reform established five super-ministries and consolidated a number of state agencies to make the supervision of macroeconomic processes more effective. The new wave of administrative reforms of 2013 onwards is expected to bring more market mechanisms and institutions into the functioning of the national economy and further limit the role of the central government.

An obvious element of marketisation is the establishment of the market-based financial system. In China, the commercialisation of the banking system commenced in the mid-1980s, with the first private banks allowed to operate in 1987 and the first foreign banks in 2006. In 1990, two stock exchanges were established in Shanghai and Shenzhen. Currently, the financial system is supervised by Western-style institutions such as the China Banking Regulatory Commission, China Securities Regulatory Commission and others, and the allocation of credit is increasingly determined by market conditions.[28] As far as the market-based price-determination mechanism is concerned, the dual price system was introduced in the first half of the 1980s, when enterprises were allowed to sell a proportion of their output outside of the plan, from 1984, by using effectively market prices. Moreover, the government gradually reduced the number of commodities whose prices were state-controlled:

> By the end of 1988, only 25 percent of commodities were subject to full scale control, leaving around 25 percent subject to floating prices (i.e. prices were allowed to vary within a specified band) and the remaining 50 percent being market determined. (World Bank, 1990, p 59, cited in Bramall, 2009a, p 351)

The OECD study shows that by the mid-2000s, '87% of producer prices and 96% of retail prices were determined by market supply and demand, compared to 46% and 69% [respectively] in 1991' (OECD,

---

[28]   A more detailed analysis of the financial system is conducted in Chapter Four, as the financial system-related policies have been identified as being among the main DS-style policies.

2009a, p 48). In the opinion of OECD experts, although challenges remain, the marketisation process has been vastly advanced: 'Market and the legal and regulatory framework for business development are well established.... The basic regulatory frameworks and institutions have been put in place for ... the financial sector. Monetary and fiscal policy instruments are fairly well developed' (OECD, 2009a, p 80).

There are a number of various reforms that are classified as microeconomic restructuring in the process of post-socialist transformation. The scholarly literature on China usually discusses: the ownership reform; the separation of various economic and institutional agents in the process of the economic decentralisation of a centrally planned economy; and the restructuring of socialist industry.

The policy concerning ownership rights of the means of production is often considered the defining feature of systemic arrangements. In capitalism or in a market economy, those means can be owned privately, collectively or by the state. In socialism or in a state-command economy, it is the state or the public who are believed to be the owners. Thus, the process of privatisation is seen as a crucial element of transformation from state-command to the market. Moreover, for the purpose of this book, this reform is important from the perspective of establishing the economic actors of China's variation of the developmental state. Privatisation is seen as the main element of the post-socialist ownership rights reform. However, it is especially visible in China that privatisation is only one of the processes that is taking place in the sphere of ownership. For example, as described by Guo (2003, pp 556–7), during the first period of ownership reform (1979–87), the reformers focused on decentralisation of management and thus on the expansion of managerial autonomy of SOEs; in the second stage (1987–92), reformers focused on separation of ownership and management by introducing a system of 'contracted managerial responsibility' (see Bolesta, 2006); and only in the third period (from 1992), did reformers focus on transformation to a mixed structure of ownership, with the public sector dominant and various types of ownership coexistent. In general, however, ownership rights have been defined obscurely, despite the perception of them being a vital element of the construction of a market economy.

Ownership reform began in rural areas. According to Walder (2002), China's rural economy was 'privatised' in three distinctive though overlapping phases, namely: the abandonment of rural agriculture and the division of land into family plots; the emergence of private household production and the marketing of non-agricultural goods and services; and the formal transfer of public enterprise assets accumulated over the reform period into the hands of private owners. Although individual user rights were established through the household responsibility system (HRS), collective ownership rights remained the prime focus in the 1980s. In fact, Bowles and Dong (1994, pp 73–4) see the initial reform process as enforcing the social nature of ownership, via, for example, the creation of collectively owned township-and-village enterprises (TVEs), which rapidly appropriated a significant share of national output at the expense of state-owned firms. TVEs are often considered to be an outcome of 'vaguely defined ownership rights' (Weitzman and Xu, 1994) and of limitations in private property rights, and are referred to as '(typically industrial) business unit[s] that belong to all residents of a rural community where [they are] usually located' (Che and Qian, 1998, p 2). They have played an extraordinary role in rural development in terms of generating both growth and employment. They are seen as collectively owned enterprises located in villages (Weitzman and Xu, 1994) or community enterprises, as opposed to SOEs and European-style cooperatives (Che and Qian, 1998). Although their nominal owners are the local residents who established them, the real control rests in town and village governments (Chang and Wang, 1994).

A lack of clearly defined property rights and the ideologically rooted anxiety towards the term 'private' did not stop private businesses from being established. During the initial reform periods, companies usually existed as individual (*gèt*) rather than private firms (*s yíng*). A 'red hat' practice, where privately owned companies or hang-on households (*guàhù*) were registered as cooperatives with local governments, popular in the Wenzhou model of development (Parris, 1993), was a good example. Despite the economic reforms, the restrictions on private means of production were being lifted gradually, and the Wenzhou model was a good example of adapting traditional institutions of central planning and a lack of private property rights to modern conditions (Liu, 1992, p 699), even prior to the reform period, and of engaging privately owned firms in disguise in activities regulated by market forces.

As a result of Deng Xiaoping's *nánxún* of 1992, privatisation accelerated. The 15th CCP Congress (1997) gave it an additional stimulus. Although it is often believed that the Congress, to some extent, only sanctioned the ongoing process (Gallagher, 2005, p 46), its provisions were seen by local governments as an encouragement to develop a private business-based economy; thus, they began widespread privatisation (Cai, 2002). Many of the TVEs and other firms owned by local governments changed their status, mostly as a result of insider privatisation (Li and Rozelle, 2003). By the end of the millennium, more than 90% of rural enterprises were privatised. In addition to informal privatisation in rural areas, informal privatisation was conducted via companies' internationalisation, where the international expansion of the PRC's firms in the 1980s and 1990s was often accompanied by the illicit privatisation conducted by the members of *nomenklatura* and their associates, who would appropriate the assets of state firms using offshore legal environments (Ding, 2000a). However, despite the privatisation drive, land has remained in state hands and 'land ownership rights [cannot be sold]. The transfer of land use rights can [exclusively] be achieved through negotiations' (Guo, 2003, p 561). This policy's proponents often argue that privatisation would: cause waste of land and human resources; undermine access of the Chinese agricultural sector to credit; discourage investment; and inhibit the ability to provide public goods (Bowles and Dong, 1994).

The mid-1990s' drive to privatisation took place under the slogan *zhu dà fàngxi o* (*Keep the larger and let the smaller go*) and was meant to address the issue of some SOEs' deteriorating performance. Naturally, the government started to privatise SOEs earlier (Yao, 2004); however, the general policy emphasis was on managerial and organisational changes to improve performance rather than on changes in ownership. Yao (2004) describes the privatisation policy of the mid-1990s as *g izhì*, that is, 'change of the system', preferred in Chinese narration due to the ideologically derived long-term reluctance to use the term 'privatisation'. 'G *izhì* included contracting and leasing ... selling to private owners, employee-holding, incorporation, listing on the stock market, restructuring of internal and external governance, and bankruptcy' (Yao, 2004, p 254).

Guo (2003), however, rightly points out that the government's intention has never been to rely extensively on the private sector. Even during the Jiang Zemin era of rapid privatisation, the state intended to tie its industrial policy to SOEs. One form of retaining control, at the same time, as strengthening the position of companies by increasing their assets, was creating large conglomerates (*q yè jítuán*). The preference for large companies was very much a model of some developmental states, as examined in the following chapters. Many well-known Chinese companies operating on the international market are the products of domestic mergers and acquisitions, propelled by the late 1990s' policies to create large business entities capable of competing with multinational corporations (MNCs). Despite the ongoing privatisation, the Hu–Wen regime only reinforced the policy of preference for SOEs as the main actors of certain developmental activities, gradually adding new industrial sectors to Guo's (2003) list of state 'commanding heights' of the national economy. This list, composed of preferential sectors for state-owned firms, included: infrastructure industries (energy, raw materials and transportation); pillar industries (mechanical, metallurgical, electrical, chemical, building, machinery, petroleum, natural gas); high-tech industries (information, telecommunication, biological technology); financial and banking systems; foreign trade and international economic cooperation; new material technology (Guo, 2003, p 558). In order to make SOEs more competitive, other reform activities focused on commercialisation of companies via management system changes (eg the introduction of the management responsibility system), via marketisation of the business environment (introduction of modern accounting, partial replacement of subsidies through bank loans and encouragement to use consulting companies) and via separation of powers (more competences were transferred to firms' management via reductions in allocative policy from above and in government coordination) (see You, 1998; Jefferson and Rawski, 1999b; Zhang, 2000).

The separation of economic powers and the decentralisation of the decision-making process, sometimes also categorised as economic liberalisation, have been important elements of post-socialist microeconomic restructuring in China. One should remember that the PRC under Mao was perhaps one of the least centralised centrally planned economies. As a large, populous and underdeveloped country it lacked, to some extent, the necessary capacity and machinery for effective central planning. The systemic reforms even saw an increase in decentralisation and economic power delegation into the lower levels of state administration and into the business entities, as 'the reformist leadership of China identified the decentralisation of economic decision-making power as a major strategy for reforming the economic system and achieving economic growth' (Zheng, 1999b, p 1166). As a consequence, China's 'central control is limited by local autonomy' (Breslin, 2007, p 61). Inevitably, the delegation of decision-making powers loosened central government control and allowed local authorities to strengthen in various spheres, such as investment, trade and privatisation. In response, the policy of selective political and economic re-centralisation was implemented by the central government in the 1990s. Premier Zhu Rongji implemented fiscal re-centralisation to consolidate the tax base and to reroute some financial resources to the central authorities. Nevertheless, the idea of decentralisation continued to be influential within China's leadership. Jiang Zemin claimed that 'conferring needed powers on local authorities, giving them more flexibility to adapt measures to local conditions, and unleashing their initiative and creativity in developing their local economies are beneficial to strengthening the vitality of the whole economy' (Jiang, 2010, p 460). However, it is also believed to be in opposition to the centralist model of the developmental state.

The transformation of socialist industry is another important feature of post-socialist microeconomic restructuring. The overall industrial policy, however, is also crucial for the understanding of the DS model, and is therefore discussed in Chapter Four. It is important to note here that China has been undergoing a dual industrial process during the reform period. The first is associated with the restructuring of heavy socialist industry, and is characteristic of most post-socialist states. The second is related to industrialisation, as China, being considered a developing country, has been under-industrialised compared to CEE and former Soviet Union (FSU) countries.

Some of China's economic reforms have indeed been consistent with DS-style institutionalisation. The economic liberalisation of the state-command economy, with its selective character to maintain a type of political control by the state, is a prime example. The controlled loosening of limitations to international trade has been a clear sign of a post-socialist economy drifting towards re-engagement with the global economy, a necessary policy from the perspective of the DS model. At the same time, post-socialist market institutionalisation has been an indispensable process if we were to think about constructing a genus of the DS model. However, some microeconomic restructuring can be seen as clearly not complying with classical DS requirements. A lack of properly defined property rights and the general weakness of the private business sectors, partly caused by some state-sponsored discriminative practices, as examined later in this book, have perhaps created obstacles to an effective state–business alliance. Moreover, the process of administrative decentralisation has weakened the central government's influence, as compared to the historically centralist DS cases.

The chronology

Let us here present the chronology of China's post-socialist transformation. According to Guo (1999, p 41), post-socialist China went through five transformation phases: an economy regulated mainly by planning and supplementally by the market (1978–84); a commodity economy with a plan (1985–87); a socialist commodity economy (1988–89); a combination of a planned and market economy (1989–91); and a socialist market economy (since 1992). According to

Ma Kai – the then chairman of the NDRC – the establishment of the socialist market economy was completed in 2005 (*People's Daily Online*, 2005). Breslin (2004) distinguishes between the stages of reforms and the phases of economic opening up. He divides the reforms into the period of policy formulation (1978–84), the period of abandoning the old system (1984–94) and the period of an 'attempt to build a new system of macroeconomic control based on law and regulation rather than [sustained] through state planning control' (since 1994) (Breslin, 2004, p 1). Bramall (2009a) sees the initial 18 years of reforms as a specific, Dengist type of market socialism, whereas the subsequent years are seen as a transition to capitalism. For him, the ideological turn is believed to be Deng Xiaoping's death.

The year 1978 is considered to be the starting point of the transformation. The political decision authored by Deng Xiaoping was reached during the 3rd plenum of the 11th CCP Congress. It was recognised that only reforms and putting an end to the PRC's isolationism would allow China to achieve dynamic socio-economic development, and, consequently, in the long run, to catch up with the developed states. Economic modernisation, as much as in historical DS cases, became the main state agenda. Deng, the author of the general idea and not unambiguous target of the new policy, entrusted the plan's realisation to Zhao Ziyang, a proponent of the market, who until 1989, as initially the premier and then the CCP's secretary general, was responsible for implementing systemic reforms and development policy. It was Chen Yun, however, who in the first years of the reforms, namely, during the readjustment period, was considered to be the most influential in economic policymaking (Zhao, 2009). Some scholars question Deng's reformist intentions, suggesting that the Politburo only sanctioned the reforms initiated by farmers and, indeed, the provincial leadership of the CCP in Sichuan (Zhao Ziyang) and Anhui (Wan Li) provinces, and later adopted a more lenient attitude towards systemic deviations, such as the Wenzhou model.[29]

The entire process of reforms was characterised by a conflict of visions within the state leadership. According to Solinger (1982, p 68, cited in Breslin, 2007, p 46), five areas of conflict would involve the extent of market regulations, the degree of decentralisation, the pace of growth versus stability, the position of heavy industry and the extent of promotion of foreign trade. Needless to say, these areas of conflict seemed to have been solved to a large degree in historical

[29] Huang (2008) presents an important account of pre-reform economic activities of the 'informal sector' as illustrative examples of bottom-up changes.

developmental states: the extent of market regulations would allow guided interventionism; the state would remain centralist; the pace of growth would be paramount, though neo-authoritarianism would secure stability; heavy industry would belong to the targeted sector; and trade would extensively be promoted by various means.

China's post-socialist transformation commenced in rural areas, where the partial introduction of market mechanisms allowed for the creation of a commodity market for agricultural products, and where the ownership reforms transformed the commune-based production into individual-based production. Moreover, 'a host of restrictions were lifted on non-agricultural activities' (Wong, 1988, p 3). These reforms 'drastically altered the organisation of production and the distribution of output in the countryside' (Perry and Wong, 1985, p 10). By 1983, de-collectivisation was almost complete, and by 1984, the commune system was abolished. It prompted a dynamic development of the rural economy (Wong, 1988). The reforms gained support from the majority of peasants, as did the agrarian reforms in the developmental states of Japan, Korea and Taiwan, implemented for the political benefit of the state elites, as discussed in Chapter Four.

The period between 1978 and 1982 is often referred to as the 'readjustment' (Solinger, 1982). It was characterised by market reforms in rural areas, as well as by slow opening up of the economy to the outside world (establishment of Special Economic Zones [SEZs]) and by shifting priorities in industrial production. By diverting investment from heavy to light industries, the government hoped for an acceleration of socio-economic development (Zhao, 2009). It was aimed at putting the national economy on the track of steady development by correcting economic imbalances. Chen Yun argued that 'three balances' related to budget, bank loans and demand–supply had to be achieved if the economy was to be run well (Bachman, 1986, p 298).

In 1984, the reforms were more directly extended to urban areas and were intended to expand productive forces. They involved the continuation of ownership rights liberalisation and price marketisation, as well as further opening up by establishing new special zones (open coastal cities, open zones – including two river deltas, two provinces, two peninsulas, open cities on the Yangtze river and open border cities) and by allowing foreign companies to establish their presence. Economic liberalisation and opening up was reinforced by Zhao Ziyang's strategy to develop coastal provinces as the most suitable for international trade and foreign investment due to their location and a higher overall level of development. Reforms continued to be implemented until 1989; however, their opponents consolidated in the mid-1980s (the so-called Anti-Bourgeois Liberalisation Campaign started in 1987), reaching momentum during the Tiananmen Square events (1989). As a consequence, the market reforms were brought to an interim standstill and some advocates of far-reaching economic liberalisation, including Zhao Ziyang, were removed from power. The 'Tiananmen interlude' (Naughton, 2007), serving as an interim period for consequent state ideology reformulation, lasted until the *nánxún*.

The reforms proceeded after the Deng Xiaoping propaganda trip around the country's southern provinces, where, as an icon of the Chinese political scene, he continued to lobby in favour of further systemic changes. He emphasised that the Chinese people 'should be bolder than before in conducting reform and opening up to the outside and have the courage to experiment' (Deng, 1994, p 360). Deng's insistence on reform acceleration effected the most significant state policy reformulation during China's PST. Ideologically, 'rather than viewing the national interest as being served by protecting key sectors from the market, the national interest was now viewed as being best served by forcing market competition and creating a more efficient market economy' (Breslin, 2007, p 52). In 1995, Jiang Zemin declared: 'To invigorate the economy, we need to further loosen control over all economic activities that should be regulated by market forces' (Jiang, 2010, p 456). Consequently, socialist modernisation ideals present in the reforms' course over the 1980s were mostly lost during the uncontrolled drive towards the market in the 1990s (Lin, 2006), and China turned away from the possible path of market socialism towards capitalist development (Bramall, 2009a). Thus, the 'embedded socialist compromise', where market reforms were accompanied by the political task of protecting those who might suffer (Breslin, 2007, p 45), was compromised and abandoned. Indeed, the second half of the 1990s marked the increasingly intensive PRC authorities' compliance with the market capitalist doctrine, culminating in China joining the WTO in December 2001.

The Hu–Wen regime, however, presided over another ideological reformulation. Hu's scientific concept of development (examined later), for example, was aimed at addressing the negative side effects of Jiang Zemin's alleged drive towards capitalism (see Fewsmith, 2008b). The subsequent 17th CCP Congress in 2007 reinstated the social priorities of the systemic transformation in view of the increasing inequalities and marginalisation of parts of society, often resulting in social unrest. While the priorities could mostly be achieved through strengthening the abilities of the indigenous population regarding socio-economic development by some sort of preferential treatment, the Western-centred perspective was that by doing this, the state administration drifted away from the systemic arrangements implemented due to China's accession to the WTO, which was perceived as a sign of desisting market-oriented reforms. Indeed, in policy terms, during the Hu–Wen period, external economic liberalisation was put on hold or even reversed in some aspects, such as industrial sector accessibility, as discussed in Chapter Four, whereas internal economic liberalisation seemed to have continued at a slower pace, as seen in the regulatory reforms of the domestic economic environment (OECD, 2009a, 2010). This attempt to return to more explicit state interventionism could be perceived as resorting to the means preferred by some historical developmental states. In social terms, this change has apparently had positive results, as claimed by Fock and Wong (2008), as more resources have been channelled to rural areas' education and health-care services, and as certain unofficial tax practices have been curbed.

The rapid development and systemic transformation of China, as well as often turbulent contemporary changes in the emerging global economy will require that the Xi–Li administration make adequate adjustments. The history of China proves that the change of its policy and policy objectives also requires appropriate modification of the state ideology and then a convincing justification for the modification rationale. The Xi–Li administration is broadly perceived as favouring further economic liberalisation, market institutionalisation and microeconomic restructuring (*The Economist*, 2013). If this proves to be true, a turn towards new policy and ideology is soon to come. This ideology is very important in the Chinese narration of the post-Mao reforms and opening up.

The Chinese perspective

There is, indeed, the important question of how *gǎigé kāifàng* (*reform and opening up*) are perceived in China and by Chinese policymakers. We have mentioned some terms that were coined during the reform process to explain and/or justify certain policies. We have briefly discussed some perceptions prevailing among Chinese academics and the political elite. As China is abandoning socialism and aggressively deviating from Marxism (Morgan, 2004), the ideology-based explanations on the part of the CCP often seem to require more and more terminological acrobatics. From the economic perspective, this is partly concentrated on the justification of the nominal communist organisation to preside over a process of an effective drifting away from socialism.

As far as political reformulation is concerned, Chinese authoritarianism is sometimes referred to by the Chinese as 'collective democracy' or 'Chinese democracy'. The concept of collective democracy has been based on a negation of Western-style democracy. Neo-Marxists – a strong group among PRC scholars – believe that Western democracy is 'a mechanism of competition which allows the *bourgeoisie* to abuse the working class' (Shih, 1999, p 24). Thus, Western democracy is nothing more than a dictatorship by the *bourgeoisie*. Stressing individual rights – visible especially in the US system – is a result of the middle class being actively involved in the forming of capitalism, the middle class being oriented towards protecting its own interests. In China, the government was considered to be, to a large extent, the driving force behind the systemic transition and it was the state that had been building a system based on collective ownership. As a consequence, collective democracy corresponds to the economic system. Social structures in China have a collective character, which lays the foundation for a 'collective culture', whereas in the West, this culture is individualistic. According to some analysts associated with the CCP, there is no contradiction between pluralism and collectivism, and the ecstatic acceptance of democracy by CEE countries and the use of all its privileges was a collective act, because even in a Western-style democracy, any decision must be supported by a group. As a result, there is no functional difference between both system variants (Shih, 1999). The Chinese authorities represent an opinion that a non-democratic system (in the Western sense of the word) does not necessarily have to be worse than Western democracy, and they sometimes try to argue that when it comes to conducting stringent economic reforms, it is better. Another argument is that even if one recognises that the final product of political reforms should be Western-style democracy, it has still not been proved that the political transition must be a linear process.

As far as economic reforms are concerned, there is plethora of domestic analyses that explain China's development trajectory. The three mainstream theories include: Deng Xiaoping's theory of socialism with Chinese characteristics; Jiang Zemin's theory of three represents; and Hu Jintao's scientific concept of development (Rong, 2009; Hu, 2011). These are all perceived as the continuation of the Mao Zedong's thought on Marxism–Leninism (Hu, 2011). In the domestic ideological debate, the systemic changes are usually referenced against Marxism. It is important to stress again that, in official propaganda, the reform process has never been about abandoning socialism. On the contrary, it has been about various paths and methods to build a socialist society and a socialist state, leading eventually to communism. Neither was there any official contemplation of releasing the CCP from the burden of being the primary and, in practice, the only political power centre. Deng (1994, p 248) claimed that 'without the Communist Party there would be chaos, or at least instability'. The deputy director of the Economics Institute of the Chinese Academy of Social Sciences (CASS), Liu Shucheng, distinguished four periods of ideological formulation of the reforms: socialist modernisation and economic development (1978–84); restructuring of the economic system via change in the relationship between plan and the market (1984–92); establishment of the socialist market economy (1992–2002); and completion of the establishment of the socialist market economy regime (since 2002).[30]

In 1978, economic modernisation and economic opening up to the outside world became the CCP's policy objective. In 1980 and 1981, Mao Zedong's 'left tendencies' were criticised; nevertheless, the CCP reaffirmed its dedication to Marxist ideological, political and organisational foundations and its adherence to four cardinal principles (Ding, 2010). Deng brought back Zhou Enlai's idea of four modernisations of agriculture, industry, national defence and science/ technology. In 1982, he declared it necessary to build 'socialism with Chinese characteristics' (Rong, 2009), which would become his paramount theory. It is important to mention that, for Deng, there was no contradiction between the market and socialism, as the former, together with planning, were means and the latter was an institutional arrangement. Later on, in 1992, as a result of *nánxún*, he would reiterate that:

> a planned economy is not equivalent to socialism, because there is planning under capitalism too; a market economy is not capitalism, because there are markets under socialism too. Planning and market forces are both means of controlling economic activity. The essence of socialism is liberation and development of the productive forces, elimination of exploitation and polarisation, and the ultimate achievement of prosperity for all. (Deng, 1994, p 361)

Nevertheless, in the early 1980s, planning was assigned a major role, whereas the market became a supplementary force. Chen Yun, in his theory of a 'bird in a cage', explained that the cage (the plan) should not be too tight, as it would suffocate the bird (the market), but a lack

---

[30] A presentation during the 'International Seminar on 30th Anniversary of China's Reforms and Opening Up', Beijing, CASS, December 2008.

of a cage would allow the bird to fly away (Bachman, 1986, p 298). In 1984, the socialist economy was identified as a 'commodity economy' to prevent, as claimed by Zhao Ziyang (2009), an ideological conflict with the opponents of the market. On the ideological front, the CCP's Central Committee Resolution on Reform of the Economic System addressed political economy, combining basic Marxist principles with China's socialist practices (Ding, 2010). In 1987, Zhao Ziyang used the term 'primary/initial stage of socialism'. Incorporated into the theoretical foundation of the 13th CCP Congress, it served as an ideological justification for more reforms deviating from Marxist theory. As China was at the initial stage of socialism (and it would take around 100 years to complete, as counted from the moment of the establishing of the PRC), it could use a variety of means, including those that are market related, in order to advance the development of socialism. It was similar to what Dirlik (2005) called post-socialism – a departure from the socialist path in order to achieve it in the long term. Jiang Zemin claimed that 'because China is in the primary stage of socialism, it must allow economic entities under diverse ownership forms to develop side by side' (Jiang, 2010, p 598). After the *nánxún*, during the 14th CCP Congress, the term 'socialist market economy' was officially recognised as the socio-economic system of China. The 15th CCP Congress called the theory of constructing socialism with Chinese characteristics the 'Deng Xiaoping theory', and inscribed it into the CCP's constitution as its guiding ideology. It stated that the CCP took Marxism–Leninism, Mao Zedong's thought and Deng Xiaoping's theory as the guidelines for its actions (Ding, 2010).

The biggest ideological contribution of Deng Xiaoping's successor, Jiang Zemin, was to include into the CCP constitution the three represents (*s ngè dàibi o*) during the 16th Party Congress in 2002. As a result, the CCP now formally represents not just the Chinese proletariat, but also China's advanced productive forces, China's advanced culture and 'the fundamental interests of the overwhelming majority of the Chinese people' (Breslin, 2007, p 71). This moment could be perceived as implicitly marking an official ideological transformation from communism to nationalism as the state ideology. Despite Jiang's insistence on adherence to four cardinal principles, three represents (announced already in 2000) intensified the scholarly debate on the reform path China may take in the future (Jia, 2004). Three represents illustrate the evolution of the CCP's position prompted by changes in economic, social and political conditions, and a more vocal assertion of its role as the state party. Jiang attempted to balance the politically liberal, or at least Marxist-remote, three represents not only with the more dynamic assertion of power by the CCP and the curbing of political activity, but also by bringing back Deng Xiaoping's concept of a *xi ok ng* society (initially mentioned in 1979) or a moderately well-off society, where all Chinese citizens would achieve a relatively 'comfortable' standard of living. Later on, in its policy objective of refocusing on social development rather than economic growth, the Hu–Wen regime, which replaced the Jiang regime, would emphasise the *xi ok ng* society concept.

Gradually, the rhetoric of the Hu–Wen administration would gear towards its own new concepts. In further interpreting Marxism's applicability to Chinese circumstances, President Hu Jintao introduced a scientific concept of development or a scientific outlook on development (*k xué f zh n gu n*) supported by the idea of 'harmonious society' (*héxié shèhuì*) (Fewsmith, 2008a). Premier Wen Jiabao added 'five balances', balancing: between urban and rural development; development among regions; between economic and social development; between man and nature; and between domestic development and opening up to the outside world (Wen, 2004, cited in Fock and Wong, 2008, p 2). Announced by Hu in 2003 and incorporated into the CCP constitution during the 17th CCP Congress in 2007, the scientific concept of development was supposed to provide 'an elementary answer to the significant theoretical and practical problems of "realising what kind of development and how to develop"' (Ding, 2010). It called upon scientific reasoning in defining the development trajectory; thus, in practice, it left a gateway for deviating from economic ideologies. It claimed to 'put people first' and 'advance people's interests', thus focusing more on human development in various well-being-related dimensions, rather than on pure economic indicators, which often seem to disguise the real developmental picture. Consequently, in theory, it emphasised the quality of growth over its dynamics (Chen, 2011). According to some Chinese scholars, the concept directly related to sustainable and balanced development, with an energy-saving and environment-friendly society, and aimed at creating an innovation-oriented country (see *China Daily*, 2007b). It was a response to the challenges that China has faced not only in the process of climbing the ladder of development, but also as a result of its growth model. In 2007, Hu Jintao declared that Deng Xiaoping theory's three represents and the scientific concept of development constituted the sinicisation of Marxism. Sustainable and balanced development based on scientific principles should result in the creation of a socialist harmonious society, as discussed during the sixth plenary session of the 16th CCP Congress in 2006 and during the 17th CCP Congress. A harmonious society is a vision of a modern, educated and affluent society guided by principles of 'honest, friendly and harmonious relationships and just, fair and open competition between social members' (*People's Daily Online*, 2007), functioning in an institutional environment of rule of law and a developed legal system and institutions. From an economic perspective, in the harmonious society:

> competition will optimise the distribution of resources, foster technological progress, develop social productivity and raise overall national [economic] strength.... Labour, knowledge, technology and capital [will be] all factors of wealth creation, which can make profits and should be respected so long as they [make] contributions to society. (*People's Daily Online*, 2007)

All those aspirations found their place in 'the Chinese dream' – a not unambiguous slogan of the new Xi–Li administration. According to Kuhn (2013), the Chinese dream's goal is a prosperous country, national revival and the people's well-being. It is believed that it was inspired by the book *The Chinese Dream: The Rise of the World's Largest Middle Class and What It Means to You* by Helen Wang (2010). The concept refers to the continuation of socio-economic progress by achieving the *xi ok ng* society by the time of the CCP's 100th anniversary and a modern high-income economy by the time of the PRC's 100th anniversary. In addition to traditional collectivism, it is believed to promote individualism, particularly among the youth. The concept is also believed to refer to political targets, mostly in the context of international relations, in order for China to become an affluent powerhouse in the global arena.

Although a scientific concept of development opens up more space for deviating from Marxism and related ideologies and the Chinese dream sketches the directions of change, so far, neither *xi ok ng* nor the harmonious society have materialised in any acceptable form. On the contrary, disparities are growing, some people experience extreme poverty and marginalisation, and describing the natural environment as heavily polluted is a vast understatement. Nevertheless, China has been developing rapidly, outperforming most, if not all, post-socialist economies in the pace of economic growth, as examined later in this chapter.

Post-socialist transformation – the comparison

China's transformation is a genus of post–socialist transformation. The assumption, however, is also that China is a post–socialist developmental state. On average, PST states are known for their moderate to low developmental dynamics. DS cases are known for their extraordinary growth. Consequently, China's developmental dynamics should be, to some extent, exceptional as compared with other post-socialist states.

In much of the scholarly literature, the exceptionality of China's transformation is usually claimed as such on the basis of distinctive initial conditions. Indeed, the differences in post-socialist transformations depended on a number of reasons, such as the initial conditions (political, economic, geopolitical, geographical, social) and the choices made by the authorities throughout the period of post-socialist transformation. The importance of choice of policy mix derives from the fact that the differences among states were not limited to the development level of the countries as a whole, but also to the development level of certain sectors of their economies. Moreover, particular sectors had different importance for different economies. In deciding the direction of the reforms, one had to take into consideration all the above-mentioned elements. Undertaking the same sectoral reforms in different states would bring about different results and would have a different impact on the development of the economy.

Although political institutions in the socialist world initially seemed similar, regional differences in development were significant.[31] It is hardly acceptable to claim that states such as Poland, the Czech Republic, Slovakia, Hungary and Slovenia belonged to the category of developing countries when commencing post-socialist transformation. China and Vietnam, on the contrary, have been considered a part of the developing world, though do not belong to the group of least developed countries (LDCs) (LDCR, 2004). In fact, in 2011, China was officially declared an upper-middle-income country. At the beginning of systemic changes, the level of development in CEE was much higher than in the East Asian socialist states. In the year 1989, GDP per capita in China was USD391 and in Vietnam USD97, as compared with the Soviet Union at USD5,204, Poland at USD2,139 and Hungary

---

[31] The developmental differences may partly be attributed to the fact that some CEE countries tried to reform their centrally planned economies before the year 1989, as was the case in Poland and Hungary in the 1980s and Yugoslavia already in the 1960s, and some, such as Romania and Bulgaria, did not.

at USD3,043 (UNStats, 2005).[32] The developmental situation of countries would also be characterised by various factors, for example: the level of industrialisation and the position of each industry within the economy; the degree of urbanisation, with its consequences for societal composition; and populations' socio-economic conditions, such as income disparities, educational base, accessibility to health care and so on. Predominantly rural and poorer China stood in clear contrast to the more industrialised and more extensively urbanised Soviet Union and Eastern Europe, where societies were better educated, in general, healthier and better fed.

Second, geopolitical or, rather, geo-economic location has been another initial condition determining development trajectory. Due to the initial post-socialist economic contraction in the Soviet Union, as well as the entire CEE region, states recorded heavy losses in international trade, which then subsequently worsened the socio-economic situation.[33] The European Economic Community (EEC) states were not a sufficient alternative. Unimpressive economic growth of 2.4% (EU-15) in the years 1980–89 (UNCTAD HS, 2005) and the protectionist access barriers to the EEC market did not initially allow for the adequate dynamics of trade relations. At the same time, China was a part of the region that was consistently showing pro-growth tendencies (since the 1960s), and at the beginning of the 21st century became, as it seems, the driving force of the global economy. Asian Tigers – Korea, Taiwan, Hong Kong and Singapore, as well as Japan – offered excellent trade and economic cooperation opportunities, together with other Southeast Asian fast developers. Moreover, China had the advantage of easy access to private capital and consequently investment stimulating economic growth. China's government could count on foreign investments from the Chinese living in Southeast Asia and North America. Inhabitants of Taiwan, Hong Kong, Macao and Singapore, as well as prosperous *Huáqiáo* from Indonesia, Thailand and Malaysia, have been a leading economic force, with great financial potential and the first and prime group to invest in China upon the opening of SEZs.

Third, internal political conditions also influenced the scope of systemic changes. While Deng Xiaoping's reforms in rural areas were

---

[32] It is another issue, however, as to how reliable the data is that refers to the socialist period of these countries. Nevertheless, it can be assumed that the developmental disparities within the Eastern bloc were indeed significant.

[33] During the state-command period, most of the trade took place among the Council for Mutual Economic Assistance (COMECON) states.

met with nationwide appreciation, as the need for change in socio-economic conditions was indeed great, the reforms of the CEEFSU leaders were so discredited before 1989, as they failed to deliver adequate growth and improvements in the standard of living, that there was no national agreement on economic changes without reforming the political system (see McCormick and Unger, eds, 1995). Partly because of the pre-Second World War tradition, but mostly because of the proximity of the Western democratic states, the pressure on the CEE countries' authorities to introduce political reforms was growing. China did not witness such strong revisionist movements – the drive for democratic changes was not as strong as in the CEE. Moreover, the early agrarian reforms gave the Chinese authorities a better position for the continuation of self-designed changes.

The differences in the initial reform design and initial local conditions are clearly seen in a comparative analysis of the USSR and PRC (see Gill, 1995; Nolan, 1995). Embarking on a transformation path, the Soviet Union was extensively urbanised with a dominant, though highly ineffective, industrial sector of mostly state-owned enterprises. Agriculture had been collectivised. The social security system did function in both cities and villages. Introducing reforms in rural areas of the same nature as in China, based on de-collectivisation, could have met some resistance. At the same time, the urban workforce was relatively well educated. Industrial reforms would mean extensive structural changes, imperative to increasing efficiency, and socially costly redundancies. Moreover, central planning had been a dominant economic model for many decades and the reforms would break the state's monopoly and could weaken the authorities. In the PRC, rural areas suffered from extensive poverty. The state's industrialisation had been less extensive, potential 'industrial' opposition less influential and the level of society's education lower than in the USSR. Paradoxically, more extensive poverty in China than in the Soviet Union allowed the CCP to introduce reforms that the Communist Party of the Soviet Union (CPSU) could not politically afford to implement.

It is often assumed that as a result of initial conditions, China's development path during the period of transformation has brought relatively more positive effects. Chinese authorities are believed to have benefited from certain advantages to intensify the country's development, namely, societal support for change, inexpensive labour, access to foreign investment, the proximity of potential export markets and a higher incidence of poverty. However, Nolan (2004) argues that the very different interim outcomes of the reforms in China and in Russia are the results not of initial conditions, but of policies chosen by the states' leaderships. This is due to the fact that 'despite the differences, [both respective national economies] possessed large possibilities for accelerated growth with the introduction of market forces in an incremental fashion, in a stable political environment with an effective state apparatus' (Nolan, 2004, p 8).

Indeed, China chose selective economic liberalisation and gradual and cautious institutional and administrative adjustment, as its 'approach to economic reform was experimental and evolutionary' (Nolan, 2004, p 7). In Russia, after the *glasnost* and *perestroika* period, authorities began fast liberalisation and privatisation as, after following the 'transition orthodoxy of revolutionary political change' (Nolan, 2004, p 7), the authorities implemented an economic shock therapy. Consequently, there seems to be a distinctive difference between the Russian and the Chinese states in dealing with the endeavour of reform, namely, the passive role of the Russian state and the active role of the Chinese state. The ability of the Chinese state to intervene is at the core of Unger and Cui's (1994) argument that the main difference between the Russian and Chinese processes of transformation lies in the philosophy of the reforms aspired to in the case of China and disregarded in Russia by three historical events: first, US interventionism in its agricultural sector in the 19th century, which is considered to have laid the fundamentals for the further development of the country; second, the subordination of foreign capital to national development strategies and pioneering a successful partnership between government and business in the East Asian tigers; and, third, the emergence of the regimes of cooperative competition in most developed parts of continental Europe, in particular, in Northern Italy, Catalonia, Denmark and Southwest Germany, where companies would compete, but nevertheless pull together their financial, commercial and technological resources.

The most unordinary feature of China's transformation is related to the fact that development policies rather than systemic reforms have been the most important part of China's transformational endeavour, which, as examined later, resulted in significant developmental advancements. This is not as much a novelty as it is unfortunately rather an unorthodox mode of behaviour among the post-socialist states. Although a good system cannot replace development policy and development policy cannot be an antidote for the lack of systemic reforms (Kolodko, 1999a), many policymakers in CEE, at least in the initial stages of transformation, forgot about this simple truth, focusing exclusively on the reforms of the system. Their short-sightedness was motivated by neo-liberal economic doctrine, reaching its peak popularity in the late 1980s and early 1990s.

There have been many attempts to categorise various paths of post-socialist transformation. For example, among 'great institutional transformations', Balcerowicz (1997, pp 170–1) recognised the European and Asian post-communist transformation. Initially, both the Asian and the European states were ruled by party-state communist regimes, the political system was blocked and the economy was centrally planned. Among the Asian states, the budget redistribution scale was rather small, whereas in the European countries, it was rather large. The economy consisted, to a large extent, of an easy-to-be-privatised agricultural sector (states of Asian transformation) and of socialist industry (states of European transformation). In the case of the Asian transformation model states, the reforms were limited to the economic system, whereas in the case of the European transformation model states, the changes encompassed both the political and the economic spheres.

Winckler (1999) has divided the states into two groups, namely, the 'European–Soviet *big bang*' group and the 'Asian gradual economic reforms only' group, allocating China, together with Vietnam and Laos, to the latter group. The division derives from the gradual versus radical discourse and takes into account what are believed to be the main processes of the transformation – economic and political reformulations. Winckler (1999) has also presented an interesting division based on states' geopolitical proximity to and dependency on the Soviet Union. In this case, the Soviet peripheral states would comprise the former Soviet republics and the CEE states, although not necessarily Yugoslavia and Albania, who followed their own independent socialist path. Mongolia, bound by political and economic ties, would also belong to this group. North Korea's dependency on the Soviet Union changed into economic dependency on China and a rather high degree of political independency. Vietnam, although heavily dependent on economic assistance from the Eastern bloc, drifted towards economic and political independence after having embarked on *doi moi* reforms. Despite the fact that at the beginning of its existence, it was the USSR's periphery, the People's Republic of China, because of its size and capacity, could not later on be considered a Soviet periphery state, if a periphery of any political construction at all.

Moreover, Winckler (1999) examined various features of Asian post-socialist transformation by presenting different variables influencing the systemic changes. Asian models differ according to the level of the appropriation of states by the ruling communist regimes described as *totalitarianisation* and the form of power personification, both being decisive on the reform preferences of the political elites. For example,

China is believed to have been more extensively totalitarianised than Vietnam and Laos.

He also points out that there were three initial waves of reforms in the process of the Asian post-socialist transformation. The first one, generated internally by the disappointing outcomes of socialist economies, took place at the end of the 1970s. In China and Southeast Asia, it brought a limited economic liberalisation and some political changes. The second wave, in the mid-1980s, was a consequence of the first. The first changes brought positive results in the socio-economic sphere, especially in China; therefore, one expected a continuation. It was generated internally and externally as both the Soviet *glasnost* and *perestroika* introduced by Mikhail Gorbachev and Deng Xiaoping's reforms in rural areas served as examples for other Asian countries. The economic reforms were advanced in China and commenced in Vietnam, as well as, to some limited extent, in Mongolia and North Korea. Some very limited liberalisation in the political sphere took place in China. The third wave, generated externally in 1989/90 by the 'Autumn of the Nations' in Central CEE, which commenced with the Polish roundtable negotiations between the Solidarity movement and the communist regime, accelerated economic reforms in Asian countries (except for North Korea) and reversed political changes everywhere except Mongolia.

Focusing on developmental issues, Kolodko (2001a) established four groups of post-socialist countries, taking into account the variation in the pace of their economic growth: first, those who are catching up, and consequently are able to maintain a long-term economic growth at least twice as fast as that of developed capitalist countries; second, those who manage not to increase the developmental distance with the developed nations and maintain economic growth levels close to or slightly higher than the developed nations; third, the strugglers, who are staying behind, increasing the developmental gap; and, fourth, the leaders, whose growth is at least three times faster.[34] In his analysis, China is exceptional as the only country that, in the long term, managed to achieve an annual GDP increase significantly higher than the leaders' category's requirement.

Moreover, despite the fact that post-socialist transformation is an extremely complex process and very often unpredictable, not only

---

[34] Casting aside the discussion on the goals of post-socialist transformation, one must take into consideration that post-socialist states are in a different phase of development; therefore, the actual economic growth required for an effective catching up would vary.

in the political sphere, but also in the economic dimension – as it is often difficult to forecast the political circumstances that create the economic reality, which renders some available data on the systemic changes incoherent, consequently creating significant obstacles in the accurate measurement of existing information – some attempts have been made to establish quantitative models to measure various aspects of post-socialist transformation. Such models were created: by Jefferson and Rawski (1999a), to establish the optimal reform strategy; by Fang (1996), to estimate governmental commitment to transformation and the applicability of gradual and radical (big bang) strategies to enterprise reforms; and by Blanchard and Kremer (1997), to measure output decline as a result of the disorganisation of the socialist system.

For example, Jefferson and Rawski (1999a) decided to use the existing theory of investment and apply it to the process of economic transition:

> The model of reform ... is based on an analogy between factors affecting a firm's investment decision and factors affecting a government's choice of reform policy. Investment decisions and reform efforts share key characteristics. In both cases the agent solves a problem of economic transition – how to get from the current state of the world to a preferred state of the world. In the case of the investment decision the owner-manager maximises the firm's expected net worth; in the case of economic reform the agent maximises society's expected welfare. Both seek to understand a set of technical and intertemporal relationships in which current input – factors of production in the case of the investor, instruments of the reform in the case of the reformer – expand production capabilities and profit or welfare in the future. Both the investment process and the reform process entail costs of adjustment that involve risk and uncertainty. (Jefferson and Rawski, 1999a, pp 265–6)

Jefferson and Rawski (1999a) conclude that there is no universal recipe for successful transformation, as the optimal strategy of reforms depends on the conditions in particular states. These conditions are determined by: a nation's reform environment or the initial conditions within which the reform package is formulated; the extent of substitutability or complementarity among reform instruments; the costs of adjustment; the level of uncertainty concerning the effectiveness of alternative reform strategies; and a society's vision of a preferred set of post-transition institutions.

As far as the measuring of post-socialist transformation is concerned, unfortunately, there is no universal measuring tool for the advancements of the systemic reforms. The two main indexes that may be used for measuring post-socialist economic reforms are the cumulative liberalisation index (CLI) – measuring the liberalisation of internal markets (freeing domestic prices, abolishing state trading monopolies), liberalisation of external markets (easing the foreign trade regime, including the elimination of export controls and taxes, currency convertibility) and facilitation of private sector entry (privatising enterprises, reforming the banking sector) – and the European Bank for Reconstruction and Development (EBRD) transition indicators, which measure several institutional changes concerned with structural reforms, the privatisation process, liberalisation, reform of the banking system and financial institutionalisation. In the mid-1990s, the CLI divided countries of post-socialist transformation into the following groups: advanced reformers (CLI greater than 3) were Slovenia, Poland, Hungary, the Czech Republic and Slovakia; high intermediate reformers (CLI less than 3 but greater than 2) were Bulgaria, Estonia, Lithuania, Latvia, Romania, Albania and Mongolia; low intermediate reformers (CLI less than 2 but greater than 1.3) were Russia, Kyrgyzstan, Moldova and Kazakhstan; and slow reformers (CLI less than 1.3) were Uzbekistan, Belarus, Ukraine and Turkmenistan (Melo et al, 1996). The transition indicators, whose value for the period between 1989 and 2012 is presented in Table 2.1, is estimated using a scale from 1 (a lack of reforms of the socialist system) to 4.3 (a level at which free market economy standards have been reached for each sector of the economy). There are, however, several problems with utilising these indexes: first, in the case of the CLI index, there is no comprehensive data covering the years of transformation for all the post-socialist states; and, second, the EBRD transition indicators do not include China.

Despite the fact that it is often perceived as an easy task, evaluation of the process of political reformulation within the post-socialist world does not seem straightforward and causes some confusion. This is mostly due to a rather high degree of ambiguity regarding the factors that determine the genus of a political system. The often accepted division into three categories (totalitarian, authoritarian and democratic systems) does not accurately reflect differences among the post-socialist states. Moreover, additional categories are constantly emerging. Zakaria (1997) coined a term 'illiberal democracy'. The term disguises the autocratic practices of the leaders, who although chosen in elections, do not maintain democratic standards. Illiberal democratic regimes 'combine

Table 2.1: Transition Indicators (1989-2012)

		1989	1990	1995	2000	2005	2010	2012
ALBANIA	Large-scale privatisation	1.0	1.0	2.0	2.7	3.0	3.7	3.7
	Small-scale privatisation	1.0	1.0	4.0	4.0	4.0	4.0	4.0
	Governance and enterprise restructuring	1.0	1.0	2.0	2.0	2.0	2.3	2.3
	Price liberalisation	1.0	1.0	3.7	4.3	4.3	4.3	4.3
	Trade and foreign exchange system	1.0	1.0	4.0	4.3	4.3	4.3	4.3
	Competition policy	1.0	1.0	1.0	1.7	2.0	2.0	2.3
ARMENIA	Large-scale privatisation	1.0	1.0	2.0	3.0	3.7	3.7	3.7
	Small-scale privatisation	1.0	1.0	2.7	3.3	4.0	4.0	4.0
	Governance and enterprise restructuring	1.0	1.0	2.0	2.0	2.3	2.3	2.3
	Price liberalisation	1.0	1.0	3.7	4.3	4.3	4.3	4.0
	Trade & Forex system	1.0	1.0	3.0	4.0	4.3	4.3	4.3
	Competition policy	1.0	1.0	1.0	1.0	2.3	2.3	2.3
AZERBAIJAN	Large-scale privatisation	1.0	1.0	1.0	1.7	2.0	2.0	2.0
	Small-scale privatisation	1.0	1.0	1.0	3.3	3.7	3.7	3.7
	Governance and enterprise restructuring	1.0	1.0	1.7	1.7	2.0	2.0	2.0
	Price liberalisation	1.0	1.0	3.7	4.0	4.0	4.0	4.0
	Trade & Forex system	1.0	1.0	2.0	3.3	4.0	4.0	4.0
	Competition policy	1.0	1.0	2.0	2.0	2.0	2.0	1.7

		1989	1990	1995	2000	2005	2010	2012
BELARUS	Large-scale privatisation	1.0	1.0	1.7	1.0	1.0	1.7	1.7
	Small-scale privatisation	1.0	1.0	2.0	2.0	2.3	2.3	2.3
	Governance and enterprise restructuring	1.0	1.0	1.7	1.0	1.0	1.7	1.7
	Price liberalisation	1.0	1.0	3.7	2.3	2.7	3.3	3.0
	Trade & Forex system	1.0	1.0	2.0	1.7	2.3	2.3	2.3
	Competition policy	1.0	1.0	2.0	2.0	2.0	2.0	2.0
BOSNIA AND HERZEGOVINA	Large-scale privatisation	1.0	1.0	1.0	2.0	2.7	3.0	3.0
	Small-scale privatisation	3.0	3.0	2.0	2.3	3.0	3.0	3.0
	Governance and enterprise restructuring	1.0	1.0	1.0	1.7	2.0	2.0	2.0
	Price liberalisation	2.7	3.7	1.0	4.0	4.0	4.0	4.0
	Trade & Forex system	2.0	2.0	1.0	3.0	3.7	4.0	4.0
	Competition policy	1.0	1.0	1.0	1.0	1.0	2.3	2.3
BULGARIA	Large-scale privatisation	1.0	1.0	2.0	3.7	4.0	4.0	4.0
	Small-scale privatisation	1.0	1.0	3.0	3.7	3.7	4.0	4.0
	Governance and enterprise restructuring	1.0	1.0	2.0	2.3	2.7	2.7	2.7
	Price liberalisation	1.0	1.0	2.7	4.0	4.3	4.3	4.3
	Trade & Forex system	1.0	2.0	4.0	4.3	4.3	4.3	4.3
	Competition policy	1.0	1.0	2.0	2.3	2.7	3.0	3.0
CROATIA	Large-scale privatisation	1.0	1.0	3.0	3.0	3.3	3.3	3.3
	Small-scale privatisation	3.0	3.0	4.0	4.3	4.3	4.3	4.3
	Governance and enterprise restructuring	1.0	1.0	2.0	2.7	3.0	3.0	3.3
	Price liberalisation	2.7	3.7	4.0	4.0	4.0	4.0	4.0
	Trade & Forex system	2.0	2.0	4.0	4.3	4.3	4.3	4.3
	Competition policy	1.0	1.0	1.0	2.3	2.3	3.0	3.0

		1989	1990	1995	2000	2005	2010	2012
ESTONIA	Large-scale privatisation	1.0	1.0	4.0	4.0	4.0	4.0	4.0
	Small-scale privatisation	1.0	1.0	4.0	4.3	4.3	4.3	4.3
	Governance and enterprise restructuring	1.0	1.0	3.0	3.0	3.7	3.7	3.7
	Price liberalisation	1.0	2.3	4.3	4.3	4.3	4.3	4.3
	Trade & Forex system	1.0	1.0	4.0	4.3	4.3	4.3	4.3
	Competition policy	1.0	1.0	2.0	2.7	3.3	3.7	3.7
GEORGIA	Large-scale privatisation	1.0	1.0	2.0	3.3	3.7	4.0	4.0
	Small-scale privatisation	1.0	1.0	3.0	4.0	4.0	4.0	4.0
	Governance and enterprise restructuring	1.0	1.0	2.0	2.0	2.3	2.3	2.3
	Price liberalisation	1.0	1.0	3.7	4.3	4.3	4.3	4.3
	Trade & Forex system	1.0	1.0	2.0	4.3	4.3	4.3	4.3
	Competition policy	1.0	1.0	1.0	2.0	2.0	2.0	2.0
HUNGARY	Large-scale privatisation	1.0	2.0	4.0	4.0	4.0	4.0	4.0
	Small-scale privatisation	1.0	1.0	3.7	4.3	4.3	4.3	4.3
	Governance and enterprise restructuring	1.0	1.0	3.0	3.3	3.7	3.7	3.7
	Price liberalisation	2.7	4.0	4.3	4.3	4.3	4.3	4.3
	Trade & Forex system	2.0	3.0	4.3	4.3	4.3	4.3	4.3
	Competition policy	1.0	1.0	3.0	3.0	3.3	3.7	3.7

		1989	1990	1995	2000	2005	2010	2012
KAZAKHSTAN	Large-scale privatisation	1.0	1.0	2.0	3.0	3.0	3.0	3.0
	Small-scale privatisation	1.0	1.0	3.0	4.0	4.0	4.0	4.0
	Governance and enterprise restructuring	1.0	1.0	1.0	2.0	2.0	2.0	2.0
	Price liberalisation	1.0	1.0	4.0	4.0	4.0	4.0	3.7
	Trade & Forex system	1.0	1.0	3.0	3.3	3.7	3.7	3.7
	Competition policy	1.0	1.0	2.0	2.0	2.0	2.0	2.0
KYRGYZSTAN	Large-scale privatisation	1.0	1.0	3.0	3.0	3.7	3.7	3.7
	Small-scale privatisation	1.0	1.0	4.0	4.0	4.0	4.0	4.0
	Governance and enterprise restructuring	1.0	1.0	2.0	2.0	2.0	2.0	2.0
	Price liberalisation	1.0	1.0	4.3	4.3	4.3	4.3	4.3
	Trade & Forex system	1.0	1.0	4.0	4.3	4.3	4.3	4.3
	Competition policy	1.0	1.0	2.0	2.0	2.0	2.0	2.0
LATVIA	Large-scale privatisation	1.0	1.0	2.0	3.0	3.7	3.7	3.7
	Small-scale privatisation	1.0	1.0	4.0	4.3	4.3	4.3	4.3
	Governance and enterprise restructuring	1.0	1.0	2.0	2.7	3.0	3.0	3.3
	Price liberalisation	1.0	1.0	4.3	4.3	4.3	4.3	4.3
	Trade & Forex system	1.0	1.0	4.0	4.3	4.3	4.3	4.3
	Competition policy	1.0	1.0	2.0	2.3	3.0	3.3	3.7

	1989	1990	1995	2000	2005	2010	2012
LITHUANIA							
Large-scale privatisation	1.0	1.0	3.0	3.0	4.0	4.0	4.0
Small-scale privatisation	1.0	1.0	4.0	4.3	4.3	4.3	4.3
Governance and enterprise restructuring	1.0	1.0	2.0	2.7	3.0	3.0	3.0
Price liberalisation	1.0	2.3	4.0	4.0	4.3	4.3	4.3
Trade & Forex system	1.0	1.0	4.0	4.0	4.3	4.3	4.3
Competition policy	1.0	1.0	2.0	2.7	3.3	3.3	3.7
MOLDOVA							
Large-scale privatisation	1.0	1.0	3.0	3.0	3.0	3.0	3.0
Small-scale privatisation	1.0	1.0	3.0	3.7	3.7	4.0	4.0
Governance and enterprise restructuring	1.0	1.0	2.0	2.0	2.0	2.0	2.0
Price liberalisation	1.0	1.0	3.7	3.7	4.0	4.0	4.0
Trade & Forex system	1.0	1.0	4.0	4.0	4.3	4.3	4.3
Competition policy	1.0	1.0	2.0	2.0	2.0	2.3	2.3
MONGOLIA							
Large-scale privatisation	1.0	1.0	1.0	2.0	3.0	3.3	3.3
Small-scale privatisation	1.0	1.0	2.7	3.7	4.0	4.0	4.0
Governance and enterprise restructuring	1.0	1.0	1.7	2.0	2.0	2.0	2.0
Price liberalisation	1.0	1.0	3.3	4.3	4.3	4.3	4.3
Trade & Forex system	1.0	1.0	2.7	4.3	4.3	4.3	4.3
Competition policy	1.0	1.0	1.7	1.7	2.0	2.7	2.7

		1989	1990	1995	2000	2005	2010	2012
MONTENEGRO	Large-scale privatisation	1.0	1.0	1.0	1.7	3.3	3.3	3.3
	Small-scale privatisation	3.0	3.0	3.0	2.0	3.7	3.7	3.7
	Governance and enterprise restructuring	1.0	1.0	1.0	1.0	2.0	2.0	2.3
	Price liberalisation	2.7	3.7	2.7	3.7	4.0	4.0	4.0
	Trade & Forex system	2.0	2.0	1.0	2.3	3.7	4.0	4.3
	Competition policy	1.0	1.0	1.0	1.0	1.0	2.0	2.0
POLAND	Large-scale privatisation	1.0	2.0	3.0	3.3	3.3	3.7	3.7
	Small-scale privatisation	2.0	3.0	4.0	4.3	4.3	4.3	4.3
	Governance and enterprise restructuring	1.0	2.0	3.0	3.0	3.7	3.7	3.7
	Price liberalisation	2.3	3.7	4.0	4.3	4.3	4.3	4.3
	Trade & Forex system	1.0	3.0	4.0	4.3	4.3	4.3	4.3
	Competition policy	1.0	2.0	2.7	2.7	3.3	3.7	3.7
ROMANIA	Large-scale privatisation	1.0	1.0	2.0	3.0	3.7	3.7	3.7
	Small-scale privatisation	1.0	1.0	2.7	3.7	3.7	3.7	3.7
	Governance and enterprise restructuring	1.0	1.0	2.0	2.0	2.3	2.7	2.7
	Price liberalisation	1.0	1.0	4.0	4.3	4.3	4.3	4.3
	Trade & Forex system	1.0	1.0	4.0	4.3	4.3	4.3	4.3
	Competition policy	1.0	1.0	1.0	2.3	2.3	3.0	3.3

		1989	1990	1995	2000	2005	2010	2012
RUSSIA	Large-scale privatisation	1.0	1.0	3.0	3.3	3.0	3.0	3.0
	Small-scale privatisation	1.0	1.0	4.0	4.0	4.0	4.0	4.0
	Governance and enterprise restructuring	1.0	1.0	2.0	2.0	2.3	2.3	2.3
	Price liberalisation	1.0	1.0	3.7	4.0	4.0	4.0	4.0
	Trade & Forex system	1.0	1.0	3.0	2.3	3.3	3.3	4.0
	Competition policy	1.0	1.0	2.0	2.3	2.3	2.3	2.7
SERBIA	Large-scale privatisation	1.0	1.0	1.0	1.0	2.7	2.7	2.7
	Small-scale privatisation	3.0	3.0	3.0	3.0	3.3	3.7	3.7
	Governance and enterprise restructuring	1.0	1.0	1.0	1.0	2.3	2.3	2.3
	Price liberalisation	2.7	3.7	2.7	2.3	4.0	4.0	4.0
	Trade & Forex system	2.0	2.0	1.0	1.0	3.3	4.0	4.0
	Competition policy	1.0	1.0	1.0	1.0	1.0	2.3	2.3
SLOVAKIA	Large-scale privatisation	1.0	1.0	3.0	4.0	4.0	4.0	4.0
	Small-scale privatisation	1.0	1.0	4.0	4.3	4.3	4.3	4.3
	Governance and enterprise restructuring	1.0	1.0	3.0	3.0	3.7	3.7	3.7
	Price liberalisation	1.0	1.0	4.0	4.0	4.3	4.3	4.3
	Trade & Forex system	1.0	1.0	4.0	4.3	4.3	4.3	4.3
	Competition policy	1.0	1.0	3.0	3.0	3.3	3.3	3.7

		1989	1990	1995	2000	2005	2010	2012
SLOVENIA	Large-scale privatisation	1.0	1.0	2.7	3.0	3.0	3.0	3.0
	Small-scale privatisation	3.0	3.0	4.0	4.3	4.3	4.3	4.3
	Governance and enterprise restructuring	1.0	1.0	2.7	2.7	3.0	3.0	3.0
	Price liberalisation	2.7	3.7	3.7	4.0	4.0	4.0	4.0
	Trade & Forex system	2.0	2.0	4.0	4.3	4.3	4.3	4.3
	Competition policy	1.0	1.0	2.0	2.7	2.7	3.0	2.7
TAJIKISTAN	Large-scale privatisation	1.0	1.0	2.0	2.3	2.3	2.3	2.3
	Small-scale privatisation	1.0	1.0	2.0	3.3	4.0	4.0	4.0
	Governance and enterprise restructuring	1.0	1.0	1.0	1.7	1.7	2.0	2.0
	Price liberalisation	1.0	1.0	3.3	3.7	3.7	4.0	4.0
	Trade & Forex system	1.0	1.0	2.0	3.3	3.3	3.3	3.3
	Competition policy	1.0	1.0	2.0	2.0	1.7	1.7	1.7
TURKMENISTAN	Large-scale privatisation	1.0	1.0	1.0	1.7	1.0	1.0	1.0
	Small-scale privatisation	1.0	1.0	1.7	2.0	2.0	2.3	2.3
	Governance and enterprise restructuring	1.0	1.0	1.0	1.0	1.0	1.0	1.0
	Price liberalisation	1.0	1.0	2.7	2.7	2.7	2.7	3.0
	Trade & Forex system	1.0	1.0	1.0	1.0	1.0	2.0	2.3
	Competition policy	1.0	1.0	1.0	1.0	1.0	1.0	1.0

		1989	1990	1995	2000	2005	2010	2012
UKRAINE	Large-scale privatisation	1.0	1.0	2.0	2.7	3.0	3.0	3.0
	Small-scale privatisation	1.0	1.0	2.0	3.3	4.0	4.0	4.0
	Governance and enterprise restructuring	1.0	1.0	2.0	2.0	2.0	2.3	2.3
	Price liberalisation	1.0	1.0	3.7	4.0	4.0	4.0	4.0
	Trade & Forex system	1.0	1.0	3.0	3.0	3.7	4.0	4.0
	Competition policy	1.0	1.0	2.0	2.3	2.3	2.3	2.3
UZBEKISTAN	Large-scale privatisation	1.0	1.0	2.7	2.7	2.7	2.7	2.7
	Small-scale privatisation	1.0	1.0	3.0	3.0	3.0	3.3	3.3
	Governance and enterprise restructuring	1.0	1.0	2.0	1.7	1.7	1.7	1.7
	Price liberalisation	1.0	1.0	3.7	2.7	2.7	2.7	2.7
	Trade & Forex system	1.0	1.0	2.0	1.0	2.0	2.0	1.7
	Competition policy	1.0	1.0	2.0	2.0	1.7	1.7	1.7

Source: EBRD (2013).

free and fair elections with systematic curtailment of freedoms and rights' (Zakaria, 1997). Various attempts at creating political system/ democracy indexes do not seem to have been firmly established in the scholarly literature. For example, The Economist Intelligence Unit's Index of Democracy, which divides systems into full democracies, flawed democracies, hybrid regimes and authoritarian regimes, is yet to develop into a credible form of evaluation of political systems. Often, the Freedom House (FH) index is mentioned as a suitable tool, being the only index scheme that examines political freedoms covering around 200 states and territories for a significant period of time, despite the fact that it is seldom perceived as a valid instrument for the evaluation of the degree of freedoms in a given country due to the inadequate methodology of the index's creation. FH indicators allocate states to three categories: free, partly free and not free. Although it seems obvious that free countries will be the democratic ones and not free either totalitarian or authoritarian, the partly free states may fall into the 'close to being a democracy' category[35] or the 'still pretty much authoritarian' category.

However, although the nature of political reformulation is important in defining the systemic features of post-socialist states, it is a secondary issue in this book. What is important here is the assessment of the developmental achievements of the states in post-socialist transformation.

The developmental exceptionality of China's post-socialist transformation

To measure development is not actually a straightforward task. There are many ways to do so (see Piatkowski 2013). Bramall (2009a) divides the approach to measuring development into two groups: the opulence approach, which estimates material wealth; and the capability approach, which refers, according to Amartya Sen, to 'a person's "capability" … to the alternative combinations of functionings that are feasible … to achieve…. The capability set represents the freedom to achieve: the alternative functioning combinations from which this person can choose' (Sen, 1999, p 75, cited in Bramall, 2009a, p 8).

In the developmental state context, Leftwich (2000, p 173) uses GDP growth and believes that a developmental state would have an average annual economic growth of at least 4% for a period of 25 years, or preferably 30 years. Indeed, the quantitative examination would need to

---

[35]   Or perhaps be an electoral democracy but not a liberal democracy.

be conducted over a sufficiently long time frame, as the phenomenon of developmental advancements is conditioned long-term. Perhaps the time frame proposed by Leftwich is empirically justifiable, as it applies to a long-term phenomenon. However, while using economic growth as the most common and, indeed, most widely accepted indicator is convenient, it is, nonetheless, sometimes questionable. This is not to say that the dynamics of economic growth is insignificant in the analysis of developmental advancements, but to stress that growth does not necessarily need to mean development. There are certain other indicators that determine development in its socio-economic form and should be taken into consideration, such as Human Development Index (HDI), which also includes the level of education and the health performance of a society. On a number of occasions, the values of GDP resulting from economic growth have been misleading as to the level of development and the real standard of living enjoyed by a society. This is due to the fact that:

- economic growth does not always translate into developmental advancements (eg Turkmenistan);
- states sometimes realise more effective socially oriented policies that contribute to the overall well-being of its citizens without high GDP 'at its disposal' (eg Cuba); and
- as a consequence, and as mentioned earlier, GDP per capita as a pure economic indicator does not fully capture other indices crucial in determining the standard of living.

Moreover, in the post-socialist world, the overall achievements measured by economic growth should be presented vis-a-vis transformational or transitional (as it can be called) depression generated during the transformation period through negative economic growth, and indeed very common among PST states. The size of the depression would partly indicate the extent of ill-formulated reforms and development policies implemented or the existence of political circumstances such as violent conflicts. In countries where transitional depression was indeed significant, limiting the analysis to economic growth distorts the overall developmental picture, as the example of Bosnia and Herzegovina illustrates. Despite positive economic growth, calculated as an annual average for the period of post-socialist transformation, Bosnia and Herzegovina is only currently regaining its pre-transition size of the national economy. Consequently, the value of average economic growth can sometimes tell us very little about the change in the size of the economy. This is because of extensive losses generated at the beginning of transformation. The methodological problem, however, arises from the difficulties in fully illustrating the extent of economic contraction. Data about the length of post-socialist transitional depression or, indeed, the annual rates of negative economic growth, in each particular case, do not provide an adequate picture of the transformational losses, nor does the extent of the deepest plummet. How deep the depression has been is one issue, and how long it has lasted is another.

As far as the suggested HDI is concerned, Bramall (2009a) questions the assignment of arbitrary weights of one third to each of the HDI components, which are: life expectancy, knowledge and opulence. He believes that 'HDI obscures more than reveals' (Bramall, 2009a, p 13). Instead of HDI, he favours the change in life expectancy as the best measurement of progress.

For the clarity of presentation, in this section, the achievements or lack thereof in the socio-economic sphere will be estimated by the HDI change, GDP growth and change in the size of the economy. Figure 2.2 illustrates GDP growth and HDI change for the first 15 years of transformation (1990–2005) and shows that the general trend, in all the examined cases,[36] was that growth was accompanied by development.

Naturally, there were some differences among the countries, where growth would translate into development more efficiently, partly due to the fact that economic growth as an indicator can obscure the developmental picture in the post-socialist world. It is interesting to note certain regularities as far as political systems are concerned. Liberal democracies, or countries declared as politically free, have all experienced positive economic and HDI growth. However, both the HDI and GDP changes were rather moderate compared to the fast-developing East Asian post-socialist economies (China, Vietnam and Laos). Those who recorded negative tendencies all belong to the group of former Soviet republics.

Between the years 1990 and 2005, when all the countries were already in post-socialist transformation or (in the year 1990) were on the verge of doing so, China experienced the largest positive change in the HDI and the highest economic growth. If we compare the average annual change in the HDI value for a later period, we can see that China maintains a strong position (see Figure 2.3). If we compare the average annual GDP growth dynamics, China is still the leading economy (Figure 2.4).

---

[36] Due to limited data on HDI, not all the countries are covered.

Figure 2.2: GDP [gross domestic product] and HDI [Human Development Index] change in post-socialist economies

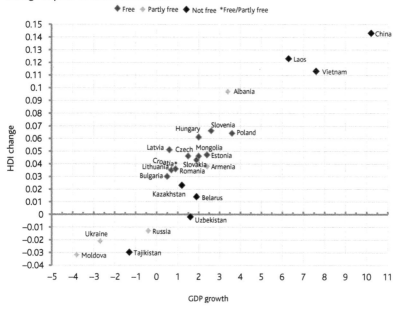

Note: As far as the type of political system is concerned, the states have been divided into the following groups: free (mid grey), partly free (light grey) and not free (black). As the post-socialist transformation is an ongoing process, during the surveyed period (1990–2005), some states would change their political regimes. Therefore, an additional classification had to be introduced, namely, free/partly free, in the case of Croatia.

Source: Author's calculations based on HDR (2002, 2007/08), EBRD (2007), WEO (2008) and FH (2006).

The comparative quantitative analysis of the developmental achievements of China suggests its rather unique character. China has been by far the fastest-growing economy among post-socialist countries. As far as HDI change is concerned, here, too, China is exceptional. Between the years 1990 and 2012, China experienced the largest positive change in the HDI, of 0.204 (HDR, 2013). The countries that most resemble China's development dynamics are Vietnam and Laos. The China–Vietnam–Laos similarities should not, however, be overestimated. It is difficult to compare little Laos, a country of 237,000 square kilometres and a population of 6.8 million, with China – the most populous state in the world with a population of almost 1.4 billion people, the second-largest economy and the third-largest territory. Yet, Laos has been achieving a significantly lower level of economic growth. Vietnam, although significantly larger than Laos, still lacks the comparable parameters (population estimated for 2013 at 92 million, and a territory of 330,000 square kilometres).

Figure 2.3: Average annual change in the HDI [Human Development Index] (2000–2012) (%)

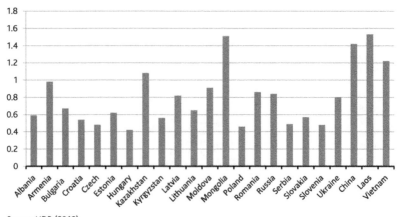

Source: HDR (2013).

Figure 2.4: Average annual GDP [gross domestic product] growth (1989-2012) (%)

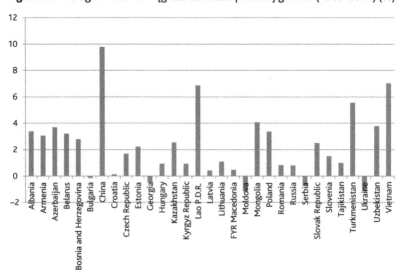

Source: WEO (2013) and EBRD (2013).

How do the developmental achievements of China and other PST countries, however, compare to those in the historical DS cases? Based on Leftwich's suggestion, the simplest answer to the question of which post-socialist states qualify for a DS-like pace of development is all those countries whose annual economic growth has exceeded 4% from the beginning of transformation. However, as explained earlier, one should utilise a more adequate measurement tool for socio-economic development, namely, HDI change, in order to evaluate where PST states are, as compared to the historical developmental states. Due to data limitations, one needs to carefully consider which time frame to use for the DS cases. Although the time frame for the PST economies is, in a sense, given, it is difficult to establish a corresponding period for the developmental states. Japan is now one of the most developed countries in the world, as opposed to many PST states; therefore, a comparison in real time does not make sense. It is probably the 1950s, 1960s and 1970s that should be perceived as the most important developmental era of Japan. In fact, what is called by Maddison (2007, p 68) the period of super-growth in Japan took place between 1952 and 1978. The same applies to Korea, where the DS core period occurred in the late 1960s, 1970s and 1980s. Taiwan (not included in Figure 2.5) experienced its successful developmental period from the 1960s until the early 1990s. Consequently, for the clarity of presentation and reinforcement of the previous argument, as well as due to the limited data available as far as the relatively newly established HDI is concerned, two 15-year-long periods, 1975–90 and 1980–95, were chosen to be used in the comparative analysis of the proven cases of developmental states with the PST economies. In the case of the PST states, the surveyed period was 1990–2005.

If we exclude Japan, whose developmental *apogeum* took place earlier than the surveyed period, among the PST states, only China (0.143), Laos (0.123), Vietnam (0.113) and perhaps Albania (0.097) managed to match or surpass the HDI dynamics of South Korea and Singapore (often mentioned as a DS case alongside the Asian Three). Among the CEE states, the best dynamics were experienced by relatively poor Albania (0.097) and the richest Slovenia (0.066). Among those who scored 0.05 or more were Poland (0.064), Hungary (0.061) and Latvia (0.051). In the surveyed period, among the developmental states, only 'post-developmental' Japan scored below 0.05 (once). The figures clearly show that the PST economies, with the exception of China, Laos, Vietnam and Albania, did not manage to achieve the developmental dynamics characteristic of the developmental states at the beginning of systemic transformation.

Figure 2.5: HDI [Human Development Index] change among post-socialist and developmental states

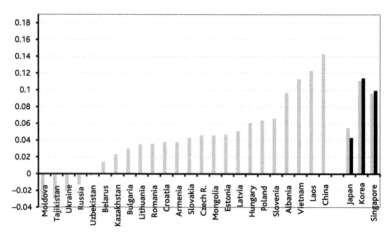

Note: In the case of PST states, the surveyed period is 1990–2005. In the case of developmental states, the surveyed period is 1975–90 (light grey) and 1980–95 (black).

Source: Author's calculations based on HDR (2002, 2005, 2007/08).

As we might need to resort to an analysis of GDP growth due to a broader available comparison base than that for HDI, Leftwich's requirement poses another difficulty among the post-socialist states, as indicated earlier. The post-socialist economic depression would be most significant at the beginning of transformation, thus immensely reducing the base for the calculation of subsequent rates of growth. Consequently, although some countries could perhaps fulfil the Leftwich requirement as to the average rate of annual growth, they would not achieve actual positive developmental results. The Leftwich requirement is applicable in non-turbulent economic circumstances, where the annual rate of growth does not record an extensive negative value at the beginning of the surveyed period. Consequently, a certain adjustment must be made. The Leftwich requirement of annual 4% growth needs to be replaced by an estimation of the increase in the size of an economy, which would be generated by a continual, uninterrupted annual economic growth of at least 4%, as presented in Table 2.2.

Table 2.2: The change in the size of an economy at an annual GDP [gross domestic product] growth rate of 4%

Year no	Size of economy (%)
1	100
2	104
3	108.2
4	112.5
5	117
6	121.7
7	126.5
8	131.6
9	136.9
10	142.3
11	148
12	153.9
13	160.1
14	166.5
15	173.2
16	180.1
17	187.3
18	194.8
19	202.6
20	210.7
21	219.1
22	227.9
23	237
24	246.5
25	256.3

Figure 2.6 illustrates that only China, Vietnam, Laos and Turkmenistan managed to achieve the required value of GDP increase. On the other hand, it is believed that in the case of Turkmenistan, this growth has not produced any relevant developmental achievements, as it is almost exclusively related to the acceleration of natural gas production, on the contrary to China, Vietnam and Laos, who, to a large extent, translated the economic growth into a positive change in HDI.

However, regardless of the base year, China has significantly outperformed Vietnam and Laos. For example, if we look at the 25-year period of 1988–2012, China's economy grew by nine times, whereas those of Laos and Vietnam grew by five times. If we measure the first 24 years of reforms in each country (the base year for China is 1979, for Vietnam 1986 and for Laos 1989), China's economy grew over eight times and Vietnam's and Laos' over four times (calculated using WEO, 2013).

The above quantitative analysis proves the developmental exceptionality of the Chinese post-socialist transformation. This exceptionality is not entirely unique, as there are certain similarities

Figure 2.6: The change in the size of national economies (1989–2008; 1989 = 100%)

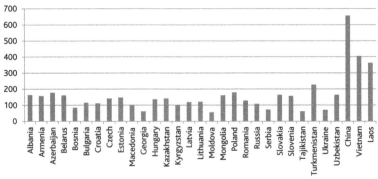

Source: EBRD (2009) and WEO (2013).

between China and some other states. China is, however, the fastest-growing post-socialist economy over the long term. Moreover, as far as the comparison with historical developmental states is concerned, China, indeed, by far exceeded Leftwich's requirement in terms of GDP growth and, as evidence suggests, the pace of Korean and Japanese growth during their DS transition (see Maddison, 2007), and recorded better HDI dynamics than historical developmental states (HDR, 2002, 2005, 2007/08).

Naturally, China's general developmental results should be downgraded by the ever-increasing high level of inequalities measured by the Gini coefficient.[37] Indeed, despite its overall achievements, the PRC has experienced significant failures in certain social spheres. Some groups of society have been marginalised due to an extremely large volume of redundancies in the industrial sector, price liberalisation and the subsequent price decrease of agricultural goods in the agricultural sector, and, as claimed by Huang (2008), due to the abandoning of policies that can be described as rural economic liberalisation aimed at the development of, what he calls, entrepreneurial capitalism. He claims that growing inequalities, especially the rural–urban divide, should be attributed to the 1990s' reversal in state policies of developing market instruments for peasants to set up businesses and to reorient the activities into non-agrarian sectors. A lack of access to free education and health services by rural migrants in urban areas, due to the *hukou* system, or indeed a predicament in accessing health care and the education system by rural inhabitants in rural areas, due to the dissolution of community

---

[37] China's Gini coefficient has been among the largest within the group of post-socialist countries, reaching 46.9 in the year 2004 (HDR, 2007/08).

medical schemes and the common practice of levying tuition fees by primary education establishments, contribute immensely towards the growth of inequalities and further marginalisation. Huang (2008) points out that as an effect, illiteracy increased significantly in the first five years of the new millennium and the general health of the nation deteriorated. Nevertheless, China's post-socialist transformation has brought some spectacular developmental improvements (OECD, 2010) and re-established China as an economic superpower in the international arena.

CHAPTER THREE

The politics of development

Chapter One concluded that the concept of the developmental state, despite its alleged shortcomings, may still be considered a useful tool in addressing inadequate developmental dynamics in some poor countries. The concept itself will still be applicable as long as the globalisation process requires significant corrections in order to achieve more equitable development and as long as disguised interventionist forces shape the global economy. Moreover, when the neo-liberal economic ideology has been discredited, the guiding role of the state in development, as embedded in the concept of the developmental state, resurfaces as, indeed, an interesting option. Having analysed the process of post-socialist transformation in China and China's developmental exceptionality among post-socialist economies in Chapter Two, one needs to address the question as to the similarities and differences between China's development trajectory and the historical DS cases. The analysis needs to be conducted in two sets of dimensions: the policy dimension addressed in Chapter Four; and the ideological background, together with political and economic arrangements, discussed in this chapter, as drawn predominantly from specific DS features presented in the scholarly literature.

In order to comparatively analyse the Chinese case, one needs to refer to the countries whose economic, geopolitical and cultural proximity are the closest. Needless to say, these constitute the 'consensus candidates' (Stubbs, 2009) or the 'Asian Three' (Weiss, 2000), namely, Japan, Korea and Taiwan. In order to focus on the largest DS economies, as China itself is a large economy, the comparative analysis will mostly be concerned with Japan and Korea. Naturally, there are significant differences between China, Japan and Korea. The relatively close geopolitical locality, a history of interactions resulting in a comparable culturally determined social structure and membership of the group of large economies creates, however, a more suitable platform for a mutual comparative analysis.

Economic nationalism

It is believed that a developmental state can be introduced in the social conditions of a nationalist state. Indeed, Johnson (1982) and others suggest a direct link between nationalism and the DS model. He points out that in the Japanese and Korean cases, the creation of the DS model was seen 'as the means to combat Western imperialism and ensure national survival' (cited in Woo-Cumings, 1999, p 6). Stubbs (2009, p 9) argues that this nationalism was related to the tense political situation in the region and the constant threat of war. Rowen (1998) emphasises that a particular type of nationalism was among Kuznets' three main requisites for successful development and that it is 'found in greater abundance in East Asia than in other developing regions'. The sociological analysis of a nationalist state in East Asia is beyond the scope of this book and may as well constitute a separate work. In fact, it may be difficult to compare Chinese and Korean post-colonial nationalism with the imperialist nationalism of Japan, with both nationalisms having their roots in the historical paths of all three countries. In the case of Japan, this nationalism can perhaps be divided into the period until the end of the Second World War (aggressive) and the period afterwards (benevolent and of economic character) (Nish, 2000). In all cases, from the perspective of their impact on the social environment of the developmental state, these nationalisms seem to translate into a collective consciousness, not merely in the form of personal identity, but also in the broad acceptance of the fact that the development trajectory concerns everybody and that collective effort must take place in order for it to be realised. China, Japan and Korea are well known for their collectiveness as an element of societal interaction. It is believed that in the case of China, the collectivist philosophy serves as the basis for the justification for the political regime and the nature of the economic changes (see Shih, 1999).

Does a developmental state require a nationalist society, as is broadly believed? If indeed this is the case, then this very nationalism, 'based on the claim of a community of feeling grounded in the past which overrides particularist attitudes and ideologies' (Kuznets, 1966, p 13, cited in Rowen, 1998, p 9), must translate into societal mobilisation behind state-level developmental targets. Japan and Korea seem to have managed to achieve an adequate level of societal mobilisation, which, however, should not be seen as a display of unconditional compliance with the actions of governments. In the case of Korea, this process was directly related to the coercive authoritarianism of Park Chung Hee, which was based on the experiences of the abusive Japanese colonial regime. As far as Japan is concerned, it is associated with the effective policy of industrialisation initiated by the Meiji administration, during which economic development became a means to nationalist purposes (Raphael and Rohlen, 1998). In the case of China, societal acceptance of systemic transformation seems to derive from actual development trajectory and developmental results. The initial societal support for economic changes is, however, believed to be attributed to a lack of adequate developmental achievements prior to the reform period and a coercive communist regime.

Chinese nationalism is a well-researched topic (see Fewsmith, 1995, 2008a; Friedman, 1995; Unger and Barme, 1996; Zheng, 1999a; He and Guo, 2000; Wei and Liu, 2001; Gries, 2004; Liew and Wang, 2004; Zhao, 2004; Hughes, 2006): 'Nationalism is hardly a new force in China; indeed it is a leitmotif underlying twentieth-century Chinese politics' (Fewsmith, 2008a, p 103). The notion of 'saving the Chinese nation' had been present at least since the defeat in the first Opium War (1842) (Yang and Lim, 2010). Post-imperial nationalism rose during the May Fourth Movement (Wu, 2008), as 'after the fall of culturalism in the late nineteenth century [and the period considered to be one of national humiliation], the Chinese political elite deemed necessary to promote nationalism as a new force for unity' (Zhao, 2000, p 28). Townsend (1992, p 98) reminds us that it is the common perception, which he does not necessarily agree with, that a 'rise of nationalism' distinguishes modern China from its imperial past. The main political power centre in post-imperial republican China became the nationalist movement – the Kuomintang (*Guómíndǎng*). Undoubtedly, the second Sino-Japanese war, which commenced in 1937, contributed further to nationalism becoming an important state ideology (Wei and Liu, 2001). Indeed, the modern history of China has had elements of nationalism, also during the state-command period. In the analysis of China's socialism, Lin (2006) underlines that Chinese socialism was nationalist in nature. It was considered to be a means in overcoming poverty and backwardness. The cosmopolitan idea of creating a unified socialist world of equal citizens regardless of their initial state affiliation was always a secondary issue. This nationalism, deeply rooted in the tradition traced back to long before the socialist era, enforced during republican times and strengthened during Cold War rivalries, when China had to deal with the US-led blockade and the Soviet Union's expansion of influence, has been preserved in Chinese society and is present while new developmental directions of the nation are being designed.

In his study, Hughes (2006) presents the changing landscape of Chinese nationalism during the reform period, illustrating its main linkages, namely, to economic policy, to foreign policy and to security issues. He discusses Deng Xiaoping's employment of the concept of patriotism 'to establish a linkage between certain areas of policy making' (Hughes, 2006, p 87), in order to frame subsequent strategy formulations. He underlines that the emergence of nationalism during the reform period signifies the creation of a more important ideological policy instrument than before, while China is becoming internationally more affluent. Nationalism is used to legitimise the CCP's claim to power, its reforms track and chosen development path (Hughes, 2006; Breslin, 2007). Therefore, as Shirk (2007, p 11) pointed out, 'the Communist Party embraced nationalism as its new ideology in an age when almost nobody believes in communism anymore', to the extent, however, that the state leadership became fearful that the unfolding ideology may enable society to escape close state-sponsored surveillance (see also Fewsmith, 1995; Breslin, 2007) – hence, for example, more and more attempts to control the Internet and especially social media by increasing surveillance and blocking content and websites and by introducing new restrictive laws concerning what can be posted.

Hughes' (2006) study examines nationalism's external conditionality, which is globalisation and external security, as well as internal factors, which are internal security and a continuous ideological struggle within the state apparatus as to the direction of reforms. This internal struggle (see Fewsmith, 2008a; Shirk, 2007) is an important feature of China's transformation, and its pronounced character distinguishes it from historical developmental states. Unsurprisingly, in the allegedly capitalist country with the allegedly communist regime, this results in multilayered, though often implicit, ideological debate. Consequently, nationalism surfaces as at least a partial remedy to the ideological chaos featuring China's transformation and development. The internal ideological debate, with its extensive ambiguities, would distinguish the contemporary nationalists or a 'New Left' (Hughes, 2006, p 75) (those who advocate the strengthening of the state role) from liberals. Hughes (2006, p 70) acknowledges that the picture is more complex and it includes 'various schools of thought, such as the "Right" and the "Left", and more recently "neo-authoritarianism", "liberalism" and the "New Left"'. Fewsmith (2008a, p xvii) positions the New Left as comprising the new nationalists, post-modernists and neo-statists.

Chinese nationalism is often analysed in reference to the three policy areas mentioned earlier: economic policy, foreign policy and security policy. All of these types seem to fall within the general DS nationalist agenda and its purpose: to mobilise the nation to a collective endeavour. For example, Deng's rhetoric of 'national unification policy' (Hughes, 2006), continued by Jiang's appeals to national unity (see Jiang, 2010) is nothing less than an attempt at societal mobilisation behind state policies. Internal and external security issues have often been used for steering nationalism and for mobilising the nation against alleged threats. The external enemies posing a threat to territorial integrity would usually comprise of the US and Japan (Li, 2001; Gries, 2004, Gries et al, 2011), but also of the Taiwanese government, as well as those who question, for example, the One-China policy. Nationalistic displays related to security issues have been common and ranged from dubious naval activities around the Spratly and Diaoyu islands to 'spontaneous' protests at Ritan Lu – the location of the Japanese embassy in Beijing. The nationalistic rhetoric was especially visible around important dates of China's recent history. Events, such as disturbances in the Olympic torch relay in the European states prior to the 2008 Beijing Olympic Games and support for the Dalai Lama during his visits to third countries were often portrayed as a plot by the outside world against China and the Chinese people. To describe this type of nationalism, Zhao (2000) used Shambaugh's phrase 'defensive nationalism' – assertive in form, reactive in essence, but not particularly aggressive. Indeed, foreign policy has always been subject to 'assertive nationalism' when China's economic interests or territorial possessions were questioned (Whiting, 1995).

It is often believed that in the early 1990s, Chinese nationalism radicalised, as it aimed at '[defending] the Chinese model of development, [endorsing] political authoritarianism, and [seeking] sources of legitimacy and identity in traditional Chinese culture' (Wu, 2008, p 467). An element of it was the emergence of cultural nationalism, as a negation of Western values as remedies to China's and the world's problems (Fewsmith, 2008a, p 121). However, the main feature of what Gries (2004) called a 'new nationalism' was its pragmatism – pragmatic in the nature of advancements of national interests domestically and internationally, with a specific self-contentedness or pride of the reforms' successes, described by Whiting (1995) as affirmative nationalism. It is an increasingly common perception that China's nationalism indeed became a pragmatic nationalism (Zhao, 2000; Hughes, 2006), especially in the way it navigates China's foreign trade policy, as presented in Chapter Four, and it justifies economic activities within the borders of the PRC. Fewsmith (2008a), however, underlines that there was, at the same time, a rise in what he calls 'popular nationalism' – a mixture of populism and nationalism, whose supporters would, nevertheless, criticise the government for insufficient defence of Chinese interests, and in economic terms, for compliance with the wishes of international corporations. Fewsmith (2008a) also points out that since the 1990s, more attention has been paid to the issue of nationalism as being the ideological background for the mode of China's socio-economic development.

Indeed, as far as economic nationalism is concerned, especially in the last two decades, but also throughout the modern era, it has been an important part of Chinese nationalism, as was Japanese and the Korean nationalism during their DS core activity period and at the beginning of the 21st century, China became the prime example of a state whose economic nationalism contributed to extensive developmental achievements. China's economic nationalism is the result of its 'East Asian heritage' rather than 'post-socialist heritage', as for many post-socialist states, this concept remained estranged when they embraced neo-liberal economic doctrine. Pei (1998) claims that in the East Asian conditionality, political nationalism would need to be replaced by economic nationalism to maintain the political legitimacy of authoritarian regimes. In the case of Japan, 'a transformed version of Meiji economic nationalism [was] evident throughout society in the post-war years, and leaders defended and reinforced it' (Raphael and Rohlen, 1998, p 291). This economic nationalism is not exclusively related to the mobilisation of the nation, but is exemplified in the economic policy of the subordination of all economic activities to the overall developmental strategy and clear preference for domestic economic agents in the realisation of developmental endeavours. Its essence can be defined as '[pursuing] national economic interests through shielding the national economy against outside influences and [implementing] aggressive and discriminatory policies against foreigners' (Cai, 2010b, p 11). In the case of China, this has been especially visible in the categorisation of industrial sectors according to the access regulations for foreign entities, commonly referred to as the Catalogue (Breslin, 2006) and examined later in this chapter.

In the 1980s, economic nationalism was realised partly by the gradual process of economic liberalisation, where the incremental and closely monitored opening up would, on the one hand, give time for domestic economic agents to consolidate and strengthen their position, and, on the other, would not allow foreign actors to immediately penetrate the domestic market. In the 1990s, despite the increase in political nationalism, economic nationalism had to be relegated to being a secondary state doctrine, as far as its instruments were concerned, at least in the interim period, in view of the imperative to comply with the wishes of international power centres when China was at the final stages of negotiating its accession to the WTO. However, Hughes (2006, p 26) points out that:

by the end of the 1990s, the particular form of Chinese techno-nationalism had become quite explicit in Jiang Zemin's elevation of scientific and technological personnel to the status of a revolutionary vanguard leading the nation to wealth and power under his ideology of the 'three represents'.

Moreover, economic nationalism motivated the consolidation of the state-owned business sector at that time.

The change in the leadership in 2002 was broadly believed to signal a reorientation of the overall policy. The Hu–Wen regime is often perceived as the one that reinstalled the principles of China's economic nationalism through increased state interventionism and the reversal of economic liberalisation. Although economic nationalism and economic liberalisation do not need to contradict each other, taking into consideration the current degree of interconnectedness of national economies and their mutual interdependence, China's authorities most likely consider this reversal as the means to advance economic nationalism, which, as Scissors (2009) points out, is necessary in their opinion for the realisation of developmental targets. Despite the Xi–Li administration's supposed dedication to further economic liberalisation, it is difficult to imagine that economic nationalism will cease to be the prime state ideology in its reform and opening up conduct.

The alleged intensity of China's economic nationalism led the US administration to publicise this nationalism's 'evils', namely:

> mercantilist tactics, including: the aggressive [and, as it is presumed, unjustified] use of antidumping and safeguard measures, manipulation of its exchange rate, provision of subsidies to SOEs, condoning violation of intellectual property rights, explicit and implicit demands of technology transfer in exchange for market access, blocking foreign industry from government procurement, adaptation of unique technical standards, and discriminatory implementation of health and safety standards. (Kennedy, 2008)

Indeed, China's economic nationalism, as much as the Korean and Japanese DS-related nationalisms, is characterised by maintaining an environment of dominance of domestic economic agents where foreign agents play merely additional supporting roles. The features of contemporary China's economic nationalism can be observed from various perspectives: as laws and regulations (including ad hoc quasi-regulatory actions), as policies, and as a sectoral approach. As a result of WTO accession, the Chinese government was obliged to eliminate certain trade/market access barriers. This, however, did not change the state's overall conviction of a necessity to protect the internal market while advocating liberalisation worldwide. Consequently, other, non-WTO related, often implicit constraints have since been applied to favour domestic economic agents by either blocking or deterring foreign competitors.

Procurement practices seem to be among the most vivid examples of China's economic nationalism. Public procurement practices involve prohibition of wholly foreign-owned companies and joint ventures registered in China from bidding in certain sectors that are increasingly reserved for products and goods made by Chinese domestic companies. Sometimes, even when the wholly foreign-owned companies and joint ventures are accepted for a bid, they do not seem to have a chance of winning the tender, usually due to 'technical reasons'. According to the *20013/2014 Position Paper* (PP), a yearly publication by the EU Chamber of Commerce in China, 'the *Government Procurement Law* and the *Bidding and Tendering Law* continue to discriminate against foreign-invested enterprises in China' (PP, 2013, p 16).

China's economic nationalism can sometimes be seen through ad hoc governmental decisions and the behaviour of its authorities. In June 2009, a circular prepared by the National Development and Reform Commission (NDRC) and by eight other ministries was distributed among various levels of decision-making authorities, which contained 'strong advice' to purchase Chinese products while spending the RMB4 trillion stimulus aimed at reviving the economy during the global economic crisis. It suggested that 'priority must be given to domestic products for all government-invested projects' (PP, 2009, p 111), and warned against engaging 'in any discrimination against domestic products' (PP, 2009).

The Chinese government very much adopted a sectoral approach in its strategy of favouring domestic economic agents, in which certain branches of the national economy were considered to have strategic importance. This results in prohibition of the penetration by foreign economic agents, or in significantly limiting their scope of possible activities: 'From 1995, this differential approach to foreign investment was formalised in "The Catalogue Guiding Investment in Industry" [or the Foreign Investment Catalogue], which, on an industry-by-industry basis, shows where investment is prohibited, restricted, encouraged or permitted' (Breslin, 2006, p 21). Breslin (2006) analysed the different sectors that, in the mid-2000s, were prohibited from foreign investment (eg essential services, the defence sector, heavy pollutant product industries and those illegal under Chinese law), encouraged (export-oriented, high-tech and *pro forma* those who could not be restricted under the WTO regulations) and restricted (those deemed to be central to national economic development, such as certain foods, medical products, raw materials, power plants, chemicals, etc). These branches where penetration is most severely limited are sometimes referred to as 'absolute control' industries and include armaments, power generation and distribution, oil and petrochemicals, telecommunications, coal, civil aviation, and shipping (see CTI, 2009). The Catalogue is on occasion amended (1997, 2002, 2004, 2007). However, the fifth amendment of the Catalogue (December 2011) brought little positive change, if any (PP, 2013). Although a sectoral opening-up trend could be observed before and after WTO accession, the common perception has been that the 2000s were marked by the tightening of control and an increase in the number of industries with limited foreign access (PP, 2009, 2010), and the 2010s seem to be characterised by little progress.

Market access is also restricted by granting a privileged position to the well-established domestic SOEs. For example, the energy sector is almost fully controlled by the state and state-controlled enterprises. This includes oil and gas exploration (also shale gas), refineries, and wholesale and retail business. The government is 'tightly reserving domestic energy sector opportunities to domestic companies' (PP, 2009, p 207). The banking sector is also affected to a distinctive degree. Foreign banks, including domestically incorporated foreign banks, do not enjoy the same rights as domestic banks as far as opening new branches and introducing new services and obligatory deposits are concerned, to name a few. The same applies to foreign insurance companies and related services.

Some of the most effective institutions in barring foreign economic agents from participating in the Chinese domestic market using standardisation practices, discussed in Chapter Four, are the General Administration of Quality Supervision, Inspection and Quarantine (AQSIQ) and the Certification and Accreditation Administration (CNCA) in the sector of agricultural and food products. The most well-known cases have been related to the procedures for European meat to be allowed to access the Chinese market. Despite evident shortages of meat and meat products in China – caused not, as some tend to believe, by interim conditions such as natural disasters and so on, but by long-term structural shortcomings and environmental conditions – and despite the fact that the situation will deteriorate in the long term, the Chinese authorities have often been very reluctant to open the domestic market to many of the European meat producers. Multilayered and multi-staged procedures have taken years and have been subject to indiscriminate delays on the Chinese side, often implicitly motivated by political reasons.[38]

The preceding sketch of China's economic nationalism should not be perceived as a list of complaints that foreign governments and companies address to the Chinese authorities. This is merely an indication of the current policy without, so to speak, taking sides. Although Chinese government practices may cause outrage among some members of the international community and are subject to notorious criticism from many developed countries, they are not unique in their form. Chinese companies often face certain constraints in the European market, for example, in the construction market.[39] Moreover, 'buy Chinese' is not a unique idea. Americans would often openly propagate 'buy American' or discourage purchasing goods 'made in China'. The British food industry notoriously labels its products with the British flag and notes such as 'British beef' and so on, implicitly encouraging their purchase.

In sum, it can be plausibly argued that China's economic policy, which will be subject to additional examination in Chapter Four, is extensively characterised by economic nationalism. In the political elite's quest to control the pace and direction of development, as well as to strengthen domestic economic agents, certain sectors of the national economy are protected and access to some is limited, regardless of the economic *rationale*. The authorities use various incentives and deterrence techniques to achieve their goals. On theoretical grounds, the Chinese leadership simply do not believe in Adam Smith's rhetoric, but rather in Friedrich List's argument that 'free competition between advanced factories in England and relatively backward factories of other manufacturing countries would ... simply lead to the destruction of the industries of the weaker states' (List, 1909 [1841], p 48, cited in Levi-Faur, 1997, p 366). China is perceived by the Chinese elite as the weaker state in this equation, which needs economic nationalism in the form of favouring/discriminating and constraining/encouraging, or rather the regulating and guiding of various economic agents for the overall benefit of national development.

---

[38] For example, a Dalai Lama visit significantly delays the negotiations for the host country of that visit.

[39] The companies who participate in the bids in the construction market are often required to have some experience in the EU market. Many Chinese companies, despite significant achievements in China and outside, lack this type of experience.

The political arrangements

Economic nationalism might sometimes be associated with the genus of political system. However, the significance of political regimes was examined in Chapter One. The DS model in Korea during its core period and contemporary China share the characteristics of the political system, namely, its authoritarian form of a rather strongly coercive character. In the case of Japan, the democratic system was accompanied by the mechanism of shielding the development trajectory. Indeed, Japan, during its DS-proper period, managed:

> to retain many 'soft authoritarian' features in its governmental institutions, and extremely strong and comparatively unsupervised state administration, single party rule … and a set of economic priorities that seems unattainable under true political pluralism during such a long period. (Johnson, 1987, p 137)

In the post-socialist world, some countries became democratic and some did not. As far as China is concerned, the late 1980s' economic reforms contributed to the emergence of the concept of new or neo-authoritarianism, sometimes believed to be an interim period leading eventually to political freedom (Fewsmith, 2008a; Hughes, 2006). The concept advocated the establishment of a strong authoritarian state with a clear target to preside over economic modernisation and the catching-up trajectory. To a large extent, it was modelled on the experiences of South Korea and Taiwan, and by the early 1990s, gained the support of central leadership. This is not to say that there was no political liberalisation intended. Some limited progress towards wider popular participation in constructing policy recommendations has been made, as discussed in Chapter Two. This suggests a deeper commitment to Evans's embeddedness, and perhaps a long-term gradual liberalisation of the political sphere, in terms of some civil rights. It should not, however, be mistaken for a process of full democratisation, as was eventually the case of Korea and Taiwan. China remains fully, so to speak, an authoritarian state, where the role of the electorate is played by, what Shirk (2007, p 40) and others call, a selectorate – 'a group of people within the Party who have effective power to choose the leader'.

An authoritarian state, however, does not guarantee a strong, 'capable' state, a somehow crucial condition for a developmental state and, indeed, embedded in the concept of neo-authoritarianism. In the post-socialist world, the threat of Myrdal's soft state is indeed great, as even the case of Russia illustrates (Rutland, 2009). On the one hand, deficiencies in legislation have been a common feature, as systemic transformation has been a complicated and multilayered endeavour, encompassing various strata of societal existence, including reformulation of the legal system and laws. This process has been taking place in a relatively short period of time. On the other hand, a lack of obedience to rules and law enforcement has been distinctively visible in the former Soviet republics, where due to the inadequate sequence and/or sectoral intensity of reforms, the states have found themselves in complete disarray. Powerful groups pursuing their own goals, in collision with the overall interest of the country, have been a constant feature of the former Soviet republics, as well as some CEE states. Naturally, the resistance of public control has always been present in CEE, also prior to the reforms, and derives from the aversion to political elites inherited from the communist times.

Japan and Korea are considered not to have been soft states during their DS periods. In Korea, the reimposition of the developmentally uncompromising state took place during the general Park Chung Hee era and was related to the form of the military regime (see Kim, 1997; Woo, 1991). According to Amsden (1989, p 142), the process of transformation from a weak state unable to defend itself against foreign aggression to a strong state capable of mediating market forces took over a century. The strong state in Japan seemed to derive more from certain structural arrangements serving the development trajectory. A well-prepared and educated bureaucracy, which traces its roots back to the Meiji administration, largely independent from both society and political elites, would have the institutional and intellectual capacity to run the state in such a way as to achieve extensive developmental goals via creating an adequate environment for domestic business to thrive in the designated economic sectors (see Johnson, 1987).

China has never been seen as a soft state, as opposed to India, another large Asian developing economy with extensive potential for growth, and to Russia, the second-largest post-socialist economy. In fact, neo-authoritarianism enforced the perception of China as a strong state. The toughness of the regime in Beijing towards its citizens contributed to the somewhat distorted picture of China as a very strong state, in addition to being a harsh state. The PRC fulfils, however, some requirements of Myrdal's soft state and is characterised by certain important weaknesses, which may affect the overall development trajectory. These weaknesses are presented in what follows.

First, there are undoubtedly certain influential groups originating from the People's Liberation Army (PLA) leadership, local government officials and business circles who contribute to the mafianisation of economic relations (ie the creation of corruption-prone, non-transparent ties between business and the state administration). Especially during the period of accelerated privatisation present at the provincial level, the temptation of the illegal acquiring of large amounts of state assets resulted in an increasing 'grey zone' of economic activities. Moreover, the process of administrative decentralisation has eroded state capacity in a number of sectors, including the fiscal extraction (Wang and Hu, 2001) necessary for the process of industrialisation. It created a 'weak centre and strong localities' (Hu and Wang, 1993, cited in Fewsmith, 2008a, p 143) and weakened the state's ability to control the business sector (Wang, 1997). This erosion of state capacity may have a profound negative impact on the genus of systemic economic and political changes (Breslin, 2007).

Second, a lack of obedience to legal regulations and policies adopted at the centre, and an overall crisis in law enforcement, especially at the local level, has been endemic throughout the transformational period. Although the broad discretion of ministries and other state executive bodies allows for flexibility and the rapid adjustment of the National People's Congress's general laws, it also leaves significant space for over-interpretation, abuse and the distortion of the initial ideas behind the laws. Moreover, too many agencies produce regulations and supporting guidelines, which results in a regulatory chaos of conflicting and unclear rules (OECD, 2009a, pp 70–1), as has been the case of the anti-monopoly law, for example. Law implementation and interpretation has become one of the biggest issues as far as state management is concerned and is often debated publicly. It is widely considered that China's legal regulations, for example, those referring to natural environment protection, intellectual property rights and others, have complied with international standards; however, their enforcement has been disastrously ineffective, as seen by the amount of illegally produced goods available on the market and by the appearance now and then of scandals related to environmental pollution. This environmental pollution is profoundly visible in all big and many medium-sized cities in China. The analysis of the effectiveness of law implementation in China, especially in such a sensitive and crucial area as environmental protection, suggests a certain inability of the state to govern.

Finally, Shirk (2007) points out that due to the systemic arrangements, and despite the overall appearance, China has been, politically, a very fragile state, especially during the Hu–Wen regime. This is partly because neither President Hu nor Premier Wen were uncontested totalitarian dictators and, therefore, could be effectively challenged by the selectorate if the internal economic and/or political situation deteriorated or if China's international position weakened. Shirk argues that the state leaders must follow three basic rules in order to maintain their grip on power, namely: avoiding public leadership splits; preventing large-scale social unrest; and keeping the military on the side of the CCP. Any of these occurrences have the potential to politically destabilise China. An open split in the leadership may even effect a military confrontation. Large-scale social unrest, a possible side effect of the state-sponsored nurturing of nationalism and unbalanced development, may turn against the political elite and trigger protests around the country if large parts of society conclude, using currently available information technology, that the leadership is unfit to govern. The military has always complied with the wishes of the CCP. However, it is sometimes believed that the marshals and generals possess the ability to stage an effective *coup d'etat* if they profoundly disagree with state policy, for example, in reference to national security.

Indeed, China may exhibit some signs of becoming a soft state and, indeed, being a weak state while maintaining the status of a politically harsh or hard state. Limiting societal and political entrepreneurship as a means to enforcing a harsh state cannot be seen as the prevention of the formation of a soft state.[40] Additionally, China's political structure produces a number of possible triggers of conflict, as determined by Shirk (2007). From the developmental perspective, this may lead to the distortion of the development path and to the further polarisation of society, or, indeed, to a political situation in which a developmental reversal takes place.

However, before the final judgement as to the strength of the Chinese state, one needs to establish how much the alleged legal chaos and economic 'grey zone' activities are the state's failures and how much they take place simply because the state tolerates them or, indeed, supports them. The legal chaos prevents some unwanted foreign economic agents from acquiring a powerful position on the Chinese market, and, thus, can perversely be seen as the means to realise Wang's (1997) and Hu's neo-authoritarian postulates of promoting certain domestic economic actors. A lack of enforcement of environmental regulation does not inhibit the nominal value of economic growth and

[40] It is important to reiterate that the concept of a soft state is not related to the level of political repression present in a given state, as the Chinese example illustrates, neither to the idea of an economically liberal or interventionist state. It relates to a state's ability to exercise certain powers effectively in order to secure the realisation of policies. In the context of this book, these powers relate to development policies.

allows for the realisation of the 'growth at all costs' doctrine. A lack of effective intellectual property rights (IPR) allows for better diffusion of innovative technology. Naturally, those benefits might be short-lived and counterproductive in the long term, when China becomes an important source of technology, when the quality of economic growth deteriorates due to lack of environmental considerations and when ineffective privileged companies born out of an initial lack of competition will be unable to provide competitive products. Nevertheless, in the short term, it seems to be a successful strategy. Moreover, although there are undoubtedly certain power centres in China that, following Myrdal's logic, could contribute to the weakening of the state despite the fact that they are often associated with the ruling elites, and, as Breslin (1992) and Shirk (1993) point out, there is a constant struggle among the PRC leadership, the state's overall priorities are being implemented and the state is by far the strongest power centre able to exercise enormous influence over the other alleged power centres. Since the Tiananmen events in 1989, the state leadership has successfully managed to continue a 'peaceful rise' and to avoid creating circumstances that could generate state-wide conflict.

The existence of authoritarianism in China prompts the question of the legitimacy of power, partly as the means to alleviate a potential state versus society conflict. Among the majority of post-socialist states, legitimacy is derived from democratic elections, in which it is the nation that votes political parties into power. The leaders are accountable to their nations and can be replaced in the process of popular voting. In authoritarian states, such a mechanism does not exist; hence, political/democratic legitimacy is not enjoyed by the ruling elite. Consequently, the state leadership needs to search for other types of legitimacy, such as, for example, developmental legitimacy. On the other hand, however, it does not mean that in democratic states, the developmental legitimacy of the ruling elite to power cannot exist. Nevertheless, most of the democratic post-socialist governments do not seem to effectively seek this type of legitimacy, as their 'promotion' to power is the result of the democratic vote.[41] In fact, none of the post-socialist states from CEE and, especially, from the former Soviet Union achieved

---

[41] 'Promotion' often does not depend on how well you do, only on how well/badly your opponents do. In the year 1997, Poland seems to be a good example of this. After a period of fast economic growth, the governing Social-Democratic Party lost the elections despite gaining more votes than in the previous elections that promoted it to power. This was due to the consolidation of the opposition into one main political bloc.

developmental dynamics comparable to those of developmental states, and thus their respective political elites probably cannot aspire to possess developmental legitimacy.

In the case of both Korea and Japan, developmental legitimacy seemed important in power being maintained by the respective ruling elites. In Japan, developmental efforts were met with cyclic approval during democratic elections, although an important argument of a lack of political contestation should not be discounted in the analysis of factors determining the election victories of the Japanese Liberal Party. In Korea, developmental legitimacy partly served as a replacement for political rights, which Korean society extensively lacked, and was seen as an important justification for the continuation of the military regime. Camilleri (2000, p 434) claims that in the case of China:

> the [Communist] regime [believed that its] claim to legitimacy depended on restoring to China its dignity and sense of importance, expunging the humiliation suffered at Western hands, and satisfactorily managing the unfinished business of China's civil war, not to mention the Cold War.

In the post-socialist period, this seems to hold true and is partly realised by elevating China to the ranks of economic superpower through rapid development. This is why the consequent governments have aimed at retaining the developmental legitimacy, as they have empirically proven their commitment to the transformation of the economic environment and to improving people's well-being, as illustrated by the dynamics of economic growth and significant positive change in HDI. Legitimacy comes precisely from those achievements. It seems to be connected with the concept of a *xi ok ng* society, advocating the necessity to achieve a certain degree of wealth in the population, and with the concept of a harmonious society – to establish balanced and orderly societal relations. Ruling elites' developmental legitimacy is enjoyed for the time during which positive results in the developmental sphere are experienced, unlike political democratic legitimacy, which is usually awarded for a fixed term. Consequently, the current legitimacy enjoyed by the Chinese political elite may not be there once the government's policies are no longer effective in fulfilling the prime objective, which is fast and steady development. Naturally, developmental reversal and the subsequent loss of developmental legitimacy would not mean an automatic departure of the CCP from power. Nevertheless, in such a situation, to maintain the supreme political position, it could mean for the CCP a slow drift towards policies of a predatory state. In fact, it is often claimed that societal polarisation – the continuous marginalisation of parts of society and a dramatic increase in income disparities – has already called the legitimacy of the China party-state into question (Wedeman, 1997; Guo and Hu, 2004).

Continuing the issue of derivatives of the genus of the political system, one must acknowledge that the existence of an authoritarian state inevitably results in limiting the freedoms readily available to society in liberal democracies. Moreover, Leftwich (2000, p 160) believes that developmental states are characterised by 'an uneasy mix of repression and poor human rights' records. Most of the democratic post-socialist states have maintained good records of respect for political freedoms and human rights, and eliminated repressions at the beginning of the systemic transformation. Naturally, the picture has not always been positive. On occasion, liberal democracies of CEE would lose their Freedom House status as 'free' countries and become 'partly free', as opposed to former Soviet republics, who would witness human rights violations in most cases during the entire period of transformation. One should note, however, that Leftwich (2000) does not advocate political repression as an element of the developmental state. He merely notes that in a developmental state, some rights widely present in Western democracies are withheld. As far as political freedoms are concerned, as opposed to certain social, economic and development-related rights, China does not seem a mere 'tamperer' of rights, but a gross violator. Naturally, political persecution was present to a great extent in the authoritarian Korean DS and, to some extent, in the pre-DS Meiji Japan. Nevertheless, China is probably a much more significant case, where political imprisonment, intimidation of the political opposition and widespread censorship of politically related matters are practised on a large scale. The repressions, as well as Confucian values deeply rooted in society, such as the respect for hierarchy and order, create, as it is believed, a type of subordinate society, another condition listed by Leftwich (2000). However, although East Asian nations are in general seen as subordinate societies, and in the case of China, this perception is reinforced by the harshness of the political regime, it is also a fact that the number of socially related protests, as well as socially related debates in the media, conferences and gatherings, suggests a certain misperception as to the real level of societal subordination of the Chinese people. Chinese society is increasingly vocal about defending its social rights, which is acknowledged by the state leadership and translated into a gradual process of the broadening of social dialogue.

The interaction of the four actors

In DS cases, development trajectories have partly been facilitated by a certain type of internal relationship. It is believed that implementation of the developmental state concept into mainstream policies requires institutional arrangements such as relative autonomy of the state and a competent economic bureaucracy. The DS model possesses a rather difficult requirement that, in effect, defines the interrelation between four actors of the developmental state scene – the political elite, the state (economic) bureaucracy, business and society – namely, the requirement of insulation and the requirement of embeddedness, hence Evans's embedded autonomy.

Figure 3.1: Four actors of the developmental state

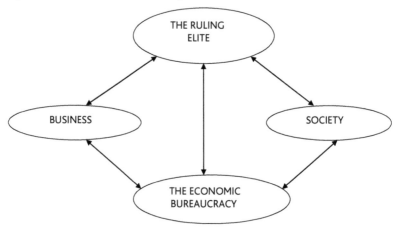

The state bureaucracy and the political ruling elite are often seen as one actor, namely, the state. However, the DS model is also characterised by a specific relation of these two. Japan showed a great deal of insulation of the bureaucracy from the political elite, whereas Korea showed dependency of the former on the latter. China is closer to the Korean case. However, the case of China brings into scope another aspect of state–bureaucracy relations not featured in the significantly smaller countries of Japan and Korea, namely, the issue of centralism. The Japanese and Korean developmental states were centralised structures, with one central authority to impose policies and regulations. China, due to its communist legacy of economic and political centralism and political harshness, is often seen as a centralised state, where policies articulated in Beijing are effectively executed throughout the country.

Their sum shapes China's overall development trajectory's direction. However, post-socialist China's development and reform paths cannot be evaluated without taking into consideration local/provincial dynamics (White, 1999; Breslin, 2007), with provinces' effectively autonomous power centres distorting state policy implementation and reorganising developmental priorities. White (1999) sees a clear difference between centralised China during the state-command times and the gradually decentralised China during the market reform period. However, even in the state-command period, China's economy was centralised to a lesser degree than the more developed states of the Eastern bloc; thus, Chinese central authorities were more constrained in implementing socialist-time state-level policies: 'Unlike the Soviet Union, where the strong ministerial system by-passed local governments and transmitted plans directly to their enterprises, the Maoist system decentralised economic and administrative power to the localities' (Oi, 1995, pp 1133–4).

Central–local relations in post-socialist China attracted significant scholarly attention. The post-socialist decentralisation, a process common among most of the former state-command economies, is believed, in the case of China, to have gone far enough to discuss federalist scenarios (Cao et al, 1999; Chung, 2006). However, Chung (1995, p 502) argues that although:

> there is no doubt that during the period of economic reform overall provincial autonomy has indeed expanded as a result of various measures of decentralisation … it seems wrong to infer that the centre is completely helpless in restricting provincial autonomy as some 'split China' scenarios project.

He points out that:

> the post-Mao reforms seem to have produced complex effects on central–local dynamics. While the decline of ideological control and the decentralisation of economic policy making have generally expanded local autonomy, the reforms have also significantly enhanced the centre's ability to acquire key information on local policy behaviour. (Chung, 1995, p 503)

In reality, the centre still remains the paramount decision-maker as far as general policies and key cadre nominations are concerned. The rotation mechanism, where high-ranking officials change positions and move to other provinces upon the decisions taken in Beijing, allows the capital to retain control, despite the internal political fighting within various factions. The fact that this control is perhaps less effective than in the cases of Japan and Korea should not preclude China from potential membership of some type of developmental states group, partly because it did not affect the general developmental dynamics to the extent that it is not comparable to the historical DS cases.

The administrative machinery, in the form of economic bureaucracy, together with the ruling elite, requires insulation from both society and business in order to fulfil its duties in managing the state's overall development trajectory. In the case of business, this state autonomy seems to be achieved to a significant degree in all three countries, China being, in this respect, the weakest case, as corruption greatly sabotages this insulation at lower administrative levels. Japan seems to be the finest example of this autonomy. On the other hand, this insulation should not prevent the creation of the state–business alliance – a mechanism necessary for facilitation of the development trajectory. This alliance had a different form in Japan than in Korea. In Japan, this relationship indeed seemed 'embedded' and characterised by conciliatory cooperation; in Korea, it took the form of coercive dependency. It is difficult to speak of a full formulation of state–business alliance in the case of China. A certain type of alliance, however, exists in two forms: first, by definition, Chinese SOEs are the tools of implementation of the state developmental strategy. This is not to say that they all serve the purpose of development. On the contrary, some are a heavy burden on the state budget and on taxpayers and function due to some 'short-termist' political reasons. Only half of all the SOEs were actually bringing in revenue at the turn of the century (Mako and Zhang, 2002) and probably only a handful of them would be able to compete with a non-state sector without the support of state regulations and without state interference into the market.[42] This is indeed an awkward type of alliance, if an alliance at all, as the dependence of one partner on the other is absolute. The energy sector seems to be the most vivid example of this relationship, as the state directly engages SOEs in the realisation of its strategy. Second, the state creates certain incentives for the development of designated sectors. These incentives are then utilised by state and non-state enterprises. This DS-style policy largely defines the state–private business alliance in China.

[42] A potential inability to compete in the conditions of a 'free' market environment can partly be illustrated by the extent of government subsidies received by some large Chinese companies. The issue is presented later in this book.

As far as state–society relations are concerned, all three countries managed to maintain a relatively high level of insulation: in China and Korea, due to, it appears, the lack of democratic procedures; in Japan, due to the lack of democratic procedures regarding the state bureaucracy and the lack of political contestation. The level of embeddedness seemed the highest in Japan. However, the Chinese state's embeddedness in society seems to be increasing, partly as a result of the 17th CCP Congress. It takes the form of the broadening of consultation channels. Although a 'public consultation procedure is not a legally guaranteed right at present' (OECD, 2009a, p 102), symposia, panel discussions and hearings have become an ever-more frequent instrument of public participation in the creation of laws and regulations. In certain circumstances, the hearings are obligatory and their results must be made public. This involves a number of procedural consequences, such as:

> that opinions from concerned parties shall be recorded and listed during the drafting of administrative and local rules. Experts shall be called upon to expound on professional or technical issues related to the drafting of regulations. During the period of examination, the investigating organ shall examine whether the drafting organ has correctly handled opinions on the draft regulation from different organisations, institutions and individuals. (OECD, 2009a, p 103)

Moreover, 'the Standing Committee of the 11th National People's Congress in April 2008 announced that it would solicit for public comments on the majority of draft and amendments coming under its review' (PP, 2009, p 91). Although the public consultation procedure constitutes only one example of increasing embeddedness, a society's influence on laws and regulations seems extremely important in a country such as China, which is undergoing institutional transformation, even if this influence is indeed limited and often illusionary, as it allows the nation's broader participation in systemic institutionalisation. The mechanism for public consultation will continue to develop, as it has been included, for example, in the reform agenda presented as a result of the 3rd plenum of the 18th CCP Congress.

In many democratic post-socialist countries, state autonomy from society seems, to a great extent, illusory, in both respects: that of political elites and that of the state bureaucracy. Politicians often define their support for policies and for legal regulations in relation to certain groups (the electorate) that they believe they represent. Those groups eventually vote them in or out. State institutions are often penetrated by political agents as far as the administration is concerned. Embeddedness of the ruling elite within society is defined by short-term accountability for the policies implemented. In the case of state–business relations, the level and nature of interconnectedness differs, in some cases, resembling Latin American political capitalism.

In sum, it can plausibly be argued that China is in the process of achieving Evans's embedded autonomy. The ruling elite enjoys extensive autonomy from society and, on the state level, also from certain groups of particular economic interests. As Shirk (2007) points out, however, this autonomy has some limitations. Embeddedness in the form of social dialogue continuously increases its importance in defining societal interrelations with the power centre. The CCP sees the expansion of dialogue as a crucial element of political reform enforced by the 17th Party Congress (*China Daily*, 2007a) and some subsequent laws.

However, despite the expansion of state–society consultation channels, the picture is not that positive. While discussing state–society relations, one also needs to focus on one important feature of the DS architecture, namely, the underprivileged position of the labour force, in particular, the working class: 'The exclusion of labour from [the] corporatist-style of politics of developmental Japan is ... well noted in the literature, as are the repressive labour politics of pre-democratic Korea and Taiwan' (Gallagher, 2005, p 153). This was due to the fact that the labour force was paramount for the nationalist development project (Gallagher, 2005, p 156) in the East Asian states, and thus it was believed that it needed to be effectively controlled. China, as much as Korea with the most antagonistic labour relations among the East Asian NICs (Gallagher, 2005, p 156), has been characterised by a high degree of repression towards the labour force during the reform period. Gallagher (2005, p 153) points out that 'the ideology and policies of state-led capitalist development adopted in China since the 1990s have brought this mark of developmentalism home'. This clear departure from communist ideals has, indeed, been a gradual process, which accelerated in the 1990s, with a number of new laws taking away many socialist benefits, such as prevention from being fired or lifetime employment (Solinger, 2006, p 181), and with the introduction of Jiang Zemin's three represents, which are sometimes believed to have depreciated the importance of workers (Solinger, 2003, p 948). This is the result of the CCP forming an alliance with the business sector rather than with the labour sector (Chen, 2003) and 'a radical shift in the state's relationship to the urban working class' (Gallagher, 2005, p 153). Consequently, the working class has been effectively marginalised (He,

2000) and a large underclass has been created (Solinger, 2006), whose standard of living is perhaps lower than it was during the state-command economy period. Effective institutionalised channels for articulating and advancing class interests do not exist (Chen, 2003). Uncoordinated workers are unable to effectively channel their agenda in the conditions of market hegemony (Blecher, 2002) as they are unprepared for the onslaught of global capitalism (Gallagher, 2005, p 96).

Indeed, eliminating the rights and privileges of the working class has been a distinctive feature of post-socialist transformation. Extensive socialist benefits were difficult to sustain in new market conditions. However, in CEE, this temporal privilege vacuum was soon replaced by the European continental model of extensive social rights. This has not happened in FSU and is not taking place in China. Post-socialist China remains very much like the Korean case of extensive repression of the labour force. In 2000, He wrote:

> regression in capital–labour relations is a stark phenomenon in China today. What we are witnessing is a return to conditions common during the Industrial Revolution of the nineteenth century, of which Marx wrote the classic critique in his monumental work *Capital*. In the PRC today, workers employed in firms financed [especially] by Asian capital are typically forced to toil continuously for ten or twelve hours everyday, with ... no weekend off. Workers in such firms earn very low wages, in poor and dangerous conditions. Accidents occur frequently.... Many firms producing toxicants take no protective steps of any kind. (He, 2000, p 85)

Although the level of salaries has risen dramatically since He (2000) wrote his analysis, to the extent that China is no longer able to compete with some Southeast Asian economies in the field of labour costs, this rise has been offset by the increase in the level of prices and, hence, the cost of living. Consequently, income levels have hardly improved, in addition to often unchanged working conditions.

A developmental state requires a strong and competent, developmentally oriented bureaucracy. Korea and Japan did possess such a bureaucracy during their DS core periods. Cheng et al (1998) point out that in the case of Korea, the economic bureaucracy, based on the Indian model, started to emerge in the late 1950s. However, it was the centralisation process of the 1960s, under the military regime, concerned predominantly with economic-decision powers and the establishment of the Economic Planning Board, which shaped the Korean development-focused state administration. The agencies promoting industry development obtained a strong standing, whereas foreign trade was closely integrated within industrial policy functions. Does China possess a competent state economic bureaucracy?[43] As a result of administrative reforms in the early 1990s, which seem to have put an accent on constant improvements of the bureaucracy, the professionalisation of the cadres is growing (Brodsgaard and Chen, 2009). Civil servants are relatively well paid. However, the process of the bureaucracy becoming autonomous is rather slow. Nevertheless, the ruling elite is free from societal pressure to a great extent. In time, one should expect an evolution of the public administration towards greater independence and higher professionalism in governing the country and provinces, as has been the trend for the last 20 years. Moreover, the fact that power is centred in the hands of one political structure contributes towards the stability of the administrative cadres. The developmental logic and the will to hold on to developmental legitimacy result in the selection of those who would be best equipped, intellectually and practically, to facilitate long-term policies.[44] It is clearly visible on the level of interaction with various state officials.[45] The situation in many other post-socialist states seems relatively worse. The political infiltration of the state administration situates many post-socialist countries among Latin American states, where 'appointive bureaucracy' is prevalent and dominant.

The analysis of autonomy and bureaucracy inevitably leads towards the question of corruption. Despite the fact that the relation between the level of corruption and the dynamics of developmental change in the DS model has not been firmly established, much of the scholarly literature features the discussion on corruption, as endemic corruption

[43] The pilot developmental agencies characteristic of the DS model are examined in the following section.

[44] In line with improving professionalism among the senior cadres, the CCP has introduced extensive training for their candidates for higher posts in the state administration. The system is based on the functioning of several CCP schools, namely: Party School of the CCP Central Committee (Beijing); China National School of Administration (Beijing); China Pudong Executive Leadership Academy (Shanghai); China Jinggangshan Executive Leadership Academy (Jinggangshan); China Yan'an Executive Leadership Academy (Yan'an); and China Business Executive Academy (Dalian).

[45] Personal observations.

is often considered one of the most important features of DS relational aspects, hence the necessity to address the issue at this point.

Although no political and economic system is free from corruption, the special partnership between business and the state present in historical developmental states can be seen as offering fertile ground for corruption and the forming of crony capitalism. Indeed, in Japan, Korea and other countries, corruption is on occasion a serious issue and politicians have been tried on corruption charges in a number of instances. The Korean DS case is the more interesting, as there are different opinions on the level of corruption. On one hand, it is claimed that the agreed industrial policies (determining overall industrial development and the economic actors to participate in the process) were the result of political considerations motivated by the exchange of bribes (see Kang, 2002; Sindzingre, 2006). On the other hand, some believe that the so-called targeted industries, examined in Chapter Four, enjoyed a corruption-free environment to some extent under the political umbrella of President Park Chung Hee, and the decisions concerning those industries were met using developmental and technical criteria (see, eg, Perkins, 2001). Those two statements do not need to be contradictory. Perhaps, once a company joins the privileged group due to an 'exchange of bribes', it then enjoys a corruption-free inner environment to operate in. Another group of countries vulnerable to corruption are those undergoing a systemic transition, such as post-socialist transformation. At a certain stage of the reforms, the economy in transition is characterised by a dual track of plan and market, and this is 'the major cause of corruption in the reform context because it is not a true market, but a plethora of networks protected by cards and bureaucrats' (Meaney, 1989, p 210, cited in Gong, 1997, p 277). As a result, White (1996, p 149) argued that 'political and bureaucratic corruption … remains a consistent aspect of the developmentally successful East Asian NICs (with the exception of Singapore) and has reared its hydra-head in the post-communist "transitional" societies of Central and Eastern Europe'.

Consequently, China, undergoing post-socialist transformation and attempting to shape many of its 'relational aspects' of economic and administrative actors in the DS manner, has been the subject of extensive examinations in the context of corruption. Historically, socialist China was prone to corruption, as were all Eastern bloc members. It was the 'socialist mode of corruption', shaped by the very features of state-command economy, namely, the monopoly of power held by the communist party, state ownership of property and the central planning of production (Kwong, 1997). In the conditions of the high degree of regulatory and distributive powers of the state administration, where almost all economic decisions were met by the monopolistic bureaucracy, socialist corruption (Gong, 1997) would always be a natural problem. However, what has been stressed by many scholars is that the level of corruption increased dramatically during the reform period (see White, 1996; Kwong, 1997), especially in the mid-1990s after the *nánxún* (Gong, 1997; Wedeman, 1997). Despite some neo-liberal explanations of the supposedly negative correlation between economic liberalisation and the intensity of corruption, the increase in corruption during the market reform period is hardly a surprise and in the Chinese mode of incremental transformation, would be difficult, if not impossible, to avoid. 'The cake' (ie the national economy) became bigger due to economic growth, the control over it less tight due to marketisation, and the supervision roles of the state more ambiguous due to transitional chaos. Moreover, 'the void of moral authority was filled ... with growing materialism and hedonism' (Kwong, 1997, p 119). Therefore, 'market reforms in the 1990s did not reduce corruption so much as they merely altered its characteristics' (Gong, 1997, p 277). In his analysis of post-socialist corruption in China, White (1996) named several explanations of the phenomenon, as presented by scholars: 'spiritual corruption' – due to contamination by capitalist thoughts and practices; transitional corruption – an 'inevitable accompaniment of the transition from central planning to a market economy, "a half-way house", in which market relations are developing, yet state agencies still retain a great deal of power and the unreformed political system pervades the economy' (White, 1996, p 154); and, finally, corruption caused by rent seeking.

There is agreement among the scholars and policymakers, including those representing Chinese political power centres, that in post-socialist China, corruption is a significant problem in both rural (Oi, 1991) and urban areas (Meaney, 1991), and that it is indeed related to the process of post-socialist transformation to a great extent. For example, Guo and Hu (2004) discuss the administrative monopoly in the transformational period as the main source of corruption in China, as opposed to the state capture-based corruption dominant in CEEFSU. This monopoly ensures that the interests of state monopolies in many sectors are well safeguarded and result in active rent seeking by the government because of the intermingling of its functions of governing and enterprise management. Gong (1997) admits that the formation of cadre entrepreneurs and their role in the economy is highly problematic: 'The rent accumulated by the sector monopoly ... is the loss of social welfare reflected in the monopoly price. [It also] includes various illegal fees collected by monopolistic sectors under various pretexts' (Guo and Hu, 2004, p 275). However, White (1996) questions rent-seeking theory as the leading explanation for rampant corruption in China. He argues that it does not explain the differentiation in corrupt practices in various places despite similar conditions, and does not address the issue of its increase during the reform period. He distinguishes three main corrupt practices in China: class A (clearly illegal in formal terms); class B (pervasive entrepreneurial practices by various state agents); and class C (pervasive networks of personal ties commonly known as *guānxi*).

One of the main types of corruption is institutional corruption (Wedeman, 1997) or organisational corruption (Lu, 2000), characterised by the exploitation of public authority by an organisation for its material gain: 'Institutional corruption involves the pursuit of gain by institutions acting collectively and relying on the authority or resources of the organisation to generate or extract income improperly' (Wedeman, 1997, p 806). Wedeman (1997, p 807) identifies a variety of forms of institutional corruption in contemporary China:

> These include the improper levying of fees, arbitrary fines and forced apportionment of funds – known colloquially as the 'three disorders' (*sān luàn*); unauthorised, and often coerced, fund raising; the siphoning of money out of budgetary and extra-budgetary accounts into off-the-books slush funds or 'small treasuries' [or 'small coffers'] (*xiǎo jīnkù*); the erection of illegal export and import barriers in support of local protectionism; and the systematic misappropriation of funds by local governments and bureaus.

Lu (2000) identifies several patterns of this type of corruption, namely: exacting revenues without clear legal mandates through *sān luàn*; unaccounted for, unreported and underreported funds, partly in the form of *xiǎo jīnkù*; irregular use of regulatory power for predatory purposes; generation of profit through the spin-off 'economic entities'; and the disposal of impounded revenues.

The corruption in China is to a great extent a provincial and local phenomenon, where lucrative privatisation and public procurement contracts are brokered. Indeed, for Ding (2000b, p 2), ownership changes comprise the major source of corruption in China. This does not just include the process of privatisation, which, in itself, is highly corruption-prone. Chen (2002) points out that corruption is prevalent in the new forms of SOE management (eg in the factory director responsibility system) and 'takes place in various links of the whole process of SOEs' production and business' (Chen, 2002, p 61), such as procurement (inferior product for superior price) and sale (hiding income to evade taxation). Naturally, rampant corruption accompanies privatisation and shareholding transformation as a result of 'organisational corruption and predation committed by government-appointed SOE directors and their collaborators in the party-state apparatus' (Chen, 2002, p 69).

Despite repeated anti-corruption campaigns and the official propaganda that the government pays close attention to the problem, supported by the examples of trials of high-ranking dignitaries such as the former CCP Shanghai chief Chen Liangyu or the leaders of the Food and Drug Administration, Zheng Xiaoyu and Cao Wenzhuang, the Chinese authorities have failed to break extensive business–political connections, as well as to stop building new relationships. Those connections and relationships have little in common with the DS concept of state–business alliance, defined as a type of cooperation agreement to facilitate the long-term development trajectory, and, to some extent, exhibit elements of the appropriation of the state characteristic of predatory states.

The corruption in China has both a political and economic impact. For example, according to Lu (2000, p 285):

> organisational corruption bears counter-developmental effects at least in three aspects. It disrupts and distorts the market, hurts investment, and reduces competitiveness. It harms state capacity in steering a healthy course of economic transition. It weakens the integrity of the bureaucracy and has an adverse effect on the institutionalisation of government structure and procedures.

Not only does it erode economic achievements by siphoning off economic benefits, it also endangers social stability and development in the long term (Guo and Hu, 2004) as it generates poverty (Chen, 2002). Nevertheless, DS-style corruption can actually have the opposite effect. Bramall (2009a) points out that some studies prove that corruption can be growth-promoting. He argues that, normally:

> corruption does lead to a deadweight loss.... However, if [it] has the effect of transferring resources to a growth-promoting class – as it seems to have done in South Korea – the net effect will be strongly positive.... Everything depends on the use to which the rents from corruption are put. (Bramall, 2009a, p 20)

This use is determined by the conduct of public officials, which White (1996, p 155) described as 'unorthodox', as it may bring clear corporate and public benefits and contribute to stimulating economic development. Bramall (2009a, p 20) concludes that although 'it is certainly arguable that corruption in China is not growth-promoting, [this] possibility cannot be dismissed *a priori*'.

Politically, however, corruption in China can lead to a crisis of legitimacy (Wedeman, 1997; Guo and Hu, 2004), partly due to the corruption-promoted rise in inequalities, which can generate social unrest (Chen, 2002). With no democratic mechanism for siphoning off popular pressure, state stability can be significantly affected. Therefore, it is the political rather than economic consequences of corruption that may affect the Chinese developmental model, by destabilising the party-state and inhibiting its abilities to preside over an effective catching-up trajectory. Naturally, East Asia has witnessed high long-term economic growth in politically unstable countries such as Thailand. The relationship between political stability and the dynamics of economic growth is more complex and by all means not straightforward. Nevertheless, due to various social and political factors, stability remains of vital importance in the PRC.

Corruption in China, however, seems to differ from that in many FSU states. It is prevalent especially in the undemocratic former Soviet republics. Kyrgyzstan (ranked 154), Tajikistan (ranked 157), Turkmenistan and Uzbekistan (ranked 170) are rated among the most corrupt states in the world, according to Transparency International. China, with a score of 39 (ranked 80) is situated in the middle of the ranking of post-socialist states (Transparency International, 2012). It is a significant fact that all the former Soviet republics except for the Baltic states and Georgia experience higher levels of corruption than China. For example, Ding (2000b) argues that as far as corruption related to privatisation is concerned, the situation was much worse in Russia, where the state was stripped of its assets as part of spontaneous and often illegal appropriation. In China, due to a lack of official mass privatisation campaigns, 'the [Chinese] managers and officials have had to design more subtle schemes to transform public assets into private property' (Ding, 2000b, p 26). On the other hand, China's ownership reform cannot be compared to the relatively corruption-free process in CEE (Walder, 2004; Breslin, 2007).

The economic arrangements

In the case of China, it seems beyond any doubt that the systemic transformation has been aimed at the significant acceleration of socio–economic development. This is repeatedly communicated in official documents, media and scholarly reports, as well as via the state leadership (see Deng, 1988). The developmental objective was also seen as the target of China's institutional arrangement prior to the reform era. Johnson (1999) argues that in order to accelerate development, China and North Korea chose communist modernisation, whereas Japan and South Korea chose a capitalist developmental state model. In this respect, the objective has not changed. However, communist modernisation did not achieve the expected results; hence, the authorities chose to adjust the model of development.

The pursuit of the improved welfare of society has remained the priority and is being achieved more effectively than prior to the reform period. One can, at most, question the imbalances of the Chinese achievements in the social strata of development. On the other hand, however, 'Japanese people's standard of living did not change anywhere near as much as the change in the Japanese gross national product' (Johnson, 1999, p 5). The initial pre-DS industrialisation in Korea involved little quality change for impoverished rural and urban residents. In fact, social disparities featured throughout the entire period of the Korean DS model. Nevertheless, the development trajectory was successfully maintained during the DS core activity period in both countries. In the case of Japan, it resulted in becoming the second-largest economy[46] and a developed nation. In the case of Korea, it meant an overcoming of backwardness comparable to that of early post-colonial African states and eventually becoming a developed state. China's example seems similar to a great extent, as socio–economic development has been conceptually detached from social welfare, that is, the overall developmental objective from social policies. In China, where the social elements of economic transformation have been neglected, the entire process of accelerating development is focused on the overall target and not on the benefits for certain social groups. This leads to the situation in which developmental advancements are accompanied by mounting social-related failures. On one side, there is impressive economic growth and change in the overall value of HDI; on the other, income disparities are among the highest in the former Eastern bloc. While a moneyed Chinese middle class is growing, some

---

[46] Only recently was Japan overtaken by China as the second-largest economy.

people are only marginally better off. In fact, due to the dismantling of the cooperative health-care system in rural areas and the deteriorating educational base therein, some groups are experiencing a decrease in their standard of living. The efforts at reinstalling universal medical coverage in rural areas and at eliminating ambiguous and unofficial, though common school fees, initiated by the Hu–Wen administration will only alleviate the negative effects of previous policies in the long term. A geographical diversity in transformational gains has prompted economic migration. Economic migrants, however, stumble on various obstacles while pursuing new employment opportunities outside their areas of residence, in the form of discriminatory practices based on the provisions of the *hukou* system, a practice that requires that each individual is registered within a particular geographical area, usually his/her or his/her parents' place of birth, and limits his/her rights outside of this area. This leads to the marginalisation of a large part of society, which is unable to benefit from the state's developmental achievements. Societal marginalisation is an increasingly important issue and, as a side effect of systemic transformation, one of the greatest concerns of the authorities as it is responsible for a number of social unrests (see He, 2000; Chen, 2003; Gallagher, 2005), which, as claimed by Shirk (2007) and many others, threaten the position of the political elite.

In general, however, the overall development trajectory has been effectively maintained, bringing extensive developmental achievements in China. These achievements are far greater than in other post-socialist countries. However, despite the fact that in both Japan and Korea, the pace of economic growth during the DS core activity period was faster than the change in people's welfare, none of the two countries experienced the societal disintegration and marginalisation characteristic of that taking place in China. On the contrary, it is believed that in Japan and Korea, the developmental state eventually contributed to social cohesion.

As far as the economic aspects of the process of post-socialist transformation is concerned, there seems to be a common agreement that the PST is about abandoning socialism and creating capitalism. The Chinese economy is becoming a market economy. Despite the heavy and extensive presence of the state sector in the economy, the private sector is expanding at a significant pace. Although many developed countries do not recognise China's market economy status (MES), the features of China's economy are essentially of a market character and certain alternative systemic and policy solutions, such as extensive state interventionism, as exemplified by close control and tight regulations regarding, for example, the energy sector, should merely be seen as a market economy variation. In fact, some of the steps taken by the leadership even suggest that China's development resembles, to some extent, Smith's capitalist development. As pointed out in Chapter Two, the process of capital accumulation is a significant part of the overall economic activities and a vital instrument in strengthening the state's ability to guide the development trajectory. The wealth comes from trade and not from agriculture.

Among the post-socialist states, there have been periods of following what was seen as liberal economic ideologies and more interventionist doctrines; hence, each state's policy would represent a mix of those two.[47] It is noteworthy, however, that, contrary to common opinion, critics of the allegedly inevitable transitional trajectory of post-socialist states guided by neo-liberal principles were indeed present at the beginning of the post-socialist transformation, mostly among political scientists, but also among some economists. Consequently, there was an alternative, unlike what some would want to believe. White and Wade (1988, p 1) underlined that 'late development', which the states in post-socialist transformation have experienced, should have been seen 'primarily in terms of Listian "political economy"', concretely as a process in which states have played a strategic role in taming domestic and international market forces and harnessing them to a national economic interest'. Particularly in the era of globalisation and the increasing interconnectedness of economic processes, 'taming' and then 'harnessing' seem of great importance.

The Korean and the Japanese DS cases were examples of an interventionist state – a DS-type interventionism in which the states would guide the developmental process, more directly in Korea than in Japan, where in the former, certain business entities would be ordered to do certain things and prohibited from doing others (see Wade, 1990; Graham, 2003). This type of interventionism would, in general, be seen as less intrusive than classical interventionism or, indeed, socialist interventionism. Nevertheless, neither Korea nor Japan could be described as 'low intervention countries'.[48]

---

[47] The discussion on state interventionism has a long history indeed, with important consequences in the post-socialist world. It is important to note, however, that the dispute in the post-socialist countries concerns internal economic ideologies that impact the type of domestic policies implemented, and should not be associated with the ambiguous global debate about the norms and rules of the global economy. Naturally, those subjects are prone to be mixed and confused in the course of debate.

[48] A term used by Wade (1992, p 284) in his analysis of Korea and Taiwan.

What kind of interventionism, then, is contemporary Chinese interventionism? Is the Chinese state a DS-type interventionist state? Through the introduction of market mechanisms, initially in the rural part of the national economy, the degree of state interventionism was bound to diminish. Moreover, in the 1990s, China's government accelerated the pace of economic liberalisation. During the negotiations concerning the PRC's accession to the WTO, the state's withdrawal from some parts of economic life was forced by the necessity to comply with the broadly accepted WTO rules: 'The agricultural sector was partly opened.... China committed to extensive changes in laws and regulations governing entry [to its domestic market]' (OECD, 2009a, p 54). Additionally, as much as throughout the state-command period, effective central planning remained an unaccomplished issue. At the beginning of the reforms, the degree of effective interventionism would be limited by the fact that China, a predominantly underdeveloped and poor country, but foremost a very large entity, would have some difficulties in enforcing centrally generated policy guidelines in actual local policies. This often seems to be proved by the disparities between provincial-level actions and state-level policy recommendations.

On the other hand, the communist legacy and a lack of democratic norms and procedures would suggest that the state has all the means to intervene in every aspect of political, social and economic life. Despite the process of economic liberalisation, China has been perceived as an interventionist state since the beginning of the systemic reforms. Deep into the transformation process partly characterised by this economic liberalisation, the 17th CCP Congress (2007) implicitly reiterated the Chinese authorities' commitment to extensive interventionism in the national economy and economic relations for supposed developmental benefits. The authorities rightly saw the previous waves of economic liberalisation as the means to achieve better developmental dynamics. Once, in their view, these means were exhausted, they did not hesitate to resort to extensive interventionist policies. The opportunity arose during the global economic crisis (2008/09), when most of the large economies resorted to financial stimulation to combat the negative effects of the crisis. In the case of China, where socio-economic development largely depends on international trade, at a time of a dramatic decrease in world consumption, the necessity for direct control over certain economic activities seemed obvious. In simplistic terms, the state had to replace the diminishing international consumption of Chinese products with domestic consumption (partly via infrastructure development), and it used a large fiscal stimulus in order to achieve this. The most important long-term incentive for increasing state interventionism, however, despite various market mechanisms in this field, has proven to be global climate change. It is often believed that the current mode of economic development needs to be dramatically altered if we are to avoid a long-term developmental catastrophe caused by global warming. In addition to inter-state cooperation, this requires extensive state intervention, especially in a country responsible for a significant share of the world's environmental pollution and greenhouse gas emissions. Despite some claims to the contrary, relying predominantly on strict market forces in the fight against global warming and increasing environmental pollution just does not seem to be an adequate solution.

Consequently, the Hu–Wen regime had favourable conditions, both internally and externally, to reverse the course of economic liberalisation and to increase state interventionism. Without doubt, growing internal inequalities, the global economic crisis, the international issues concerned with climate change and extensive domestic environmental pollution gave the Chinese elite reasons for a more broad intervention in economic affairs, as could be seen by the general shift in the content of economic policy (see PP, 2009). This has been happening despite some improvements in the market regulatory environment (see OECD, 2009a). It remains to be seen whether the new leadership's explicit declaration to avert the course will be implemented.

In sum, it can be argued that from an economic systemic perspective, China has been very much an interventionist state. This interventionism is clearly seen in the earlier analysis of Chinese economic nationalism. The country has transformed from a state-command economy into a market economy, but has maintained strong interventionism throughout the period of transformation. It is believed that the Chinese state is very much involved in what White and Wade (1988) seem to discourage, namely, direct production and direct regulation, and falls beyond guided interventionism.

The DS interventionism is characterised by the presence of a powerful economic bureaucracy. This prompts the question as to who 'intervenes' on behalf of the government as far as maintaining, securing and also designing and redesigning the development trajectory is concerned. Upon close examination of state-level administrative relations, institutional prerogatives and policy competences, it can be concluded that the paramount government institution supervising the developmental directions and modernisation efforts in China is the descendant of the State Planning Commission – the National Development and Reform Commission (NDRC). The NDRC finally took its present shape after the State Planning Commission had been renamed the State Development Planning Commission (SDPC) (in 1998) and had merged with the State Council Office for Restructuring the Economic System (SCORES) and with a part of the State Economic and Trade Commission (SETC) in 2003. According to official documents, the NDRC 'is a macroeconomic management agency under the State Council, which studies and formulates policies for economic and social development, maintains a balance of economic aggregates and guides the overall economic system restructuring' (NDRC, 2007).

As the agency responsible for the development of the country and therefore an organisation that contributes greatly towards the formulation of the Five-Year (Development) Plans (which serve as main guidelines for the short-term developmental and reform agenda), the NDRC must be firmly positioned within the governmental structure to be capable of enforcing its recommendations and of effectively supervising the activities of other agents. The chairman of the NDRC, selected from the members of the Central Committee of the CCP, is an extremely influential person (with the rank of the deputy premier), whereas some of his deputies are ranked at ministerial level. The NDRC was labelled a 'super-ministry' in the 2008 administrative reform,[49] reflecting its influential position among other ministries.

Another important institution concerned to a great extent with the country's development is the Ministry of Commerce (MOFCOM), whose main mandate is to formulate development strategies, guidelines and policies for domestic and foreign trade and international economic cooperation (MOFCOM, 2007). This is because China's development is fuelled by international trade, similar to the historical developmental states.[50] MOFCOM, although often considered a 'normal' ministry, enjoys a very influential position in the governmental structure, as opposed to some so-called 'super ministries' created as a result of the 2008 administrative reforms.

It is worth investigating the competences and functions of the NDRC and the institutions largely believed to have constituted the core of the economic bureaucracy in the DS of Japan and Korea. The differences among them seem to reflect the overall state role during

---

[49] As a result of the 2008 administrative reforms, five so-called super-ministries were established, namely: the Ministry of Industry and Information; the Ministry of Human Resources and Social Security; the Ministry of Environmental Protection; the Ministry of Housing and Urban–Rural Construction; and the Ministry of Transport. A ministerial-level energy commission was also created.

[50] The issue is elaborated in the following chapter.

the Japanese and the Korean DS core periods, as well as contemporary China. The Japanese MITI acquired more of a guiding role, especially for the leaders in targeted industries and export activities. The Korean EPB and the Chinese NDRC seemed more in direct control of certain developmental aspects, as far as strategy formulation and policy implementation are concerned. Although MITI would play some role in other sectors of the Japanese national economy, such as investment in plants and equipment, pollution control and the energy sector, it would focus mostly on the strategy of industrial development. Although it would coordinate general policies concerning international trade, its role in export facilitation would be limited to export competitiveness issues, whereas the overall export strategy would be developed with extensive participation of the Ministry of Finance and the Ministry of Foreign Affairs. As far as general developmental planning is concerned, it was not a main concern of MITI, as the Japanese Economic Planning Agency would be the paramount agency in this respect. Johnson (1982) accurately described the role of MITI as compared to other state institutions in his examination of so-called deliberate councils – advisory bodies drawn from independent experts, who would advise the Japanese authorities on accepting or dropping certain policy proposals. Among 246 deliberate councils (as of 1975), only 36 were attached to MITI. The most important MITI-affiliated council was the Industrial Structure Council, whereas the Economic Council was attached to the Economic Planning Agency (see Johnson, 1982). Nevertheless, if we accept that the main component of classical DS development was industrialisation, then MITI would play a major role in this particular process. This is, however, the main difference between the Korean EPB, the Chinese NDRC and the Japanese MITI. The Korean and the Chinese paramount economic bureaucracy agencies would play an important role in overall developmental strategy formulation, not only within industrial policy. The EPB would be, however, more economically intrusive than the NDRC: 'From its initiation, EPB came to have a powerful say over ministries through the budget' (Cheng et al, 1998, p 102), as it effectively controlled the amount of financial resources obtained by ministries. Amsden (1989, p 82) points out that the Korean agency would even determine microeconomic projects to a great extent. In the Chinese administrative system, this role is rather reserved for specific ministries and, most commonly, local-, provincial- or county-level authorities. The EPB seemed also to possess a stronger political position than the NDRC currently enjoys, as it would be accountable directly to the Office of the President and the president himself. The leader of the EPB would be guaranteed a position equal to that of a vice premier, and the Board would be in charge of the budget allocation to other ministries, as mentioned earlier. The NDRC is accountable to the leadership of the State Council and has no budgetary allocation powers. Its strength derives from the fact that NDRC recommendations become governmental policies to be implemented by the ministries. It seems not embedded, however, in the CCP structure, although it seems hardly possible that the NDRC leader would not be a member of the CCP Central Committee. Moreover, the EPB directly infiltrated other ministers, unlike the NDRC, by having its agents officially placed in the ministries' departments who would monitor sectoral progress. Nevertheless, the NDRC does possess the power to monitor the implementation of recommended policies. The EPB and NDRC are similar as far as their analytical role is concerned. The important 'intellectual arm' of the EPB was the Korea Development Institute (KDI), whereas one of the main tasks awarded to the NDRC is to analyse and examine macroeconomic processes and socio-economic development in all sectors of the national economy.

The 2013 policy shift, partly related to the 3rd plenum of the 18th CCP Congress, suggests that China's leadership intends to move closer to the Korean DS model in the way that it supervises the reform and development process, giving the head of the state additional instruments to influence economic transformation. Among the postulates was the establishment of a small leading group to coordinate reforms, which would report to the president. It was decided that the large bureaucracy of the NDRC would be best suited to prepare policy guidelines and enforce their implementation, but the final coordination would need to rest within a small group close to China's leader. The new construction would allow the head of the state a closer insight into the reform process and greater ability to act. A type of this model was part of the Korean DS model, where the EPB would closely cooperate with and report to the president.

In conclusion, it is important to make the final comparison of certain ideological, political and economic arrangements of China's development trajectory with those in the historically proven DS cases of Japan and Korea. All three countries are characterised by a type of nationalism that results in societal mobilisation behind developmental targets. Economic nationalism is a prevalent feature of the state ideology, which affects the policies and regulations. The political systems differ, as the Japanese DS enjoyed a democratic environment, with the institutional functions structured to facilitate long-term developmental strategies, whereas in Korea, authoritarianism featured throughout the DS 'core activity' period, with state institutions subordinate to the overall development plan. China's political environment remains authoritarian. All three states can be considered strong states; however, contemporary China exhibits some potential for fragility. From the DS perspective, the degree of China's institutional decentralisation can be perceived as a weakness, as it inhibits the state's ability to implement policies.

In all three cases, including democratic Japan, the legitimacy of the ruling elite to power is drawn from developmental achievements, along with nationalist promises. Undoubtedly, a fast pace of long-term development to enable effective catching up has been the paramount target of economic restructuring and industrialisation in all cases. This developmental objective was achieved in Korea and Japan and is being achieved in China in a market economic environment. The market system of the DS model is characterised by a certain type of interventionism, which translates into a guided market economy. China's economy is characterised by the presence of extensive interventionism to regulate the market.

The economic bureaucracy necessary for a DS-type interventionist state was extensive and well organised in the Korean and Japanese DS cases. It is also an important part of the Chinese administrative structure. In all three cases, the economic bureaucracy was dominated by one paramount agency. Nevertheless, in Japan, this agency had the least broad area of competence.

State autonomy is present in all three cases. Evans's embedded autonomy is most clearly visible in the Japanese case. The frames for the state–business alliance are yet to be fully formulated in China. Currently, they are seen as extremely corruption-prone. Although, in the case of Korea, civic freedoms were greatly repressed during the DS period, China has the most coercive regime in the group, with the worst record of respecting human rights. At the same time, the repression of the labour force is a distinctive DS feature of contemporary China.

CHAPTER FOUR

The policies of development

Strategically designed state-level long-term development policies aimed at state transformation so that it can become a developed country within a relatively short period of time are a crucial part of DS characteristics. This chapter focuses on the main group of DS-related policies and establishes to what extent they are also part of China's developmental efforts during the transformation period. Policy selection has been decided upon the policies' conformity with and importance for the DS model, as featured in the scholarly literature.

The perceptions on industrial policies

Developmental states' economic modernisation efforts have often been referred to as a process of state-led industrialisation. Indeed, the process of industrialisation and, thus, industrial policy seem to be central elements of the DS, as industrialisation, also seen as a part of the process of the departure from an economic system dominated by rural activities, that is, urbanisation, is the core of historical DS transformation. The literature on industrial policies is rather extensive and detailed.

Ha-Joon Chang (1999a) points out that there is no unambiguous definition of industrial policy (IP) and that the term is often used in reference to too narrow a spectrum of economic activity, namely, state subsidies policy, or too broad a spectrum, namely, any economic activity related to industry. Indeed, Cimoli, Dosi and Stiglitz (2009, pp 1–2) claim that industrial policy:

> comprises policies affecting "infant industry" support of various kinds, but also trade policies, science and technology policies, public procurement, policies affecting foreign direct investments, intellectual property rights, and the allocation of financial resources. Industrial policies, in this broad sense, come together with processes of "institutional engineering" shaping the very nature of the economic actors, the market mechanisms and rules under which they operate, and the boundaries between what is governed by market interactions, and what is not.

Rodrik (2007, p 3) sees industrial policies as 'policies that stimulate specific economic activities and promote structural change, thus, are not [exclusively] about industry *per se*'. However, for Lindbeck (1981), those policies do not involve monetary and fiscal measures. For Haggard (2004, p 64), industrial policies comprise 'selective interventions designed to influence the allocation of resources among different activities'. This selectiveness seems to be at the core of the discussion on definitions of industrial policies:

> When we talk about 'industrial policy', the majority of us do not mean any policy that affects industry [but] 'selective industrial policy' or 'targeting' – namely, a policy that deliberately favours particular industries over others, against market signals, usually to enhance efficiency and promote productivity growth. (Chang, 2009, p 2)

'Against market signals' is the cause of the debate between proponents and opponents of the applicability of industrial policy as a developmental tool, in other words, whether industrial policy actually matters (Haggard 1990):

> The traditional rationale for selective industrial policy (i.e. policies intended to promote specific industries as against general policies to promote industrialisation) has been made in terms of 'market failures' that arise when competitive markets either do not exist or are incomplete, in situations, for example, when there are information asymmetries, scale economies, or externalities. (ul Haque, 2007, p 3)

Its opponents question the correlation between the policies and the dynamics of economic growth (see Krugman, 1983; Quinn and Jacobson, 1989; World Bank, 1993; Page, 1994; Pack and Saggi, 2006; Woo, 2011). Their objections concern the effectiveness of governments addressing market imperfections and constructing adequate counter-policies, and governments' ability to eliminate rent seeking and corruption associated with industrial policy (see Rodrik, 2007). Its proponents claim that 'industrial policies [are] intrinsic fundamental ingredients of all development processes' (Cimoli et al, 2009, p 2; see also Zysman and Tyson, 1983; Zysman and Schwartz, 1998; Amsden, 1989; Wade, 1990; Chang, 2002; Rodrik, 2008), despite their shortcomings. Graham (1992) claims that industrial policy opponents misread the history and that industrial policy has always been present in some form, even in the US during Reagan's deregulation period.

There is a plethora of literature on industrial policy, its features, history and applicability. Initially, the justification for industrial policy would come from the perception that market forces are incapable of the structural change of the economy necessary in the process of socio-economic development:

> Development is fundamentally about the structural change: it involves producing new goods with new technologies and transferring resources from traditional activities to new ones.... Poor countries remain poor because markets do not work as well as they could to foster the structural transformation that is needed. (Rodrik, 2007, pp 6–7)

Therefore, 'there was broad consensus around the basic assumption that development required [a] non-marginal change that market forces alone could not generate' (Shapiro, 2007, p 2). Chang (2009) points out that, since the 18th century, the history of rapid development of currently affluent states is dotted with interventionist practices framed within industrial policy. Indeed, Alexander Hamilton – the first US Treasury Secretary – and Friedrich List are considered to be main historical proponents of industrial policy (see Hamilton, 2008). Thanks to Gerschenkron (1962) and others, it became a conceptual tool in fighting underdevelopment. However, a 'neoclassical backlash' resulted in industrial policy being questioned as to its developmental role, as its application was allegedly linked to poor economic performance (Shapiro, 2007). Although neo-liberal economic doctrine is in retreat, 'the context for the design of industrial policy has profoundly changed as a result of new rules governing international trade, the rise of global value chains and marketing networks, and other aspects of globalisation' (ul Haque, 2007, p 1).

Most of the recent scholarly literature on industrial policy is associated with the rapid development of East Asian states. Regional socio-economic advancements have been closely linked among the main historical DS cases of Japan, Korea and Taiwan, not merely in the context of the wild-geese-flying pattern (Akamatsu, 1962), but also due to long-term political and economic interaction, particularly intense during Japanese colonialism (Cumings, 1984; Wade, 1990; Kohli, 1994; Doner et al, 2005). As far as industrialisation is concerned, East Asian states are often compared with Latin American countries; the latter believed to be the first developing nations to industrialise. The main difference between the two regions is usually framed within the debate on outward (ie export-driven) and inward (ie domestic consumption-driven) industrialisation in East Asia and Latin America, respectively. However, according to Chang, the East Asian type of industrial policy involves:

> a lot more than handing out subsidies and providing trade protectionism (e.g., tariffs, import bans, quotas, domestic regulations at least partially intended to curb imports). [According to him], industrial policy measures in East Asia included: (i) coordination of complementary investments (the so-called Big Push); (ii) coordination of competing investments through entry regulation, "investment cartels", and (in declining industries) negotiated capacity cuts; (iii) policies to ensure scale economies (e.g., licensing conditional upon production scale, emphasis on the infant industries starting to export from early on, state-mediated mergers and acquisitions); (iv) regulation on technology imports (e.g., screening for overly obsolete technologies, cap on technology licensing royalties); (v) regulation on foreign direct investment (e.g., entry and ownership restrictions, local contents requirement, technology transfer requirements, export requirements); (vi) mandatory worker training for firms above a certain size, in order to resolve the collective action problem in the supply of skilled workers due to the possibility of "poaching"; (vii) the state acting as a venture capitalist and incubating high-tech firms; (viii) export promotion (e.g., export subsidies, export loan guarantees, marketing help from the state trading agency); (ix) government allocation of foreign exchanges, with top priority going to capital goods imports (especially for export industries) and the bottom priority to luxury consumption good imports. (Chang, 2009, p 3–4)

In this large group, Chang (1999b) pays special attention to the coordination of complementary and competing investments, the advantages of the economy of scale, and the imperative of structural change, which is encouraged via the policies mentioned above.

In his 'classic' work on Japanese industrialisation, Johnson (1982) distinguished two basic components of industrial policy in Japan, corresponding to micro- and macro-aspects of the economy: the first was industrial rationalisation policy; and the second was industrial structure policy:

> Industrial rationalisation means: (1) the rationalisation of enterprises, that is, the adoption of new techniques of production, investment in new equipment and facilities, quality control, cost reduction, adoption of new management techniques, and the perfection of managerial control; (2) the rationalisation of the environment of enterprises, including land and water transportation and industrial location; (3) the rationalisation of whole industries, meaning the creation of a framework for all enterprises in an industry in which each can compete fairly or in which they can cooperate in a cartel-like arrangement of mutual assistance; and (4) the rationalisation of the industrial structure itself in order to meet international competitive standards. (Johnson, 1982, p 27)

Industrial structure policy:

> concerns the proportions of agriculture, mining, manufacturing, and services in the nation's total production; and within manufacturing it concerns the percentages of light and heavy and of labour-intensive and knowledge-intensive industries. The application of the policy comes in the government's attempts to change these proportions in ways it deems advantageous to the nation.... The heart of the policy is the selection of the strategic industries to be developed or converted to other lines of work. (Johnson, 1982, p 28)

Kagami (1995) underlines that throughout the period of Japan's rapid growth, there were many IP definitions that appeared in the scholarly literature, ranging from all MITI activities, via most policies intervening in national industry, to selective actions within certain industries. He focuses his IP analysis on market limitations as the main reason to implement industrial policies and, following Goto and Idre, divides them into traditional and recently added market failures, and market imperfections. He pays special attention to the economy of scale concept (internal and external), as Chang does, and to Marshallian externalities and start-up costs. The 'internal' economies of scale concern the decreasing cost of production per unit with the increasing volume of production and with the accumulated knowledge of workers (so-called dynamic economies of scale); 'The "external" economies of scale mean that the average production cost in related industries declines in proportion to a production expansion in the main industry' (Kagami, 1995, p 121), for example, in the case of 'network effects' or 'Marshallian externalities', when improvements in the main industry trigger improvements in related industries thanks to knowledge dissemination. Kim (1985, p 16), in his analysis of Korea, considers industrial policy to be 'all government policy measures that are aimed at promoting the development of [national] industry'. However, he distinguishes between those industrial promotional measures that exert an economy-wide impact and those whose impacts are industry-specific. In his analysis of Taiwan, Wade (2003, p 30) sees industrial policies as functional and sectoral. Baek (2005, p 492) divides Chinese industrial policy into industrial organisation policy and industrial readjustment policy. According to him, the latter is the legacy of the socialist past and the existence of socialist heavy industry, as examined later in this chapter. For Bramall (2009a, p 397), industrial policy, as selective assistance to some enterprises (as also understood by Brandt et al, 2008), has, in various ways, featured in modern China during the central planning and market economy periods.

It is peculiar how the content of industrial policy changes in different analyses of East Asia. For example, Cimoli et al (2009) exclude financial system-related policies from industrial policies, calling them *compatible macro-policies*. For Wade (2003, p 30), 'macroeconomic policies affect aggregate demand, but they also affect different industries differently, although [are] not intended to produce such differential effects, [whereas] industrial policies ... are intended to affect production and investment decisions of decentralised producers'. Moreover, Page (1994), in his attempt to discredit industrial policy, attributes East Asian developmental achievements to trade policy, setting those two apart. For clarity, one may appreciate the distinction between trade policy and industrial policy, as interrelated but, nevertheless, different sets of state activities. Due to the complexity of East Asian industrial and trade policies, it is perhaps also advisable to separate the financial sector-related activities. Much scholarly attention has been directed at the financial sector, which has played an extraordinary role in DS industrialisation (see, among others, Woo, 1991; Lee, 1992).

It is also important to note the post-socialist context of industrial policy. The socialist heritage and the pre-Second World War tradition meant that a large part of CEE states was rather extensively industrialised prior to the PST process (Baka, 2004). Zysman and Schwartz (1998) claim that during post-socialist transformation, CEEFSU industrial policy had, to a large extent, a 'back door' character. Due to a broad acceptance of Washington Consensus provisions, states did not initially design any explicit industrial policies, and the authorities often questioned their applicability. Moreover, the term had an implicitly pejorative meaning, often associated with a state-command economic system and the communist past. As a result, in the case of Poland, the 1989–91 'shock therapy' threatened to trigger deindustrialisation rather than industrial transformation, as industrial production fell by 30% (Klein, 2007, p 191). Nevertheless, during the realisation of the economic policy called Strategy for Poland (1993–97), the state authorities 'reconciled' with the idea of industrial policy (see Kolodko, 1999a). It focused on the consolidation and restructuring of domestic companies (Comisso, 1998). In Russia, industrial policy has been neglected during most of the PST period (Kolodko, 2004a). Contemporarily, some scholars call for it to be reinstated (see Louvert, 2005), and some claim that it is indeed already happening in some industries, such as the high-tech industry (Fushita, 2009). The question, however, is how post-socialist transformation affected industrial policy in China. The issue will be examined later.

Coming back to DS-style industrial policies, the general approach to industrialisation in developmental states is concerned, first, with import substitution industrialisation (ISI) and then with export-orientated industrialisation (EOI), as discussed in Chapter One. These processes are accompanied by the gradual technological and, thus, value-added upgrading of the content of industrial production. Historical experiences prove that the scope and intensity of DS industrialisation allows for a significant expansion of production and the subsequent reorientation of the economy towards export, as the initial domestic capacities of absorbing the production volume come to exhaustion. This exhaustion is, nevertheless, an expected effect of industrialisation, as, first, a relatively poor society of an early developmental state consumes less than the societies in developed nations and, second, it is international trade that is expected to bring about rapid development. Export-led growth is seen as an important engine behind DS developmental achievements. Consequently, trade policy is a vital element of the DS architecture, in addition to a general industrialisation policy. Moreover, DS economic reorganisation, as much as PST systemic reformulation, takes place in a relatively short period of time. Thus, the state needs to possess additional tools for the creation of certain incentives to stimulate the development of industries, production and export. In the systemic conditions of a market economy, characteristic of the developmental state, these incentives can be partly materialised through specific financial policies. The financial system is perceived as the bloodstream of the market economy, enabling economic activities to take place. Consequently, the usage of financial system-related instruments is also of great significance. It is important to note, however, that the interconnectedness of a state financial policy, state-led industrialisation and state-encouraged trade results in rather bleak barriers as to which policy instruments should be attributed to the particular set of policies. Moreover, state industrialisation policy, trade policy and state financial policy are together and separately a broad spectrum for examination. A thorough analysis of each would need to constitute a separate book. Theoretical considerations in Chapter One, however, deliver some important conclusions as to which elements of these state policies should be perceived as being at the core of the DS model. The DS-type state interventionism is a 'guiding' type of interventionism. This means that the state manages the development trajectory via a certain pool of incentives. Those incentives encourage business, partly via Wade's 'big followership', to engage in certain activities in certain economic sectors. Consequently, industrialisation, international trade-related policies and financial policies should be examined from the point of view of encouraging commerce and industrial development.

There is empirical evidence, as illustrated later in this chapter, that, in general, DS trade policy includes the erecting of certain barriers for imports and the establishing of incentives for export. In fact, export seems in the classical DS case a more important component of DS-related economic activities, as the import policy selectively deters foreign products from the market at the same time attracting desirable commodities, and enables domestic production to thrive without foreign competition, whereas export policy fuels the entire process of national development by delivering financial assets to the economy. In the DS model, it is a strict selectivity of imports and extensive support for the export of certain products that matter. Therefore, the essence of DS trade policy is the policy of (selective) import discrimination and (selective) export support, which, to a great extent, determines the volume and the genus of export and, thus, to a considerable degree, domestic production. Consequently, in the process of the economic expansion of historical DS cases, domestic production was absolutely crucial. The assortment of production is a derivative of the industrial structure of a country, which is a result of the policy of industrialisation. Therefore, the export offer of a developmental state is the effect of the policy of industrial development, that is, the policy of selecting and developing certain industries. The policies of import discrimination, export support and industrial development are supported by certain activities within the financial sector of the economy. The state utilises financial system-related policies to encourage industrial production and international trade.

The comparative analysis of DS-relevant policies is affected by the time distortion factor. In the case of Japan, the DS-proper period is believed to have taken place from the 1950s until the early 1980s. In the case of Korea, the DS is counted roughly from the mid-1960s until the early 1990s. In the case of China's development trajectory during the period of systemic transformation, as a contemporary phenomenon, its commencement should probably be traced to the late 1970s. Different time frames mean that the respective processes have taken place in different global institutional environments (ie different international conditionalities) and at different stages of human social and technological development. This significant fact influences the reforms implemented and the policies followed by a state.

In Japanese industrialisation policy, the first half of the 20th century was crucial in establishing Japan as a production base, as well as the state working out the initial mechanisms of support for preferential industrial sectors. The institutional formation commenced as early as in the 1870s during the 'Meiji restoration'. In Korea, the industrialisation policy can be traced back to the early 1930s, and state institutional reorganisation to the beginning of the 20th century and Japanese colonial rule. In China, the transformation period was preceded by the state–command economy (fully institutionally formalised in 1956 and lasting until 1978) and the communist political regime (since 1949). Naturally, the differences in political and institutional background between China and the other two states have also had an impact on the reforms and policies implemented.

The issues concerned with the policy of industrial development, the policy of import discrimination and export support, and the state financial policy of support for industrial development and international trade, in the cases of Japan and Korea, are well researched. There are an increasing number of analyses that attempt to examine Chinese financial, industrial and trade policies in comparison with those of Japan, Korea and other Asian or developing countries due to the increasing role of China on the international economic scene and significant developmental achievements during the last three and a half decades. Most of those analyses do not seem to address the similarities and differences from the perspective of the existence of certain features of the DS model. This is probably because the notion of the developmental state lost its attractiveness, due to the factors mentioned earlier in this book. As stated in Chapter One, however, the DS model may still remain an interesting developmental option. Therefore, the following sections of this chapter will examine the three most evident DS sets of policies previously mentioned in the case of China, with references to the historical developmental states of Japan and Korea.

Broadly speaking, the DS model is believed to be an institutional and policy option/alternative for some relatively poor countries in their quest of accelerating socio-economic development and eventually catching up with developed states. Consequently, the initial conditions of a DS must be similar to those in many developing countries, that is, the agricultural sector constitutes a major component of the overall national economy. The significant share of rural, agrarian-focused production in the economy is often seen as the predicament in overcoming underdevelopment. Consequently, the necessary background for the establishment of the DS is to commence the reorganisation of the agrarian sector and agrarian relations. Indeed, the DS-related, as well as China-related, literature is concerned with the rural development and agrarian reforms necessary for subsequent effective industrialisation. Therefore, those processes will also be presented here in a comparative perspective.

Agrarian reforms and rural industrialisation

Rural area reforms are usually not considered an element of the developmental state's architecture. However, considering the starting point of the DS transformation, that is, the relative backwardness of the DS economies and thus a domination of the agrarian sector within the national economy, it is plausible to claim that rural changes are more than implicitly involved in the making of a DS. This is due to the fact that the industrialisation of underdeveloped countries is linked to 'de-ruralisation' or urbanisation, and includes a shift from the dominance of primary industry to secondary and tertiary, which is accompanied by a transfer of the labour force from agrarian and agrarian-related jobs to industrial jobs. It is symptomatic that land reforms have featured in early or pre-developmental state periods, predominantly, to create political conditions for industrialisation and to increase the effectiveness of food supply. Interestingly, with all their differences, the land reforms of the late 1940s were, to some extent, similar in Japan, Korea, Taiwan and China, and involved the distribution of land from the wealthiest, but nevertheless often unproductive, elements of rural society. Their political aim was to weaken the landlord class – usually a rich and influential, conservative caste – which is a factor to consider when implementing extensive modernisation efforts in the form of state-led industrialisation, and to gain the support of the less affluent parts of society and, at the same time, in the non-communist countries, to avoid a possible peasant rebellion leading to a change of the political system. In the case of the PRC, landlords were natural enemies of the new regime. In Japan, the reforms were initially carried out by the US administration; in Taiwan, by the newly arrived and not locally affiliated Nationalist government. There was much more to rural transformation than just land reform. The economic, and thus developmental, aim was to increase productivity and accelerate rural development (see Alesina and Rodrik, 1994; Cumings, 1984; Donner et al, 2005; Jeon, 1995; Wade, 1990); in the case of Taiwan and Korea, partly in preparation for possible military conflict with communist China and communist North Korea, respectively. For example, rural development policies in South Korea 'involved the creation of a corporatist network of public–private and parastatal organisations that gave subsidised loans to improve farmers' housing, provided technical training, expanded irrigation and access to fertiliser, and disseminated seeds for higher yield varieties of rice' (Wade, 1982, cited in Donner et al, 2005, p 342). Improving rural infrastructure was also an element of rural development in China during the state-command period and rural industrialisation, 'primarily as a way of modernising agriculture (by supplying farm machinery, chemical fertiliser and the steel and concrete needed for irrigation systems)' (Bramall, 2009a, p 119). Bramall (2009a, p 94) argues that the land reforms in the CCP-controlled territories prior to 1947 were radical and aimed at an egalitarian distribution of land, whereas those implemented between 1947 and 1953 focused on an interim phase of the rich peasant economy (characteristic of Japan and Korea) to increase production. However, eventually, by the mid-1950s, the rural economy was fully collectivised, creating a very different structure from that in Japan and Korea. Therefore, in terms of rural economy, the initial conditions of the historical DS cases and in post-Mao China were dramatically different. However, a common denominator was that despite all these changes, agriculture was in all cases considered to have a merely supporting role for industrialisation and remained a rather neglected sector of the national economies. In China, this applies to both the state-command and the market economy periods.

The developmental states of Japan and Korea began their period of rapid industrialisation with agriculture being in the hands of private small-scale owners (Kim and Lee, 2003; OECD, 2009c). China's fast post-socialist development started with the reforms of non-private large-scale unit agriculture. Typically for most socialist states, China's rural economy was characterised by collective ownership. Naturally, there were exceptions to collectivism within the Eastern bloc. For example, in Yugoslavia and Poland, the bulk of agricultural production was from small-scale private farms (see Johanssen, 2001). Therefore, the post-socialist land reform in Poland was limited to the privatisation of large state-owned agriculture production units (PGR) of marginal meaning to the rural economy. However, other countries embarked on the de-collectivisation path as much as China. Johanssen (2001, p 12) points out that 'most of the countries have chosen to reform the communist agricultural system and most have chosen to adopt the principle of private ownership', despite poorly defined property rights or a lack of legal sanctioning of private land. 'Furthermore, in general the restitution policy has been the dominant method in Central Europe, whereas distribution to farm workers [has] dominated among the CIS [Commonwealth of Independent States] countries' (Johanssen, 2001, p 12). In this respect, China, with its land distribution to farmers without legal ownership entitlements, hardly seems an exception, and exhibits one of the post-socialist patterns.

The ineffectiveness of collective farming, especially visible in the Soviet Union, prompted Chinese authorities to resort to the systemic solution, imitating the rural conditions in Japan and Korea, so as to embark on a similar type of rapid industrialisation – hence the distribution of land to smallholders. Naturally, the ideological constraints prevented the communist government from transferring land ownership rights; nevertheless, the household responsibility system brought extensive positive results in terms of food production. Moreover, the DS rural environment was by no means optimal and hardly the most effective solution. Japan and Korea heavily relied on grain supply from the US in the 1960s and 1970s (Cumings, 1984) as the growth of agricultural output was rather slow (Bramall, 2004). Nevertheless, it was created as a political condition for DS industrialisation and was partly determined by geographical conditions, rather than was chosen as the best option for rural development. Despite this, it proved more effective in supplying food than the collective socialist system.

In China – a large country with a number of historical incidences of malnutrition – the change in agricultural production mode was paramount. Agrarian reforms also had political motives – by creating better conditions for development in rural areas, the CCP gained social support for its modernisation efforts. By creating small farming units rather than large *latifundia*, the authorities made sure that the rural power centres were fragmented and weak. The process of rural industrialisation accelerated during the reform period, despite it also being a visible element of late Maoism. As restrictions were lifted on non-agricultural activities, many peasants turned away from farming, commencing a period of dynamic transfer of the labour force from agriculture to industry and services – a phenomenon observed in developmental states. As a result, in the mid-1980s, over 100 million rural peasants were working in non-farm activities (Wong, 1988, p 3). Sanctioning the existence of non-state enterprises in rural areas effected a mushrooming of rural enterprises, among them TVEs, who rapidly increased their share in the national market and continued to engage a large part of the national workforce. The transfer of the labour force is also visible through the increase in the number of migrant workers from rural to urban areas (OECD, 2009b). A dynamic transfer of the labour force from agricultural to non-agricultural industrial jobs also featured in the periods of high growth in Japan and Korea (see OECD, 2009c).

Land reform and rural industrialisation during the post-socialist transformation brought positive developmental results in the non-urbanised territories of the PRC. Naturally, one may question the extent of those changes. The dissolving of cooperative health-care services and the deterioration of accessibility to the educational base may suggest a socio-economic regress in some aspects. Nevertheless, there seems to be agreement that in the PST period as much as during the state-command period, rural areas, as compared to urban territories, have been neglected by the authorities. As a result, the urban–rural income gap continues to grow. A lack of adequate attention seems in some ways odd in a country that hosts over 20% of mankind and only 7% of the Earth's arable and husbandry land, which is rapidly decreasing due to environmental pollution and climate change. The explanation seems to lie within the model of China's development. As much as in historical DS cases, agriculture plays an auxiliary role in the process of economic modernisation and the sector is aimed at supporting industrialisation. Therefore, in economic terms, the preoccupation is with securing a steady supply of food and labour. This is evident in most countries undergoing rapid industrialisation, also outside of the East Asia realm. Nevertheless, East Asia is a very explicit example of the disadvantageous position of the rural economy.

The developmental state policy of industrial development

In our analysis, a DS policy of industrial development can probably be summarised as a policy that determines which industries are targeted for development and why, and what assortment will be produced as a result and by what sort of economic agents. This policy defines the change in the national industrial structure enabled by 'sequencing and targeting' and can thus be seen as Johnson's macroeconomic industrial structural policy. It also relates to his microeconomic industrial rationalisation policy, as it involves, among other things, rationalisation activities within industries and the institutional environment to effect a gradual technological upgrade of selected industries and as it impacts directly on the companies' capabilities. It decides in which sectors the 'big push' takes place. In short, the DS policy of industrial development is about the philosophy of upgrading by learning and then by innovating, and is sustained via the mechanism of targeting industries for industrial change by using certain types of economic agents, as discussed below.

Industrialising by learning and by innovating

The developmental states' initial phase of industrialisation 'has come about as a process of learning rather than of generation of inventions and innovations' (Amsden, 1989, p 4), as the late developers were in the position to 'borrow' existing technologies (see Gerschenkron, 1962). Therefore, the DS industrial targeting, examined later in this chapter, would need to be primarily focused on those industries that would contribute to the broad strategy of the overall catching up, rather than exclusively singling out sectors associated with advanced technologies. In the DS conditionality, these industries would usually possess the potential for their products to become widely desirable on the international market, as DS growth would be export-led. For a developmental state to be able to maintain a certain competitive advantage and sometimes also domination on the international scene in the production of certain goods in the long term would require not only the utilisation of geo-economic superiority, as reflected in the tradition of the manufacturing of particular goods and a favourable locality for the transportation and retail (selling) of its industrial products, but also constant upgrading, which would allow the production to be receptive to the international market. In other words, the changes in global international trade relations and consumption patterns would have to be met by adequate reactions on the supply side for industrial production to be sufficiently profitable. Eventually, this demand would be generated by supply, as a developmental state would move from copying existing technologies and, subsequently, products to inventing technologies and, subsequently, products.

In practice, preferential treatment of what would be adequately technologically advanced production became an important feature of the developmental state, and indigenous innovation has been a vital element of the East Asian developmental model (Evans, 1998). Adequate levels of innovation would be achieved via investment in R&D and/or import of technologies. The quality of R&D could be achieved through the attraction of foreign specialists and experts, as well as foreign technologies, in the short term, whereas long-term effects would be achieved via the creation of a local intellectual base composed of scientists and engineers. This would necessitate a constant nurturing of human capital via the expansion of the training base/facilities.

Although Japan is considered to belong to the 'late developers' group, hence the initial process of innovation would suggest an importation and duplication of technologies, Japan's rather early developmental start in the late developers group, as well as a general lack of a generic Asian policy of major FDI attraction, suggest that throughout the DS core period, Japan, to some important extent, relied on its own R&D. Indeed, already at the beginning of the 20th century, Japan's expansion in cotton textile production was attributed to the utilisation of new technologies and adequate managerial coordination based on indigenous experiences and patterns. Mass and Miyajima (1993) point to the establishment of experimental industrial laboratories aimed initially at developing new technologies in the textile industries, as far as the dyeing of material is concerned, as an example of R&D orientation. This policy, as well as the earlier efforts of the Meiji administration focused on the development of the educational base (see Brinkley, 1904), resulted in a very high position of Japan in the ranking of the Human Capital Index, even among developed nations. The subsequent 'targeting' of industries for development during the DS core period took into consideration the advantages of becoming innovative, hence offering technologically more advanced products. This is not to say that Japan refrained itself from importing necessary technologies during the DS–proper period. On the contrary, US companies were especially targeted for the transfer of technology. Initially, 'Japan imported ... technology for its basic and high-growth industries, and imported the greater proportion of this technology from the United States' (Johnson, 1982, p 16). The government was in charge of technology transfers and no technology would enter the country without MITI's approval (Johnson, 1982). Based on the Foreign Capital and Foreign Exchange Control Law, 'the Japanese government allocated its scarce foreign currency selectively to those firms capable of adapting and improving import technology, in order to encourage the importation of advanced technology and to promote a domestic technology base' (Sakakibara and Cho, 2002, p 678). Subsequently, 'technological development was supported by direct and indirect production and R&D subsidies, the encouragement of multifirm research consortia, [and] the discouragement of foreign direct investment in sectors in which it was technologically feasible for Japan to enter' (Noland, 2007, p 255). The proof of a strong R&D base was delivered during the early 1970s, when Japan commenced reorganisation of its industrial sector towards future promising branches, such as the computer industry and electronics. As a result, by the late 1970s, Japan became the world leader in semiconductor technology, following the MITI's vision of a 'technology-based nation'. Nevertheless, R&D expenditure remained relatively low as compared with advanced economies and increased significantly only by the mid-1980s. Despite the fact that direct support for private R&D had been introduced already in the early 1950s, 'the size of the incentives provided through tax breaks, subsidies, and low-interest loans was modest. [So was the] budgetary contributions to research conducted in universities and national research institutions' (Sakakibara and Cho, 2002, p 678).

Korea found itself in favourable conditions, as far as the process of learning and innovating was concerned, already prior to the establishment of the DS model. The state was seen by its coloniser – Japan – as an important supply base for further Japanese expansion in Asia; hence, the development of the country was viewed by the Japanese as crucial. This is why Korea's rapid and extensive industrialisation commenced under Japanese rule. The first Korean companies[51] derived their innovation by imitating Japanese firms and by heavily relying on transfers of technology from Japan. During the DS core period, Korea continued to rely on foreign technologies for its industries, partly benefiting from US overall assistance. Nevertheless, in the early 1980s, the government commenced the reorganisation of the development trajectory into knowledge- and information-intensive industries, in which local R&D would play a crucial role. Cho et al (1996) call this period the 'creative knowledge-intensive era'. The alleged initial low position in rankings on the Human Capital Index (see Noland, 2007) resulted in Korea's government paying more attention to the education of scientists and engineers. Chun (2002) points out that, for that reason, science-profiled high schools were supervised by the Ministry of Commerce and Industry and not by the Ministry of Education.[52] As early as in the 1960s, the government established the Korea Institute of Science and Technology, which was responsible for

---

[51] The companies set up in Korea were initially the Japanese *zaibatsu*.

[52] For an analysis of the importance of R&D during Korea's industrialisation, see Amsden (1989).

developing industrial technology, and the Korea Development Institute, which was responsible for conducting research on development policy. Foreign specialists were continuously attracted via income and career-development incentives. Korea became a good example of effective human capital accumulation (Kim et al, 1995; Lee, 1997). Sakakibara and Cho (2002), however, claim that the Korean government did not play an important role in direct R&D promotion until the 1981 amendment of the 1971 Technology Development Promotion Law. Instead, R&D was mostly promoted indirectly through general policies of broad objectives. For example, state support for certain companies would create conditions for the targeted firms to develop their own R&D base: 'The new policy [as a result of the amendment] was geared toward both direct and indirect promotion of technology-intensive industries' (Sakakibara and Cho, 2002, p 679).

China's tactics in developing innovative industrial branches seems similar to that present in the initial stages of the DS in Korea, as well as partly in Japan. Despite gradually becoming a source of technology (PP, 2013), it still heavily relies on the import of technologies. Its domestic market, large in terms of potential consumers and proven capacity to grow rapidly, made it easier for the Chinese government and Chinese firms to attract the inward transfer of foreign technology. The authorities 'have been able to demand and entice technology transfers on a large scale from eager investors vying for the opportunity to market and manufacture their goods there' (Linden, 2004, p 4). According to Linden (2004, p 5), the absorptive capacity for technology is a distinctive feature of contemporary China, as compared with other East Asian countries. Technology transfer on a large scale also took place during the state-command period from the Soviet Union, prior to Khrushchev's thaw. However, during the times of economic opening up, the process accelerated significantly, especially in the special zones created for export production.

This is not to say that China has been entirely unsuccessful in nurturing a domestic research base. During the state-command period, it had a relatively well articulated innovation system (Linden, 2004). Although not without significant foreign assistance, it managed, for example, to develop a nuclear weapon programme. It recorded a number of innovations in food production (Bramall, 2009a). During the systemic transformation period, government efforts were initially focused on improving the research base: 'The research institutes were corporatised and encouraged to obtain funds by competing for state-funded grants, performing contract research for enterprises or by licensing their technology for a fee' (Liu and White, 2001, cited in Linden, 2004, p 6). According to Lee et al (2006), the PRC can be perceived as a good example of the relatively effective strategy of 'forward engineering', in which the initiative rests in research centres and other academic institutions with intellectual potential who in order to implement the results of their research, are engaged in the establishment of the manufacturing base: 'Forward engineering is a top-down mode of technological development where the creators of scientific knowledge themselves further process the new or nascent knowledge until it could be applied to commercial uses' (Lee et al, 2006, p 20). Three important computer equipment manufacturers, that is, Lenovo, Founder and Tsinghua Tongfang, were all established by and affiliated with academic institutions (Lee et al, 2006).

The imported technologies serve as the basis for the development of local technologies and consequently local industries. This happens in a number of industrial sectors. Two very vivid examples are in the areas of renewable energy and transportation. In 2007 China overtook Japan and Germany as the biggest producer of solar panels in the world. Its Suntech company became the biggest manufacturer. In 2009, China became the biggest wind turbine manufacturer in the world. Currently, there are a number of Chinese companies whose position on the global solar energy-related market is increasing, Yingli Solar (originating from Hebei province) being, in addition to Suntech, another prime example. As far as wind energy is concerned, the two largest companies, Sinovel and Goldwind, who account for a large share of China's production (CCM, 2010), also became global players. However, although China has become the biggest producer of solar panels and wind turbines, the technology utilised in this production is predominantly from foreign sources. Representatives of the PRC's Ministry of Environmental Protection openly admit that China does not possess advanced technologies in this respect and is forced to import them.[53] However, as Chinese companies such as Suntech and Yingli Solar are becoming world leaders within their sector, they are being forced to increasingly rely on their own R&D to maintain their affluent position on the international market.

The second example is the construction of China's high-speed railway system.[54] For this purpose, CNR – the leading Chinese producer of trains – purchased German technology from Siemens and has since been

[53] Personal communication at the Chinese Ministry of Environmental Protection, Beijing, 11 August 2009.

[54] High-speed railways are considered here those capable of 330 km/h.

modifying it for domestic purposes.[55] As a result of this cooperation, the Beijing–Tianjin high-speed railway line was opened in 2008. In 2009, the 1,054 km railway line, which connects the southern city of Guangzhou with the Central China city of Wuhan, became operative. The third line connecting Beijing with Shanghai was opened in 2011. Since then, the length of high-speed railway system has been gradually increasing with the assistance of other foreign companies, such as Bombardier and Kawasaki Heavy Industries.

China's dynamic inward transfer of technologies is conducted partly without consideration and respect for intellectual property rights (IPR), as has been the cases with the automobile industry, the food processing industry, computer software and others, involving, for example, German carmakers and a French food production chain. In 2007, the Chinese car manufacturer Shuanghuan was accused of copying one of the BMW and Mercedes models. The dispute between a French company, Danone, and a Chinese company, Wahaha, was related to the latter copying the products of the former. Although IPR are well incorporated into the Chinese legal system and a National IPR Strategy[56] of the PRC has been launched, the enforcement of the regulations on the ground is very limited. This seems to be a deliberate policy of the authorities aimed at short-term benefits. In the long term, however, this policy may prove counterproductive by discouraging international cooperation and by exposing Chinese companies to their own IPR infringement.

The insufficient development of domestic technological capacity and the existence of a relatively poor R&D base has implicitly been emphasised in the 2006–2020 Programme for Science and Technology Development prepared by the PRC's Ministry of Science and Technology. The Programme outlines the key industries that enjoy preferential treatment from the state due to their innovative character, namely, biotechnology, information technology, new materials technology, advanced manufacturing technology, new energy technology, marine technology, advanced agricultural technology and, in particular, biomedicine, nanotechnology and ICT technology, commercial aircraft technology, and satellite technologies. It is intended that the expenditure on R&D will reach 2.5% of GDP by 2020. There are currently over 4,000 official research centres registered throughout the country, with an estimated 250,000 full-time scientists (NBS, 2008), 54 economic and technological development zones

---

[55] With the assistance of Siemens' engineers based in the headquarters of the CNR branch for high-speed trains in the city of Tangshan.

[56] Issued by the State Council on 5 June 2008.

(ETDZ) and 53 high-tech industry development zones (HIDZ) (Alder et al, 2013). The Programme states that the authorities intend to establish an additional 50 state research centres, 100 state-owned laboratories and 300 industrial technological centres. The Programme for Science and Technology Development and national-level projects are complemented by regional activities and initiatives by various organisations. Many provincial governments create special entities, as exemplified by HIDZ, in which foreign investors who bring know-how can enjoy extensive assistance from local authorities.

The limited development of the domestic research base and a lack of efficiency in utilising existing research establishments for economic innovativeness is why foreign partners remain the key to the further innovation of China's national economy. The EU is the main source of innovative technologies for China, with German industrial companies such as Siemens (seen as the leader in technology transfer to the PRC) at the forefront.

There are, however, various barriers and obstacles to the effective delivery of new technologies to the Chinese market: first, a persistent lack of respect for IPR, as previously mentioned. The *2007/2008 Position Paper* published by the EU Chamber of Commerce in China lists the lack of enforcement of IPR regulations as one of the most significant barriers for European companies to access and operate on the Chinese market, which would consequently lead to enhancing the level of innovativeness of the Chinese economy (PP, 2007).[57] The second barrier to the effective delivery of new technologies to the Chinese market are the regulations that force foreign firms to disclose sensitive technological information when gaining access to the Chinese market:

> In various circumstances, companies are required to apply for technical and/or regulatory approval of a product (e.g. medical or cosmetic product) or for the authorisation to build a plant. Such enterprises are required to disclose to Chinese governmental agencies highly confidential information, information that goes beyond the scope necessary for the approval concerned. (PP, 2009, p 77)

[57] It is believed that European small- and medium-sized enterprises (SMEs) possess the largest innovative capacity on the EU market. However, SMEs are especially anxious to cooperate with Chinese partners or establish their base in China due to the relatively high possibility of their technology being illegally transferred to other local actors of the market. IPR is usually one of the most important topics in discussions between the EU Commissioner of Trade and representatives of the PRC government.

Moreover, regulations concerning the requirement for a majority share of Chinese companies in joint ventures in various industrial sectors are perceived as also affecting the willingness of foreign firms to cooperate and to deliver their know-how.

Despite numerous IPR violations, foreign companies are keen to be part of the strategy of 'trading market for technology'. China opens its lucrative domestic market for those companies who bring in innovative technologies. With its population of almost 1.4 billion people, the country constitutes a great consumer market and thus represents incomparable opportunities for foreign commercial entities to conduct business activities. Many foreign firms are ready to benefit from access to this market in exchange for their know-how. Establishment of the Shanghai Bell joint venture in 1984 was perhaps the first effective implementation of this strategy (Lee et al, 2006).

In sum, it can be stated that all three countries, China, Japan and Korea, have considered imitation and then innovation as important elements of the policy of industrial development. The sources of innovation varied: Japan relied mostly on its own resources; China relies predominantly on the import of technologies; whereas Korea seems to have been an in-between model, in which technology-copying was gradually replaced by its own R&D. Undoubtedly, China intends to achieve the same position in this respect: 'The indigenous development of intellectual property is a point of national pride' (Linden, 2004, p 2).

All three countries were characterised by inward technology transfer, with Japan being perhaps the least dependent case. During its rapid growth period, China has acquired technology by all means available, with and without consideration for IPR. Due to the attractiveness of its domestic market capacity as the main factor creating international supply, and the chosen DS-style development path of technological upgrading creating the demand, the technology transfer to China has indeed been impressive, to the extent that a number of Chinese companies, initially using imported know-how, managed to become world leaders in certain sections of knowledge-intensive industries in a very short time. Huawei is perhaps the prime example. In the case of Japan, the source of technology was the US; in the case of Korea, it was Japan and the US. In contemporary China, it is the EU and, to some extent, Japan, Korea and the US.

In the context of the PSDS model, it is important, however, to return to the initial conditions for technological advancements of developmental states' and China's economies. Bramall (2009a, p 385) claims that without certain developments during the socialist period, China's inward technology transfer, even less its own R&D

development, would not be possible. He specifically points to education expansion and defence industrialisation in the late Maoist period, which created a 'technological inheritance' crucial for developing the capacities for the subsequent economic modernisation during the systemic transformation. Perhaps China's socialist period can be seen as the Japanese colonial period in Korea and Taiwan and the Meiji restoration in Japan, in terms of performing initial industrialisation. In the 1930s, the Japan-led industrialisation of Taiwan involved the development of food processing, plywood, textiles, pulp and paper, cement, chemical fertiliser, aluminium and copper refining, petroleum refining, and shipbuilding industries (Wade, 2003, p 74). In Korea, it involved textiles, the processing of raw materials, mining, iron, steel, hydroelectric power and shipbuilding (Kohli, 1994, p 1280). Industrial development in socialist China focused on heavy industry, including defence and machinery. Defence industrialisation is often believed to be a driving force for economic growth in developing countries (Benoit, 1978; Ross, 1991), as well as a catalyser of industrial upgrading.

The earlier-mentioned initial high ranking in human capital gave Japan an advantage in commencing a process of economic modernisation in the 1950s. Korea's lack, to some extent, of the same human capital power, despite Japanese industrialisation, forced the government to rapidly intensify the efforts to improve the educational base (Lee, 1997; Chun, 2002). The societies of socialist states were on average better educated than the level of GDP per capita would suggest (see Cereseto and Waitzkin, 1986) – the case of Cuba being a distinctive contemporary example (Gasperini, 2000). There is empirical evidence of improvements in China's educational base in the 1960s and 1970s, especially at primary and secondary level (see Gao, no date; Huang, 2008; Bramall, 2009a). From the 1960s, China began to converge with Korea and Taiwan. As a result, its human capital stock at the beginning of *gǎigé kāifàng* was of a better quality than in Korea and Taiwan in the 1960s (see Godo and Hayami, 1999). Thus, it is legitimate to claim that the relative readiness for transformation, in terms of society's skills and education, is attributable to its socialist past. The 'socialist inheritance' put China in a better position to embark on DS-style industrialisation than would be the case of many non-socialist developing nations. The same could theoretically apply to FSU states, as they dramatically increased the level of their societies' education during the state-command period.

The targeting

In the DS conditionality, certain industrial sectors were deliberately targeted by the state for development, due to their real or potential value for the national economy. During the DS core period, the Japanese government's targeting encompassed various sectors. In the early days of the 'DS-proper' period, the priority was given to the production of coal, iron and steel as a part of the 'priority production programme' (Kuchiki, 2007, p 7). It should be seen as a continuation of the pre-war heavy industry development then focused on military equipment, which would accompany the expansion of textile production from the late 19th century. Later, the focus also included electric power building and shipbuilding, as well as petrochemicals to produce synthetic fibre and chemical fertiliser, among other things. According to Cumings (1984, p 2), this assortment of targeting represented the second phase of Japan's industrialisation, which commenced in the 1930s and was completed by the mid–1960s. The late 1940s' efforts were mainly focused on the reconstruction of pre–war industrial sectors, whereas the theme of the 1950s' industrialisation became industrial catching up (Kagami, 1995). In a way, Japan followed the traditional development path of the early second half of the 20th century, also present among socialist countries, whereby heavy industry was seen as the engine of development in the 1950s as part of the reconstruction efforts after the Second World War. A similar recovery after the Korean War determined the initial targeting policies of the South Korean government during its pre-DS-proper period, which included cement and glass, as well as refined oil products. Nevertheless, attention was directed shortly afterwards towards light industry (Mah, 2010). During the 1950s, communist China embarked on the development path through preferential treatment for heavy industry, including iron and steel production, as did communist North Korea, with rather different final results due to some ill-designed policies.[58]

In the 1960s, the Japanese government continued to promote heavy as well as chemical industries (HCI). Heavy industry remained strategic at least until 1970 (Kobayashi, 1993, p 81). However, more focus was directed towards machinery and the automobile industry. Although the Korean government also started paying more attention to HCI as a potential export-oriented production, production was nevertheless dominated by light industry, including textiles (Kim, 1985, p 6).

[58] In the case of China, the 'great leap forward' was a very illustrative example of an ill-designed policy. Moreover, it is important to note that during the first decade after the Korean War, it was North Korea that was better developed than South Korea.

In the 1970s, Japanese targeting focused on machine production and electronic industries, including the computer industry. Undoubtedly, it was partly caused by the 1973 oil shock, as a result of which a number of energy-intensive industries, such as aluminium, chemicals and steel, found themselves in decline. Despite that, in 1973, Park Chung Hee announced the strategy of heavy-chemical industrialisation in Korea (Jeon, 1995, p 74). HCI became a priority sector (Haggard and Moon, 1986; Amsden, 1989). As much as in Japan during the 1950s, the production of iron, steel, petrochemicals and non-ferrous metals became strategically important. The government also promoted the construction of shipyards (Kim, 1985, pp 8–9).

From the late 1970s, high-tech products became the main target for the Japanese government's preferential treatment and the governmental support for R&D increased. In the late 1970s, the Koreans accelerated the development of HCI, with the emphasis on industrial machinery, steel and electric equipment, whereas in the 1980s, similar to Japan, they redirected their attention to knowledge- and information-intensive industries (see Cho et al, 1996; Mah, 2010). The change from labour-intensive to knowledge-intensive industries in both cases was also dictated by the rapidly increasing cost of labour (Cho et al, 1996; Kimura, 2009). Needless to say, the targeting of industries was consequently reflected in the assortments of export goods.

The policy of targeting in China shows certain similarities with and differences from Japan and Korea. As mentioned earlier, the 1950s were characterised by heavy industry development. This strategy was only marginally adjusted during the late state-command period, when the machinery sector for rural industrialisation became a more visible element of industrial targeting. As a result, 'between 1953 and 1978 per capita production of coal quintupled, that of steel increased by 11 times, and that of electricity increased by 16 times' (Naughton, 2007, p 329).

'After 1978, China diversified into a range of relatively low-technology, labour-intensive consumer goods that had been neglected under the planned economy' (Naughton, 2007, p 330). As early as in April 1979, the Executive Intelligence Unit reported that China turned away from heavy industry and shifted towards light industry (EIR, 1979). China's industrial development took a reverse direction from the classical mode, where labour-intensive light industry development preceded more capital-intensive HCI and machinery. This was precisely due to the fact that the PRC commenced the process of post-socialist transformation. During the socialist period, it followed Soviet-style HCI development, creating an illusion, as put by Naughton (2007), that it already passed the developmental phase of early, labour-intensive manufacturing development. Due to developmental necessities, however, heavy industry was not abandoned as a whole and the significant transformation of this industrial sector commenced. Already in 1981, the industry resumed growth (Tidrick and Chen, 1987).

To some extent, the simultaneous development of HCI and light, especially textile, industries characterised pre-DS Japan and Korea. However, Japan abandoned textile industry as a targeted sector early on, followed by a similar decision in Korea in the late 1960s. In China, light industry still seems important, at least in terms of job creation. Within the manufacturing sector, textile production still engages the largest number of workers. In the year 2008, total employment exceeded 20 million people. However, by no means can it be currently considered a targeted industry, as governmental support seems limited to some provisions related to export. The state has withdrawn from textile production, which is now in the hands of private Chinese producers, joint ventures and foreign companies with their production bases located in China. However, many foreign firms are gradually shifting their production to countries with lower labour costs.

The HCI reorganisation and development of the 1980s included an increase in production of steel, iron, coal and oil. The targeting of steel and iron should be associated with both international demand and Chinese domestic demand, related particularly to infrastructural expansion. The process of socio-economic development had to be accompanied by adequate infrastructure building. Indeed, it was often claimed that a lack of infrastructure development was one of the factors that hindered developmental advancements in China prior to the systemic reforms. This is why the Chinese authorities decided to heavily invest in the sector during the reform period. Between 1982 and 1989, around RMB293 billion was spent on 261 projects (Ke et al, 2009). A good indication of infrastructural development is the length of motorways built. The first motorway, Jingjintang highway, was constructed in 1993. By the end of 2013, the total length exceeded 100,000 km. Moreover, the acceleration of economic growth would require intensification of the domestic production of energy. In fact, the targeting of the development of the energy industry was entirely motivated by domestic necessities, with the exception of the recent development of the renewable energy sector, aimed, to some extent, at the international market as a response to growing international demand.

In addition to construction and petrochemicals, Kuchiki (2007) named other industrial sectors that became listed as targeted in the mid-1990s: the automobile industry and the electronics and machinery industries. Indeed, both sectors resemble the priority sectors in the middle stages of the Japanese and Korean DS. In fact, the results of the middle DS period targeting are still part of the world's production assortments, where especially Japanese cars and Korean domestic appliances maintain dominant positions in certain layers of the international market. Naughton (2007, p 332) underlines that:

> since 1995 new patterns of structural change have emerged in Chinese industry.... First, the overall shift toward light, diversified manufactures clearly came to an end after 1995. Traditional light industry products typical of the early stage of industrialisation declined dramatically as a share of China's industrial output.... Food products, textiles, garments, and leather goods dropped from 24% to 17% of total industrial sales. Instead, newly emerging industries with higher technological content grew robustly. Electronics and telecommunications equipment increased its share from 4.6% to 10.5% of total industrial sales.

The mid-1990s' targeting in China is currently also increasingly visible on the world stage. China became a main supplier to the outside world of a number of goods manufactured within the electronics and machinery industries. Among others, it manufactures: 80% of the world's digital cameras and DVD players; 70% of air conditioners and microwave ovens; 60% of electric cookers, refrigerators and notebooks; 50% of phones, electronic fans and colour TV sets; and 25% of cars. It is also the number one producer of washing machines.[59] According to the China Machinery Industry Federation, the four major machinery-related industries became automobiles, power equipment, machine tools and construction machinery.[60]

The increase of technologically advanced products in the share of production volume and the gradual turning towards knowledge-intensive industries became a feature of China's industrial development at the beginning of the 21st century. For example, establishing semiconductor joint ventures with leading foreign semiconductor firms has been one of China's key industrial development strategies (Hu and Jefferson, 2008). It was also a distinctive feature of Japan and Korea at the late stages of their DS-proper period. However, China's contemporary policy of industrial targeting cannot be simply summarised as a return

[59] Data compiled from National Bureau of Statistics of China and Ministry of Industry and Information Technology of China.

[60] Personal communication, Beijing, 10 July 2009.

to labour-intensive production after a period of socialist development, and then a gradual increase of capital-intensive industries, with a clear focus on technological upgrading. The populous and underdeveloped country's industrial development strategy seems to have no choice but to adhere to the diversification mentioned by Naughton (2007), perhaps in the broadest manner possible. Indeed, currently in China, the areas of targeting are extensive and go beyond the classical industrial sectors. This is due to the fact that it could be extremely difficult for such a vast and populous country to focus entirely on a handful of industries in order to nurture national development.

First, it is sometimes claimed that the agricultural sector enjoys 'guiding' interventionism, where reorganisation, modernisation and technological innovations are aimed at enhancing capacity in food production (see OECD, 2009b), despite the common perception of the inadequacy of government measures. The most populous nation in the world, plagued by a plethora of famines, continually gears its policies towards the rather difficult task of securing food self-reliance. Indeed, diverting attention from the agricultural sector did have severe consequences in China's history. This is why China's government currently tries to put a stronger emphasis on rural development (see Fock and Wong, 2008).

Second, HCI, controlled to a great extent by SOEs, is still being targeted, partly to secure the international position using comparative advantage, as in the case of the shipbuilding industry (characteristic for the early Japanese and mid-Korean DS), and partly to satisfy the local market in need of infrastructure expansion. Many special enclaves still attract investment in HCI. For example, the Nantong Economic and Technological Development Area (NETDA) specialises in chemical industries, and this is the profile that the local authorities intend to maintain.[61] As a result of this targeting, China's infrastructure, including roads, railways, bridges and buildings, has been growing rapidly. The country is currently host to the biggest number of skyscrapers, the fastest train in the world (and the only maglev technology-based train for public usage, connecting Shanghai city with Pudong airport), the longest bridge and the highest railway.

Third, the targeting involves the machinery and electronics industries due to their labour-intensive character, in addition to being capital-intensive, and the possibility for their long-term competitive advantage. As a result, China has become an important producer of automatic data-

[61] Personal communication with the representatives of NETDA, Nantong, 29 November 2009.

processing equipment (eg notebook computers), telecommunication equipment and components (eg mobile phones), household electrical appliances (eg refrigerators, air conditioners), electronic products (eg digital cameras, TV sets), as well as motor vehicles and their components, vessels (eg ships) and construction machinery (eg cranes, excavators, etc), among other things.

Despite the policy of combining labour- with technology-intensive production, certain traditional industrial sectors such as light industry remain extremely important for sustainable development, though they can hardly be described as targeted. Further development of labour-intensive traditional branches of the national industry remains very important, as the labour transfer from the rural economy to the industrial economy must continue.[62] Although some scholars predict a slow but firm departure from labour-intensive production in places such as the Pearl River Delta due to increasing labour costs, the overall status of China's economy still requires the extensive development of labour-intensive industries. In order to proceed with the de-ruralisation process, one needs to continue a steady increase in the absorption capacities of the urban parts of the national economy.

Fourth, the energy production and environmental protection-related industries are gaining in importance in the process of China's fast socio-economic development (see Chatham House, 2007; Wei et al, 2011). Indeed, China's international expansion, partly aimed at securing imports of oil and natural gas from all corners of the world (see Downs, 2006; Rosen and Houser, 2007), as well as the reorganisation and the modernisation of domestic mines in order to achieve greater efficiency, with the grand support of and the decisive role of the state, are clear examples not only of the level of demand for energy, but also of the intensity of targeting efforts. This is caused by the fact that energy shortages have been a real obstacle in economic development and China's energy efficiency is at a disastrously low level (Naughton, 2007), making it an important environmental factor, since around 70% of electric power from fossil fuels and 70% of energy is used in industrial production. Moreover, the situation will become increasingly difficult as in order to maintain the current pace of development, by 2030, China will need an additional 1,300 GW (gigawatts) of energy production capacity.

Consequently, since the late 1990s, industrial development has been compelled to take into account the necessity of limiting usage of

---

[62]   Anecdotal data suggests that out of the over 700 million rural population, there were 293 million people employed in rural areas in 2007.

energy in industrial production, as well as curbing the pollution emitted that accompanies the process.[63] Thus, energy production-associated industries, such as coal mining, oil exploitation and transportation, and nuclear plant building, as well as the renewable energy sector, are increasingly important. Due to deteriorating environmental conditions and to climate change, which affects the entire planet, industrial development must involve activities aimed at limiting air, soil and water pollution, including CO_2 emissions,[64] as much as increasing energy efficiency. A lack of a certain quality of water and energy supply interruption is an often-occurring predicament that affects Chinese industrial output. Due to environmental crises, the standard of living is decreasing, for example, in the coal-intensive production provinces of Central China, with Lifeng (the Shanxi province) being one of the most polluted cities in the world.

Despite the fact that China has become the biggest polluter on the planet and that its energy efficiency is at an extremely low level, it must be acknowledged that those issues remain of concern to the Chinese authorities and that certain sectoral policies in this respect are being introduced. The Ministry of Environmental Protection (MEP) has launched a number of initiatives that became state policies, such as green credit, green insurance, green security and green trade:[65]

[63] It can plausibly be argued that until the summit in Rio De Janeiro in June 1992, which produced the United Nations Framework Convention on Climate Changes (UNFCCC) (an international treaty whose objective is to stabilise greenhouse gas concentrations in the atmosphere at a level that would prevent dangerous changes to the climate), little attention was paid to environmental and climate issues in constructing developmental models.

[64] China accounted for a quarter of global CO_2 emissions and 57% of the global increase in carbon emissions in the first decade of the 21st century (Hallding et al, 2009, p 12). The European Commission estimates that by the year 2020, per capita greenhouse gas emissions in China will exceed that of Europe.

[65] The policy of 'green credit' ensures that good environmental performance is a criterion for companies to obtain bank loans. As far as 'green insurance' is concerned, companies will be required to buy insurance from insurance companies based on their environmental risk assessment. For heavy industries, 'green security' means that companies within this sector will need to reach specific environmental standards in order to be listed on the stock exchange. According to the policy of 'green trade', products that are highly polluting and environmentally dangerous shall enjoy no trade privileges (see PP, 2009, p 38).

> The Circular Economy Promotion Law came into effect on 1st January 2009. It establishes a legal framework for developing the economy, raising energy efficiency [and] protecting the environment.... China has also implemented various tax incentives and subsidies to support sustainable development. (PP, 2009, p 38)

Of the November 2008 economic stimulus,[66] 38% was designated for green and eco-friendly projects. The Chinese government has repeatedly pledged to reduce energy intensity and began to focus on reducing the carbon intensity in the process of industrial production, as indicated by Premier Wen Jiabao during his speech in New York prior to the G20 summit in Pittsburgh (24–25 September 2009). Moreover, China participates in the Near Zero Emission Coal (NZEC) Initiative, which examines 'the merits of various options for carbon (CO^2) capture, transport and geological storage (CCS)' (NZEC Summary Report 2009).[67] At the same time, provincial and local authorities attempt to implement policies aimed at supporting green development, often in collaboration with the Ministry of Science and Technology – Shanghai's fund to encourage energy conservation and emission-reduction projects being a good example.

Naturally, from the perspective of historical DS experiences, energy sector targeting seems nothing more than a supporting activity for the DS core targeting, whereas environmental protection was hardly an issue in the DS cases. Contemporarily, the necessity for energy security makes the energy sector by all means a targeted industry, not merely in its supporting role of other industries. Moreover, the environmental protection-related industries constitute an integral element of any feasible long-term developmental model.

Fifth, the sectors that are currently subject to extensive targeting were, indeed, the final DS targeting objectives in Japan and Korea, namely, the new innovative technologies in knowledge- and information-intensive industries. This policy of targeting is aimed at replacing the 'made in China' philosophy with the 'made by China' doctrine, to use the words of a CCTV (China Central Television) commentator

---

[66] The November 2008 economic stimulus was the package of financial assistance for a number of sectors of China's national economy to avert the negative effects of the global economic crisis.

[67] CCS technology is at an experimental stage. It is aimed at eliminating CO^2 from the atmosphere by capturing it at its source and then depositing it among geological formations underground.

during the national parade commemorating the 60th anniversary of the establishment of the PRC. Chinese authorities create fiscal and administrative incentives for companies bringing innovative technologies, often attempting to discriminate against those firms who are not in the possession of know-how. The law is constructed in such a way that the transfer of technology to Chinese companies is almost inevitable. At the same time, it is advocated on the international scene that a transfer of innovative technologies to China, preferably on a non-remunerable basis, is a necessary condition for alleviating the effects of climate change and environmental pollution.[68]

To reiterate, there are certain similarities and differences between China's targeting and the targeting of the two other states. Japan and Korea went from the pre-DS-proper period's favouring of light industries, through labour-intensive HCI and machinery industries, to capital-intensive electronics. Eventually, both countries focused on new technology-, knowledge- and information-based industries, without, however, the hindering of their supremacy in some electronics and machinery sectors that they had achieved. China's process of industrial development during the post-socialist period has been consistent to a large extent with Japan's and Korea's: light, including textile, industry; then HCI; subsequently machinery and electronics; and eventually knowledge-intensive technologies. In this respect, it is fashioned on the DS model, with two significant differences, however. First, due to China's capacity, a number of industrial sectors are targeted simultaneously, with, as it seems, similar intensity. This is not to say that the Japanese and Korean governments adhered to a policy of single industry support; however, the shift in support seemed, indeed, more pronounced. Second, there are some types of industries that did not constitute main targets in developmental states, such as agriculture, the environment and energy, but do feature in China's policy of targeting. Although Japan included environmental policies as part of its industrial upgrading and transformation (Kagami, 1995), the importance of those three sectoral policies within general state policies has increased only contemporarily, due to climate change, rapidly increasing environmental pollution and dwindling natural resources.

---

[68] In the years 2007–2011, I visited a number of special zones situated in such diverse places as the historical industrial bases of Liaoning province, the opening-up policy's offspring in Zhejiang and the underdeveloped Western China development hubs in Sichuan. In the overwhelming majority of cases, local authorities would stress that the pool of incentives to establish a business presence was linked to high-tech investments.

China's industrial targeting also needs to be seen in the post-socialist context. As a result of state-command industrial planning, 'at the start of reform, Chinese industry had already attained a substantial size. Chinese factories and mines employed more workers in 1978 than the combined total of all other third-world nations' (Brandt, 2008, p 569). The dominance of the heavy and defence industries resulted in two processes: first, the unusual character (Naughton, 2007) of developing light industries, having had experience in developing HCI industry, against the common developmental pattern; and, second, a part of industrialisation policy has been focused on industrial restructuring rather than industrial development. Both phenomena are explained by post-socialist transformation. The reasons for resorting to a light industry development strategy are well known: a necessity to create a large amount of industrial jobs in a relatively short period of time in order for the country to abandon its underdeveloped pattern of rural economy dominance; the short supply of light industry products as a result of HCI domination;[69] a lack of financial resources to develop exclusively capital-intensive industries at the beginning of the transformation; a necessity to embark on a rapid development trajectory while performing a costly and long restructuring of heavy industry; and, finally, the desire to partly reorient the national economy to export production. Indeed, initially, the labour-intensive products of the light industry became the main export goods. As far as heavy industry restructuring is concerned, the reform primarily took the form of liberalisation of allocation mechanisms to allow more market-based incentives, ownership changes leading to partial autonomy, price deregulation and changes in labour relations. At the same time, technological upgrading, usually by means of foreign technology, and changes in managerial practices allowed for the modernisation of the sector. These modernisation efforts have allowed the industry to increase quality and diversify production, catering predominantly for domestic infrastructure development. As a result, some large Chinese companies such as LiuGong[70] even began to operate on the international market, including the EU.[71]

---

[69] In the 1970s, 'China's industries were still able to produce to only a level that supplied the population with severely rationed cloth and non-grain food commodities' (Huang et al, 2008, p 469).

[70] LiuGong is believed to be world's 20th and China's largest construction equipment manufacturer.

[71] In 2011, LiuGong acquired HSW (Huta Stalowa Wola) – the leading Polish steel producer.

Throughout the DS core period in Japan and Korea and the transformation period in China, all the earlier-mentioned sectors enjoyed the preferential treatment described in the sections concerned with financial- and trade-related policies. This preferential treatment would be the direct consequence of the strategy of targeting. The mechanism of targeting was sustained in a similar way in all three cases, that is, by a certain degree of control over production, distribution and consumption. This control was more stringent in Korea than in Japan. Again, due to the time-distortion factor, the economic environment seems more liberal in contemporary China than it was in Korea and Japan during their DS 'core activity' periods. Despite what has been seen as a return to interventionist practices by the Hu–Wen administration and the attempts at strengthening the status of the national economy as a 'regulated market economy' (*China Daily*, 2007a), production, distribution and consumption is decided mostly by market demand and not by the state administration.

Historically, after the Second World War, the Japanese government supervised production and product distribution via the state policy of the direct allocation of goods and rationing measures (Kagami, 1995, p 125). This continued during the 'priority production programme' via the technology import approval mechanism and close monitoring of developmentally related spending on infrastructure (roads, harbours, hydroelectric power). However, subsequently, the Japanese DS model was characterised by a certain policy elasticity and, thus, a more liberal economic environment than in other DS cases. Contrary to Korea, Japanese industrial policy was flexibly revised (Cho et al, 1996). 'Deliberation councils', consisting of representatives of the state administration, business and other knowledgeable circles, were good examples of dynamic adjustment in state policy (see Johnson, 1982). The loosening of state control was connected with the mid-1960s' partial liberalisation drive and then with the late 1970s' government's promotion of further economic liberalisation. In Korea, the first attempts to relinquish direct targeting in favour of more prominence for market forces were initiated in the late 1970s (Haggard and Moon, 1986). The real liberalisation policies, however, started to be implemented from the early 1990s (Chang et al, 1998). In the initial period of systemic reforms in China, the government directly controlled all production, distribution and consumption, except for the partly liberalised agricultural market. This was the legacy of the socialist period. The loosening of state control took place in the 1990s while on the path to WTO accession. Although the gradual economic liberalisation has witnessed some retrenchments since, as some policymakers called for the closer monitoring and regulating of production and export, the extent of control in contemporary China, as Perkins (2001) points out, cannot reach the level of the Korean DS model, especially in the most developmentally successful years of Park Chung Hee's rule, during which the decision on the nature and volume of both production and exportation was, to a great extent, reached in the presidential office and then forcefully negotiated with Korean firms. Direct targeting of specific industries and specific companies was an integral part of the policy of industrial development (Kim, 1985). Perkins (2001) also underlines that in Korea, effective control was not too difficult in terms of achieving the desired manufactured volumes, as half of the value-added production was in the hands of 200 or so companies. As far as Chinese companies are concerned, this big country hosts a vast number of economic agents, and despite the fact that some industrial sectors are controlled by a handful of privileged companies, national development cannot be facilitated by a small group of large enterprises, as was the case in Korea.

The business actors

This leaves us with the issue of the economic actors/agents facilitating the DS strategies, as well as China's current development, and, more specifically, with the question as to what group of companies would become 'national champions', to use the DS-related terminology:

> Below the level of the state, the agent of expansion in all late-industrialising countries is modern industrial enterprise, a type of enterprise that Chandler (1977) described as large in scale, multidivisional in scope, and administered by hierarchies of salaried managers. (Amsden, 1989, p 9)

In Japan, the initial facilitation of pre-DS textile and military production expansion was conducted by family-controlled conglomerates (*zaibatsu*), which significantly increased their role in industrial production during the governmentally motivated cartelisation efforts of the 1920s. Most of them, however, were dissolved in the late 1940s as a result of the introduction of the anti-monopoly law. In view of a certain economic liberalisation forced upon Japan, when it became an IMF Article VIII country and an OECD member in 1964, the *keiretsu* conglomerates came into play as the only organisations capable of maintaining Japanese firms' competitive advantage on the international market via the economy of scale. A number of internationally well-known companies were either vertical or horizontal *keiretsu*, namely, Mitsubishi Group, Honda Group, Toyota Group, Nissan Group and Daihatsu Motors. At the same time, fully or partially (under various arrangements) government-owned companies have been present in the Japanese developmental state (Johnson, 1982; Nielsen, 1982) and played an important role until the mid-1980s' reform (Nakamura, 1996). In the case of the Korean DS, the main enterprises were privately-owned *cheabols* (Kim, 1985), whose origins can be traced back to the Japan-led industrialisation of Korea and the presence of the *zaibatsu* on the Korean market. Kyongbang, Kongsin, Paeksan, Hwasin and Mokpo belong to the oldest *chaebols* (Kohli, 1999, p 118), and among the most famous are Samsung, Hyundai and LG. In the early 1970s, 46 *chaebols* controlled 37% of value added in manufacturing (Perkins, 2001, p 5).

In the case of China, the question of which companies could be the main actors/facilitators of the process of development – whether private as well as some state companies, as was the case of Japan, or closely monitored private companies, as was the case of Korea – continues to be perceived as an open question. Huchet and Richet (2002, p 173) name several groups of companies that dominated the early stage of China's systemic reforms:

> large state-owned enterprises run from the central government; small to medium-sized businesses in the state and collective sector set up in urban areas and run by local governments; ... small firms in rural zones registered as collective enterprises and run by local governments; [and] private firms on the fringe of the centrally planned system; especially in trade and services.

The subsequent economic liberalisation and deepening of the ownership reform resulted in an increase of privately owned companies:

> Since the mid-1990s ... new categories of Chinese groups with more complex control structures [emerged]: major financial holding companies in the public sector specialising in services ... commonly called 'red chips' (CITIC, COSCO, China Resources, Beijing Enterprise); major state groups controlled by the central government and operating in protected sectors; state sector and collective groups that are leaders in competitive fields and have earned greater autonomy from their overseeing [mainly local] administration; joint ventures a majority of whose capital is

controlled by a foreign company and firms 100% controlled by foreign multinationals; small groups in the state and collective sector controlled by local governments; private groups in competitive sectors that increasingly operate under the control of the main owner; small private and family collective commercial firms in the service sectors in urban and rural areas. (Huchet and Richet, 2002, pp 173–4)

Despite the ongoing reforms, in the mid-1990s, the authorities reaffirmed their dedication to supporting SOEs: 'Five hundred and twelve large SOEs were designated as priority companies by government industrial policy' and 'the medium and large-scale high-technology industry as well as the security-related sector were selected among SOEs as strategic sectors of vital importance'(Baek, 2005, pp 488, 489). At the end of 1990s, the 'hundred largest [SOEs operated] in areas that [were] still strongly regulated and largely protected from both internal and international competition' (Huchet and Richet, 2002, pp 175–6). Currently, SOEs dominate some of the targeted industries. The largest companies, such as Sinopec and PetroChina (petroleum), Shenhua Group (coal mining) (both in the energy-related sector), China Telecom (telecommunications), Baoshan Iron & Steel (heavy industry), and CCCC (China Communications and Construction Company) (construction), to mention but a few, are all state-owned. It is the overall state policy to entrust the development of targeted industries and, subsequently, the realisation of developmental objectives in the hands of Chinese SOEs. Those enterprises are, by definition, easier to control and influence, to the extent that 'Beijing [is able to set] non-profit orientated goals for state-owned enterprises to accomplish, and thereby [can use] the SOEs to further its industrial policies. These goals may require that SOEs make suboptimal decisions for political … purposes' (Haley, 2007, p 2). Moreover, Huang (2008) suggests that the favouring of large SOEs has taken place at the expense of other companies, especially private Chinese SMEs, as an element of building a 'state-led capitalism' where private indigenous entrepreneurship is repressed and the dominance of state firms is ensured by extensive support. Consequently, the current policy suggests that the central government has indeed chosen the actors for the implementation of the developmental strategies. Therefore, some insight into the ability of the main economic actors to facilitate China's development trajectory may be provided by the analysis of the reforms of SOEs, which is, in itself, a well researched topic (see You, 1998; Jefferson and Rawski, 1999b; Zhang, 2000; Bolesta, 2004, 2006). On the other hand, the emergence of private enterprises may result in them taking over the targeting policy's implementation in at least some less politically sensitive sectors, once they have gained the authorities' consent. The policy of building the national economy's innovation capacities, which is very important for successful contemporary development, can be realised (under state guidance) via private companies. The European example shows that a significant part of know-how is generated in small- and medium-sized private enterprises. The last two decades of lack of significant developmental achievements in Japan is often attributed to the fact that large SOEs and *keiretsu* multi-conglomerates with complicated and conservative managerial structures, which impact decision-making processes, among other things, failed to secure an adequate innovativeness of the Japanese economy, which, in turn, slowed down, reaching recession point at a certain stage. The clear case study is Sony, a long-time innovator in the electronics industry, which has failed to manufacture a breakthrough innovative product comparable to the invention of the walkman.

The developmental state policy of import discrimination and export support

Despite the rather late development of the Japanese DS export–oriented regime, all the East Asian DS examples prove that export was an important drive behind the fast socio-economic development. Trade policy would involve the establishment of barriers for import and incentives for export. Import substitution industrialisation (ISI) would include import barriers; export-oriented industrialisation (EOI) would involve export promotion. Nevertheless, it is very difficult to categorise the plethora of policy instruments used by the developmental states. In this section, we deal with general trade policies, custom duties and quantitative measures rather than incentives, which are broadly referred to as subsidies. Those are analysed in the next section.

According to Prebisch (1950), developing countries should introduce import substitution strategies in their developmental quest as due to the dominance of the export of their primary commodities and the import of industrial products, they suffer unfavourable terms of trade. Consequently, the general DS trade policy was characterised by 'import substitution' and then by 'export orientation'. Those concepts, however, should in no way be seen as opposite. On the contrary, in the DS model, the natural consequence of the successful policy of import substitution was the gradual introduction of export orientation policies. In Japan, the dual strategy was already present during the years 1914–38 (Mass and Miyajima, 1993, p 153), when the state became a world-leading textile exporter. The earlier-mentioned cartelisation process was accompanied by increased import tariffs and anti–dumping laws. After the Second World War, Japan followed a similar path. Up until 1975, it was domestic consumption, and thus ISI, which drove its economic growth (Johnson, 1982, p 16). All international trade was under the government's direct control (until the early 1950s) (Kimura, 2009). Later, two factors caused the steady climb of the rate of average trade tariffs, namely: the gradual reduction of tariff exemption for machinery; and the increase in tariffs on food imports. For example, sugar customs duties were hiked from 15% in 1951 to 100% in 1959 (Yamazawa, 1975, p 386). Import substitution production was additionally enhanced in the DS-proper period via the exercising of strict control over imports, mostly via quota systems, whereby, in the 1960s, almost 500 types of goods were under the import quota system (Sakoh, 1984, p 531), including steel products (as early as in 1950). Economic liberalisation moved Japan closer to an EOI pattern. However, this liberalisation focused on eliminating quota-style quantitative restrictions, whereas tariffs continued to be important tools in restraining imports. The agreements brokered during the General Agreement on Tariffs and Trade's (GATT's) Kennedy Round (1964–67) effected a gradual decrease in Japanese tariffs from the late 1960s. In the early 1970s, the government implemented a number of effective tariff reductions on mining and manufacturing products, as well as on agricultural goods (Yamazawa, 1975). In the late 1970s, the measures to prevent imports and promote exports were gradually eliminated, whereas, in the early 1980s, a policy of import promotion took place in order to balance the Japanese trade surplus.

'Until the late 1950s, Korea was a typical inward–orientated economy' (Nam, 1995, p 154). The early DS period was characterised by import substitution production. Soon after Park Chung Hee took over power, EOI became the dominant focus (Jeon, 1995). The government introduced various export incentives. Nevertheless, export was closely monitored to the extent that the decisions on the product type, the exporter and the targeted market were greatly influenced by the state administration. Moreover, the 'Ministry of Commerce and Industry set annual export targets for officials connected with export administration' (Kim, 1985, p 30). At the same time, protection of the domestic market played an important role. The government tightened import controls, while general import tariffs rose to 40%. The diversification and exemptions of tariffs allowed the government to steer the inflow of goods and capital. For example, intermediate goods for export production and some capital goods for special uses or specific industries were imported duty-free (Nam, 1995). Imposed import quotas were proportionally awarded to companies, according to their export volume (the export–import link). Although the first attempts at import liberalisation had already taken place in the late 1960s, the effective policy took shape in the 1980s. In both cases, Japan and Korea, export incentives predominantly took the form of various financial system-related policies; thus, the topic is examined in the following section.

Tariffs and quotas were extensively used by developmental states to manage international trade. Selective discrimination of imports and selective support for exports, the latter especially via various financial incentives, were important features of historical DS cases. However, those policies have been, in particular, affected by the time-distortion factor due to the evolution of the international economic order and international economic rules. Due to globalisation, which 'adds more actors to the policy process in developing states and … increases the power of "external" actors over state policy' (Breslin, 2003, p 228), the degree of openness of national economies worldwide during the time of China's systemic transformation has been significantly greater than during the DS core periods of Japan and Korea. As a result, 'compared to the growth takeoffs of Japan and Korea, China's opening occurred at an earlier stage and went further' (OECD, 2009a, p 35). Thus, one must take into consideration that the process of state guidance of China's development trajectory is affected by the fact that the Chinese authorities are unable to use certain mechanisms, for example, import/export limits, barriers and quotas, readily available during the times of the Japanese DS and the Korean DS. This situation is exacerbated by the fact that China became a member of the WTO. Its path to WTO accession (1986–2001), as well as its accession's consequences, are well documented (see Lardy, 2002; Zweig, 2002; Breslin, 2003, 2007). Domestically, there has always been opposition to joining the WTO; however, both the then President Jiang Zemin and Premier Zhu Rongji eventually supported the idea. Internationally, the negotiation process was aimed at ensuring that China would not obtain benefits derived from the status of a developing economy, despite its persistent claim to being one. As a result, 'China's accession protocol entailed significant concessions far exceeding the obligations of previous "developing country" members' (Breslin, 2003, p 221). During the first five years of membership, it was obliged to effect a significant reduction in trans-border barriers as 'the agreement mandated a further reduction in tariffs in a wide range of sectors along with the conversion of quotas into tariff equivalents' (OECD, 2009a, p 54).[72] The average tariff levels fell from 15.88% to 9.82% (OECD, 2009a, pp 152–3).[73] Further liberalisation in the field is expected and required, and any protectionist behaviour is usually met with reaction from the EU and the US, as expressed during the High Level Economic Dialogue meetings between the EU and the PRC, and as proved by the US on occasions engaging the Chinese in the WTO dispute settlement mechanism. Moreover, China's participation in the OECD's 'enhanced engagement' programme – through which several large developing economies, including India, Brazil, Indonesia and South Africa, aim to improve their economic, as well as political, transparency and adhere to market economy rules in their economic-related conduct – puts additional pressure on the Chinese government to refrain from using protectionist policies. Thus, it is difficult to argue with Zweig (2002) and Lardy (2002) that China's trade policy is, to a large extent, determined by foreign factors and international pressures.

Consequently, the Chinese authorities had to find the means and mechanisms to cope with this international conditionality, characterised by a high degree of intrusiveness into domestic economic affairs, and to benefit from the distinctively different institutional arrangements of the global economic order than that during the Japanese and Korean DS core periods. It is believed that, to a large extent, China has been successful in achieving this, as the contemporary Chinese economic expansion illustrates. China's interventionist attitude and economic nationalism resulted in the broad usage of non-tariff means to hinder imports (eg standardisation) and promote exports (eg political and developmental cooperation with other developing countries) as a way to circumvent the effects of economic liberalisation.

Some means of import discrimination have been examined in Chapter Three in the section on economic nationalism, where access to the market is limited by laws, regulations, policies, sectoral activities and ad hoc actions, in place of customs duties. One of the main policies in this respect involves China's standardisation practices. According to PP (2009, p 140), with 22,900 national standards, 40,000 industry standards and 14,000 local (provincial, municipal) standards, China has

---

[72] One should not confuse the obligation to reduce tariffs, imposed by international agreements that China chose to be a part of, with the general change in the state ideology to increase state interventionism, especially visible after the 17th CCP Congress.

[73] Not to mention that in the year 1992, the average tariff level was around 42% (see Ianchovichina and Martin, 2004; OECD, 2009a, pp 152–3).

more standards than all the European states combined and no systematic structure to govern them. Moreover, 'the Chinese standardisation infrastructure is growing extremely fast, and with this growth inevitably comes growing complexity' (PP, 2009, p 140). There are conflicting regulations on various levels, especially as far as industry standards are concerned, and access to information regarding procedures is limited. The country seems to remain behind its WTO commitments to adjust national standards to international norms. Indeed, unwilling to accept and adopt international standards and certification procedures, the Chinese authorities effectively utilise standardisation procedures to constrain market access and discriminate against foreign products. One case clearly demonstrates the level of determination to use this tool. In October 2008, during the EU–China trade negotiations concerning the free flow of certain groups of goods, in response to Peter Mandelson's (the then EU Commissioner for Trade) questions as to why China would not allow access of European medicines to its market, knowing that they had to go through very detailed and exhaustive scrutiny in order for them to be sold in the EU, Chen Deming (the PRC's Minister of Commerce) replied that 'we Asians are different. That's why we need to employ our own procedure and our own standards'. Although one can understand that, in general, China is often unwilling to accept international standards to allow market advantage for domestic producers, the response of Chen Deming was, to put it mildly, astonishing.[74] However, it is important to stress the selectivity of import discrimination rather than its indiscrimination, as some import is in fact encouraged and supported, namely, that of intermediary goods for the purposes of production/assembly (see Zhou and Latorre, 2013).

Coming back to the issue of ISI, in the case of China, import substitution has always been an important component of the overall developmental strategy during the socialist and post-socialist periods. In the conditions of state command, without appropriate market mechanisms of financial intermediation and the persistent lack of so-called hard currency funds, ISI was perhaps the only way to industrialise and, indeed, it was vigorously implemented by Premier Zhou Enlai in the early 1970s (Bramall, 2009a). In terms of instruments, 'by the mid-1980s, China had moved from a planned trading system to a system of high tariffs, multiple nontariff barriers, and abundant administrative discretion, a system that was in many ways typical of developing country ISI strategies' (Naughton, 2007, p 385). Because of the socialist heritage,

[74]   I personally witnessed this exchange of opinions at the MOFCOM headquarters.

trade barriers had to be redefined rather than erected. Thus, socialist-style trade barriers were replaced by custom tariffs for subsequent WTO negotiations (Naughton, 2007).

It is export, and thus EOI, however, that became an increasingly visible element of China's developmental advancements. In 2009, the country became the biggest exporter in the world, which was the result of the long-term state-level export support policy, as from the early 1980s, China's authorities created a wide pallet of incentives for export production. The policy was clearly visible in the creation of special zones in which manufacturing would be export-oriented. As opposed to Japan, where the DS model was not characterised by the existence of some special designated geographical structure to play a significant role in export expansion, in this regard, China resembled some Southeast Asian countries, with their special zones to attract FDI and export-processing zones (eg in the Philippines and Malaysia) (see Ge, 1999; Ishida, 2009), and, indeed, Taiwan, which established the first Asian export-processing zone in Kaoshiung, and Korea, which established an export-processing zone in Masan city. Indeed, the special zones – where relaxed taxation policies and other indirect incentives are applied to attract foreign capital – have been a pillar feature of the Chinese development trajectory. The special arrangements were created for special economic zones (SEZs) in: Shenzhen, Zhuhai, Shantou and Xiamen (1979–80); Hainan (1988); the open coastal cities of Dalian, Qinhuangdao, Tianjin, Yantai, Qingdao, Lianyungang, Nantong, Shanghai, Ningbo, Wenzhou, Fuzhou, Guangzhou, Zhanjiang and Beihai (1984); open zones in the Yangze river delta and the Zhujiang (Pearl) river delta; the triangle of the South Fujian, the Liaodong and Shandong peninsulas; the Hebei and Guangxi provinces (1985); the Shanghai–Pudong zone (1990); open ports of the Yangtze river (Chongqing, Yueyang, Wuhan, Huangshi, Jiujiang and Wuhu); and the 13 open border cities (Yining, Bole, Tacheng, Erenhot, Manzhouli, Heihe, Suifenhe, Hunchun, Ruili, Wanding, Hekou, Pingxiang and Dongxing). In addition, 54 economic and technological development zones (ETDZ), 53 high-tech industry development zones (HIDZ), 60 export-processing zones, and 15 bonded zones (Alder et al, 2013) have been created in various parts of the country. The goal of all special zones has been support for the grand development plan of the country via export-oriented production, as well as via attracting capital, new technologies and managerial skills to improve the effectiveness of the entire Chinese economy. It is believed that the special zones significantly contributed to economic growth (Alder et al, 2013). Therefore, the current Xi–Li administration seems to be fond of the special zone idea, as exemplified by the launching of the Shanghai Pilot Free Trade Zone in September 2013.

Currently, although, according to Alder et al (2013), some incentives are still in place in ETDZs and HIDZs, namely, tax and custom duty deductions, discounted land-use prices, no regulations on labour contracts, and special treatment on bank loans, special zones do not enjoy the same privileged position as previously due to economic liberalisation throughout China and the process of the unification of business tax rates. Moreover, Chinese 'classical' export products have already achieved a satisfactory international position, and the conditionality of international trade relations should secure their long-term participation in the global market, despite the growing competition from other emerging economies. Thus, extensive governmental support does not seem to be necessary. Naturally, both the EU and the US have, on occasion, threatened to impose tariffs and other barriers on Chinese products, using a vast range of arguments, from politically motivated to economically related anti-dumping measures, and this may, in theory, affect the position of Chinese products on the global market. Nevertheless, the Chinese authorities learned to negotiate those threats by skilfully adopting Western rhetoric advocating the necessity of the liberalisation of the international market and the abolition of trade barriers.

The PRC government has utilised certain tools in order to promote Chinese export expansion. There is a special state-level and, indeed, influential agency that promotes international trade, namely, the China Council for the Promotion of International Trade (CCPIT),[75] and its quasi-commercial wing, as opposed to the CCPIT's governmental character, the China Chamber of International Commerce (CCOIC). The CCPIT focuses not only on export promotion, but also generally on international trade cooperation, including the promotion of the importation of new technologies. In many ways, it is similar to the

---

[75] According to the official website, the CCPIT (established in May 1952) comprises VIPs, enterprises and organisations representing the economic and trade sectors of China. It is the most important and largest institution for the promotion of foreign trade in China. The aims of the CCPIT are to operate and promote foreign trade, to use foreign investment, to introduce advanced foreign technologies, to conduct activities of Sino-foreign economic and technological cooperation in various forms, to promote the development of economic and trade relations between China and other countries and regions around the world, and to promote mutual understanding and friendship between China and the economic and trade circles of all nations around the world, in line with the law and government policies of the PRC (CCPIT, 2008).

Japan External Trade Organisation (JETRO), created in 1958, and the Korea Trade Promotion Corporation (KOTRA), which was established in 1962 as a governmental agency to promote export-related activities and to assist the companies involved in exports, as well as to conduct overseas marketing.[76]

Other export-incentive tools can be described as being part of the process of China's overall international economic expansion. Negotiations regarding trade barrier elimination (as was the case in establishing a free trade agreement between China and the Association of Southeast Asian Nations [ASEAN]) and the realisation of development projects in exchange for access to natural resources (as is the case in cooperation with African countries, periodically reviewed during meetings of the Forum on China–Africa Cooperation [FOCAC]) are aimed at promoting Chinese products and at opening additional markets for Chinese goods. For example, the China–ASEAN Free Trade Agreement (CAFTA), which took effect in January 2010, created more opportunities for Chinese exporters in one of the most dynamically growing regional markets, as the custom tariffs were reduced from an average of 12.8% to 0.6% (for Chinese exports to ASEAN) and from 9.8% to 0.1% (for Chinese imports from ASEAN). At the same time, this enabled closer economic ties with countries that serve as an important base for raw materials and energy resources for the Chinese economy. China's economic expansion is particularly visible in smaller ASEAN economies, namely, Myanmar, Laos and Cambodia.[77] The policy of economic expansion in the developing world is sustained via developmental assistance through financial instruments and direct investments. In 2009, Premier Wen Jiabao, in his speech during the FOCAC summit, emphasised that China would provide African states with USD10 billion worth of credit on preferential terms, forgive debts of the poorest African countries, liberalise trade barriers, invest in 100 energy production projects, send 50 teams of agriculture and food experts, and donate RMB500 million for medical supplies, among other things. Some estimate that between 2004 and 2009, the value of China's development-related projects in Africa was around USD14 billion, whereas total investment in 2013 reached USD40 billion. As a result of economic activities, Chinese exports to Africa doubled from USD37 billion to USD73 billion between the years 2007 and 2011 alone (CCS, 2007, 2009; The China Analyst, 2012).

---

[76] The Korean government also developed a system of trade companies specialising in export (*chonghap sangsa*) (Kim, 1985).

[77] Personal observation from visits to ASEAN states, January–April 2012.

The political rhetoric, backed by some scholars' opinions, suggests that the policy of export support will be relegated to a category of less importance in the long term. Indeed, in 2007 and 2008, tax deductions for exporters were significantly reduced. In January 2008, an extra customs tax was imposed on the export of agricultural products. The official propaganda stressed the importance of more extensive import of goods in order to decrease the foreign trade imbalance. This seems to be in line with Japanese policies of the early 1980s. Moreover, the authorities realise that export dependency might negatively influence the economy, as illustrated by the loss of tens of millions of jobs during the global economic crisis of 2008/09, as its status depends greatly on the international economic situation. In fact, the Chinese model of export dependency has often been criticised as making the national economy excessively vulnerable to external shocks and foreign economic agents. Therefore, the policy of boosting domestic consumption is being vigorously implemented so that domestic consumption becomes the main pillar of economic growth. What has to be stressed, however, is that regardless of whether China's GDP growth will be fuelled by domestic consumption, which is nevertheless a remote perspective, exports will remain important for the national economy. There are structural long-term factors that determine the position of exports within Chinese economic activities. The most populous country in the world, with scarce arable land and the continuous diminishing size of what is available for cultivation, will be forced to accelerate the volume of agricultural importation in order to feed its increasingly affluent and expected-to-be-well-fed population. Despite official propaganda, it will not be achievable exclusively with domestic resources. The consequent import of goods will have to be met by maintaining a certain level of export dynamics in order to shape the necessary balance. Moreover, development of the labour-intensive industries necessary in the process of shifting the rural populations to non-agrarian employment will continue to put pressure on export expansion, as a large volume of manufacturing will not be absorbed domestically. In addition, the globalisation process, in a way, already requires national economies to maintain a high volume of exchange, as trade contributes to economic innovation by pushing towards greater competitiveness. Consequently, the policy of export support will have to be maintained in one way or another. In fact, the 2008/09 global economic crisis forced the Chinese authorities to temporarily reverse the policy trend of a slow departure from support for export activities due to a dramatic fall in export volume. At a time of a rapid decrease in consumption around the world, China has attempted to maintain a high level of international retail of its products by various actions in the sphere of the policy of export support together with the policy of financial support, including fiscal means such as the reintroduction of a preferential tax treatment for certain export sectors, for example, the textile and toy industries.

The developmental state financial policy of support for industrial development and exports

As far as the DS financial policy of support for industrial development and exports is concerned, I will focus my analysis on those main financial policies and financial reforms that facilitated the development of industrial production and the development of exports. Some of these were mentioned in previous sections of this chapter in reference to trade and industrial development policies.

Woo-Cumings (1999, p 10) sees finance as the nerves of the developmental state. Sindzingre (2006, p 6) claims that 'financing the developmental state could be achieved at the external level via foreign direct investment, debt, and aid, and at the internal level via taxation – public revenues and spending – domestic private savings and investment'. East Asian countries are believed to be privileged in a way, as far as the potential availability of domestic financial assets is concerned, since their nations are characterised by a widespread preference for a high rate of savings. It is worth mentioning, however, that high savings featured in Korea only in the late 1970s, and the industrial policy was initially financed primarily from foreign loans. Moreover, the high saving rate within Chinese society is not culturally motivated, as some would like to believe, but is forced both by the relatively low purchasing power of the population, leading to long periods of saving before goods such as cars, property and so on can be purchased, and by a poorly developed financial sector, which results in limited options for private credit, hence making it impossible to obtain loans for such purchases. Our interest here, however, does not lie in the broad issue of financing the developmental state, but rather in the question of how financial policies support the developmental state's activities in terms of industrial production and export.

It is important to note here that the effects of financial policies have often been questioned as to their real influence on actual industrialisation and socio-economic development, especially in the case of Japan (see Sakoh, 1984; Noland and Pack, 2003). The criticism usually comes from opponents of the industrial policy. Indeed, it is often difficult to find a correlation between specific policies and the increasing dynamics of the development of certain industries and sectors of the national economy. Nevertheless, the lack of a proven positive correlation does not mean that there is no negative correlation in the absence of certain policies. In other words, to give an example, the fact that the direct link between financial subsidies for HCI and the pace of development of HCI may be difficult to establish does not mean that in the case of a lack of those financial subsidies, HCI would develop at a similar pace. One should also take into consideration that the usage of financial and fiscal instruments towards specific industries is most likely to produce some effects in other sectors of the economy, not necessarily, as it may sometimes be argued, in a negative sense.

To nurture the development of certain industries, as well as to boost exports, the DS financial policy of support would involve the direct and indirect channelling of financial assistance to them via banks or state institutions in the form of credit subsidies and other subsidies, regulatory actions such as domestic tax policies and price control mechanisms, and monetary policies, such as the manipulation of interest rates and exchange rates. All those policies are sometimes classified as subsidy-related (see Magnus, 2006; CTI, 2009). The entire history of the DS model in Japan and Korea has featured extensive interventionism in the financial sector. The same applies to China throughout the period of systemic transformation.

Monetary policy and the banking sector

Unlike in many post-socialist countries, including Poland, where the monetary policy of the central bank has focused on maintaining a low level of inflation and, to a considerable degree, ignored developmental necessities in favour of financial stability, monetary policy in developmental states was always subordinate to developmental targets, and was often realised via maintaining an artificial rate of exchange in order to boost exports (China throughout the reform period; Korea in the early 1960s), or via multiple exchange rates (Japan and Korea during some years of DS model functioning, as well as in China), which would allow for the market adjustments necessary in order for the exporters to maintain an adequate level of international competitiveness. In fact, in the case of Korea, to a great extent, it was the Economic Planning Board that, during the Park Chung Hee times, realised monetary policy due to its proximity to the state leader. A similar situation applies in the case of China, where the People's Bank of China (PBC) does not enjoy any freedom, and is merely a tool in the overall development policy, as has been seen in the policy of the foreign exchange rate (see Lardy, 2005; Yu, 2010; Morrison and Labonte, 2011). The flexible management of the exchange rate regime has been a part of China's strategy of export development (OECD, 2009a). To enhance international competitiveness, the exchange rate was devalued on three occasions in the 1980s and the dual exchange rate system was introduced in 1981.[78] In order to further enhance the level of competitiveness of Chinese exports, the PRC maintained an undervalued RMB pegged to the US dollar. Under international pressure, as well as because of certain internal conditions, in June 2005, the RMB was revalued at 2.1%, and the daily allowable rate fluctuation was set at 0.03%, which was subsequently extended in 2007 to 0.05%. It was only in 2013, after the 3rd plenum of the 18th CCP Congress, that the CCP announced a plan to make the RMB fully convertible in the foreseeable future, hinting towards liberalisation of exchange rate policy. The case of the controlled gradual de/revaluation of the RMB proves that monetary policy is entirely subordinate to developmental objectives. The undervalued RMB increases the international competitiveness of Chinese exports, as indicated earlier. A liberalisation of this course, insisted on by the Western world, would have, at least in the short term, a negative impact on developmental dynamics, despite the arguments about creating a healthier financial environment and cheapening imports, which is important for the PRC as far as the trade imbalance and the cost of supply of energy resources and raw materials are concerned. This policy of maintaining an undervalued currency was a common practice among the developmental states. In the case of Japan from the 1950s until 1971, the Yen was pegged to the dollar at the value of 360, as was the Korean Won in the 1970s. Due to the rapid development of the Japanese economy, which would have led to currency appreciation, at the end of the 1960s, the Yen was significantly undervalued (Yamazawa, 1975), hence the series of revaluations in the 1970s.

The lack of policy freedom for central banks was similar to the lack of freedom (to various degrees) in the entire banking sector. In Korea, especially during the fast development of the Park Chung Hee era, the banking sector was closely controlled by the state and fulfilled developmental objectives. In 1962, 'the structure of the Monetary Board, the supreme authority overseeing monetary policies, and the management and administration of the Bank of Korea and the management and operation of the banking system as a whole, were altered drastically' (Lee, 1992, p 190). Banks were nationalised. The

---

[78] The exchange rate regime was subsequently reunified in the year 1994.

central bank became an arm of the Ministry of Finance, and the powers of the finance minister as the chair of the Monetary Board were expanded. Its budget would be overseen by the EPB and the flow of export and policy loans would be influenced by the Ministry of Commerce (Woo, 1991, p 159). The Bank of Korea enjoyed significant supervisory powers over commercial banks (Euh and Baker, 1990, p 10). This control was even tightened in 1972 as a result of an emergency decree intended to 'dramatically improve the financial structure of businesses, primarily by relieving them from the burden of private money market loans' (Chun, 2002, p 24). As a result, 'the role of banks, both commercial and specialised, became that of credit-rationing outlets for the government as the allocation of credit was tightly controlled by the Ministry of Finance' (Lee, 1992, p 190). At the same time, this policy became a tool to influence businesses, as 'by controlling their access to credit the government controlled their decisions on resource allocation and thus the pattern of industrial development' (Lee, 1992, p 189). Financial liberalisation came in the early 1980s 'as part and parcel of stabilisation' (Woo, 1991, p 189), together with the general trend of the opening up and phasing out of industrial policy. Major commercial banks were privatised (Nam, 1995).

In Japan, the environment looked more relaxed. Although the post-Second World War reconstruction-related investments were financed by the state's Reconstruction Finance Corporation, in the 1960s, the dominant lending/investment was done by private banking (Sakoh, 1984, p 523). Nevertheless, such governmental organisations as the Export-Import (ExIm) Bank and Development Bank of Japan played an important role in the process of financing development (Suzuki, 1987) and also in encouraging other banks to finance specific projects. Moreover, in the Japanese DS arrangements, under the 'main bank system', a large enterprise would be informally bound to one particular bank, from which it would draw its financial assets, among other activities (see Aoki and Patrick, 1994). This created a certain degree of safety associated with the fact that financial assets would be entrusted to an organisation often partly controlled by the enterprise or that this organisation would hold considerable equity holdings in the enterprise. In both cases, that of the DS in Japan and that of the DS in Korea, the banking sector was a semi- or non-independent component of the financial sector, which was an infrastructure to provide services to the economic actors of the DS model.

In the case of China, despite Xu's (1998) claims that the political elite saw it as an important part of transformation, the financial sector has been less developed than even in the early years of the DS model in Korea and Japan. Initially, the banking sector was dominated by four state-owned, so-called, policy banks, each with its division of competence, that is, to which sectors financial resources should be channelled. For example, the Agricultural Bank of China would facilitate transactions in rural areas, whereas the Industrial and Commercial Bank of China would do the same in urban territories. The Bank of China would be engaged in foreign transactions. Nevertheless, the underdeveloped financial sector is believed to have played an important role in the development of rural areas in the 1980s. Huang (2008) points out that due to the relaxation of state policies and support from government officials, the Agricultural Bank of China began a broader crediting of non-state businesses by expanding the range of businesses eligible for loans (eg private rural enterprises in addition to household businesses) and by eliminating certain regulatory obstacles (eg waving the loan-guarantee requirement for some costumers). Its limited capacities, in view of the rapid development of the rural economy, were supported by: rural credit cooperatives (RCCs), structures enjoying relative autonomy who became the main source of funds for rural businesses; rural cooperative foundations (RCFs), which accumulated capital from certain activities related to the privatisation process; and by informal finance, that is, private business entities tolerated by officials (Huang, 2008). At the same time, however, in urban areas, 'most credit continued to be allocated on the basis of the plan [as opposed to market allocation] at interest rates fixed by the authorities' (OECD, 2009a, p 36).

Huang (2008) underlines that rural financial liberalisation came to an end, and the subsequent 'financing repression' of the 1990s reversed the process. Banks were ordered to change their lending priorities from private to other businesses, and within the rural economy, they were encouraged to support agricultural activities rather than non-agricultural enterprises. Bureaucratic control over RCCs was tightened to the extent that it significantly affected their lending abilities. There was a crackdown on informal financing. All the banks began to realise the governmental policy of investment according to the leadership's wishes (central and local), mainly into SOEs. In particular, the China Construction Bank (one of the four big state-owned banks) would focus its activities on assisting SOEs in the process of additional capitalisation.

The policies were subsequently relaxed and the limits of activities abolished after the 1994 reform, as a result of which the PBC acquired the formal role of a central bank.[79] Nevertheless, the preference for a

[79] The PBC acquired an informal role as the central bank in 1983 (OECD, 2009a, p 36).

state-owned sector prevailed. The arbitrary channelling of funds into politically motivated projects without proper economic justification, present also in the DS model of Korea, in the case of China, resulted in extensive non-performable loan (NPL) problems, so called 'bad loans', which still remain unsolved today and are likely to continue to contribute to the level of fragility of the Chinese financial sector.[80] Currently, while private banks are free to operate and, due to WTO regulations, foreign banks have the right to operate their businesses in the PRC, the large state-owned banks are still the ones awarded programmes related to the development plans of the state, especially in the area of infrastructural activities, as well as financial services pilot projects. Naturally, this is met with significant opposition from several foreign banks, such as Standard Chartered, who upon fulfilling the high capitalisation requirement to enter the Chinese market, would like to participate in lucrative financial services projects.[81] In sum, one may argue that the Chinese state-owned policy banks can be perceived as the financial sector's state agents for supporting the developmental strategy.[82] This approach is consistent with the Korean DS model.

Subsidies

In all the DS countries, the banks have realised a policy of indirect subsidies, offering preferential rate loans for designated sectors and designated enterprises. These were usually described as policy loans or subsidised general loans (Woo, 1991, p 163). The mechanism was based on subsidised interest rates (Kim, 1985, pp 36–7), and the market distortion in Korea became so significant that export loans had negative real interest rates (Woo, 1991, p 164). Woo (1991) distinguished three ways of generating policy loans in Korea: from the banking system, the fiscal-type taken out of the state budget and from the National Investment Fund (since 1974). In the 1970s, policy loans accounted for

---

[80] According to the OECD, the situation is improving. For example, the ratio of NPLs to the overall volume of loans from the banking system fell from 18% in 2003 to 6.2% in 2007 (OECD, 2009a, p 47).

[81] Information obtained during a personal communication with a representative of Standard Chartered in Beijing, 6 December 2007.

[82] It does not mean that they are the most efficient supporters of this strategy. In fact, they enjoy their status because, first, the government feels more confident in relying on financial support from the organisations it fully controls and, second, the effectiveness of other banks, especially the large foreign banks, is compromised by the fact that they face a large amount of discriminatory treatment on the Chinese market.

over 40% of domestic credit. Preferential loans were initially granted for the textile industries and later for export and all HCI sectors, including transport infrastructure, energy and defence. In Japan, 'capital channelling to preferred sectors was implemented through direct subsidies, indirect subsidies through state-owned or dominated banks, and preferential tax breaks such as accelerated depreciation on investment' (Noland, 2007, p 255). Policy loans mostly benefited the targeted industries: iron and steel production, electric power, and shipbuilding. A direct credit allocation to selected industries on concessional terms was supplemented by direct governmental subsidies. However, Kimura (2009) claims that the government needed to exercise significant pressure on banks, especially the Development Bank of Japan, to provide policy loans, as contrary to Korean authorities, its involvement in providing direct subsidies was much smaller. Gradually, the policy loans were phased out in both Japan and Korea during the process of economic liberalisation.

Direct subsidies featured already in pre-DS Japan for the designated textile production industry. The Japanese government used the Fiscal Investment and Loan Programme in the endeavour of selective investment in targeted sectors and enterprises, whereas in Korea, this role was fulfilled by the National Investment Fund. In Japan, the initial purpose of the direct allocation of foreign reserves was to purchase foreign technologies. It is important to reiterate that the preferential policy of direct and indirect subsidies was directed not only at targeted industries, but also at particular enterprises. In Korea, especially during HCI targeting, the subsidies were given to certain enterprises who managed to gain favour from Park Chung Hee.

In China, subsidies play a prominent role in economic affairs and support the development of the targeted industries (see Haley and Haley, 2013). Direct and indirect subsidies have been seen as a favourable tool and the Park Chung Hee policy of designated enterprise targeting has been used towards large Chinese SOEs active within the so-called pillar industries, namely, automobile, machinery, electronics, petrochemical and construction. They include governmental grants and governmental interest subsidies, debt forgiveness and loan guarantees at no cost, preferential lending rates for companies investing in western China, and for high-tech companies (see Wong et al, 1995). Although the official propaganda of the 15th CCP Congress insisted on privileged financial treatment for SMEs, the large SOEs have been the major beneficiaries of the main four state-owned banks' loans, guaranteed through, for example, 'specific project financing'. The most vivid examples of subsidies provided in various forms to a handful of companies were presented in *An Assessment of China's Subsidies to Strategic and Heavyweights Industries* (CTI, 2009), submitted in 2009 to the U.S.–China Economic and Security Review Commission of the United States Congress. The report named several companies that exceeded the value of RMB1 billion in subsidies received, namely: Huaneng Power International Inc. (HPI), one of the leading power producers engaged in developing, constructing, operating and managing large-scale power plants throughout China – the total value of subsidies has been estimated at over RMB1.9 billion in various forms, including governmental grants (RMB423 million) for the construction of desulphurisation equipment; China Blue Chemical Ltd, a company producing mineral fertilisers and chemical products – RMB1.7 billion worth of subsidies; China Telecom Co. Ltd – RMB5.3 billion; China Shenhua Energy Ltd, a major coal producer that also operates railway, port and power businesses – RMB4.9 billion; Air China Ltd – RMB2.5 billion; COSCO, one of the world's largest companies in the shipping industry – RMB2.8 billion; Dongfeng Motor Group Co. Ltd – RMB1.6 billion; Chalco (Aluminium Corporation of China Ltd) – RMB3.4 billion; and, finally, PetroChina – a staggering RMB37.5 billion. The assessment report divided China's subsidies into two groups: practical subsidies that 'reward companies for accomplishing a social policy goal, such as investing in disadvantaged regions to alleviate unemployment'; and strategic subsidies 'that seek to advance the overall economic well-being of the country by earning foreign exchange, promoting technological development, developing an industry that the government views as being important, or otherwise enhancing China's industrial competitiveness' (CTI, 2009, p vi). The subsidies are also awarded to foreign firms that operate in the targeted industries and are considered important from the perspective of China's sectoral development. The report did not include estimates related to subsidies associated with the November 2008 economic stimulus. A significant part of the stimulus is believed to have been spent on direct subsidies to a handful of favoured enterprises in the designated sectors concerned, among other things, with energy and automobile production.

These subsidies also take the form of various tax subsidies. In general, tax policies, meaning favourable treatment for certain activities, that is, lower taxes, tax deductions, tax exemptions and special depreciation for tax purposes, were all used towards targeted sectors and enterprises in the case of Japan and Korea. In Japan, the overall level of taxes was relatively low. In the 1950s, the Japanese government introduced various tax-incentive policies for industrial development, as well as export development, namely, special depreciation (1951), import tax exemption for the import of machinery (1952) and export–import link tax reduction (1953). The fiscal policies served to attract modern technology (Kagami, 1995). The 'inclined taxation system' provided generous corporate tax exemption arrangements in purchasing specific types of machinery and equipment, and accelerated the introduction of foreign technologies (Kimura, 2009). In Korea, 'the 1961 Tax Exemption and Reduction Control Law began to provide export firms with tax deduction measures' (Mah, 2010, p 8). The subsequent policies focused on tax exemptions and tax deductions, as well as accelerated tax depreciation on profits from export activities, in targeted HCI such as steel, chemical, shipbuilding and machinery, and eventually, in 1982, on R&D-related activities (see Haggard et al, 1994; Nam, 1995).

Scholarly literature has paid significant attention to fiscal subsidies and fiscal reforms in China (see Wong, 1991; Oi, 1992; Lin and Liu, 2000; Tsui and Wang, 2004) in the process of redefining central–local relations and local industrialisation (Wong, 1992) or state capacity (Wang and Hu, 2001). During the state-command period, China's 'fiscal system [had] two salient features: an overwhelming dependence on industry and a reliance on profits of state-owned enterprises, along with taxes, for government revenue' (Wong, 1992, p 200). Therefore, the initial fiscal reform was to 'gradually ... replace enterprise profit remittances with a series of taxes' (Wong, 1992, p 215; see also Naito, 2010). Fiscal decentralisation – the process commenced in the mid-1980s – was aimed at transferring powers to lower administrative levels in order to increase the effectiveness of tax collection and of tax utilisation and was conducive to the general characteristics of post-socialist reforms after central planning. According to Tsui and Wang (2004, p 73), it had two important features: first, it introduced fiscal contracts between successive levels of government to share locally generated revenues as well as subsidies from and remittances to the next level of government; and, second, it gave freer rein to local governments in tapping off-budget resources. Lin and Liu (2000) believe that fiscal decentralisation significantly contributed to economic growth, mainly by improving the efficiency of resource allocation. However, Wong (1991) and Tsui and Wang (2004) are not convinced about the extent of actual decentralisation and the alleged benefits to local governments. Wong (1991) claims that by the early 1990s, the fiscal system in China fell into serious disarray, as central–local and local–local relations deteriorated. Indeed, Wang and Hu (2001) state that since the early 1980s, the state's financial extractive capacity has declined rapidly. The decreasing capacity in tax collection and tax revenues transfer from local to central authorities, as well as macroeconomic imbalances, prompted Premier Zhu Rongji to implement the policy of fiscal re-centralisation in 1994. It can be argued that this process had a lot in common with a DS practice, as centralism was an important feature of the DS model. The initial aim of the new tax policy was an improvement of tax transfers to central authorities (as was also in the case of Korea). Despite the mid-1980s' reforms, the tax system changes lagged behind the dynamics of the national economy's development and only the 1994 tax reform succeeded in significantly boosting the tax revenue of the central government necessary for the continuation of the developmental endeavour. Fiscal policies remained relatively effective and rather conservative during the first years of the new millennium, as illustrated by the low fiscal deficit (Naito, 2010). On the institutional side, the reforms accelerated in 2007. According to the OECD (2009a), the years 2007–09 were 'remarkable in China's taxation history ... following the promulgation of the enterprise income tax law [and] the issuance of the revised value–added tax provisional rules' (PP, 2009, p 50), to name a few reforms. However, the 2008/09 global economic crisis prompted a wave of financial policy adjustments. The government used some fiscal measures to alleviate the effects of the slowdown in economic growth and the increase in unemployment. Yu (2010) grouped the government's responses into two categories: expansionary fiscal policy, which included relaxation of tax policies and the fiscal stimulus package of RMB4 trillion; and expansionary monetary policy, which dramatically increased the money supply through additional bank credit.

Preferential tax treatment was largely associated with industrial production in special zones and, consequently, the exporting of goods 'made in China'. Indeed, in 2006, Ernst and Young's report indicated that manufacturing companies in SEZs and ETDZs were normally granted a reduced 15% tax rate (as compared to the standard tax rate of 33%), with a full exemption for the first two years of operation and a 50% reduction for the following three years. In High-Tech Industrial Development Zones (HTIDZs), the tax could even be 7.5% for the second five-year period of operation (after the first five years of 'tax holidays') for Sino-foreign joint ventures. The spectrum of industrial sectors that would enjoy preferential tax treatment would be broad and would include: engineering; electronics; partly energy; metallurgy; chemical and manufacturing of construction materials industries; light, including textile, industry; manufacturing materials; medical and pharmaceutical industry; agriculture and forestry; construction; communications and transport industries; as well as industries associated with scientific and technical development, geological studies, and consulting services aimed at production improvements and precision instruments (Ernst and Young, 2006). The three main options used in China's fiscal policy to control the genus of industrial production and the genus of export have been tax exemptions, tax deduction (the VAT on materials would be offset against the VAT on the final product) and various tax rebates, the latter already introduced in 1985 – all three determined by the location of the manufacturer, type of production and other issues related to the degree of innovativeness and technological advancement of the product.

However, preferential tax treatment benefited predominantly foreign companies and joint ventures, and, in this respect, Chinese companies operating in geographical parts of China other than special zones were discriminated against. This subsequently changed with the introduction of the unified corporate tax rate in January 2008, as a result of which the general tax of 33% was lowered to 25%, with companies who paid the preferential 15% tax rate subject to a transition period with a gradual increase of tax to reach 25% in 2011 (naturally, with some exceptions related to location, length of operation on the Chinese market, etc). Currently, preferential tax treatment is still awarded to R&D-related investments, as in the case of Korea and Japan. Foreign investors can benefit from tax breaks if they establish companies in the government (including local government)-determined industries and areas. Those industries are usually recruited from the last group of targeted industries, namely, knowledge- and information-intensive. Another element of the current policy is that the tax-related preferential treatment is applied to pillar companies in designated sectors. A part of the subsidies awarded to the large Chinese companies mentioned earlier has been in the form of tax subsidies, such as refunds of VAT, preferential and concessionary tax rates, exemption from certain tax surcharges, and other tax exemptions and tax credits for purchases of domestic equipment.

It is important to note that the Chinese government proved to be flexible in the use of tax policies to encourage or discourage international trade, depending on the internal and external economic situation. Despite the general long-term policy of withdrawing preferential tax treatment for exports, associated with the strategy of boosting domestic consumption, during the global economic crisis, certain tax privileges were temporarily restored. In October 2008, China raised tax rebates for 3,486 items from various labour-intensive industries and high value-added sectors (*China Daily*, 2008), and continued to do so until June 2009, to alleviate the effects of worldwide decreasing consumption. However, in order to fulfil its international obligations to limit the dynamics of growth in greenhouse gas emissions, it eliminated tax rebates for 406 items to discourage export manufacturing of highly polluting, highly resource-dependent and highly energy-consuming products (*People's Daily Online*, 2010). Additionally, in order to boost business activities, the government lowered the corporate tax in China's underdeveloped Western regions to 15% (*Deloitte*, 2012).

Price control and investment policy

Price control has been another common tool among the developmental states. In Japan, state-regulated pricing was aimed at achieving the desired allocation of resources. In the early stages of the DS core period, over 60,000 goods had their prices controlled. This number was subsequently reduced after the 'Dodge Line' reforms (1949–52).

China's reform period has been characterised by a dual price system, where certain sensitive goods, such as some grains, petrol, electricity, pharmaceuticals and so on, have had their prices controlled by the government. The intention of the dual system was to encourage industrial production via guarantees of state purchase of certain goods at a pre-set price. At the initial stage of reforms, however, there was almost full price control. In the mid-1980s, the price reform was aimed at partial price marketisation (Gao, 1987). By the end of the 1980s, half of the prices were market prices, whereas the other half were controlled, state-set prices. The price control mechanism is still an attractive instrument, as presented in the recovery package put forward by the Chinese authorities after significant shortcomings in energy caused by the strong snowfall in central and southern provinces during the winter of 2007/08. Nevertheless, the price liberalisation process imposed by WTO rules is extremely advanced, and the temporary attempts to administer the price level cannot be seen as a long-term element of the development policy.

Some of the financial system-related incentives presented earlier are aimed at navigating the financial resources flow into targeted industries, and can perhaps be seen as elements of overall investment policy. Naturally, investment policy can be categorised as trade-related or market-access policies – in the case of China, this would make sense in the context of SEZ and investment restrictions in certain industrial sectors. However, in the DS context, investment policy effectively channels funds to designated sectors and areas and can therefore be seen as a DS financial policy of support for industrial development.

In this respect, China went further than historical DS cases and, especially in the 2000s, large investments have also been directed towards rural areas, as agriculture seems to have become a targeted industry. Naturally, as pointed by Noland and Pack (2003), Japan also channelled large financial means towards the agricultural sector, though in the form of European-style subsidies. In China, the policy of targeting agriculture is visible in the amount of focus directed in the 11th and 12th Five-Year Plans towards development of the countryside's infrastructure and public services (Fock and Wong, 2008). The Hu–Wen regime channelled large financial resources to reconstruct education and health-care bases, whereas agricultural tax was eliminated to limit the fiscal burden on farmers. The Xi–Li administration has also promised extensive investments in rural areas.

However, as far as investment policy is concerned, an important feature of China's development model is FDI. In fact, 'in establishing an investment policy in post-Mao China, the policy was designed to gain the benefits of foreign direct investment (capital flow, job creation, export growth and the upgrading of technology and skills)' (Breslin, 2006, p 9). Furthermore, 'China's early and continued opening up to FDI ... stands in stark contrast to the experiences of other East Asian states, in particular Japan, Korea and Taiwan' (Gallagher, 2002, pp 366–7). Indeed, FDI did not seem to play a vital role in historical DS cases. Japan eventually became an important FDI exporter (Yamazawa, 1975), in addition to its historical colonial investment-related activities in Korea and Taiwan (see Cumings, 1984; Wade, 1990; Kohli, 1994). Its presence is particularly visible in China and in Southeast Asian countries such as Thailand (ASEAN's second-largest economy). In Korea, FDI seemed to play a marginal role. Nevertheless, Kim (1985) claims that the authorities were eager to attract foreign investment, especially into the special zones, such as Masan or Iri EPZ [Export Processing Zone] (see Yuan and Eden, 1992; Oh, 1993; Amirahmadi and Wu, 1995), as it played an important role in promoting the development of indigenous industries: 'Foreign capital was welcomed as long as it could contribute to the development of priority sectors, the transfer of technologies, and the enlargement of marketing contracts' (Kim, 1985, p 39). Nevertheless, 'the Korean and Taiwanese governments chose to keep their domestic economies closed and protected while taking the outward orientation [while] China's leadership opted instead for much greater integration with the global economy' (Gallagher, 2002, p 367).

In China, FDI has been an important part of investment policy and secured steady capital, technology and managerial skill flows into the country. This happened despite the prevailing 'communist' regime (Gallagher, 2002). As the largest recipient of FDI among all developing countries (Zhou and Latorre, 2013), between 1979 and 2010, China absorbed over USD1 trillion worth of foreign investment (Shambaugh, 2013). According to Tseng and Zebregs (2002, pp 5–6), 'equity joint venture companies, cooperative joint venture companies, and wholly foreign-owned enterprises have been the main forms of absorbing of FDI into China'. Initially, they were allowed only in SEZs, but already in 1986, this limitation was lifted. Although current investment is encouraged in most parts of the country, various special zones continue to have a legal and infrastructural edge in terms of attracting foreign investors. Despite the Catalogue (mentioned in Chapter Three), China remains one of the largest FDI destinations. Tseng and Zebregs (2002) name three groups of FDI determinants: economic structure (market size, abundant supply of cheap labour, infrastructure, scale effects); reduced barriers and preferential policies; and the cultural and legal environment. Foreign direct investments have been closely related to export-oriented production in the SEZs and to China's international trade, within the frames of the regional supply chains controlled by MNCs (Wong and Tsang, 2009), or what Kawai (2004) and others called the FDI–trade nexus. Zhou and Latorre (2013) emphasise that China has become a big assembly factory for MNCs; thus, 'FDI play a significant role in the rapid increase in vertical intra–industry trade' (Zhou and Latorre, 2013, p 2), as evidenced by the high foreign content of Chinese export (Zhou and Latorre, 2013, p 3). Between the years 1985 and 2008, East Asian economies provided 63% of foreign investment to China (Xing, 2010, cited in Zhou and Latorre, 2013, p 2).

The above comparative policy analysis illustrates certain distinctive features, as well as similarities, of China's development policies with the policies of the Japanese and Korean developmental states. The examples presented here show that China's authorities seem determined to closely supervise industrial development and international trade, through various industrial, trade-related and financial policies.

Having analysed the specific features of China's development trajectory in terms of ideological, political and economic arrangements, and state-level policies, as compared to the historical DS cases, and having established the distinctive elements of China's post-socialist transformation, we now turn to the final exercise of this book. The final chapter will attempt to explain the Chinese post-socialist development trajectory and to construct the model that China is believed to be following, namely, the post-socialist developmental state model. This model is also intended to provide a broader understanding of developmental issues in the post-socialist world and beyond.

CHAPTER FIVE

China as a post-socialist developmental state

The post-socialist developmental state

In Chapters One, Three and Four, we discussed the developmental state. We now turn our focus to its post-socialist version. The post-socialist developmental state (PSDS) model is a type of developmental state (DS) model within the frames of contemporary post-socialist transformation. It fuses the two intellectual streams of the developmental state concept and post-socialist transformation (PST). Its basic features are similar to those in the DS model adjusted by the PST process and different international conditions, as compared to historical DS cases. There can be various genera of the PSDS model, as each country would have its own variation of institutional features and policy solutions, and China's development trajectory represents one of those genera. The PSDS model brings into the discussion on the DS model two important elements: first, it debates its broader than usual applicability, extending it to a very particular group of countries in systemic transformation; and, second, it confronts the model with a different international conditionality than that experienced during the high-growth period of historical developmental states.

In addition to guiding the development trajectory by many means characteristic of the classical DS model, as examined earlier, the post-socialist developmental state has the task of systemic transformation. Consequently, the role of the state, in addition to actively supporting and enabling an effective development trajectory (which has somewhat been lost in the process of post-socialist transformation due to political and economic-doctrinarian reasons), also includes presiding over economic liberalisation, market institutionalisation and microeconomic restructuring. The PSDS should be characterised by selective, and perhaps cautious, economic liberalisation, as so-called 'shock therapy' has produced extensive economic contraction in the post-socialist world and subsequently significantly impaired developmental dynamics. The economic-systemic reorganisation creates two unfavourable conditions: first, the state's attention is captured by systemic transformation and development policies are usually neglected, as was the case in the majority of post-socialist states: and, second, the process leaves the economy in interim vulnerability due to the dissolving of old institutions and the creating of new ones. This 'transformational vulnerability' negatively affects the state's ability to maintain a stable, favourable environment for development. Within the process of systemic reformulation, the mechanism of state command or central planning needs to be replaced by indicative guiding planning rather than dismantled. The old economic bureaucracy needs to be restructured along DS lines. The paramount developmental agency not only takes up the task of coordinating overall development-related efforts, but is also responsible for designing and implementing systemic reforms and preventing developmental dynamics from being affected by transformational vulnerability. In the process of industrial development, a post-socialist developmental state should partly use the advantages of historical experiences of heavy and chemical industry (HCI) development. The PSDS initially employs the state-owned enterprises (SOEs) as the state's partner in the state–business alliance, as neither indigenous development of the private sector nor post-socialist privatisation offer at first adequate privately owned resources.

In short, the PSDS model is presented with additional tasks as compared with the historical DS model, as follows:

- A task of transformation of the systemic arrangements and of state interventionist mechanisms. The new institutions and laws allow a broader scope of economic activities by non-state-owned actors and facilitate the partial withdrawal of the state from directly controlling those economic activities. They redefine the state's role in guiding development.
- A task of counteracting the 'transformational vulnerability' connected to systemic reformulation and a lack of institutions, which creates an institutional and legal vacuum (Blanchard and Kremer, 1997). The DS model could be focused on development, whereas the PSDS model needs to address the issue of the systemically unstable economic environment. This can be achieved via maintaining a firm control over the reforms (a 'strong in capacity', interventionist state), by a gradual mode of transformation (as the shock therapy would weaken the state's ability to act) and by protectionist measures motivated by economic nationalism.
- A task of ensuring a capable partner for the state in the state–business alliance. The DS experiences suggest that this partner ought to represent a private sector. However, what seems to be

more important in the DS context is that it is a partner who can be effectively influenced. The post-socialist experiences suggest that it is difficult to extract such a partner from the private sector as discussed later.

- A task of reorganisation of the industrial sector. Unlike pre-DS countries, socialist states were extensively industrialised, and at the point of transformation, possessed a large industrial sector, dominated by heavy industry. The PSDS policy of industrial development would thus need to involve the restructuring of socialist industry to remain important for national development and to fit the frames of the post-socialist developmental state.

As far as the contemporary conditionality is concerned, the PSDS task of nurturing development is both easier and more difficult. There are essentially two groups of factors that need to be considered currently, and could have been ignored in the past. First, the global economic order is more intrusive. Consequently, a sophistication of trade and financial sector-related policies is necessary, as custom tariffs, quotas and arbitrary export–import link mechanisms, which were readily available for historical DS cases, may not be at the state's disposal contemporarily due to globalisation processes. A post-socialist developmental state needs to use its remaining domestic policies, such as fiscal policies and entry procedures, among other things, to encourage and to deter economic activities, and is required to increasingly negotiate its obligations and privileges in international forums. The second group of factors encompasses broad issues related to environmental pollution, climate change and the scarcity of energy and other resources. They constitute an integral part of any contemporary developmental model, and are believed to have an increasingly negative impact on the Chinese development trajectory. Environmental issues and climate change need to be taken into consideration as they affect the quality and pace of developmental changes. In the PSDS model, the imperative to consider environmental degradation as a threat to the development trajectory could specifically result in: the development of environment protection-related policies, regulations and mechanisms, as well as effective policies of adaptation and mitigation; the incorporation of environmental considerations into the strategy of sectoral development; and the development of a low-carbon and low-pollutant economy in general, through the reorganisation of the energy sector, transportation sector and industrial production, in order to gradually increase the share of green growth. However, the positive effects of globalisation are that a contemporary post-socialist developmental state has easier access to knowledge, that is, information and technologies. It seems, therefore, much easier to increase the quality of human capital as compared with the historical DS cases.

The constraints of the PSDS model are similar to those of the DS model, as discussed in Chapter One, meaning that in order to retain PSDS status, three sets of endogenous conditions must not occur extensively, that is, there is no broad departure from the DS institutional environment and policies, the pace of development continues to be relatively high, and the states in question are not as developed as so-called Western countries. Naturally, the PSDS countries must be recruited from formerly socialist states. Consequently, they must be effectively undergoing the process of systemic transformation from a state-command economy to a market economy. However, the completion of this process does not need to mean the termination of the PSDS model. A post-socialist economy remains post-socialist after the PST process has been completed. Perhaps a highly developed post-socialist state can still be a PSDS if it became a transformative state (see Weiss, 2000).

The PSDS model is largely in opposition to some general guidelines of economic conduct broadly advocated by affluent members of the so-called international community, such as limiting the role of the state and extensively liberalising national economies. Despite the failure of this neo-liberal economic doctrine, as illustrated not only by the growing disparities in Latin American countries in the 1990s and meagre developmental results of post-socialist states, but also by the 2008/09 global economic crisis, the terms associated with the DS and thus PSDS model in relation to state economic policies, such as 'economic nationalism', 'interventionism' and especially 'protectionism' (an instrument of economic nationalism), still seem to have a pejorative meaning. This is not due to the evident superiority of one set of policies and regulations over another, but due to the intense worldwide propaganda that poorly disguises the economic interests of the most affluent participants of international economic relations.

China and the post-socialist developmental state model

China's mode of post-socialist development has a number of similarities with the historical developmental states, as examined in this book, and may be perceived as an attempt to apply the provisions of neo-Listian political economy to the contemporary conditionality of systemic reformulation and to a new set of internal and external institutional features and processes. Although many aspects of China's development trajectory hardly seem a surprise, as it would be expected that the Chinese authorities would draw some lessons from neighbouring patterns of, indeed, very successful development, if we consider that China is undergoing a process of post-socialist transformation, which the historical developmental states did not, then its reform path and thus development trajectory seem highly unordinary when compared with other post-socialist cases. Indeed, many directions of China's transformation and development trajectory have been determined by the fact that China is following a type of DS model. This model can be described as a post-socialist developmental state model as it is based on the classical institutional and policy solutions of the DS model in the conditionality of post-socialist transformation. As has been analysed earlier, there is a plethora of policy and institutional choices that one may classify as determined by DS provisions.

As far as political-systemic reforms are concerned, China, as opposed to most Central and Eastern European (CEE) and some former Soviet Union (FSU) countries, did not undergo a process of democratisation. Instead, it chose to maintain a type of authoritarianism. This choice was motivated, among other things, by the Chinese Communist Party's desire to retain political control of the state. A legal prohibition of political contestation seemed to be the easiest solution. In the DS context, this was closer to the Taiwanese and the Korean cases than the Japanese case. The Japanese pattern would perhaps be difficult to establish in post-socialist China. The Japanese soft authoritarian institutions were not only required to preside over economic modernisation and development, but also used to shield the development trajectory from the democratically elected political elite's potential short-termist populism (see White, 1998), this populism being so prevalent in the newly established post-socialist democracies.

Naturally, political reformulation without liberalisation is hardly exceptional among post-socialist states. Many former Soviet republics have continued undemocratic practices. However, China's authoritarianism exhibits features of neo-authoritarianism or, as described by Woo-Cumings (1999) and Fewsmith (2008a), new authoritarianism, which advocates a strong, undemocratic state to guide the developmental advancements of a country. Contrary to many FSU countries, Chinese authorities effectively sought developmental legitimacy to stay in power. This indeed seems a rarity in the post-socialist world, but is nevertheless a rule among DS cases. The developmental and modernisation obsession among China's ruling elite during the process of systemic transformation has been clearly visible. Whereas in CEE, the motive of gaining political freedoms and establishing democracy prevailed, in the PRC, it was the acceleration of socio-economic development that justified reforms and opening up (see Deng, 1994; Jiang, 2010).

Retaining an authoritarian state was also aimed at creating a strong and capable state, following what White (1998) called a pessimistic view that authoritarianism is better suited for fast development in a developing country. Despite the purported erosion of state capacity (see Wang, 1997; Wang and Hu, 2001; Shirk, 2007), the authorities have attempted to strengthen their power and control (Howell, 1998) over society and the business sector. It is visible in their practice of forging links and relations with and influencing the newly emerging social structures (Dickson, 2001) that are the result of systemic changes. In the DS context, these links are intended to maintain an uneven relationship with other state actors (Leftwich, 2000), for example, through the policy of suppressing the labour force (Solinger, 2006), common in the historical DS cases (Gallagher, 2005). Indeed, the position of the working class is believed to have deteriorated during the PST process (He, 2000), partly due to ideological reformulation (see Solinger, 2003). At the same time, although the authoritarian regime is believed to be relatively autonomous and insulated despite a clamour of pressure, studies show that it strives for embeddedness through social dialogue (PP, 2009, 2010) to create some form of Evans's (1995) DS-style embedded autonomy, as examined in Chapter Three. This 'keeping at bay' of the various societal structures emerging during post-socialist transformation and attempting to effectively control societal interaction, in a way expected of the nominally communist regime, is accompanied by a gradual extension of negotiation and consultation channels with society and business, via experiments with rural democracy (O'Brien and Li, 2000), public soliciting of new laws (PP, 2009) and an increased consideration of public opinion (eg communicated through the Internet). This is because the Chinese authorities are searching for their own pattern of embedded autonomy (Evans, 1995) with a subordinate society (Leftwich, 2000).

As far as the economic aspects of the process of transformation are concerned, China's lack of approval of the Washington Consensus contrasts with many CEE and FSU countries, which at different stages of their transitions, followed its provisions. The Consensus was in dramatic opposition to the regulations prevailing and policies followed in the East Asian development model. The Chinese authorities chose a proven regional option rather than a theoretical framework with little evidence of success, despite the fact that it was often argued that the acceleration of economic growth required radical changes and rapid liberalisation and China was believed to be implementing the policy of 'growth at all costs'. Naturally, the political *rationale* for incremental changes was to maintain stability and control. Nevertheless, this is hardly a gradual pace of reforms, which indicates the affinity of the Chinese development trajectory with the DS model. Rather, it is the reform selectivity, focused on maintaining a tight grip over economic freedom in certain sectors of the national economy, partly via access barriers and investment limitations (see the Catalogue), and on establishing a strong domestic business base through market-distortive mechanisms. From a theoretical perspective, a strong domestic sector does not have to be an indispensable element of successful development. In fact, to enhance the competitiveness of their national economies, many post-socialist countries chose to partly liquidate their inefficient domestic industrial sectors or hand them over to foreign, so-called strategic, investors (Poznanski, 2000), who would provide know-how and raise the level of capitalisation. This policy was in line with many neo-liberal recommendations (Sachs, 1993, 1994). Despite suffering from common socialist countries' maladies of ineffective industries, China opted for a different variant of improvements and focused on the state-supervised strengthening of its domestic business base and state-controlled restructuring of companies. The process required time, resources and selective opening up, rather than broad and swift economic liberalisation, as it would be largely against so-called market forces. Theoretically, it was a more difficult and lengthier road to follow. However, it was a choice dictated by the DS logic as it would allow for the business sector to be retained in domestic hands.

China's post-socialist marketisation has also featured DS institutionalisation. In addition to establishing institutions characteristic of capitalist economies (OECD, 2009a), the reform focused on creating economic bureaucracy with an influential pilot agency to preside over economic modernisation. The powers of the National Development and Reform Commission (NDRC) almost equal those of the Korean Economic Planning Board (EPB) and far exceed those of the Japanese Ministry of International Trade and Industry (MITI). Moreover, a new coordinating body supervised by the head of state is being created. None of the CEEFSU countries structured their administrations to include such a prominent developmental agency, either due to the perception that economic planning is a relic of the past, or because the authorities would not search for developmental legitimacy and would secure their claim to power with other means. The two largest post-socialist economies of CEEFSU, Russia and Poland, lacked what could be described as a powerful economic bureaucracy and, suffice it to say, they did not seem to make any effort to create one. In the case of Poland, there was a ministry responsible for the privatisation of state assets known as the Ministry for Ownership Transformation (*Ministerstwo Przekształceń Własnościowych*), but there was no Ministry for Development. As far as central planning is concerned, the Chinese political elite saw it not only as compensating for economic liberalisation (Lau and Qian, 2000), but also as the DS-style 'plan-rational' to guide development (see Woo-Cumings, 1999). China did not relinquish extensive state interventionism, and state withdrawal from the economy was rather limited compared with many CEE states. In fact, during the PST period, it searched for new means and instruments of intervention to control various entities and processes. In the case of post-socialist Poland, state intervention and therefore also central planning were rapidly replaced by market forces (Kolodko, 1999a, 2001a); in the case of Russia, it was even without basic market institutionalisation at first.

State interventionism is common within the continental Western Europe capitalist model. The differences between classical European interventionism and DS interventionism were discussed in Chapter One: to developmentally catch up with developed nations (the DS model); to secure/maintain societal cohesion in the process of development (the Western European model). Chinese interventionism is much closer to the DS type in terms of general ideology. Despite usual official propaganda, it is not about social cohesion and the elevation of the less affluent parts of society – as proven by rapidly growing income disparities and the institutional discrimination of the less affluent rural part of society and the industrial working class – but about guiding the general process of socio-economic development.

Extensive state involvement in economic affairs has resulted in rampant corruption. Its intensity increased during the PST process (White, 1996; Kwong, 1997). Corruption is often rightly blamed for the developmental incapacity of ruling elites. More odd is that China's authorities do not pay sufficient attention to the problem, despite official propaganda. The reason being that in the DS model, corruption did not extensively affect the developmental trajectory due to it often being growth-promoting, as it would divert the resources to more effective economic entities (Bramall, 2009a). Although this does not need to be the current case in China, its real impact is to some extent questionable. Moreover, corruption serves some DS purposes, such as the deterrence of unwanted foreign economic agents and activities.

As far as the paramount state economic ideology is concerned, Levi-Faur (1997) distinguished three principal schools of political economy, namely, economic socialism, economic liberalism and economic nationalism. By employing this simplistic division, we can observe the difference between China and most of the other post-socialist countries. As a result of post-socialist transformation, China has replaced economic socialism with economic nationalism, as opposed to the economic liberalism preferred by most post-socialist states. Although a lack of full marketisation in a number of CEEFSU countries, as presented in reports of the European Bank for Reconstruction and Development (EBRD, 2001, 2005, 2008), may suggest that some countries have still not fully embraced economic liberalism as their main state ideology – and after over 20 years of transformation, may see it as unnecessary, hinting towards economic nationalism as a preferred philosophy in an increasingly interdependent and volatile world – China's economic nationalism has shown distinctive features of the DS model, not merely in the state's ability to mobilise the nation behind common developmental goals, but also in the state's ability to protect its domestic market. It is visible in: prohibitive procurement practices demanding, among other things, local content; discriminatory use of labour and competition laws aimed at targeting foreign entities; and arbitrary decisions related to economic activities, guided by ambiguous regulations of local and state authorities. Moreover, China's DS-style nationalism has not only been prominent in the economic sphere, but concerns a broader policy area of national economy, foreign affairs and security (Hughes, 2006). Security issues, in perhaps a more pronounced manner, were especially important in the context of East Asian nationalism (Cumings, 1984; Camilleri, 2000), although they do play a prominent role in contemporary China as well.

As far as China's development policies are concerned, it can plausibly be argued that they are to a great extent similar to the classical DS development policies and deviate from ordinary post-socialist policies. Rural policies in post-socialist China included a distribution of land to farmers rather than its restitution, as was the case in most CEE countries (Johanssen, 2001). Naturally, restitution would probably mean a partial return to feudal relations or at least to the rich peasant economy of the early 1950s (Bramall, 2009a). However, the CCP-controlled regime could have abandoned this policy and maintained the large commune units established in the late 1950s. It would be economically justifiable if only appropriate managerial changes and market institutionalisation took place in rural areas in the process of abandoning state command. For example, Poland's fragmented agrarian production structure, continuously dominated by smallholders, is rightly blamed for its ineffectiveness and the generating of social problems (see Borzutzky and Kranidis, 2005) and contrasts with states such as the Czech Republic, where large units remained mostly intact. At the same time, the revisionist pressure present in most CEE countries that led to restitution was not present in China. Moreover, empowering the farmers through land distribution could theoretically weaken the CCP position, whose persistent inadequate attention throughout the state-command period and prioritising of urban development resulted in rather limited support in rural areas. However, by creating family units and a household responsibility system, Deng Xiaoping addressed two important issues: first, it enabled a rapid rise in the volume of production, as China was experiencing food shortages; and, second, it nevertheless empowered farmers and created conditions for more effective wealth generation, bolstering rural support for the new economic policies. Increasing the volume of production and gaining support for further policies were very much the targets of the South Korean and Taiwanese land reforms (see Cumings, 1984; Wade, 1990; Alesina and Rodrik, 1994; Jeon, 1995; Doner et al, 2005). By fragmenting arable land, the Chinese authorities did not perhaps choose the optimal strategy for rural development. However, rural development was not of paramount importance, despite official propaganda. Rural policies served the purpose defined within the frames of the DS model and were to play an auxiliary role in industrial development. The 'targeting' of the rural economy seems only to be a relatively recent phenomenon.

The policy of industrial development was a permanent feature of socialist states (Brada, 1984). However, this policy was extensively neglected in the CEEFSU region during post-socialist transformation, at least at the beginning of transition, as it was believed that the best industrial policy is no industrial policy (Husan, 1997). The subsequent attempts to revive industrial policies after the dismantling of the planning bureaucracy and extensive external economic liberalisation were not effective. In Poland, as in other countries, they took the form of industrial restructuring, aimed at gradual advancements in the level of sophistication of the industrial product. In China, the policy of industrial development has not been abandoned during the post-socialist transformation. On the contrary, it has been characterised by all the features presented by Chang (1999b, 2009) in his analysis of East Asian industrial policy (see Chapter Four). The natural tendency of socialist states for import-substitution industrialisation (ISI) (despite the existence of Council for Mutual Economic Assistance[83]) has been supplemented by export-oriented industrialisation (EOI) in the

---

[83] Which China was not a member of.

post-socialist era, and industrial development was tuned into the DS pattern of gradual change in industrial targeting from labour-intensive to capital- and technology-intensive sectors. However, in order to follow what is often considered to be a classical developmental path, post-socialist China initially reversed its targeting and went from capital-intensive HCI to labour-intensive light industry development. This is not to say that it did not begin HCI restructuring, as it did. It is to stress that at the beginning of transformation, light industry development became the focus, despite the socialist heritage of having a more developed HCI sector. Naughton (2007) argues that it was due to the fact that the socialist development of HCI created an illusion of skipping the light industry development period. Nevertheless, China could have focused its efforts on the industrial restructuring of existing HCI, broadly considered to be more advanced, where it must have gained expertise and experience, and then continued to climb the developmental ladder. The reasons for light industry development are clear and convincing, as discussed in Chapter Four. Among them was also the desire to increase China's participation in international trade. The fastest way was perhaps by the rapid expansion of technologically not-intensive branches, which required a large number of workers with limited skills. As much as in other DS countries, China's industrial selection – the (supposedly developmentally reversed) choice of light industry, the (time-consuming) industrial restructuring of HCI and the gradual focusing on those industries with advanced technological content – was determined by the PRC's willingness to more extensively engage in international trade, as China's growth was intended to be export-led (Woo, 1999). Empirical evidence from the analyses of developmental states suggests it was export that was mostly responsible for securing dynamic economic growth in an underdeveloped country whose domestic purchasing power would not allow for internal consumption to be the initial driving force for socio-economic development. Naturally, other post-socialist states also considered international trade an important developmental factor; however, they never utilised the East Asian experiences to the extent that China chose to (Kokko, 2002). Export-led economic growth is an exception among post-socialist countries and the rule in developmental states.

Indeed, in its industrial targeting, China was guided not merely by gradual technological improvements in its production content, which is a common developmental pattern, but also by the content's international market receptiveness, which is more affiliated with the DS-style export-driven pattern of growth. Chinese authorities chose to develop industrial sectors previously not associated with China. In order to achieve this, they created an ambitious national research and development (R&D) programme accompanied by intensive inward technology transfer (Linden, 2004) characterised by an ambiguous attitude towards intellectual property rights (IPR) (PP, 2007).

The plethora of instruments used by the state in order to channel capital, technological and skill resources to the targeted sectors, partly illustrated in the closely monitored foreign investment policy, is overwhelming. Foreign technologies and expertise have been attracted, on one hand, by potential business opportunities and, on the other, by special investment conditions. Moreover, various aspects of monetary policy have not been aimed at macroeconomic stabilisation, but have focused on developmental issues. As in other DS cases and as opposed to most post-socialist CEE countries, the banking sector has not become an independent element of the market economy. The People's Bank of China (PBC) and the state-owned policy banks are developmental tools, and their decisions are based on the government's necessities to advance its agenda. China utilises DS-style indirect (rate manipulations, rebates and exemptions) and direct subsidies (direct payments) to targeted sectors and enterprises. Fiscal (tax) subsidies are also important instruments (see Wong et al, 1995).

It is often believed that in the contemporary international conditionality characterised by the process of globalisation, engagement in international trade is usually necessary for developmental advancements. Therefore, export promotion became a natural element of external economic activities. Most post-socialist countries have specialised agencies to assist exporters to gain access to new markets. In this respect, DS-style export promotion is perhaps not unusual. What is distinctive, however, is the domestic machinery to make exports more competitive by navigating financial system-related incentives. Chinese authorities not only resorted to political means of development cooperation with less developed countries and negotiated trade agreements with potentially important partners, but also employed comprehensive state regulatory machinery. An artificial exchange rate of the undervalued RMB is maintained to make exports more internationally competitive (Mehrotra and Sanchez-Fung, 2010; Yao et al, 2011). Export-oriented production is supported by various palettes of subsidies, as examined earlier. Moreover, what has been a distinctive feature in DS trade policy is import discrimination. China has used a number of tariff (eg import custom taxes) and non-tariff, including bureaucratic, barriers to selectively prevent imports. In order to comply with World Trade Organization (WTO) regulations, it developed a range of additional instruments to prevent its domestic market's penetration by foreign products and economic entities, for example, via very strict and ambiguous standardisation procedures (PP, 2009) or a deliberate ignoring of its own IPR regulations. It constructed a Catalogue of industries where a foreign presence is either limited or entirely forbidden due to ambiguous national security reasons.

However, not all of post-socialist China's solutions are perceived to be in line with DS arrangements and not all DS recipes are believed to have been implemented. For example, the authorities chose to rely on SOEs as partners for the state in state-led industrialisation. It contradicts the idea of the DS state–business alliance, which is based on public–private partnership. In both Japan and Korea, private companies were crucial in the development of various industries. China apparently chose to ignore this fact, at least as far as targeted capital-intensive industries are concerned.

Indeed, a developmental state would choose the most effective agents for implementation of its development strategy. In many aspects, it would be private companies. On average, they are more efficient in delivering results, as they have more clearly defined targets, that is, maximisation of profit, and more clearly defined beneficiaries, that is, the stakeholders. The SOEs are usually implicated in ambiguous 'extracurricular' activities and social targets, which may inhibit their effectiveness. Naturally, private companies in the DS environment were not free from these kinds of pressures. This was the case in both Japan and Korea. Nevertheless, the logical choice for post-socialist states would be to make sure that there is a supply of private companies. In the post-socialist conditionality, this could be achieved in two ways: first, via the privatisation of state companies. Socialist economies were characterised as hosting a number of relatively large SOEs. The second method would be to create an institutional environment for the growth of the indigenous private sector. The second option is, however, a time-consuming process, with ambiguous and often unpredictable results. Therefore, privatisation would be an easier and, thus perhaps, preferable option.

Let us here, however, present the main features of the privatisation outcomes of the two largest CEEFSU economies, namely, Russia and Poland. In the post-socialist world, privatisation was considered to be an important element of transformation (Dehesa, 1991; Kornai, 1992) and its implementation was, indeed, encouraged to be as fast as possible (Sachs, 1993; Williamson, cited in Kolodko, 1999a). In both cases, this process was rapid and extensive (Jermakowicz et al, 1994; Baka, 2004), gained some support in their respective societies, but ended up with dubious results (Poznanski, 2000; Klein, 2007).

The post-socialist privatisation process in the two countries had two distinguishing features, leading to the same conclusion in the context of our DS-related analysis. In Poland, it resulted in most of the sizable companies being transferred to foreign owners (Poznanski, 2000), usually in the same sector, as seen in a number of industries, from alcoholic beverages (Pernod Ricard bought the most famous Polish vodka trademark Wyborowa) to defence (PZL Swidnik and PZL Mielec, the helicopter manufacturers, were sold to the Italian–British company AgustaWestland and the US firm Sikorsky Aircraft Corporation, respectively), with all the possible sectors in-between. In Russia, the privatisation process did not result in the handover to foreign stakeholders. Instead, as a result of the appropriation of state assets, a caste of oligarchs was created, who commenced large transfers of their financial assets to more secure locations abroad in anticipation of the instability of the country's political system and, as a consequence, insecurity in terms of their economic status and wealth possession. To avoid the repossession of their wealth acquired in dubious conditions, they chose to invest much of their assets in other countries and not in Russia. The process of privatisation in both countries resulted in the effective elimination of potential economic agents for DS-style state-led developmental efforts. In the case of Poland, the picture is clear: companies are usually foreign-owned, and the handful of those that are domestically owned would not be able to carry on the task as their number fell short of even the relatively limited number of Korean *chaebols*. In Russia, the appropriation of state assets, often illicit in form, was not accompanied by regulations that would prevent the flight of capital and other assets, and the state was not able to effectively coerce the business sector into supporting the developmental endeavour until very recently.[84]

The outcomes of the Polish and Russian ownership reforms illustrate the rationality of China's choice to keep SOEs and to nominate them to be the main economic agents, if it were to follow the DS-patterned development trajectory during post-socialist transformation. The Polish failure to create a domestically controlled large business sector, in addition to the SOEs being, for obvious reasons, easier to manoeuvre into the state's policies, suggests that the PRC's reliance on the state sector may not have been a choice to regret entirely. Naturally, the Chinese authorities commencing transformation in the late 1970s could

---

[84] By no means am I trying to say that today's Russian government has a clear development strategy that it imposes on its business sector. I merely state the fact that it is perhaps creating conditions for an effective DS-style state–business relationship.

not have known Poland's and Russia's experiences of the 1990s. Initially due to ideological constraints, and later perhaps having observed the developmental logic of East Asian states and the rather ambiguous results of early privatisation efforts in CEEFSU, Chinese authorities chose to keep some important companies within the state's proximity and influence. The easiest way was to maintain state ownership. The history of the Rheinish capitalism of Western continental Europe (Hall and Sockice, 2001; Bramall, 2009b) was dotted with SOEs effectively operating as vital economic agents. Chang (2009) points to the Korean POSCO and the Brazilian Emraer not only as successful SOEs, but also as enabling the states to enter new sectors of world production and to become important players. Keeping 150 or so large SOEs as actors of the developmental endeavour meant that the Chinese authorities followed rather than ignored DS recommendations. Priority was given to the stability of the state–business alliance and to the effectiveness of control over the supposed effectiveness of performance.

The fact, however, that in the case of China, the main companies in the targeted industries are state-owned does not mean that China has not followed more directly certain Japanese and Korean patterns. On the contrary, in the 1990s and during the first decade of the 21st century, there was a certain level of intensification of mergers among the SOEs, as discussed in Chapter Two. After the 15th CCP Congress (in 1997), the Chinese authorities, using the economy of scale argument, started implementing a policy of grouping companies and creating large conglomerates, similar in size to *chaebols* and *keiretsu*, as the continuation of *zhu dà fàngxi o* (Gallagher, 2005; Breslin, 2007). The earlier-mentioned Shenhua, Baoshan, Sinopec and PetroChina are examples of the policy of creating a range of very large companies, with asset capacity, which would allow them to pull in sufficient resources to compete on the international scene dominated by multinational corporations (MNCs). In the case of Japan and Korea, it was the large companies who were predominantly responsible for implementing the state's industrial production plans.[85] This is also currently the case in China.

The reliance on state firms does not need to be a permanent feature. Initially, it seemed to be the logical choice, even from the DS perceptive. The state needed to secure a business partner for the state–business alliance who was most reliable and easy to manoeuvre into the developmental agenda. Japan and Korea had strong private

---

[85]   As opposed to Taiwan, where the development trajectory was mostly facilitated by small and medium enterprises and MNCs' subcontractors.

business sectors prior to the DS-proper period; China possessed large state-owned firms prior to systemic transformation. However, China will perhaps eventually rely on private companies in its DS-style development process. Accepting the business sector into the CCP (as a result of the concept of 'three represents'), and one of its most prominent members, the business tycoon Liang Wengen, into its governing bodies, is a sign of creating a Korean model-inspired close relationship between private business and the state. The mechanism of DS-style state–business alliance based on public–private partnership is thus under construction.

Another issue concerns growing disparities, as a result of which China is already positioned among the most unequal societies. It is a common opinion that developmental state policies eventually led to a higher degree of social cohesion. However, the DS model has never been about social cohesion. In fact, Korea experienced relatively large income disparities during the DS-proper period. Perkins (1994) rightly argues that some positive effects in this respect were side effects rather than deliberate targets. With that in mind, the Chinese authorities chose to ignore social necessities and focus, as developmental states did, on overall development. This was despite the initial strategies of 'not leaving any social group behind'.

What has clearly failed to form within the post-socialist Chinese state is the DS-style centralist character. Naturally, China is not a federalist state, despite some claims that it might eventually become one (see Cao et al, 1999; Chung, 2006), and the central party-state is still the most influential power centre. The government has been keen on tightening its grip on provinces, for example, by using Zhu Rongji's fiscal re-centralisation and the mechanism of rotating the leading state cadres. However, China is a very large, populous, diverse and underdeveloped country. Therefore, the centralism present in small Korea and Taiwan, or in medium-sized Japan, is perhaps unattainable. This directly affects China's ability to be a strong capable state. From the DS perspective, this can be seen as one of the main weaknesses in the PRC following some kind of DS development pattern.

In sum, the choices of the Chinese authorities as far as institutionalisation and policies during post-socialist transformation are concerned have been, to a significant degree, determined by the concept of the developmental state. This is why China has maintained a type of authoritarian political system, but nevertheless: sought developmental legitimacy and is seeking to create some sort of embedded autonomy; in the process of reforms, implemented selective liberalisation; let development policies, guided by economic nationalism, take priority over systemic changes; has been economically rather than socially oriented in its state interventionism, partly sustained by an influential central economic bureaucracy; was growth-obsessed, with this growth being driven by exports; focused on building a strong domestic business sector and a weak labour class; developed a large palette of policy mechanisms to support exports and discriminate against imports; and chose a strategy of industrial targeting with gradual technological upgrades and international market opportunities in mind. This is why it ignored corruption and growing disparities. This is also why in search of business partners for the DS state–business alliance, it prioritised effectiveness of control over type of ownership. Naturally, due to various internal and external factors, some policies and institutional arrangements differ from those in historical developmental states. For example, international trade-related policies, as well as market access regulations, had to be redefined due to the changes in international conditions. In this respect, China has managed to adapt to a new environment, as did Japan in the late 1960s after partial liberalisation, without abandoning the paramount philosophy of state developmental intervention.

Following the analysis of DS-determined choices in China's post-socialist development trajectory, one may argue that, in general, the PSDS explains many aspects of China's political reformulation, its focus on economic growth, its genus of market economy and its pattern of international engagement. More specifically:

- The method of retaining power by a nominal communist party. The CCP could follow other autocratic regimes, that is, increase or reformulate political repression, enrich itself, and ignore the economy. In the short term, it would be easier than implementing reforms of an ambiguous target and gradually empowering the nation with economic and other means.
- The prioritisation of long-term economic growth and economic modernisation for China to become a developed and modern economy, rather than focusing on systemic reforms to become a liberal market economy.
- Extensive state involvement in the economy to preside over economic modernisation and industrial development, despite proceeding with post-socialist economic liberalisation.
- The method of interaction with the global economy by incremental and selective opening up aimed at strengthening the domestic business sector and developing an export-oriented regime, by nurturing new, international-market receptive industries, in addition

to relying on historical advantages related to socialist industrial development.

There seems to be a plethora of scholarly literature on virtually all elements of China's development and transformation, providing analyses of why and how the state leadership chose particular ways to retain power and to develop the country. Naturally, there has been a number of ways of doing this, and although today China's choice is often considered to have been a developmentally better option than that taken by many other post-socialist states, China could have followed a very different route than it did in its systemic transformation and thus post-socialist development trajectory, namely, fast democratisation, extensive liberalisation and opening up. At the beginning of the transformation, it was not clear that post-socialist economies would plummet into extensive recession. On the contrary, it was believed that they would thrive after a perhaps short period of depression. China's policy and institutional selection, as well as mode of transformation, however, was the result of embracing the PSDS model.

The future

However, the reform and policy agenda presented after the 3rd plenum of the 18th CCP Congress (December 2013) is often interpreted as a clear signal towards the state's willingness to advance and accelerate economic liberalisation. The CCP leadership has been explicit about making the market mechanism more prominent, if not decisive, in the systemic institutionalisation. International commentators, partly provoked by Chinese state propaganda, seem to believe that the unveiled reforms might be as bold as those of the historical 3rd plenum of the 11th CCP Congress. Consequently, perhaps the idea of a post-socialist developmental state has finally been rejected? This question is particularly important at a time when the international community is intensifying its criticism of China's growth model and when the discussion on global and national systemic arrangements prompted by the 2008/09 economic crisis is gaining in impetus.

Heiduk (2012) asserts that although China came out of the crisis less harmed than many other countries, its economy was, nevertheless, hit through three channels: a decrease in export demand; a decline in foreign direct investment (FDI); and a loss of productivity due to the underutilisation of the capital stock, revealing certain shortcomings in its institutional design. The existence of these shortcomings is often claimed to be caused by the fact that, as opposed to many

PST countries, in China, development policies took priority over systemic transformation; hence, the Xi–Li administration's call for the acceleration of marketisation. Although international and Chinese economists and policymakers may not have a common understanding as to favourable future systemic arrangements for the PRC, they seem to be in agreement as to the necessary short-term steps that the country needs to take to advance development. China needs to change its growth model as the current pattern has become unsustainable and obsolete. This assertion may not necessarily be derived from China's de-acceleration of economic growth – in 2012 and 2013, China's pace of gross domestic product (GDP) growth slowed down to below 8% – as it is an expected phenomenon after many years of hyper-dynamics. Rather, it is based on the examination of the economic growth's quality and developmental effects. The necessity to change the model of growth has already been anticipated in the 12th Five-Year Plan (2011–15). In his detailed analysis of the document, In der Heiden (2012) points to four main areas of improvement necessary for the change in the growth model: increasing domestic consumption; creating an advanced service sector; promoting the competitiveness of manufacturing business in general and developing emerging strategic industries in particular; and advancing green development. Ding (2012) emphasises that the change in the growth model lies at the centre of the 12th Five-Year Plan. He believes that China's 'new magic triangle' consists of mutually reinforcing phenomena that will lead to further developmental advancements: social security, growth and openness. In its recent report entitled *Urban China: Towards Efficient, Inclusive, and Sustainable Urbanization*, the World Bank (2014), together with the Development Research Center of the PRC's State Council, emphasises that the process of urbanisation will continue to be central to developmental advancements as 'the great urban transformation' (see Hsing, 2010) continues. The report calls for a new model of urbanisation and names several areas necessary of reform, namely: land management; the *hukou* system; financial discipline for local governments; the sustainability of urban finances; urban planning and design; the management of environmental pressures; and governance at the local level.

Not surprisingly, environmental degradation and climate change surface as the main issues that need to be addressed in China's new growth model. Lin and Swanson (2010) underline that:

> the environmental challenges confronting the PRC are diverse and growing, and include the following:

> land degradation; water scarcity and pollution; air
> pollution; inadequate urban environmental infrastructure;
> contamination of the rural environment; increasing
> frequency and intensity of environmental accidents; loss of
> biodiversity; and global climate change. (ADB, 2007, p 1)

Cai and Du (2008) clearly link China's environmental problems to its growth pattern (see also Song and Woo, 2008; Lin and Swanson, 2010). As a result of China's industrialisation during the socialist and post-socialist period, as well as due to the prioritisation of growth over sustainable development in the contemporary conditions of environmental degradation, the pace and, most importantly, the quality of economic growth have already diminished and are likely to diminish even more in the near future. The developmental losses will be in the form of a slowdown in economic growth, either due to lost opportunities or decreased returns, as well as in the form of a decrease in the quality of economic growth, that is to say, the lack of the growth's translation into socio-economic development. As far as lost opportunities are concerned, environmental degradation will prevent the farming of certain lands that could have been or, indeed, were farmed in the past, due to soil, air and water pollution, as well as due to weather-related anomalies altering natural conditions. Certain types of industries that rely on pure water, pure air and so on will not be developed in specific areas, despite, for example, a growing local necessity for additional employment. The same applies to certain services that could have been established and provided, but due to environmental and environmentally related social and economic reasons, will not. Lost opportunities to develop industries, agriculture and services will have a direct negative impact on GDP growth, the labour market and additional consumption opportunities.[86] Environmental degradation will diminish the returns from various economic activities. This process is related to the decreasing productivity of land, as well as of people's labour. Pollution will affect the population's health, which will impact the effectiveness and the amount of work they can provide. Radical environmental anomalies may shorten farming periods. The new weather conditions will prompt outbreaks of diseases, and soil pollution will decrease the quality of farming and husbandry lands. Those phenomena are already extensively

---

[86] In a way, prompting a spiral of events as such additional consumption could facilitate the development of more industries and services.

affecting China's development and the authorities are increasingly paying more attention to the problems.

All this hints to the fact that development strategy changes are not only necessary, but also imminent. In no way, however, do these changes seem to be affecting PSDS principles. Economic liberalisation and market institutionalisation do not need to be against the PSDS model. Although, internationally, China is forced to operate in a more liberal environment than Japan and Korea did during their DS-proper period and has thus faced strong pressures for economic liberalisation, domestically, China's regulated market economy has still some space to limit interventionism to maintain its DS character. Moreover, Japan and Korea gradually liberalised their national economies in the process of shifting priorities determined by developmental advancements. Consequently, the announced plans for economic liberalisation and market institutionalisation do not suggest a departure from the DS. China will not become a North American-fashioned or even European-styled liberal economy in the close future. In fact, many decisions seem to be in line with PSDS expectations. This is because the problems that need to be solved can only be dealt with by the state.

Therefore, the head of the state is consolidating and strengthening his powers to supervise the reforms (using a small leading group) and to increase his grip on domestic security by chairing the national security commission. In particular, the small leading group could be an important structure to coordinate the multilayered process of economic transformation. It is intended to ensure more direct control over policies, partly as it was in the Korean DS during the Park Chung Hee era. At the same time, with a mass of publicity and a general perception as a reformer, Xi Jinping is building the support of the nation, thirsty for further modernisation efforts. This support will also increase in rural areas due to the promise of the extension of the mechanisms of consultation and of radical changes in the sphere of ownership of land, to a large degree aimed at empowering rural inhabitants. On one side, the state is again portrayed as a strong and capable state and, on the other, it is making advancements in building embedded autonomy. The intended ownership of land reforms in rural areas addresses another neglected sphere during China's transformation, which is important in the DS context, namely, property rights. It has usually been argued that the genus of the DS model would be difficult to establish without properly defined property rights. Although this does not need to be a correct assertion, the promised changes will undoubtedly be in the right direction as far as the DS perspective is concerned.

Although there are indications of a possibility for less discriminatory treatment of the private business sector, both domestic and foreign, it is explicit that SOEs will remain the main economic actors in strategic industrial sectors. The CCP reaffirms that the state will continue to rely on the by-default trustworthy partner in the state–business alliance. At the same time, increasing support for the private sector comes from the conviction that its auxiliary role is crucial, as well as from the fact that the large SOEs are becoming increasingly powerful, and that this alleged power, also of a political nature, needs to be curbed.

The current reform plan is perceived as an escape forward, as the current set of growth engines is becoming obsolete and further restructuring is necessary. This is inevitable in all fast-developing economies. Despite the proposed economic liberalisation and market institutionalisation, the changes and plans indicate the continuation of DS rules within the policy and institutional framework of the PSDS model. For example, the provisions of the 12th Five-Year Plan are clearly in line with PSDS recommendations: technological upgrading and new industrial targeting. The strengthening of the central power centre, at the same time as empowering neglected rural residents, and more direct supervision of the reforms, as well as further economic liberalisation without degrading the role of SOEs, if realised, will all indicate that the PSDS is there to stay, at least for some time.

Therefore, one can assume that the future development trajectory will most likely be characterised by the Chinese authorities' continuing favouring of market-distortive mechanisms and intervention, especially visible in state development policies. They will search for new, perhaps more subtle, mechanisms for the state to preside over development in order to adapt to global changes in the international economic order and to the dynamically changing domestic situation, as has been visible with the reform and the policy agenda after the 3rd plenum of the 18th CCP Congress. The policy of industrial development will push for more technological advancements (as indicated in the 12th Five Year Plan), whereas the policy for export support will gradually be weakened during the attempt to divert the focus towards domestic consumption. It is likely that Chinese legislators will accelerate economic liberalisation and, in this respect, more effectively adopt certain norms believed to be the domain of developed, Western nations, as the authorities are already adamant that they favour more market forces. It will be hailed as a great success of the international community, but, in reality, it will be dictated by internal conditions and necessity, and international pressure would have played an important but rather auxiliary role. For example, domestic market penetration in various sensitive sectors might be permitted once they are fully controlled by Chinese companies and those companies reach the capital, technological and managerial level that will enable them to effectively deter MNCs. Intellectual property rights will be embraced once Chinese companies begin to lose more than they gain without protection. Finally, political liberalisation will lead to a liberal democracy. This was the case in Korea and Taiwan. An increasingly affluent and educated Chinese society will eventually demand non-material goods. It is sometimes claimed that contrary to official propaganda, the Chinese authorities accept the inevitability of political liberalisation and are believed to be preparing themselves and the nation. Perhaps the next generation of leaders – rumour has it that they might be Hu Chunhua (party secretary of Guangdong province) and Sun Zhengcai (party secretary in Chongqing) – will be the last state leaders chosen without nationwide democratic elections.

However, the PSDS model not only serves the purpose of explaining China's post-socialist development trajectory. In general, it offers 'transferable lessons' – to borrow the phrase from Evans (1998) – as to how to maintain an effective development trajectory during the post-socialist transformation and contemporary international conditionality. Despite neo-liberal propaganda, it can be argued that the PSDS was perhaps more desired and a more natural choice for the post-socialist states than was the neo-liberal economic model guided by the provisions of the Washington Consensus. This is visible in the analysis of China's development trajectory during the systemic transformation throughout this book. The argument can be summarised in three points.

First, due to the insufficient developmental results in socialist times, the post-socialist states of CEEFSU hoped for the acceleration of economic growth as a result of systemic transformation. In fact, it is often claimed that in CEE and in the Soviet Union, socialism collapsed rather than was dismantled (Kolodko, 1999a) due to limited developmental achievements. The DS model, on which the PSDS has been built, was the most successful developmental option in the history of the second half of the 20th century, whereas the neo-liberal model did not bring any recognisable acceleration of development in countries in which it was applied.

Second, socialist states prior to the transformation already possessed a number of institutional features necessary for the implementation of a genus of the DS model. The state-command system positioned the state as the paramount power centre to design and implement developmental plans. Socialist countries were usually unitary, centralised states. They had experience in and institutional mechanisms for central planning. Naturally, the DS plan-rational varies significantly from socialist state command. Nevertheless, the socialist experiences would have been invaluable in creating a new planning mechanism. Socialist states possessed an extensive planning bureaucracy, which could have been transformed into the economic bureaucracy of the DS model. The bureaucrats lacked the knowledge of market and market mechanisms, but possessed essential knowledge of designing centralist developmental strategies. By definition, socialist countries were interventionist and their elites decided which industries to develop and what and how much to produce. In this respect, the difference between the DS model and socialism was in the agents of the developmental endeavour and the institutional mechanisms used for industrial development. However, the concept of the state guiding industrial development via some sort of planning was closely related. The alternative to the PSDS was the neo-liberal model, where central planning and state interventionism were abandoned, the centralised state was decentralised, and the state bureaucracy was effectively dismantled. As a result, the central state was weakened and retreated from the economy. The shock therapy recommended by the proponents of the Washington Consensus would favour building new institutions 'from scratch' and ignoring the positive institutional legacy of socialism. As empirical experiences illustrate, this pattern of development was initially counterproductive, whereas in the long term, it brought limited positive effects.

Third, the socialist legacy would create some favourable conditions for the process of DS industrial development. Socialist states were relatively well industrialised and their societies were well educated. Industrialisation was key to DS-style development and human capital quality was paramount for Japanese post-Second World War advancements, whereas a lack of an adequate level of qualified cadres forced Korea to pay much more attention to nurturing a local educational base. Japan and Korea were also characterised by large enterprises as the agents for industrial development. Socialist states possessed a number of large SOEs, who, upon adequate restructuring, could become important *keiretsu- and chaebol*-style partners for the PSDS state–business alliance. Finally, socialist states had a domestically owned banking sector, considered a necessary condition for the DS financial policy of support for industrial development and international trade, as this banking sector role would go beyond that reserved in traditional Western capitalism. The neo-liberal model offered open market competition to the socialist companies, who had never operated in the market conditionality and would have to compete against experienced MNCs, leading, at best, to the shifting of industrial decision-making abroad and, at worst, to the dismantling of the industrial base. It also offered privatisation of the banking sector as a necessary restructuring activity, which would inevitably lead to eliminating banks as DS-style developmental agents.

Consequently, the Chinese authorities selected a more 'natural' institutional and policy choice of systemic transformation to facilitate the post-socialist development trajectory, despite it being unordinary. Moreover, by having adopted the PSDS model, they provided us with useful insight into possible future scenarios of China's transformation and development trajectory.

Institutional arrangements enabling state-guided development, policy solutions focusing on industrial development and a selective engagement with the global economy and state ideology defending national economic interests, as analysed in this book, can all, in one way or another, be considered as applicable to a broader audience. The main message, however, is that the role of the state (ie the ruling political elite and the administrative bureaucracy) in the process of socio-economic development of underdeveloped countries and countries in systemic reformulation is of paramount importance, and no imaginary market forces are able to effectively preside over developmental advancements. This message is particularly important at a time when the discussion on the favourable national and global institutional arrangements after the global economic crisis is broadening and intensifying, and the critics of contemporary capitalism are becoming louder.

Naturally, most of the recent economic and systemic crisis-related literature deals with the causes and consequences of the global financial crisis of 2008/09 (see, eg, Cooper, 2008; Bliss and Kaufman, 2010; Foster and McChesney, 2012). A financial crisis is, it seems, an inevitable element of the socio-economic landscape of the world. Only in the last two decades have there been several, for example, the 1997 financial crisis, which extensively affected the economies of East Asia (see Goldstein, 1998; Haggard, 2000; Klein and Shabbir, 2006), but nevertheless, as explained in Chapter One, hardly dislocated the principles of the DS model. However, the recent financial crisis in some industrial nations, which became a global economic crisis (see Stiglitz, 2010), dubbed the Great Recession (Chacko et al, 2011; Kolb, 2011), has been particularly painful, to the extent that it has often been compared with the Great Depression of 1930. Various aspects and different stages of this crisis have been given attention in numerous analyses. They often point to the 'innovativeness' of the actors of the financial markets (Albo et al, 2010), and, indeed, the financial alchemy (Nesvetailova, 2010), which triggered the crisis. It is the insufficiencies in the US model, the cradle of the crisis, which are given special attention (see

Bonner and Wiggin, 2006; Shiller, 2008; Foster and Magdoff, 2009; Kolb, 2011). In its extensive 650-page report entitled 'Wall Street and the Financial Crisis: The Anatomy of a Financial Collapse' (Levin and Coburn, 2011), the US Senate cites regulatory failures as one of the reasons for the global economic crisis. A lack of regulation explicitly and inadequate state intervention implicitly are blamed for the havoc. Therefore, *The Stiglitz Report* (Stiglitz, 2010) suggests the restoration of the state as the appropriate regulator.

A bulk of contemporary scholarly literature also deals with the issue of adjustment of the growth models and the reformulation of the global institutional order to mitigate climate change and environmental degradation (see Owen and Hanley, 2004; Lopez and Toman, 2006; Giddens, 2009; Bulkeley and Newell, 2010). As Speth (2008, p 234) puts it, 'the seriousness of looming environmental threats is slowly sinking in, driven largely by climate issues but also informed by the outpouring of serious books and articles pointing out that various breakdowns and collapses are actually possible'. Moreover, some analyses emphasise the unfairness of globalisation and its dangerous side effects (see Stiglitz, 2004; Krugman, 2000; Steingart, 2008; Panic, 2011), such as growing disparities and thus marginalisation and increasing vulnerability, particularly of the less developed countries' economies.

The critics of the financial market's lack of constraints, of the development models with inadequate attention to environmental degradation and climate change, and of globalisation as a whole, call for the overhaul of national systems and the global order. The world has not become flat and neo-liberalism did not lead to the end of history. The crisis of the capitalist systemic arrangements is perhaps more evident than ever. *The Stiglitz Report* (Stiglitz, 2010, p 1) emphasises that 'the crisis has exposed fundamental problems, not only in national regulatory systems affecting finance, competition and corporate governance, but also in the international institutions and arrangements created to ensure financial and economic stability' (see also Joyce, 2013). Many call for more explicit state interventionism. Scott (2011, p 611) states that:

> the essential lesson of the last 30 years is that self-regulation of capitalism is an ideological fig leaf that hides a superficial understanding of a system that requires the coercive powers of government to restrain the competitive urges of many of its leading players.

Griffith-Jones et al (2010) declare that it is time for 'a visible hand' in the market. Giddens (2009) calls outright for the return of some sort of planning – the necessity especially evident, according to him, in the failures in the area of the environmental protection: 'There has now to be a return to greater state interventionism, a conclusion that is reinforced by the failure of deregulation' (Giddens, 2009, p 96). Needless to say, the calls for state involvement, more prominent planning and amending the failures of deregulation hint at institutional and systemic solutions consistent with the DS and the PSDS recommendations. So, too, do Chang's (2010) suggestions on how to rebuild the world economy. He compares capitalism to a machine that needs careful regulation and steering to operate properly. He underlines that the 'government needs to become bigger and more active' (Chang, 2010, p 337), especially in developing countries, which are particularly disadvantaged as far as the effects of economic crises are concerned (see also Stiglitz, 2010).

The process of rejection of neo-liberalism is accompanied by an increase in the interest in a variation of the DS arrangements in other continents than Asia. It is interesting to see how the DS model becomes more prominent in Africa. The continent is seen as the new high-growth region, with challenges similar to those faced earlier by East Asian economies, mostly related to a large incidence of poverty. It is, then, by all means natural that the discussion on adequate development models therein also includes that which brought the biggest successes in the second half of the 20th century. The idea of constructing an African developmental state has floated around at least since the 1990s (Mkandawire, 2001) and is, indeed, believed to have peaked in the 21st century (Mbabazi and Taylor, 2005). Due to its authoritarian political arrangements and high growth, Ethiopia is often mentioned as a possible example (Desta, no date; Kefale, 2011). However, as many countries on the continent have been undergoing democratisation processes, the African developmental state has been connected with the constructing of a democratic developmental state (Edigheji, 2005; Olayode, 2005). Botswana and Mauritius have often been seen as good examples. Sometimes, Uganda and South Africa are also mentioned.

However, as far as the PSDS model is concerned, it may be useful for some post-socialist economies, especially in times of the increasing prominence of post-socialist states (see Bolesta, 2013b; Heiduk, 2013; Piatkowski, 2013), but not for all. Undoubtedly, the new member states of the European Union (EU) and the countries in the process of accession negotiations have already selected the mode that they would like to follow in terms of development. On the one hand, these states are limited in their competences by the imposition of EU regulations and, in the case of accession negotiations, by EU guidelines. On the other hand, the inevitable consequence of the multilayered convergence with the entire relatively wealthy bloc of the EU, partly via cohesion policy, immensely contributes to their developmental dynamics. Some provisions of the PSDS model might thus be useful for those states whose development trajectory depends predominantly on the institutional and policy choices made by their political elite, as they are not part of or in proximity to the EU. Undoubtedly, countries that still seem to be in the process of post-socialist transformation and are in need of development lie in the Caucasus region and in Central Asia. Russia is also a good candidate, where some PSDS-style efforts have recently taken place. Moreover, for Cuba and North Korea, who did not commit to the process of systemic transformation, some PSDS provisions might, indeed, be useful to prevent extensive economic contraction and to build fundamentals for long-term sustainable development, if the respective leaderships decide to reform the state-command system. Vietnam and Laos are already successfully implementing PSDS provisions. Mongolia can still become a PSDS in view of its recent policy reformulation and more intense state involvement in some elements of the national economy.[87] So can Myanmar. Finally, most of the PSDS features, those related to the DS model, can perhaps serve as guidelines of conduct to be considered by any developing country – as mentioned earlier in relation to the possible emergence of the African developmental states – who would like to embark on an effective developmental catching-up trajectory and is committed to withstanding the pressure of the affluent entities within the contemporary international economic and political order. This pressure may be weakening due to the intensified criticism of the current mode of world capitalism. So there is hope ...

[87]   Personal observations from consultations with the governmental officials in Ulan Bator, 21–29 August 2011.

References

ADB (Asian Development Bank) (2007) *Country Environmental Analysis for the People's Republic of China*, Manila: Asia Development Bank.

Ahrens, J. (1999) Towards a Post-Washington Consensus: The Importance of Governance Structures in Less Developed Countries and Economies in Transition. In: Hermes, N. and Salverda, W. (eds.) *State, Society and Development; Lessons for Africa*, CDS Research Report, 7, Goetingen: University of Goetingen.

Akamatsu, K. (1962) A Historical Pattern of Economic Growth in Developing Countries. *Journal of Developing Economies*, 1(1), pp 3–25.

Albo, G., Gindin, S. and Panitch, L. (2010) *In and Out of Crisis: The Global Financial Meltdown and Left Alternatives*, Oakland: PM Press.

Alder, S., Lin, Sh. and Zilibotti, F. (2013) Economic Reforms and Industrial Policy in a Panel of Chinese Cities. Available at: www.econ.uzh.ch/faculty/zilibotti/publications/AlderShaoZilibotti_CEPR_Oct28.pdf

Alesina, A. and Rodrik, D. (1994) Distributive Politics and Economic Growth. *Quarterly Journal of Economics*, 109(2), pp 465–90.

Allen, F., Qian, J. and Qian, M. (2008) China's Financial System: Past, Present, and Future. In: Brandt, L. and Rawski, T.G. (eds) *China's Great Economic Transformation*, Cambridge: Cambridge University Press, pp 506–68.

Amirahmadi, H. and Wu, W. (1995) Export Processing Zones in Asia. *Asian Survey*, 25(9) (September), pp 828–49.

Amsden, A.H. (1989) *Asia's Next Giant: South Korea and Late Industrialisation*, Oxford: Oxford University Press.

Anderson, J. (2007) Is China Export-Led? *Asia Focus*, 27 September.

Aoki, M. and Patrick, H. (eds) (1994) *The Japanese Main Banking System. Its Relevance for Developing and Transforming Economies*, New York, NY: Oxford University Press.

Arrighi, G. (2007) *Adam Smith in Beijing. Lineages of the Twenty-First Century*, New York, NY: Verso.

Aslund, A. (1991) *Gorbachev's Struggle for Economic Reform*, Ithaca, NY: Cornell University Press.

Aslund, A. (1995) *How Russia Became a Market Economy*, Washington, DC: Brookings Institution Press.

Bachman, D. (1986) Differing Visions of China's Post-Mao Economy: The Ideas of Chen Yun, Deng Xiaoping, and Zhao Ziyang. *Asian Survey*, 26(3), pp 292–321.

Baek, S.-W. (2005) Does China Follow 'the East Asian Development Model'? *Journal of Contemporary Asia*, 35(4), pp 485–98.

Baka, W. (2004) Ekonomiczne idee Okrągłego Stołu po piętnastu latach. Wnioski na przyszłość. In: Kolodko, G.W. (ed) *Strategia Szybkiego Wzrostu Gospodarczego w Polsce*, Warsaw: WSPiZ.

Balcerowicz, L. (1997) *Socjalizm, Kapitalizm, Transformacja: Szkice z przełomu epok*, Warszawa: PWN.

Balcerowicz, L. (1998) *Wolność i rozwój. Ekonomia wolnego rynku*, Krakow: Wydawnictwo Znak.

Balcerowicz, L. (2003) Post-Communist Transition in A Comparative Perspective. Presentation at the World Bank, Washington, DC, 18 November.

Beeson, M. (2004) The Rise and Fall (?) of the Developmental State: The Vicissitudes and Implications of East Asian Interventionism. In: Low, L. (ed) *Developmental States: Relevancy Redundancy or Reconfiguration?*, New York, NY: Nova Science Publishers.

Benoit, E. (1978) Growth and Defense in Developing Countries. *Economic Development and Cultural Change*, 26, pp 271–80.

Benton, G. and Lin, Ch. (eds) (2010) *Was Mao Really a Monster? The Academic Response to Chang's and Halliday's Mao: The Unknown Story*, London and New York, NY: Routledge.

Bernard, M. and Ravenhill, J. (1995) Beyond Product Cycles and Flying Geese: Regionalization, Hierarchy, and the Industrialization of East Asia. *World Politics*, 47(2), pp 171–209.

Blanchard, O. and Kremer, M. (1997) Disorganization. *Quarterly Journal of Economics*, 112(4), pp 1091–126.

Blecher, M. (2002) Hegemony and Workers' Politics in China. *The China Quarterly*, 170, pp 283–303.

Bliss, R.R. and Kaufman, G.G. (eds) (2010) *Financial Institutions and Markets: The Financial Crisis – An Early Retrospective*, New York, NY: Palgrave MacMillan.

Block, F. (2008) Swimming against the Current: The Rise of a Hidden Developmental State in the United States. *Politics Society*, 36, pp 169–206.

Boettke, P.J. (2004) Hayek and Market Socialism: Science, Ideology, and Public Policy. The 2004 Hayek Lecture at the London School of Economics, 19 October.

Bolesta, A. (2004) Management of the Chinese State-Owned Enterprises in the Times of Systemic Transformation, *Optimum-Economic Studies*, 4(24).

Bolesta, A. (2006) *China in the Times of Transformation: Systemic Reforms, Development Policy and State-owned Enterprises*, Warsaw: Dialog Academic Publishers.

Bolesta, A. (2007) China as a Developmental State. *Montenegrin Journal of Economics*, 3(5), pp 105–11.

Bolesta, A. (2013a) Myanmar's Post-Socialist Economic Transformation. *Mizzima News*, 16 March.

Bolesta, A. (ed) (2013b) *From Central Planning to Market: Poland's Transformation in a Comparative Perspective and the Lessons for Myanmar*, Bangkok: Chulalongkorn University Printing House.

Bonner, W. and Wiggin, A. (2006) *Empire of Debt: The Rise of an Epic Financial Crisis*, New Jersey, NJ: John Wiley and Sons, Inc.

Borzutzky, S. and Kranidis, E. (2005) A Struggle for Survival: The Polish Agricultural Sector from Communism to EU Accession. *East European Politics and Societies*, 19, pp 614–54.

Bowles, P. and Dong, X. (1994) Current Successes and Future Challenges in China's Economic Reforms. *New Left Review*, I(208), pp 49–76.

Brada, J.C. (1984) Industrial Policy in Hungary: Lessons for America. *Cato Journal*, 4(2), pp 485–520.

Bramall, Ch. (2004) Chinese Land Reform in Long-Run Perspective and in the Wider East Asian Context. *Journal of Agrarian Change*, 4(1/2), pp 107–41.

Bramall, Ch. (2009a) *Chinese Economic Development*, Abingdon: Routledge.

Bramall, Ch. (2009b) Out of the Darkness: Chinese Transition Paths. *Modern China*, 35, pp 439–49.

Brandt, L. and Rawski, T.G. (eds) (2008) *China's Great Economic Transformation*, Cambridge: Cambridge University Press.

Brandt, L., Rawski, T.G. and Sutton, J. (2008) China's Industrial Development. In: Brandt, L. and Rawski, T.G. (eds) *China's Great Economic Transformation*, Cambridge: Cambridge University Press, pp 569–632.

Braudel, F. (1977) *Afterthoughts on Material Civilization and Capitalism*, Baltimore, MD: Johns Hopkins University Press.

Breslin, Sh. (1992) China's Interrupted Evolution. In: Hill, R.J. (ed) *Beyond Stalinism: Communist Political Evolution*, London: Frank Cass & Co. Ltd., pp 63–83.

Breslin, Sh. (1996) China: Developmental State or Dysfunctional Development? *Third World Quarterly*, 17(4), pp 689–706.

Breslin, Sh. (1999) China: The Challenges of Reform, Region-building and Globalisation. In: Grugel, J. and Hout, W. (eds) *Regionalism Across the North–South Divide. State Strategies and Globalisation*, London: Routledge, pp 86–101.

Breslin, Sh. (2003) Reforming China's Embedded Socialist Compromise: China and the WTO. *Global Change, Peace and Security*, 5(3), pp 213–30.

Breslin, Sh. (2004) Capitalism with Chinese Characteristics: The Public, the Private and the International. Asia Research Centre's Working Paper, 104, June, Perth: Murdoch University.

Breslin, Sh. (2006) Foreign Direct Investment in the PRC: Preferences, Policies and Performance. *Policy & Society*, 25(1), pp 9–38.

Breslin, Sh. (2007) *China and the Global Political Economy*, Basingstoke: Palgrave MacMillan.

Brinkley, F. (1904) *Japan and China: Its History, Arts and Literature* (vol 12), London: T.C. & E.C. Jack.

Brodsgaard, K.E. and Chen, G. (2009) *China's Attempt to Professionalise its Civil Service*. EAI Background Brief 494, Singapore: East Asia Institute.

Brugger, B. and Kelly, D. (1990) *Chinese Marxism in the Post-Mao Era*, Stanford, CA: Stanford University Press.

Bulkeley, H. and Newell, P. (2010) *Governing Climate Change*, Abingdon and New York, NY: Routledge.

Cai, F. (2010a) The Developmental State in the Globalizing World. Paper, University of York. Available at http://www.e-ir.info (accessed 25 March 2014).

Cai, F. and Du, Y. (2008) The Political Economy of Emissions Reduction in China: Are Incentives for Low Carbon Growth Compatible? In: Song, L. and Woo, W.T. (eds) *China's Dilemma: Economic Growth, the Environment and Climate Change*, Canberra: ANU E Press and Asia Pacific Press, pp 226–42.

Cai, K. (2010b) *The Politics of Economic Regionalism: Explaining Regional Economic Integration in East Asia*, Basingstoke: Palgrave MacMillan.

Cai, Y. (2002) Relaxing the Constraints from Above: Politics of Privatising Public Enterprises in China. *Asian Journal of Political Science*, 10(2), pp 94–121.

Camilleri, J. (2000) *States, Markets and Civil Society in Asia-Pacific*, Cheltenham: Edward Elgar.

Cao, Y., Qian, Y. and Weingast, B.R. (1999) From Federalism, Chinese Style to Privatization, Chinese Style. *Economics of Transition*, 7(1), pp 103–31.

CCM (2010) *Wind Turbine Components. China Insights*, Guangzhou: CCM International Ltd.

CCPIT (China Council for Promotion of International Trade) (2008) Nature and Functions. China Council for the Promotion of International Trade. Available at: http://english.ccpit.org/Contents/ Channel_402/2006/0525/840/content_840.htm (accessed 10 October 2008).

CCS (China's Customs Statistics) (2007) *China's Customs Statistics (Monthly Exports and Imports), 220*, Beijing: General Administration of Customs.

CCS (2009) *China's Customs Statistics (Monthly Exports and Imports), 244*, Beijing: General Administration of Customs.

Cereseto, Sh. and Waitzkin, H. (1986) Economic Development, Political-Economic System, and the Physical Quality of Life. *American Journal of Public Health*, 76(6), pp 661–6.

Chacko, G., Evans, C.L., Gunawan, H. and Sjoman, A. (2011) *The Global Economic System: How Liquidity Shocks Affect Financial Institutions and Lead to Economic Crises*, New Jersey, NJ: FT Press.

Chand, G. (1965) *Socialist Transformation of Indian Economy*, Mumbai: Allied Publishers.

Chandler, A.D. (1977) *The Visible Hand: Managerial Revolution in American Business*, Cambridge: Harvard University Press.

Chang, Ch. and Wang, Y. (1994) The Nature of the Township-Village Enterprise. *Journal of Comparative Economics*, 19, pp 434–52.

Chang, H.-J. (1999a) The Economic Theory of the Developmental State. In: Woo-Cumings, M. (ed) *The Developmental State*, Ithaca, NY: Cornell University Press, pp 182–99.

Chang, H.-J. (1999b) Industrial Policy and East Asia – The Miracle, the Crisis, and the Future. A revised version of the paper presented at the World Bank workshop on 'Re-thinking East Asian Miracle', 16–17 February, San Francisco.

Chang, H.-J. (2002) *Kicking Away the Ladder. Development Strategy in Historical Perspective*, London: Anthem Press.

Chang, H.-J. (2009) Industrial Policy: Can We Go Beyond an Unproductive Confrontation? A plenary paper for Annual World Bank Conference on Development Economics (ABCDE), 22–24 June, Seoul.

Chang, H.-J. (2010) *23 Things They Don't Tell You About Capitalism*, London: Penguin Books.

Chang, H.-J., Park, H.-J. and Yoo, Ch.-G. (1998) Interpreting the Korean Crisis: Financial Liberalisation, Industrial Policy and Corporate Governance. *Cambridge Journal of Economics*, 22, pp 735–46.

Chang, J. and Halliday, J. (2005) *Mao: The Unknown Story*, New York, NY: Alfred A. Knopf.

Chatham House (2007) *Changing Climates: Interdependencies on Energy and Climate Security for China and Europe*, London: The Royal Institute for International Affairs.

Che, J. and Qian, Y. (1998) Institutional Environment, Community Government, and Corporate Governance: Understanding China's Township-Village Enterprises. *Journal of Law, Economics, and Organization*, 14(1), pp 1–23.

Chen, A. (2002) Socio-Economic Polarization and Political Corruption in China: A Study of the Correlation. *Journal of Communist Studies and Transition Politics*, 18(2), pp 53–74.

Chen, A. (2003) Rising-Class Politics and its Impact on China's Path to Democracy. *Democratization*, 10(2), pp 141–62.

Chen, J. (2011) China Should Adhere to Scientific Outlook on Development. *People's Daily Online*, 5 August. Available at: http://english.peopledaily.com.cn/90780/91342/7561184.html (accessed 5 February 2012).

Cheng, T.-J., Haggard, S. and Kang, D. (1998) Institutions and Growth in Korea and Taiwan: The Bureaucracy. *Journal of Development Studies*, 34(6), pp 87–111.

China Daily (2007a) Political Reform Will Be Pursued. *China Daily*, 15 October, p 1.

China Daily (2007b) Scientific Outlook on Development. *China Daily*, 12 October.

China Daily (2008) China to Raise Export Rebates for Textile, Garments. *China Daily*, 21 October. Available at: http://www.chinadaily.com.cn/china/2008-10/21/content_7126456.htm (accessed 21 June 2010).

Cho, D.-S., Lee, D.-H., Ryu, S.-J., Cho, D.-W. and Kim, D.-J. (1996) Comparative Study of Korean and Japanese Industrial Policies Through Content Analysis of Official Documents. *Hitotsubashi Journal of Commerce and Management*, 31(1), pp 59–74.

Chun, S.-H. (2002) *Economic Development and Fiscal Management in Korea*, research paper, Seoul: Korea Institute of Public Finance.

Chung, J.-H. (1995) Studies of Central–Provincial Relations in the People's Republic of China: A Mid-Term Appraisal. *The China Quarterly*, 142(June), pp 487–508.

Chung, J.-H. (ed) (2006) *Charting China's Future: Political, Social, and International Dimensions*, Lanham: Rowman and Littlefield Publishers, Inc.

Cimoli, M., Dosi, G. and Stiglitz, J.E. (2009) The Political Economy of Capabilities Accumulation: The Past and Future of Policies for Industrial Development. In: Cimoli, M., Dosi, G. and Stiglitz, J.E. (eds) *Industrial Policy and Development: The Political Economy of Capabilities Accumulation*, Oxford: Oxford University Press.

CIRD (China Institute for Reform and Development) (2008) *China's Reform Stepping into Its 30th Year – Retrospects and Prospects*. Haikou: China Reform Forum.

Clift, J. (2003) Beyond the Washington Consensus. *Finance & Development*, September, Washington, DC: International Monetary Fund.

Cohen, B.J. (1991) *Crossing Frontiers: Explorations in International Political Economy*, Boulder, CO: Westview Press.

Comisso, E. (1998) 'Implicit' Development Strategies in Central East Europe and Cross-National Production Networks. In: Zysman, J. and Schwartz, A. (eds) *Enlarging Europe: The Industrial Foundations of a New Political Reality*, Berkeley, CA: University of California Berkeley, pp 380–423.

Cooper, G. (2008) *The Origin of Financial Crises: Central Banks, Credit Bubbles and the Efficient Market Fallacy*, Petersfield: Harriman House Ltd.

CTI (Capital Trade Incorporated) (2009) *An Assessment of China's Subsidies to Strategic and Heavyweight Industries*, report submitted to the U.S.–China Economic and Security Review Commission, Washington, DC: Capital Trade Incorporated.

Cumings, B. (1984) The Origins and Development of the Northeast Asian Political Economy. Industrial Sectors, Product Cycles and Political Consequences. *International Organization*, 38(1), pp 1–40.

Deans, Ph. (2004) The People's Republic of China: The Post-Socialist Developmental State. In: Low, L. (ed) *Developmental States: Relevancy, Redundancy or reconfiguration?*, New York, NY: Nova Science Publishers, Inc, pp 133–46.

Dehesa, G. (1991) *Privatization in Eastern and Central Europe*, Occasional Papers 34, Washington, DC: The Group Thirty.

Deloitte (2012) *Taxation and Investment in China 2012: Reach, Relevance and Reliability*. Beijing: Deloitte Touche Tohmatsu Ltd.

Deng, X. (1988) *Chinska droga do socjalizmu*, Warsaw: Ksiazka i wiedza.

Deng, X. (1994) *Selected Works. Volume III (1982–1992)* (1st edn), Beijing: Foreign Languages Press.

Desta, A. (no date) *Emerging Challenges in Democratic Developmental State: The Case of Ethiopian Growth and Transformation*, An article from Aiga Forum. Available at: http://aigaforum.com/articles/democratic_developmental_state.pdf

Deyo, F.C. (ed) (1987) *The Political Economy of the New Asian Industrialism*, Ithaca, NY: Cornell University Press.

Dickson, B.J. (2001) Cooptation and Corporatism in China: The Logic of Party Adaptation. *Political Science Quarterly*, 115(4), pp 517–40.

Dikotter, F. (2010) *Mao's Great Famine: The History of China's Most Devastating Catastrophe, 1958–1962*, New York, NY: Walker & Co.

Ding, Ch. (2012) Social Security, Growth and Openness: China's New 'Magic Trangle'. In: Heiduk, G. and McCaleb, A. (eds) *The Role of Openness in China's Post-Crisis Growth Strategy: Implications for the EU*, Warsaw: Warsaw School of Economics Press, pp 61–76.

Ding, X.L. (2000a) Informal Privatization through Internationalization: The Rise of Nomenklatura Capitalism in China's Offshore Businesses. *British Journal of Political Science*, 30(1), pp 121–46.

Ding, X.L. (2000b) The Illicit Asset Stripping of Chinese State Firms. *The China Journal*, 43(January), pp 1–28.

Ding, X. (2010) Socialism with Chinese Characteristics and the Development of Marxism in China. *Sozialismus XXI: Übergangsprogramm zum Demokratischen Sozialismus des 21. Jahrhunderts in Europa*, Goettingen: AktivDruck Verlag. Available at: file:///C:/Users/rh13505/Chrome%20Local%20Downloads/ding_englishpdf.pdf

Dirlik, A. (2005) *Marxism in the Chinese Revolution*, Oxford: Rowman & Littlefield Publishers, Inc.

Doner, R.F., Ritchie, B.K. and Slater, D. (2005) Systemic Vulnerability and the Origins of Developmental States: Northeast and Southeast Asia in Comparative Perspective. *International Organization*, 59(Spring), pp 327–61.

Dornbush, R. (1994) Post-Communist Monetary Problems: Lessons from the End of the Austro-Hungarian Empire. *Occasional Paper*. San Francisco, CA: Institute of Contemporary Studies.

Downs, E. (2006) *China*. Energy Security Series, December, The Brookings Foreign Policy Studies, Washington, DC: The Brookings Institution.

Ducket, J. (1998) *The Entrepreneurial State in China. Real Estate and Commerce Departments in Reform Era Tianjin*, London: Routledge.

Ducket, J. (2003) China's Social Security Reforms and the Comparative Politics of Market Transition. *Journal of Communist Studies and Transition Politics*, 19(1), pp 80–101.

EBRD (European Bank for Reconstruction and Development) (2001) *Annual Report 2000*, London: The European Bank for Reconstruction and Development.

EBRD (2005) *Doklad o Procese Perehoda: Proces Perehoda i Pokazateli Stran SNG*, London: The European Bank for Reconstruction and Development.

EBRD (2007) *Doklad o Processie Perehoda. Dzien. Wperehodniy period*, London: The European Bank for Reconstruction and Development.

EBRD (2008) *Proces Perehoda i Pokazateli Stran SNG i Mongolii*, London: The European Bank for Reconstruction and Development.

EBRD (2009) *Transition Report 2009. Transition in Crisis?*, London: The European Bank for Reconstruction and Development.

EBRD (2013) Economic and Research Data. Available at: http://www.ebrd.com/pages/research/economics.shtml (accessed 10 November 2013).

Edigheji, O. (2005) A Democratic Developmental State in Africa? A Concept Paper. Research Report 105, Centre for Policy Studies.

EIR (Executive Intelligence Review) (1979) *Executive Intelligence Review, 10–16 April*, New York, NY: New Solidarity International Press.

Engels, F. (1969 [1847]) The Principles of Communism. *Selected Works*, 1, Moscow: Progress Publishers, pp 81–97. Available at: http://www.marxists.org/archive/marx/works/1847/11/prin-com.htm (accessed 2 February 2009).

Ernst and Young (2006) Special Economic Zones and Tax Exemption in China. China Competence Center, Ernst and Young.

Euh, Y.-D. and Baker, J.C. (1990) *The Korean Banking System and Foreign Influence*, London: Routledge.

Evans, P. (1995) *Embedded Autonomy: States and Industrial Transformation*, Princeton, NJ: Princeton University Press.

Evans, P. (1998) Transferable Lessons? Re-Examining the Institutional Prerequisites of East Asian Economic Policies. *Journal of Development Studies*, 34(6), pp 66–86.

Fang, X. (1996) Government Commitment and Gradualism. In: McMillan, J. and Naughton, B. (eds) *Reforming Asian Socialism: The Growth of Market Institutions*, Ann Arbor, MI: The University of Michigan Press.

FDIC (Federal Deposit Insurance Corporation) (1997) *History of the Eighties – Lessons for the Future: An Examination of the Banking Crisis of the 1980s and early 1990s*, Washington, DC: Federal Deposit Insurance Corporation.

Feng, Ch. (1995) *Economic Transition and Political Legitimacy in Post-Mao China*, New York, NY: State of New York Press.

Fewsmith, J. (1995) Neoconservatism and the End of the Dengist Era. *Asian Survey*, 35(7), pp 635–51.

Fewsmith, J. (2001) The New Shape of Elite Politics. *The China Journal*, 45(January), pp 83–93.

Fewsmith, J. (2008a) *China Since Tiananmen. From Deng Xiaoping to Hu Jintao*, Cambridge: Cambridge University Press.

Fewsmith, J. (2008b) Studying the Three Represents. *China Leadership Monitor*, 8.

FH (Freedom House) (2006) Freedom House Indicators. Available at: www.freedomhouse.org/report-types/freedom-world#. U9pHLtEcQuR

Fock, A. and Wong, Ch. (2008) *Financing Rural Development for Harmonious Society in China: Recent Reforms in Public Finance and Their Prospects*, World Bank Policy Research Working Paper 4693 (August), Washington, DC: World Bank.

Foster, J.B. and Magdoff, F. (2009) *The Great Financial Crisis: The Causes and Consequences*, New York, NY: Monthly Review Press.

Foster, J.B. and McChesney, R.W. (2012) *The Endless Crisis: How Monopoly-Finance Capital Produces Stagnation and Upheaval from the USA to China*, New York, NY: Monthly Review Press.

Friedman, E. (1995) *National Identity and Democratic Prospects in Socialist China*, Armonk, NY: M. E. Sharpe.

Fushita, H. (2009) A Study of Russia's High-Tech Industry Policy. KIER Discussion Paper Series 667 (January), Kyoto Institute of Economic Research.

Gaidar, Y. (2005) Recovery Growth as a Stage of Post-Socialist Transition?, *Studies & Analyses* 292, Warsaw: Center for Social and Economic Research, www.case-research.eu/en/node/55380

Gallagher, M.E. (2002) 'Reform and Openness'. Why China's Economic Reforms Have Delayed Democracy. *World Politics*, 54(April), pp 338–72.

Gallagher, M.E. (2005) *Contagious Capitalism: Globalisation and the Politics of Labor in China*, Princeton, NJ: Princeton University Press.

Gao, P. (no date) The Rise of Education in China Through the 20th Century. Paper submitted for the seminar EH590, LSE, London.

Gao, Sh. (1987) The Reform of China's Industrial System. In: Tidrick, G. and Chen, J. (eds) *China's Industrial Reform*, New York, NY: Oxford University Press, pp 132–42.

Gasperini, L. (2000) *The Cuban Education System: Lessons and Dilemmas*, Education Reforms and Management Publication Series 1(5), Washington, DC: World Bank.

Ge, W. (1999) *The Dynamics of Export-Processing Zones*, UNCTAD Discussion Papers 144 (December), Geneva: UNCTAD.

Gereffi, G. and Fonda, S. (1992) Regional Paths of Development. *Annual Review of Sociology*, 18, pp 419–48.

Gerschenkron, A. (1962) *Economic Backwardness in Historical Perspective*, Cambridge: The Belknap Press of Harvard University Press.

Giddens, A. (2009) *The Politics of Climate Change*, Cambridge: Polity Press.

Gill, G. (1995) The Political Dynamics of Reform: Learning from the Soviet Experience. In: McCormick, B.L. and Unger, J. (eds) *China after Socialism: In the Footsteps of Eastern Europe or East Asia?*, New York, NY: ME Sharpe, pp 54–72.

Godo, Y. and Hayami, Y. (1999) *Accumulation of Education in Modern Economic Growth: A Comparison of Japan with the United States*, Research Paper Series 4, Tokyo: Asian Development Bank Institute.

Goldstein, M. (1998) The Asian Financial Crisis: Causes, Cures, and Systemic Implications. Policy Analyses in International Economics 55, Institute for International Economics.

Gong, T. (1997) Forms and Characteristics of China's Corruption in the 1990s: Change With Continuity. *Communist and Post-Communist Studies*, 30(3), pp 277–88.

Goodman, D.S.G. (1985) The Chinese Political Order after Mao: 'Socialist Democracy' and the Exercise of State Power. *Political Studies*, 33(2), pp 218–35.

Graham, E.M. (2003) *Reforming Korea's Industrial Conglomerates*, Washington, DC: Peterson Institute for International Economics.

Graham, O.L. (1992) *Losing Time: The Industrial Policy Debate*, Cambridge, MA: Harvard University Press.

Greenfield, G. and Leong, A. (1997) China's Communist Capitalism: The Real World of Market Socialism. *The Socialist Register 1997*, 33. Available at: http://socialistregister.com/index.php/srv/article/view/5684#.VAXlqPldV8F

Greenspan, A. (2007) *The Age of Turbulence: Adventures in a New World*, New York, NY: The Penguin Press.

Gries, P.H. (2004) *China's New Nationalism: Pride, Politics, and Diplomacy*, Berkeley, CA, and London: University of California Press.

Gries, P.H., Zhang, Q., Crowson, H.M. and Cai, H. (2011) Patriotism, Nationalism and China's US Policy: Structures and Consequences of Chinese National Identity. *The China Quarterly*, 205, pp 1–17.

Griffith-Jones, S., Ocampo, J.A. and Stiglitz, J.E. (eds) (2010) *Time for A Visible Hand: Lessons from the 2008 World Financial Crisis*, New York, NY: Oxford University Press.

Guo, R. (1999) *How the Chinese Economy Works: A Multiregional Overview*, New York, NY: St Martin's Press.

Guo, S. (2003) The Ownership Reform in China: What Direction and How Far? *Journal of Contemporary China*, 12(36), pp 553–73.

Guo, Y. and Hu, A. (2004) The Administrative Monopoly in China's Economic Transition. *Communist and Post-Communist Studies*, 37, pp 265–80.

Haakonssen, K. (ed) (2006) *The Cambridge Companion to Adam Smith*, Cambridge: Cambridge University Press.

Haggard, S. (1990) *Pathways from the Periphery*, Ithaca, NY: Cornell University Press.

Haggard, S. (2000) *The Political Economy of the Asian Financial Crisis*, Washington, DC: Institute for International Economics.

Haggard, S. (2004) Institutions and Growth in East Asia. *Studies in Comparative International Development*, 38(4), pp 53–81.

Haggard, S. and Moon, Ch.-I. (1986) Institutions and Economic Policy: Theory and a Korean Case Study. Paper presented at the American Political Science Association Convention, Washington, DC.

Haggard, S., Cooper, R.N., Collins, S., Kim, Ch. and Ro, S.-T. (1994) *Macroeconomic Policy and Adjustment in Korea, 1970–1990*, Harvard Studies in International Development, Harvard Institute for International Development, Cambridge: Harvard University Press.

Haley, G.T. (2007) Statement before the U.S.–China Economic and Security Review Commission. Hearing on the Extent of the Government's Control of China's Economy, and Implications for the United States, Washington, DC, U.S.–China Economic and Security Review Commission, 24–25 May.

Haley, U.C.V. and Haley, G.T. (2013) *Subsidies to Chinese Industry: State Capitalism, Business Strategy, and Trade Policy*, Oxford and New York, NY: Oxford University Press.

Hall, P.A. and Soskice, D. (eds) (2001) *Varieties of Capitalism. The Institutional Foundations of Comparative Advantage*, Oxford: Oxford University Press.

Hallding, K., Han. G. and Olsson, M. (2009) *A Balancing Act: China's Role in Climate Change*, document prepared for the Swedish ... Presidency of the Council of the European Union, Stockholm: The Commission on Sustainable Development.

Hamilton, A. (2008) *The Revolutionary Writings of Alexander Hamilton*, Indianapolis: Liberty Fund.

Hamrin, C. (1990) *China and the Challenge of the Future. Changing Political Patterns*, Boulder, CO: Westview Press.

Hayashi, Sh. (2010) The Developmental State in the Era of Globalization: Beyond the Northeast Asian Model of Political Economy. *The Pacific Review*, 23(1), pp 45–69.

HDR (Human Development Report) (2002) *Human Development Report 2002: Deepening Democracy in a Fragmented World*, UNDP, New York, NY, and Oxford: Oxford University Press.

HDR (2003) *Human Development Report 2003: Millennium Development Goals: A Compact among Nations to End Human Poverty*, UNDP, New York, NY, and Oxford: Oxford University Press.

HDR (2005) *Human Development Report 2005: International Cooperation at the Crossroads, Aid, Trade and Security in an Unequal World*, UNDP, New York, NY, and Oxford: Oxford University Press.

HDR (2007/08) *Human Development Report 2007/2008: Fighting Climate Change: Human Solidarity in the Divided World*, UNDP, New York, NY, and Oxford: Oxford University Press.

HDR (2013) *Human Development Report 2013: Human Progress and the Rising South*, UNDP, New York, NY, and Oxford: Oxford University Press.

He, B. and Guo, Y. (2000) *Nationalism, National Identity and Democratization in China*, Aldershot: Ashgate.

He, Q. (2000) China's Listing Social Structure. *New Left Review*, 5(September–October), pp 68–99.

Heiduk, G. (2012) Introduction. In: Heiduk, G. and McCaleb, A. (eds) *The Role of Openness in China's Post-Crisis Growth Strategy: Implications for the EU*, Warsaw: Warsaw School of Economics Press, pp 5–14.

Heiduk, G. (2013) Transition Economies in Central and Eastern Europe: The Case of Poland in a Comparative Perspective. In: Bolesta, A. (ed) *From Central Planning to Market: Poland's Transformation in a Comparative Perspective and the Lessons for Myanmar*, Bangkok: Chulalongkorn University Printing House.

Howell, J. (1998) An Unholy Trinity? Civil Society, Economic Liberalization and Democratization in post-Mao China. *Government and Opposition*, 33(1), pp 56–80.

Howell, J. (2006) Reflections on the Chinese State. *Development and Change*, 37(2), pp 273–97.

Hsing, Y.-T. (2010) *The Great Urban Transformation: Politics of Land and Property in China*, New York, NY: Oxford University Press.

Hu, A.G.Z. and Jefferson, G.H. (2008) Science and Technology in China. In: Brandt, L. and Rawski, T.G. (eds) *China's Great Economic Transformation*, Cambridge: Cambridge University Press, pp 286–336.

Hu A. and Wang, Sh. (1993) *Strengthen the leading role of the central government in the transition to a market economy. A research report on China's state capacity*. Shenyang: Liaoning Renmin Chubanshe.

Hu, J. (2011) Full Text of Hu Jintao's Speech at CPC Anniversary Gathering. *Xinhuanet*. Available at: http://news.xinhuanet.com/english2010/china/2011-07/01/c_13960505.htm (accessed 30 December 2011).

Huang, J., Otsuka, K. and Rozelle, S. (2008) Agriculture in China's Development: Past Disappointments, Recent Successes, and Future Challenges. In: Brandt, L. and Rawski, T.G. (eds) *China's Great Economic Transformation*, Cambridge: Cambridge University Press, pp 467–505.

Huang, Y. (2008) *Capitalism with Chinese Characteristics: Entrepreneurship and the State*, New York, NY: Cambridge University Press.

Huchet, J.-F. and Richet, X. (2002) Between Bureaucracy and Market: Chinese Industrial Groups in Search of New Forms of Corporate Governance. *Post-Communist Economies*, 14(2), pp 169–201.

Hughes, Ch. (2006) *Chinese Nationalism in the Global Era*, London: Routledge.

Husan, R. (1997) Industrial Policy and Economic Transformation: The Case of the Polish Motor Industry. *Europe-Asia Studies*, 49(1), pp 125–39.

Ianchovichina, E. and Martin, W. (2004) Economic Impacts of China's Accession to the WTO. In: Bhattasali, D., Li, Sh. and Martin, W. (eds) *China and the WTO: Accession, Policy Reform, and Poverty Reduction Strategies*, Washington, DC: World Bank and Oxford University Press.

ICFD (International Conference on Financing for Development) (2002) Final Outcome of the International Conference on Financing for Development. Monterey, 18–22 March (adopted by acclamation at the Summit Segment of the Conference), United Nations, A/CONF/198/3.

In der Heiden, P.T. (2012) The 12th Five Year Program for National Economic and Social Development. In: Heiduk, G. and McCaleb, A. (eds) *The Role of Openness in China's Post-Crisis Growth Strategy: Implications for the EU*, Warsaw: Warsaw School of Economics Press, pp 15–37.

Ishida, M. (2009) *Special Economic Zones and Economic Corridors*, ERIA Discussion Paper Series 2009-16, Chiba: Institute of Developing Economies.

Jain, R.B. (ed) (2000) *Command Economy to Market Economy: Restructuring and Transformation*, New Delhi: Deep & Deep Publications.

Jayasuriya, K. (2001) *Governance, Post Washington Consensus and the New Anti Politics*, Southeast Asia Research Centre Working Paper Series, 2, April, Hong Kong: City University of Hong Kong.

Jefferson, G.H. and Rawski T.G. (1999a) Appendix A: A Model of Economic Reform. In: Jefferson, G.H. and Singh, I. (eds) *Enterprise Reform in China: Ownership, Transition and Performance*, Oxford: Oxford University Press, pp 265–78.

Jefferson, G.H. and Rawski T.G. (1999b) Ownership Change in Chinese Industry. In: Jefferson, G.H. and Singh, I. (eds) *Enterprise Reform in China: Ownership, Transition and Performance*, Oxford: Oxford University Press, pp 23–42.

Jeon, J.-G. (1995) Exploring the Three Varieties of East Asia's State-Guided Development Model: Korea, Singapore, and Taiwan. *Studies in Comparative International Development*, 30(3), pp 70–88.

Jermakowicz, W.W., Pankow, J. and Abramov, A.J. (1994) *Voucher Privatization in Russia: First Results and Experiences*, paper prepared under the Project of Supporting Economic Reforms in Post-Soviet States, Warsaw: CASE.

Jia, H. (2004) The Three Represents Campaign: Reform the Party or Indoctrinate the Capitalists? *Cato Journal*, 24(3), pp 261–75.

Jiang, Z. (2010) *Selected Works. Volume One*, Beijing: Foreign Languages Press.

Johanssen, L. (2001) Principles and Policies of Agrarian Reform in Post-Communist Countries: The First Building Block for a Comparative Analysis of State Capacity and Political Development. Paper presented at the DEMSTAR workshop, 28 June–1 July, Femmøller, Denmark.

Johnson, Ch.A. (1981) Introduction: The Taiwan Model. In: Hsiung, J.S. (ed) *Contemporary Republic of China. The Taiwan Experience, 1950-1980*, New York, NY: Praeger.

Johnson, Ch.A. (1982) *MITI and the Japanese Miracle: The Growth of Industrial Policy, 1925–1975*, Stanford, CA: Stanford University Press.

Johnson, Ch.A. (1987) Political Institutions and Economic Performance: The Government–Business Relationship in Japan, South Korea, and Taiwan. In: Deyo, F. (ed) *The Political Economy of the New Asian Industrialism*, Ithaca, NY, and London: Cornell University Press, pp 136–64.

Johnson, Ch.A. (1999) The Developmental State: Odyssey of a Concept. In: Woo-Cumings, M. (ed) *The Developmental State*, Ithaca, NY: Cornell University Press, pp 32–60.

Joyce, J.P. (2013) *The IMF and Global Financial Crises: Phoenix Rising?*, New York, NY: Cambridge University Press.

Kagami, M. (1995) The Role of Industrial Policy: Japan's Experience. *Revista de Economia Politica*, 15(1), pp 119–33.

Kang, D.C. (2002) *Crony Capitalism: Corruption and Development in South Korea and the Philippines*, Oxford: Oxford University Press.

Katzenstein, P. (ed) (1978) *Between Power and Plenty: Foreign Economic Policies of Advanced Industrial States*, Madison, WI: University of Wisconsin Press.

Kawai, M. (2004) Trade and Investment Integration for Development in East Asia: A Case for the Trade–FDI Nexus. Paper presented at the ABCDE Europe meeting, 10–11 May, Brussels.

Ke, Y.J., Wang, S.Q. and Chan, A.P.C. (2009) Public–Private Partnership in China's Infrastructure Development: Lessons Learnt. In: Wamelink, H., Prins, M. and Geraedlts, R. (eds) *Changing Roles: New Roles and New Challenges*, Delft: University of Technology.

Kefale, A. (2011) Narratives of Developmentalism and Development in Ethiopia: Some Preliminary Explorations. Paper submitted for the 4th European Conference on African Studies, Uppsala, 15–18 June.

Kennedy, S. (2008) Chinese Economic Nationalism: The Effect of Interests and Institutions. Background paper for the National Committee on US–China Relations' conference 'China, the United States and the Emerging Global Agenda', 13–15 July, Queenstown.

Kim, E.M. (1997) *Big Business, Strong State: Collusion and Conflict In South Korean Development, 1960–1990*, Albany, NY: State University of New York Press.

Kim, H. and Lee, Y.-K. (2003) Agricultural Policy Reform and Structural Adjustment: Historical Evidence from Korean Perspective. Paper submitted for the Workshop on Agricultural Policy Reform and Adjustment, Imperial College, Wye, 23–25 October.

Kim, J.-K., Shim, S.D. and Kim, J.-I. (1995) The Role of the Government in Promoting Industrialization and Human Capital Accumulation in Korea. In: Ito, T. and Krueger, A. (eds) *Growth Theories in Light of the East Asian Experience*, Chicago, IL: University of Chicago Press, pp 181–200.

Kim, K.S. (1985) Industrial Policy and Industrialization in South Korea: 1961–1982 – Lessons on Industrial Policies for Other Developing Countries. Kellogg Institute Working Paper 39.

Kimura, F. (2009) Japan's Model of Economic Development: Relevant and Nonrelevant Elements for Developing Economies. WIDER Working Paper 22.

Klein, L.R. and Shabbir, T. (eds) (2006) *Recent Financial Crises: Analyses, Challenges and Implications*, Cheltenham: Edward Elgar Publishing.

Klein, N. (2007) *The Shock Doctrine: The Rise of Disaster Capitalism*, New York, NY: Metropolitan Books.

Knight, J. (2012) China as a Developmental State. CASE Working Paper, WPS/2012-13, November, Oxford.

Kobayashi, Y. (1993) The Role and Significance of Japanese Industrial Policy: Its Estimation and Recent Issue. *Economic Journal of Hokkaido University*, 22, pp 69–90.

Kohli, A. (1994) Where Do High Growth Political Economies Come From? The Japanese Lineage of Korea's 'Developmental State'. *World Development*, 22(9), pp 1269–93.

Kohli, A. (1999) Where Do High-Growth Political Economies Come From? The Japanese Lineage of Korea's 'Developmental State'. In: Woo-Cumings, M. (ed) *The Developmental State*, Ithaca, NY: Cornell University Press, pp 93–136.

Kokko, A. (2002) Export-Led Growth in East Asia. Lessons for Europe's Transition Economies. European Institute of Japanese Studies Working Paper Series 142.

Kolb, R.W. (2011) *The Financial Crisis of Our Time*, New York, NY: Oxford University Press.

Kolodko, G.W. (1993) *Kwadratura pięciokąta. Od załamania gospodarczego do trwałego wzrostu*, Warsaw: Poltex.

Kolodko, G.W. (1999a) *Od szoku do terapii. Ekonomia i polityka transformacji* , Warsaw: Poltext.

Kolodko, G.W. (1999b) Transition to a Market Economy and Sustained Growth. Implications for the Post-Washington Consensus. *Communist and Post-Communist Studies*, 32(3), pp 233–61.

Kolodko, G.W. (2001a) *Globalizacja a perspektywy rozwoju krajów posocjalistycznych*, Toruń: TNOiK.

Kolodko, G.W. (2001b) Post-Communist Transition and Post-Washington Consensus. The Lessons for Policy Reforms. In: Blejer, M.I. and Skreb, M. (eds) *Transition. The First Decade*, Cambridge: The MIT Press, pp 45–83.

Kolodko, G.W. (2004a) Instytucje i polityka a wzrost gospodarczy. *Ekonomista*, 5, pp 609–34.

Kolodko, G.W. (2004b) Strategia rynkowej transformacji: gradualizm czy radykalizm? *Dziś – Przegląd Społeczny*, 8(167), pp 32–40.

Kolodko, G.W. (2008) *Wędrujący Świat*, Warsaw: Proszynski i Spolka.

Kolodko, G.W. (2011) *Truth, Errors, and Lies: Politics and Economics in the Volatile World*, New York, NY: Columbia University Press.

Kornai, J. (1992) *The Socialist System: The Political Economy of Communism*, Princeton, NJ: Princeton University Press.

Kornai, J. (2004) *What Can Countries Embarking on Post-Socialist Transformation Learn from the Experiences So Far?*, paper prepared for the Cuba Transition Project, University of Miami, Miami: Institute for Cuban and Cuban-American Studies.

Krugman, P. (1983) Targeted Industrial Policy: Theory and Evidence. *Industrial Change and Public Policy*, Kansas City, KS: Federal Reserve Bank of Kansas City.

Krugman, P. (2000) *Crises: The Price of Globalization?*, Global Economic Integration: Opportunities and Challenges, A symposium sponsored by the Federal Reserve Bank of Kansas City Jackson Hole, Wyoming, 24-26 August.

Krugman, P. (2008) Inequality and Redistribution. In: Serra, N. and Stiglitz, J.E. (eds) *The Washington Consensus Reconsidered: Towards a New Global Governance*, Oxford: Oxford University Press, pp 31–40.

Kuchiki, A. (2007) *Industrial Policy in Asia*, IDE Discussion Papers 128, Chiba: Institute of Developing Economies.

Kuhn, R.L. (2013) Understanding the Chinese Dream. *China Daily*, 19 July.

Kuznets, S. (1966) *Modern Economic Growth: Rate, Structure and Spread*, New Haven and London: Yale University Press.

Kwong, J. (1997) *The Political Economy of Corruption in China*, Armonk: Sharpe.

Lange, O. (1973) O ekonomicznej teorii socjalizmu. In: *Dzieła, Vol.2. Socialism*, Warsaw: PWE.

Lankester, T. (2004) 'Asian Drama': The Pursuit of Modernization in India and Indonesia. *Asian Affairs*, XXXV(III), pp 291–304.

Lardy, N.R. (1983) *Agriculture in China's Modern Economic Development*, Cambridge: Cambridge University Press.

Lardy, N.R. (1998) *China's Unfinished Economic Revolution*, Washington, DC: Brookings Institution Press.

Lardy, N.R. (2002) *Integrating China into the Global Economy*, Washington, DC: Brookings Institution Press.

Lardy, N.R. (2005) Exchange Rate and Monetary Policy in China. *Cato Journal*, 25(1), pp 41–7.

Lau, L.J. and Qian, Y. (2000) Reform without Losers: An Interpretation of China's Dual-Track Approach to Transition. *Journal of Political Economy*, 108(1), pp 120–63.

Lautard, S. (1999) State, Party, and Market: Chinese Politics and the Asian Crisis. *International Political Science Review*, 20(3), pp 285–306.

LDCR (The Least Developed Countries Report) (2004) *The Least Developed Countries Report 2004: Linking International Trade with Poverty Reduction*, New York, NY, and Geneva: UNCTAD.

Lee, CH.H. (1992) The Government, Financial System, and Large Private Enterprises in the Economic Development of South Korea. *World Development*, 20(2), pp 187–97.

Lee, J.-W. (1997) Economic Growth and Human Development in the Republic of Korea, 1945–1992. Occasional Paper 24.

Lee, K. and Mathews, J.A. (2010) From Washington Consensus to BeST Consensus for World Development. *Asian-Pacific Economic Literature*, 24(1), pp 1–22.

Lee, K., Jee, M. and Eun, J. (2006) *China's Strategies for Economic Catch-Up and Implications for Korea*, working paper, Seoul: Korea Institute for International Economic Policy.

Leftwich, A. (2000) *States of Development: On the Primacy of Politics in Development*, Cambridge and Oxford: Polity Press.

Levi-Faur, D. (1997) Economic Nationalism: From Friedrich List to Robert Reich. *Review of International Studies*, 23, pp 259–370.

Levin, C. and Coburn, T. (2011) *Wall Street and the Financial Crisis: The Anatomy of a Financial Collapse*. Majority and Minority Staff Report, Permanent Subcommittee on Investigations, United States Senate, 13 April.

Lewis, J.W. and Xue, L. (2003) Social Change and Political Reform in China: Meeting the Challenge of Success. *The China Quarterly*, 176(December), pp 926–42.

Li, H. and Rozelle, S. (2003) Privatizing Rural China: Insider Privatization, Innovative Contracts and the Performance of Township Enterprises. *The China Quarterly*, 176(December), pp 981–1005.

Li, N. (2001) From Revolutionary Internationalism to Conservative Nationalism: The Chinese Military's Discourse on National Security and Identity in the Post-Mao Era. United States Institute of Peace's Peaceworks 39.

Liew, L.H. and Wang, Sh. (eds) (2004) *Nationalism, Democracy and National Integration in China*, London: RoutledgeCurzon.

Lijphart, A. and Waisman, C. (eds) (1996) *Institutional Design in New Democracies: Eastern Europe and Latin America*, Boulder, CO: Westview Press.

Lin, Ch. (2006) *The Transformation of Chinese Socialism*, Durham, NC: Duke University Press.

Lin, J.Y. (2005) *Lessons of China's Transition from a Planned Economy to a Market Economy*, WSPiZ & TIGER Distinguished Lectures Series 16, Warsaw: Wydawnictwo WSPiZ.

Lin, J.Y. (2012) *Demystifying the Chinese Economy*, New York, NY: Cambridge University Press.

Lin, J.Y. and Liu, Zh. (2000) Fiscal Decentralization and Economic Growth in China. *Economic Development and Cultural Change*, 49(1), pp 1–21.

Lin, T. and Swanson, T. (eds) (2010) *Economic Growth and Environmental Regulation: The People's Republic of China's Path to a Brighter Future*, Abingdon and New York, NY: Routledge.

Lindbeck, A. (1981) Industrial Policy as an Issue in the Economic Environment. *World Economy*, 4, pp 391–405.

Linden, G. (2004) China Standard Time: A Study in Strategic Industrial Policy. *Business and Politics*, 6(3), pp 1–26.

List, F. (1909 [1841]) The National System of Political Economy. The Online Library of Liberty, Liberty Fund. Available at: http://oll.libertyfund.org/index.php?option=com_staticxt&staticfile=show.php%3Ftitle=315&Itemid=27 (accessed 5 January 2010).

Liu, A.P.L. (1992) The 'Wenzhou Model' of Development and China's Modernization. *Asian Survey*, 32(8), pp 696–711.

Liu, X. and White, S. (2001) Comparing Innovation Systems: A Framework and Application to China's Transitional Context. *Research Policy*, 30(7), pp 1091–1114.

Lopez, R. and Toman, M.A. (eds) (2006) *Economic Development and Environmental Sustainability: New Policy Options*, New York, NY: Oxford University Press.

Loriaux, M. (1999) The French Developmental State as Myth and Moral Ambition. In: Woo-Cumings, M. (ed) *The Developmental State*, Ithaca, NY: Cornell University Press, pp 235–75.

Louvert, E. (2005) *Russia: The Urgent Necessity of an Ambitious Industrial Policy*, Russian–European Centre for Economic Policy (RECEP).

Lu, X. (2000) Booty Socialism, Bureau-Preneurs, and the State in Transition: Organizational Corruption. *Comparative Politics*, 32(3), pp 273–94.

Maddison, A. (2007) *Chinese Economic Performance in the Long Run*, Paris: Development Centre Studies, OECD.

Magnus, J.R. (2006) Chinese Subsidies and US Responses. Testimony before the U.S.–China Economic and Security Review Commission, 'Hearing on China's World Trade Organization Compliance: Industrial Subsidies and The Impact on US and World Markets', Washington, DC, Tradewins LLC, 5 April.

Mah, J.S. (2010) Export Promotion Policies, Export Composition and Economic Development of Korea. Paper prepared for the 'Law and Development Institute Inaugural Conference', October, Sydney.

Mako, W. and Zhang, Ch. (2002) *Exercising Ownership Rights in State Owned Enterprise Groups: What China Can Learn from International Experience*, World Bank Note, 31 December, Beijing: World Bank.

Mao, T. (1977) On the Ten Major Relationships. In: *Selected Works of Mao Tse-tung*, Beijing: Foreign Languages Press. Available at: http://www.marx2mao.com/Mao/TMR56.html (accessed 3 June 2010).

Marx, K. and Engels, F. (1969 [1848]) Manifesto of the Communist Party. *Selected Works*, 1. Moscow: Progress Publishers, pp 98–137. Available at: http://www.marxists.org/archive/marx/works/1848/communist-manifesto/ (accessed 2 February 2009).

Mass, W. and Miyajima, H. (1993) The Organization of the Developmental State: Fostering Private Capabilities and the Roots of the Japanese 'Miracle'. *Business and Economic History*, 22(1), pp 151–68.

Mbabazi, P. and Taylor, I. (eds) (2005) *The Potentiality of 'Developmental States' in Africa: Botswana and Uganda Compared*, Dakar: Codesria.

McCormick, B.L and Unger, J. (eds) (1995) *China after Socialism: In the Footsteps of Eastern Europe or East Asia?*, New York, NY: ME Sharpe.

McMillan, J. and Naughton, B. (eds) (1996) *Reforming Asian Socialism: The Growth of Market Institutions*, Ann Arbor, MI: The University of Michigan Press.

Meaney, C.S. (1989) Market Reform in a Leninist System: Some Trends in in the Distribution of Power, Status and Money in the Urban China. *Studies in Comparative Communism*, 22(2/3), pp 203–20.

Meaney, C.S. (1991) Market Reform and Disintegrative Corruption in Urban China. In: Baum, R. (ed) *Reform and Reaction in Post-Mao China: The Road to Tiananmen*, New York, NY: Routledge.

Mehrotra, A. and Sanchez-Fung, J.R. (2010) China's Monetary Policy and the Exchange Rate. Federal Reserve Bank of San Franscisco Working Paper Series 19.

Meier, N. (2009) *China – The New Developmental State? An Empirical Analysis of the Automotive Industry*, Frankfurt am Main: Peter Lang.

Melo, M., Denizer, C. and Gelb, A. (1996) *From Plan to Market: Patterns of Transition*, Policy Research Working Paper 1564, Washington, DC: World Bank.

Migdal, J.S. (1988) *Strong Societies and Weak States: State–Society Relations and State Capabilities in the Third World*, Princeton, NJ: Princeton University Press.

Migdal, J.S. (2001) *State in Society: Studying How States and Societies Transform and Constitute One Another*, Cambridge: Cambridge University Press.

Mkandawire, T. (2001) Thinking about Developmental States in Africa. *Cambridge Journal of Economics*, 25(3), pp 289–313.

MOFCOM (Ministry of Commerce) (2007) Main Mandate of the Ministry of Commerce. Ministry of Commerce of the People's Republic of China. Available at: http://english.mofcom.gov.cn/column/mission2010.shtml.

Morgan, J. (2004) Contemporary China, Anachronistic Marxism? *Critical Asian Studies*, 36(1), pp 65–90.

Morrison, W.M. and Labonte, M. (2011) China's Currency Policy: An Analysis of the Economic Issues. CRS Report for Congress, 11 December.

Murrell, P. (1993) What is Shock Therapy? What Did it Do in Poland and Russia? *Post-Soviet Affairs*, 9(2), pp 111–40.

Myrdal, G. (1968) *Asian Drama. An Inquiry into the Poverty of Nations*, London: Penguin Books.

Naito, J. (2010) Fiscal System and Policy in China – Transition and Tasks of Thirty-Year-Reform and Opening Policy. *Japan's Public Policy Review*, 6(3), pp 511–56.

Nakamura, K. (1996) State-Owned Enterprise Reform: Lesson from Japan. In: Yuen, N.-Ch., Freeman, N.J. and Huynh, F.H. (eds) *State-Owned Enterprise Reform in Vietnam: Lessons from Asia*, Singapore: Institute of Southeast Asian Studies, pp 77–101.

Nam, Ch.-H. (1995) The Role of Trade and Exchange Rate Policy in Korea's Growth. In: Ito, T. and Krueger, A. (eds) *Growth Theories in Light of the East Asian Experience*, Chicago, IL: University of Chicago Press, pp 153–79.

Naughton, B. (1995) *Growing Out of the Plan, Chinese Economic Reform 1978–1993*, Cambridge: Cambridge University Press.

Naughton, B. (1999) China's Transition in Economic Perspective. In: Goldman, M. and MacFarquhar, R. (eds) *The Paradox of China's Post-Mao Reforms*, Cambridge: Harvard University Press.

Naughton, B. (2007) *The Chinese Economy: Transitions and Growth*, London: The MIT Press.

NBS (National Bureau of Statistics) (2008) *China Statistical Yearbook 2008*, Beijing: China Statistics Press.

NDRC (National Development and Reform Commission) (2007) Main Functions of the NDRC. National Development and Reform Commission of the People's Republic of China. Available at: http://en.ndrc.gov.cn/mfndrc/

Nesvetailova, A. (2010) *Financial Alchemy in Crisis: The Great Liquidity Illusion*, London: Pluto Press.

Nielsen, R.P. (1982) Government-Owned Businesses: Market Presence, Competitive Advantages and Rationales for Their Support by the State. *American Journal of Economics and Sociology*, 41(1), pp 17–27.

Nish, I. (2000) Nationalism in Japan. In: Leifer, M. (ed) *Asian Nationalism*, London: Routledge.

Nolan, P. (1995) *China's Rise, Russia's Fall: Politics, Economics and Planning in the Transition from Stalinism*, London: Palgrave Macmillan.

Nolan, P. (2004) *Transforming China. Globalisation, Transition and Development*, London and New York, NY: Anthem Press.

Noland, M. (2007) From Industrial Policy to Innovation Policy: Japan's Pursuit of Competitive Advantage. *Asian Economic Policy Review*, 2, pp 251–68.

Noland, M. and Pack, H. (2003) *Industrial Policy in an Era of Globalization: Lessons from Asia*, Washington, DC: Peterson Institute for International Economics.

Nordlinger, E.A. (1987) Taking the state seriously. In: Weiner, M. and Huntington, S.P. (eds) Understanding Political Development, Boston, MA: Little, Brown and Co., pp 353-90.

North, D.C. (1990) *Institutions, Institutional Change and Economic Performance*, Cambridge: Cambridge University Press.

North, D.C. (1997) *The Contribution of the New Institutional Economics to an Understanding of the Transition Problem*, WIDER Annual Lecture, Helsinki: UNU-WIDER.

Nozick, R, 1974, *Anarchy, State, and Utopia*, Oxford and Cambridge, MA: Blackwell

Nuti, D.M. (2010) *The Former Soviet Union after Dis-integration and Transition*, TIGER Working Paper Series 117, Warsaw: Wydawnictwo WSPiZ.

NZEC (Near Zero Emissions Coal Initiative) Summary Report (2009) Summary Report. China–UK Near Zero Emissions Coal (NZEC) Initiative, Beijing, September.

O'Brien, K.J. and Li, L. (2000) Accommodating 'Democracy' in a One-Party State: Introducing Village Elections in China. *The China Quarterly* (Special Issue: Elections and Democracy in Greater China), 162, June, pp 465–89.

OECD (Organisation for Economic Co-operation and Development) (2009a) *China. Defining the Boundary between the Market and the State*, OECD Reviews of Regulatory Reform, Paris: OECD.

OECD (2009b) *China*, OECD Rural Policy Reviews, Paris: OECD.

OECD (2009c) *The Role of Agriculture and Farm Household Diversification in the Rural Economy of Japan*, Paris: OECD.

OECD (2010) *China 2010*, OECD Economic Surveys, Paris: OECD.

Oh, W.-S. (1993) *Export Processing Zones in the Republic of Korea: Economic Impact and Social Issues*, ILO Working Paper 75, Multinational Enterprises Programme, Geneva: ILO.

Oi, J.C. (1991) Partial Market Reform and Corruption in Rural China. In: Baum, R. (ed) *Reform and Reaction in Post-Mao China: The Road to Tiananmen*, New York, NY: Routledge.

Oi, J.C. (1992) Fiscal Reform and the Economic Foundations of Local State Corporatism in China. *World Politics*, 45(1), pp 99–126.

Oi, J.C. (1995) The Role of the Local State in China's Transitional Economy. *The China Quarterly* (Special Issue: China's Transitional Economy), 144, pp 1132–49.

Olayode, K. (2005) Reinventing the African State: Issues and Challenges for Building a Developmental State. *African Journal of International Affairs*, 8(1/2), pp 23–43.

Otero, C. (ed) (1995) *Examples of Successful Models of Development. Country Overviews*, Washington, DC: United States Agency for International Development.

Owen, A.D. and Hanley, N. (eds) (2004) *The Economics of Climate Change*, London and New York, NY: Routledge.

Pack, H. and Saggi, K. (2006) *The Case for Industrial Policy: A Critical Survey*, World Bank Policy Research Working Paper Series 3839 (February), Washington, DC: World Bank.

Page, J. (1994) The East Asian Miracle: Four Lessons for Development Policy. In: Fischer, S. and Rotemberg, J.J. (eds) *NBER Macroeconomics Annual, Volume 9*, Cambridge, MA: MIT Press, pp 219–82.

Panic, M. (2011) *Globalization: A Threat to International Cooperation and Peace?* (2nd edn), Basingstoke: Palgrave MacMillan.

Pareto, V. (1966) *Sociological Writings*, London: Pall Mall Press.

Parris, K. (1993) Local Initiative and National Reform: The Wenzhou Model of Development. *The China Quarterly*, 134, pp 242–63.

Pei, M. (1998) Constructing the Political Foundations of an Economic Miracle. In: Rowen, H.S. (ed) *Behind East Asian Growth: The Political and Social Foundations of Prosperity*, London: Routledge, pp 39–59.

Pei, M. (2006) *China's Trapped Transition: The Limits of Developmental Autocracy*, Cambridge: Harvard University Press.

People's Daily Online (2005) China Has Socialist Market Economy in Place. *People's Daily Online*, 13 July. Available at: http://english. people.com.cn/200507/13/eng20050713_195876.html (accessed 13 March 2011).

People's Daily Online (2007) Harmonious Society. *People's Daily Online*, 29 September. Available at: http://english.people.com. cn/90002/92169/92211/6274603.html (accessed 5 February 2012).

People's Daily Online (2010) China to Eliminate Tax Rebates on Certain Export Goods. *People's Daily Online*, 23 June. Available at: http:// english.people.com.cn/90001/90778/90861/7037210.html

Perkins, D.H. (1994) There Are at Least Three Models of East Asian Development. *World Development*, 22(4), pp 655–61.

Perkins, D.H. (2001) Industrial and Financial Policy in China and Vietnam: A New Model or a Replay of the East Asian Experience? In: Stiglitz, J. and Yusuf, S. (eds) *Rethinking the East Asia Miracle*, Washington, DC: World Bank.

Perry, E. and Wong, C. (eds) (1985) *The Political Economy of Reform in Post-Mao China*, Cambridge: Harvard University Press.

Piatkowski, M. (2013) *Poland's New Golden Age: Shifting from Europe's Periphery to its Center*, Policy Research Working Paper 6639, Washington, DC: The World Bank.

Ping, J.H. (2011) The Chinese Development Model: International Development and Hegemony. In: McCormick, B. and Ping, J.H. (eds) *Chinese Engagements: Regional Issues with Global Implications*, Robina: Bond University Press, pp 167–99.

Poznanski, K. (2000) *Wielki Przekręt. Klęska polskich reform*, Warsaw: Towarzystwo Wydawnicze i Literackie.

PP (Position Paper) (2007) *European Business in China Position Paper 2007/2008*. Beijing: European Union Chamber of Commerce in China.

PP (2009) *European Business in China Position Paper 2009/2010*, Beijing: European Union Chamber of Commerce in China.

PP (2010) *European Business in China Position Paper 2010/2011*, Beijing: European Union Chamber of Commerce in China.

PP (2013) *European Business in China Position Paper 2013/2014*, Beijing: European Union Chamber of Commerce in China.

Prebisch, R. (1950) *Theoretical and Practical Problems of Economic Growth*, Mexico: United Nations Economic Commission for Latin America.

Przeworski, A. and Limongi, F. (1993) Political Regimes and Economic Growth. *Journal of Economic Perspectives*, 7(3), pp 51–69.

Quinn, D.P. and Jacobson, R. (1989) Industrial Policy through the Restriction of Capital Flows: A Test of Several Claims Made about Industrial Policy. *American Journal of Political Science*, 33(3), pp 700–36.

Ramo, J.C. (2004) *The Beijing Consensus: Notes on the New Physics of Chinese Power*, London: The Foreign Policy Centre.

Raphael, J.H. and Rohlen, T.P. (1998) How Many Models of the Japanese Growth Do We Want or Need? In: Rowen, H.S. (ed) *Behind East Asian Growth: The Political and Social Foundations of Prosperity*, London: Routledge, pp 265–96.

Reich, R. (1991) *The Work of Nations: Preparing Ourselves for 21st Century Capitalism*, Hemel Hempstead: Simon and Schuster.

Riskin, C. (1987) *China's Political Economy: The Quest for Development since 1949*, Oxford: Oxford University Press.

Robinson, M. and White, G. (eds) (1998) *The Democratic Developmental State: Politics and Institutional Design*, Oxford: Oxford University Press.

Rodrik, D. (2007) Normalizing Industrial Policy. Paper prepared for the Commission on Growth and Development.

Rodrik, D. (2008) Industrial Policy: Don't Ask Why, Ask How. *Middle East Development Journal*, 1(1), pp 1–29.

Roemer, J.E. (1994) *Future for Socialism*, Cambridge, MA: Harvard University Press.

Rong, Ch. (2009) Analysing the Theoretical System of Socialism with Chinese Characteristics. *Asian Social Science*, 5(10), pp 134–36.

Rosen, D.H. and Houser, T. (2007) *China Energy. A Guide for the Perplexed*, Washington, DC: Peterson Institute for International Economics.

Ross, A.L. (ed) (1991) *The Political Economy of Defense: Issues and Perspectives*, Westport, CT: Greenwood Press.

Rowen, H.S. (ed) (1998) *Behind East Asian Growth: The Political and Social Foundations of Prosperity*, London: Routledge.

Rutland, P. (2009) Post-Socialist States and the Evolution of a New Development Model: Russia and China Compared. In: Hayashi, T. and Ogushi, A. (eds) *Post-Communist Transformations: The Countries of Central and Eastern Europe and Russia in a Comparative Perspective, SRC Slavic Eurasian Studies, 21*, Sapporo: Hokkaido University, pp 49–71.

Sachs, J. (1989) *Social Conflict and Populist Policies in Latin America*, NBER Working Paper 2897, Cambridge: National Bureau of Economic Research.

Sachs, J. (1993) *Poland's Jump to the Market Economy*, Cambridge, MA: The MIT Press.

Sachs, J. (1994) Shock Therapy in Poland: Perspectives of Five Years. The Tanner Lectures on Human Value, 6–7 April, University of Utah, Salt Lake City.

Sachs, J. and Woo, W.T. (1994) Structural Factors in the Economic Reforms of China, Eastern Europe, and the Former Soviet Union. *Economic Policy*, 18, pp 101–45.

Saich, T. (2001) *Governance and Politics of China*, New York, NY, and Basingstoke: Palgrave.

Sakakibara, M. and Cho, D.-S. (2002) Cooperative R&D in Japan and Korea: A Comparison of Industrial Policy. *Research Policy*, 31(5), pp 673–92.

Sakoh, K. (1984) Japanese Economic Success: Industrial Policy or Free Market? *CATO Journal*, 4(2), pp 521–48.

Schneider, B.R. (1999) The Desarrollista State in Brazil and Mexico. In: Woo-Cumings, M. (ed) *The Developmental State*, Ithaca, NY: Cornell University Press, pp 276–305.

Schumpeter, J.A. (1942) *Capitalism, Socialism and Democracy*, New York, NY: Harper & Row Publishers.

Scissors, D. (2009) Deng Undone. The Costs of Halting Market Reform in China. *Foreign Affairs*, 88(3), pp 24–39.

Scott, B.R. (2011) *Capitalism: Its Origins and Evolution as a System of Governance*, New York, NY: Springer.

Sen, A. (1997) Human Rights and Asian Values: What Lee Kuan Yew and Li Peng Don't Understand about Asia. *The New Republic*, 217(2/3), pp 33–40.

Sen, A. (1999) The Value of Democracy. *Development Outreach*, Summer, pp 5–9.

Serafino, N., Turnoff, C. and Nanto, D.K. (2006) *U.S. Occupation Assistance: Iraq, Germany and Japan Compared*, CRS Report for Congress RL33331, 23 March, Washington, DC: Congressional Research Service.

Serra, N. and Stiglitz, J.E. (eds) (2008) *The Washington Consensus Reconsidered: Towards a New Global Governance*, Oxford: Oxford University Press.

Shah, P.J. (ed) (2001) *Profiles in Courage: Dissent on Indian Socialism*, New Delhi: Centre for Civil Society.

Shambaugh, D. (2013) *China Goes Global: The Partial Power*, New York, NY: Oxford University Press.

Shapiro, H. (2007) *Industrial Policy and Growth*, DESA Working Paper 53, New York, NY: United Nations.

Shih, Ch. (1999) *Collective Democracy: Political and Legal Reform in China*, Beijing: Chinese University Press.

Shiller, R.J. (2008) *The Subprime Solution: How Today's Global Financial Crisis Happened, and What to Do About It*, Princeton, NJ, and Oxford: Princeton University Press.

Shirk, S.L. (1993) *The Political Logic of Economic Reform in China*, Berkeley, CA: University of California Press.

Shirk, S.L. (2007) *China Fragile Superpower. How China's Internal Politics Could Derail its Peaceful Rise*, New York, NY: Oxford University Press.

Shleifer, A. and Vishny, R.W. (1994) The Politics of Market Socialism. *Journal of Economic Perspectives*, 8(2), pp 165–76.

Sindzingre, A. (2006) Financing the Developmental State: Tax and Revenue Issues. Presentation at the Overseas Development Institute (ODI), London, 5 April.

Singer, P. (1980) *Marx. A Very Short Introduction*, Oxford: Oxford University Press.

Skousen, M. (2007) *The Big Three in Economics: Adam Smith, Karl Marx and John Maynard Keynes*, Armonk: Sharpe.

Smith, A. (2003 [1776]) *The Wealth of Nations*, New York, NY: Bantam Dell.

Solinger, D.J. (1982) The Fifth National People's Congress and the Process of Policymaking: Reform, Readjustment and the Opposition. *Issues and Studies*, 18(8), pp 63–106.

Solinger, D.J. (2003) State and Society in Urban China in the Wake of the 16th Party Congress. *The China Quarterly*, 176, pp 943–59.

Solinger, D.J. (2006) The Creation of a New Underclass in China and its Implications. *Environment & Urbanization*, 18(1), pp 177–93.

Song, L. and Woo, W.T. (eds) (2008) *China's Dilemma: Economic Growth, the Environment and Climate Change*, Canberra: ANU E Press and Asia Pacific Press.

Speth, J.G. (2008) *The Bridge at the Edge of the World: Capitalism, the Environment, and Crossing from Crisis to Sustainability*, New Haven, CT, and London: Yale University Press.

Steingart, G. (2008) *The War for Wealth: The True Story of Globalization, or Why the Flat World is Broken*, New York, NY: McGraw-Hill.

Stiglitz, J.E. (1993) Market Socialism and Neoclassical Economics. In: Bardham, P.K. and Roemer, J.E. (eds) *Market Socialism. The Current Debate*, New York, NY: Oxford University Press.

Stiglitz, J.E. (1998) *More Instruments and Broader Goals: Moving Towards The Post-Washington Consensus*, WIDER Annual Lecture, Helsinki: UNU-WIDER.

Stiglitz, J.E. (2002) *Globalization and Its Discontents*, New York, NY: W.W. Norton & Company, Ltd.

Stiglitz, J.E. (2004) Globalization and Growth in Emerging Markets. *Journal of Policy Modeling*, 26, pp 465–84.

Stiglitz, J.E. (2010) *The Stiglitz Report: Reforming the International Monetary and Financial Systems in the Wake of the Global Crisis*, New York, NY, and London: The New Press.

Stubbs, R. (2009) What Ever Happened to the East Asian Developmental State? The Unfolding Debate. *The Pacific Review*, 22(1), pp 1–22.

Suzuki, Y. (1987) *The Japanese Financial System*, Oxford: Clarendon Press.

Sylwestrzak, A. (1996) *Historia doktryn politycznych i prawnych*, Warsaw: PWN.

The China Analyst (2012) *Regional Focus: China–Africa, the Beijing Axis*, Hong Kong. Available at: www.thebeijingaxis.com/tca/editions/the-china-analyst-sept-2013/211-regional-focus-china-africa

The Economist (2013) The Xi Manifesto. *The Economist*, 23–29 November, pp 35–6.

The Economist (2014) What's Gone Wrong with Democracy. *The Economist*, 1–7 March, pp 47–52.

Tidrick, G. and Chen, J. (eds) (1987) *China's Industrial Reform*, New York, NY: Oxford University Press.

Townsend, J. (1992) Chinese Nationalism. *The Australian Journal of Chinese Affairs*, 27, pp 97–130.

Transparency International (2012) Corruption Perceptions Index 2012, www.transparency.org/cpi2012/

Tseng, W. and Zebregs, H. (2002) Foreign Direct Investment in China: Some Lessons for Other Countries. IMF Policy Discussion Paper PDP/02/3 (February).

Tsui, K.-Y. and Wang, Y. (2004) Between Separate Stoves and a Single Menu: Fiscal Decentralization in China. *The China Quarterly*, 177, pp 71–90.

ul Haque, I. (2007) Rethinking Industrial Policy. UNCTAD Discussion Papers 183.

UNCTAD HS (United Nations Conference on Trade and Development's Handbook of Statistics) (2005) *UNCTAD Handbook of Statistics 2005*, New York, NY, and Geneva: UNCTAD.

UNFCCC (United Nations Framework Convention on Climate Change) (1992) United Nations Framework Convention on Climate Change. Available at: http://unfccc.int/2860.php (accessed 10 October 2009).

Unger, J. and Barme, G. (eds) (1996) *Chinese Nationalism*, Armonk, NY: M.E. Sharpe.

Unger, J. and Chan, A. (1995) Corporatism in China: A Developmental State in an East Asian Context. In: McCormick, B.L. and Unger, J. (eds) *China After Socialism: In the Footsteps of Eastern Europe or East Asia*, Armonk, NY: Sharpe, pp 95–129.

Unger, R.M. and Cui, Z. (1994) China in the Russia Mirror. *New Left Review*, 208, pp 78–87.

UNStats (United Nations Statistics Division) (2005) United Nations Statistics Division, United Nations. Available at: http://unstats.un.org/unsd/snaama/dnllist.asp (accessed 15 June 2006).

Von Mises, L. (1951) *Socialism. An Economic and Sociological Analysis*, New Haven, CT: Yale University Press.

Wade, R. (1982) *Irrigation and Agricultural Politics in South Korea*, Boulder, CO: Westview Press.

Wade, R. (1990) *Governing the Market: Economic Theory and the Role of Government in East Asian Industrialisation*, Princeton, NJ: Princeton University Press.

Wade, R. (1992) East Asia's Economic Success: Conflicting Perspectives, Partial Insights, Shaky Evidence. *World Politics*, 44(2), pp 270–320.

Wade, R. (2000) Governing the Market. A Decade Later. LSE DESTIN Working Paper Series 00-03 (March).

Wade, R. (2003) *Governing the Market: Economic Theory and the Role of Government in East Asian Industrialisation*, 2nd Edition, Princeton, NJ: Princeton University Press.

Walder, A.G. (2002) Privatization and Elite Mobility: Rural China, 1979–1996. Stanford Institute for International Studies A/PARC Working Paper.

Walder, A.G. (2004) The Party Elite and China's Trajectory of Change. *China: An International Journal*, 2(2), pp 189–209.

Waldner, D. (1999) *State Building and Late Development*, Ithaca, NY: Cornell University Press.

Wang, H.H. (2010) *The Chinese Dream: The Rise of the World's Largest Middle Class and What It Means to You*, Brande: Bestseller Press.

Wang, Sh. (1997) The State, Market Economy, and Transition. Department of Government and Public Administration, The Chinese University of Hong Kong.

Wang, Sh. and Hu, A. (2001) *The Chinese Economy in Crisis: State Capacity and Tax Reform*, Armonk: East Gate.

Wedeman, A. (1997) Stealing from the Farmers: Institutional Corruption and the 1992 IOU Crisis. *The China Quarterly*, 152, pp 805–31.

Wedeman, A. (2003) *From Mao to Market: Rent Seeking, Local Protectionism, and Marketization in China*, New York, NY: Cambridge University Press.

Wei, G. and Liu, X. (eds) (2001) *Chinese Nationalism in Perspective: Historical and Recent Cases*, Westport, CT: Greenwood Publishing Group.

Wei, Y., Liu, L., Wu, G. and Zou, L. (eds) (2011) *Energy Economics: CO2 Emissions in China*, Beijing and Berlin: Science Press and Springer.

Weiss, L. (2000) Developmental States in Transition: Adapting, Dismantling, Innovating, not 'Normalizing'. *The Pacific Review*, 13(1), pp 21–55.

Weitzman, M.L. and Xu, Ch. (1994) Chinese Township-Village Enterprises as Vaguely Defined Cooperatives. *Journal of Comparative Economics*, 18, pp 121–45.

Wen J. (2004) *Report on the Work of the Government*, Delivered at the 2nd Session of the 10th National People's Congress). March 5. Available at: www.people.com.cn/GB/shizheng/1024/2394441.html

WEO (World Economic Outlook) (2008) *Financial Stress, Downturns and Recoveries*, Washington, DC: International Monetary Fund.

WEO (2013) WEO Database. Available at: www.imf.org/external/pubs/ft/weo/2013/02/weodata/weoselgr.aspx (accessed 10 November 2013).

White, G. (1984) Changing Relations between State and Enterprise in Contemporary China: Expanding Enterprise Autonomy. In: Maxwell, N. and McFarlane, B. (eds) *China's Changed Road to Development*, Oxford: Pergamon, pp 43–60.

White, G. (1987) The Impact of Economic Reforms in the Chinese Countryside: Towards the Politics of Social Capitalism? *Modern China*, 13(4), pp 411–40.

White, G. (ed) (1988) *Developmental States in East Asia*, New York, NY: Macmillan Press.

White, G. (1996) Corruption and the Transition from Socialism in China. *Journal of Law and Society*, 23(1), pp 149–69.

White, G. (1998) Constructing a Democratic Developmental State. In: Robinson, M. and White, G. (eds) *The Democratic Developmental State: Politics and Institutional Design*, Oxford: Oxford University Press.

White, G. and Wade, R. (1988) Developmental States and Markets in East Asia: An Introduction. In: White, G. (ed) *Developmental States in East Asia*, New York, NY: Macmillan Press.

White, L.T. (1999) *Unstately Power: Volume 1 and 2, Local Causes of China's Intellectual, Legal, and Governmental Reforms*, Armonk: Sharpe.

Whiting, A.S. (1995) Chinese Nationalism and Foreign Policy after Deng. *The China Quarterly*, 142, pp 295–316.

Williamson, J. (1990) What Washington Consensus Means by Policy Reform. In: Williamson, J. (ed) *Latin American Adjustment: How Much Has Happened?*, Washington, DC: Institute for International Economics.

Williamson, J. (2002) *Did the Washington Consensus Fail? Speeches, Testimony, Papers*, Washington, DC: Institute for International Economics.

Williamson, J. (2008) A Short History of the Washington Consensus. In: Serra, N. and Stiglitz, J.E. (eds) *The Washington Consensus Reconsidered: Towards a New Global Governance*, Oxford: Oxford University Press, pp 14–30.

Winch, Ch. (1998) Listian Political Economy: Social Capitalism Conceptualised? *New Political Economy*, 3(2), pp 301–16.

Winckler, E.A. (ed) (1999) *Transition from Communism in China: Institutional and Comparative Analyses*, Boulder, CO: Lynne Rienner Publishers.

Wong, Ch. (1988) Interpreting Rural Industrial Growth in the Post-Mao Period. *Modern China*, 14(1), pp 3–30.

Wong, Ch. (1991) Central–Local Relations in an Era of Fiscal Decline: The Paradox of Fiscal Decentralization in Post-Mao China. *The China Quarterly*, 128, pp 691–715.

Wong, Ch. (1992) Fiscal Reform and Local Industrialization: The Problematic Sequencing of Reform in Post-Mao China. *Modern China*, 18(2), pp 197–227.

Wong, Ch., Heady, C. and Woo, W.T. (1995) *Fiscal Management and Economic Reform in the People's Republic of China*, Hong Kong: Oxford University Press.

Wong, J. (2004) The Adaptive Developmental State in East Asia. *Journal of East Asian Studies*, 4, pp 345–62.

Wong, P.-Y. and Tsang, Sh.-K. (2009) FDI-Driven Trade and Economic Growth in China. A revised version of a paper presented at the HKBU China Studies 20th Anniversary Conference 'China Studies: Past, Present and Future', 23 May.

Woo, J.-E. (1991) *Race to the Swift: The Role of Finance in Korean Industrialization*, New York, NY: Columbia University Press.

Woo, W.T. (1999) The Real Reasons for China's Growth. *The China Journal*, 41, pp 115–37.

Woo, W.T. (2004) Serious Inadequacies of the Washington Consensus: Misunderstanding the Poor by the Brightest. In: Teunissen, J.J. and Akkerman, A. (eds) *Diversity in Development: Reconsidering the Washington Consensus*, The Hague: Forum on Debt and Development (FONDAD).

Woo, W.T. (2011) The Changing Ingredients in Industrial Policy for Economic Growth. Paper presented at the Asia-Pacific Research and Training Network (ARTNeT) Symposium 'Towards a Return of Industrial Policy?', 25–26 July, ESCAP, Bangkok.

Woo-Cumings, M. (ed) (1999) *The Developmental State*, Ithaca, NY: Cornell University Press.

World Bank (1990) *China – Between Plan and Market*, Washington, DC: World Bank.

World Bank (1993) *The East Asian Miracle: Economic Growth and Public Policy*, Washington, DC: World Bank.

World Bank (2014) *Urban China: Toward Efficient, Inclusive, and Sustainable Urbanization*, Washington, DC: World Bank and Development Research Center of the State Council, P.R. China.

Wu, G. (2008) From Post-Imperial to Late Communist Nationalism: Historical Change in Chinese Nationalism from May Fourth to the 1990s. *Third World Quarterly*, 29(3), pp 467–82.

Xia, M. (2000) *The Dual Developmental State: Development Strategy and Institutional Arrangements for China's Transition*, Aldershot: Ashgate.

Xing, Y. (2010) Facts About and Impacts of FDI on China and the World Economy. *China: An International Journal*, 8(2), pp 309–27.

Xu, X. (1998) *China's Financial System under Transition*, New York, NY: St Martin's Press.

Yamazawa, I. (1975) Trade Policy and Changes in Japan's Trade Structure – With Special Reference to Labour-Intensive Manufactures. *The Developing Economies*, 3(4), pp 374–99.

Yang, H. (2008) Decentralisation and Governance Transition: Understanding Administration Reform in China. Paper prepared for the Workshop in Political Theory and Policy Analysis Conference, Indiana University, spring.

Yang, L. and Lim, Ch.-K. (2010) Three Waves of Nationalism in Contemporary China: Sources, Themes, Presentations and Consequences. EAI Working Paper 155.

Yao, Sh., Luo, D. and Loh, L. (2011) On China Monetary Policy and Asset Prices. The University of Nottingham China Policy Institute Discussion Paper 71.

Yao, Y. (2004) Government Commitment and the Outcome of Privatization in China. Governance, Regulation, and Privatization in the Asia-Pacific Region, NBER East Asia Seminar on Economics 12.

You, J. (1998) *China's Enterprise Reform: Changing State/Society Relations after Mao*, London: Routledge.

Young, A. (2000) The Razor's Edge: Distortions and Incremental Reform in the People's Republic of China. *The Quarterly Journal of Economics*, 115(4), pp 1091–35.

Yu, Y. (2010) The Impact of the Global Financial Crisis on the Chinese Economy and China's Policy Responses. TWN (Third World Network) Global Economy Series 25.

Yuan, J.-D., Eden, L. (1992) Export Processing Zones in Asia: A Comparative Study. *Asia Survey*, 32(11) (November), pp 1026–45.

———

Zakaria, F. (1997) The Rise of Illiberal Democracy. *Foreign Affairs*, 76(6), pp 22–43.

Zhang, W.-W. (2000) *Transforming China: Economic Reform and Its Political Implications*, Basingstoke: Macmillan.

Zhao, S. (2000) Chinese Nationalism and Its International Orientations. *Political Science Quarterly*, 115(1), pp 1–33.

Zhao, S. (2004) *A Nation-State by Construction: Dynamics of Modern Chinese Nationalism*, Stanford, CA: Stanford University Press.

Zhao, Z. (2009) *Prisoner of the State. The Secret Journal of Zhao Ziyang*, New York, NY: Simon & Schuster.

Zheng, Y. (1999a) *Discovering Chinese Nationalism in China: Modernization, Identity, and International Relations*, New York, NY: Cambridge University Press.

Zheng, Y. (1999b) Political Incrementalism: Political Lessons from China's 20 Years of Reform. *Third World Quarterly*, 20(6), pp 1157–77.

Zhou, J. and Latorre, M.C (2013) The impact of FDI on the production networks between China and East Asia and the role of the U.S. and ROW as final markets. MPRA Paper 51384, November.

Zweig, D. (2002) *Internationalizing China. Domestic Interests and Global Linkages*, Ithaca, NY: Cornell University Press.

Zysman, J. and Schwartz, A. (eds) (1998) *Enlarging Europe: The Industrial Foundations of a New Political Reality*, Berkeley, CA: University of California Press.

Zysman, J. and Tyson, L. (eds) (1983) *American Industry in International Competition: Government Policies and Corporate Strategies*, Ithaca, NY, and London: Cornell University Press.

Index

Note: page numbers in italic type refer to figures and tables.

A

administration see bureaucracy
Africa 210, 253
'African socialism' 61
Agricultural Bank of China 216
agricultural sector
  development of 193
  domestic investment in 224
  and foreign investment 137–8
  under state-command 70–1
  see also rural economy; rural policies
Akamatsu, K. 10, 21
Albania 109
Allen, F. 71
American system 2
Amsden, A.H. 15, 17, 140
Armenia 109
Arrighi, G. 32–3, 66–7
'Asian socialism' 61
authoritarianism
  and 'collective democracy' 96
  and developmental state 139–45
  legitimacy of power 26, 143–4
  neo-authoritarianism 139, 140, 231
  in post-socialist developmental state 231–2
  relationship with development 22–6
Azerbaijan 109

B

Baek, S.-W. 51
Balcerowicz, Leszek 63
banking sector 86, 137, 214–17, 238
Beeson, M. 43
Beijing Consensus 67
Belarus 110
BeST Consensus 52, 68
'big followership' 17, 174
Block, F. 46
Bosnia and Herzegovina 110, 119
Bramall, Ch. 92, 118, 120, 156–7, 187–8
Breslin, Sh. 49–50, 76, 84, 92–4, 99, 136–7, 205–6, 224
Bulgaria 110
bureaucracy
  in China 78, 85–6, 146–8, 152, 162–5
  in developmental states 27–8, 38–9, 151–2
  institutions 162–5, 233–4

relationship with business 148
relationship with ruling elite 146–8, 152
business actors
  in industrial policy 200–3
  in post-socialist developmental state 239–42
  relationship with state 31, 141, 148
  state-business alliance 16–18, 39, 148, 228–9, 239, 241–2, 248
  see also corruption; SOEs

C

Cai, F. 246
capitalism
  in China 75–7, 94, 160
  and developmental state 30–1
  see also market economy; neo-liberalism
capitalist development, problems of 3
'Catalogue Guiding Investment in Industry' 84, 134, 136–7
catching up
  and developmental state time frame 12–13
  see also technology transfer
CCP (Chinese Communist Party) 69, 74, 78–80, 97, 98–9, 132
CEE (Central and Eastern Europe)
  industrial policy in 173
  influences on transformation in 101–2, 103
  institutionalisation in 233–4
  rural policy in 235–6
  see also Poland
central planning 32, 34, 73–4, 249–50
centralisation 146–8
  see also decentralisation; re-centralisation
chaebols 201
Chan, A. 52
Chand, Gyan 61–2
Chang, H.-J. 36, 37, 168, 170, 241, 253
Chen, A. 155–6
Chen Yun 82, 92, 93, 98
China
  authoritarian state in 139, 140, 231–2
  bureaucracy in 78, 85–6, 146–8, 152, 162–5
  capitalism in 75–7, 94, 160

corruption in 141, 153–7, 234
developmental legitimacy in 144–5, 231
domestic financial assets in 212
financial policies
  banking sector 86, 137, 215–17, 238
  investment policy 223–5
  monetary policy 213–14, 238
  price control 86, 223
  subsidies 218–19, 220–3
future for 244–9
historical economic growth 1
industrial policies
  business actors 141, 148, 201–3,
   239–42
  learning and innovating 183–8
  perspectives on 172, 175
  targeting 189, 190–200
market economy in 159–60
nationalism in 130–8, 235
political freedoms in 145
political reform in 78–81, 96, 231–2
  as PSDS *see* post-socialist
   developmental state
  PST in *see* post-socialist transformation
relational aspect of state in 146–7, 148,
  149, 150–1
rural reform in 87–8, 93, 176–9, 224,
  235–6, 247
socialism in 51, 68–9, 72–7, 96–8, 131,
  188
state interventionism in 161–2, 234
status as developmental state 49–53,
  230–44
strength of state in 140–3, 232
trade policies 205–12, 238–9, 248
China Chamber of International
  Commerce (CCOIC) 209
China Council for the Promotion of
  International Trade (CCPIT) 209
China-ASEAN Free Trade Agreement
  (CAFTA) 210
'Chinese dream' 100
Chung, J.-H. 147
Cimoli, M. 167–8
class see ruling elite; rural elites; working
  class
climate change 162, 195
  see also environmental issues
coalitions
  as part of policy formulation 14–15
Cohen, B.J. 21
Cold War 29–30, 42
collective democracy 96
collective ownership rights 88
collectivism 130, 178
colonialism 2
commodity economy 98
communism 3, 55–7

conglomerates 89, 200–1, 241
coordinated market economy 17
corporatist state 52
corruption 18, 42, 45, 141, 152–7, 234
Croatia 110
Cumings, B. 16, 28, 29, 30, 36, 189
cumulative liberalisation index (CLI) 108

D

dazhai model 70–1
de-collectivisation 93
debt crisis 65
decentralisation in China 90–1, 147
  and developmental state 50
  fiscal 220
  and political reform 80
  and state-command 71
  and strength of state 141
defence industrialisation 188
defensive nationalism 133
democracy
  Chinese collective democracy 96
  in Japan 139
  legitimacy of power 26, 143–4
  relationship with development 22–6
democratisation 57–8, 80–1
Deng Xiaoping 84, 92, 94, 97
developing countries, Chinese relations
  with 210
development
  and end of developmental states 12–13
  measuring 118–20
  models of 1–5
   see also developmental state; post-
    socialist developmental state
  regional differences before
   transformation 101–2
  relationship with political system 22–6
  role of financial policy 212–13
  role of industrial policy 169
  role of industrial revolution 1–2
  role of state 3–4, 41
developmental legitimacy 143–5, 231
developmental state (DS)
  China's status as 49–53, 230–44
  concept of 3–4, 7–8, 40–1
  contemporary relevance of 41–9
  economic arrangements 30–9, 158–66
  and economic nationalism 20–2,
   129–38
  geographical aspects 9–11
  influence in China 5–6
  policies 18–20, 173–5
   financial *see* financial policies
   industrial *see* industrial policies
   rural 176–9
   trade 174, 203–12
  political arrangements 22–30, 139–45

post-socialist and historical comparisons
123–6, 228–9
and post-socialist transformation in
China 72, 77, 85, 91, 242–3
relational aspects 13–18
business-ruling elite 146–8
corruption 152–7
state-business 148
state-society 149–51
time frame for 11–13, 175
transferable lessons 48–9
see also post-socialist developmental
state
Dickson, B.J. 79
Ding, Ch. 245
Dirlik, A. 76–7
domestic consumption 211, 248
domestic economy
protection of 136–8
see also import discrimination policies
Doner, R, F. 15, 17
Dosi, G. 167–8
Du, Y. 246
dual transition 77

E

East Asia
development and geopolitical location
29–30, 42
developmental state in 10–11, 48
industrial policies in 169–72
political systems and development in 24
economic arrangements, of developmental
states 30–9, 158–66
economic bureaucracy 38–9
economic growth
early period of 1
market compared with state-command
systems 59–60
see also GDP
economic liberalisation
as aspect of post-socialist transformation
58, 59
in China 83–5, 134–5, 244, 248–9
and financial crisis 44–5
and nationalism 134–5, 235
and trade policies 205–6
economic migrants 159, 179
economic nationalism 20–1, 129–38, 235
Economic Planning Board (EPB) (Korea)
164–5
economic reform, in China 83–91, 96,
232–4
economics, relationship with politics 2–3
economies of scale 171–2
education 182–3, 188
electronics industry 192, 193–4
elites see ruling elite; rural elites

embedded autonomy 14, 18, 23, 50–1,
150, 232
embeddedness 18, 149
energy industries 184, 191, 194–5, 196
environmental issues
Chinese policy on 195–6
and developmental trajectory 229,
245–7
and industrial policy 194–6
need for state intervention 162, 252
neglected in China 141, 142–3
and renewable energy 184, 191
Estonia 111
European Bank for Reconstruction and
Development (EBRD) 108
European Union (EU) 186–7, 253–4
Evans, P. 14, 18, 23, 38, 48–9
exchange rate 214
export dependency 211
export support policies 203–4, 208–12
in China's post-socialist developmental
state 238
financial support 213–14, 219–20,
221–3, 225
future in China 248
export-oriented economy 76, 237
export-oriented industrialisation (EOI)
19, 203, 208
export-processing zones 208
external political influences on
development 28–30, 42

F

FDI (foreign direct investment) 224–5
Fewsmith, J. 133–4
financial crisis 42, 44–5, 244, 251–2
financial policies
banking sector 86, 137, 214–17, 238
investment policy 223–5
monetary policy 213–14, 238
price control policy 86, 223
relationship with development 212–13
relationship with industrial policies 172,
174–5
subsidies 217–23
financial system
reform in China 86–7
under state-command in China 71
fiscal decentralisation 220
fiscal re-centralisation 221
Fonda, S. 10
food sector 137–8
foreign investment 136–8, 222, 224–5
foreign trade
importance to China 75–6
see also technology transfer; trade
policies
forward engineering 184

free market economy 33
Freedom House (FH) index 118
FSU (Former Soviet Union)
  corruption in 157
  industrial policy in 173
  institutionalisation in 233–4
  see also Russia

G

Gaidar, Yegor 63
Gallagher, M.E. 150
GDP
  as indicator of development 119, *121*,
    122, 124–5
  market compared with state-command
    systems 59, *60*
geo-economic position, regional
  differences before transformation 102
geographical aspects
  of developmental state 9–11
  of post-socialist transformation 60–2
Georgia 111
Gereffi, G. 10
Global Economic Crisis 136, 161, 162,
  196, 211, 212, 221, 223, 230, 251, 252
global economy 37, 42–3, 44, 45–6
globalisation
  impact on China's trade policy 205–6,
    211
  impact on post-socialist developmental
    states 229
  inequities of 45, 47
gradual reform 63–4, 81–3, 105
'Great Leap Forward' 70
Guo, R. 91
Guo, S. 33, 58, 87

H

Haggard, S. 10, 16, 18, 19, 27, 28
Hamilton, Alexander 2
harmonious society 75, 99–100
Hayashi, Sh. 22–3
He, Q. 151
heavy and chemical industries (HCI) 189,
  190–1, 193, 237
Heiduk, G. 244
household responsibility system (HRS)
  88, 178, 236
Howell, J. 8, 50–1
Hu Jintao 99, 141–2
Huang, Y. 126–7, 202, 216
Huchet, J.-F. 201–2
Hughes, Ch. 131–2, 134–5
human capital 182–3, 188
Human Development Index (HDI) 119,
  120–2, 123, 124, 181, 182
human rights 145
Hungary 111

I

ideology 234–5
  see also nationalism
import discrimination policies 203–8,
  238–9
import-substitution industrialisation (ISI)
  19, 203, 207
importation of technology see technology
  transfer
In der Heiden, P.T. 245
India 61–2
industrial policies
  defining 167–8
  of developmental states 18–20, 179–80
    business actors 200–3
    learning and innovating 180–8
    targeting 189–200
    financial support for 212–13, 217–20,
      221–2, 223–4
  future in China 248
  perceptions of 167–76
  of post-socialist developmental state
    236–8, 250–1
  relationship with trade and financial
    policy 172, 173–5
  under state-command 71
industrial rationalisation 171
industrial revolution 1–2
industrial sectors
  categorisation and investment in 134,
    136–8, 224–5
  targeting and development of 189–200,
    237–8
industrial structure policy 171
industrial upgrading 20, 30
  see also technology transfer
industrialisation, and establishment of
  developmental state 176–9
industry, restructuring of socialist 91, 229
inequalities
  in developmental states 16, 158–9
  and globalisation 45, 47
  and marginalisation in China 75, 126–7,
    150–1, 159, 242
infrastructure development 191, 193
innovation
  and industrial development 180–8
  and knowledge-intensive industries
    196–7
institutional corruption 155
institutions of developmental state 26–7,
  38–9, 162–5, 233–4
  to promote exports 209–10
  see also bureaucracy
intellectual property rights (IPR) 143,
  185, 186, 238, 239
interventionism see state interventionism

investment policy
  in developmental states 223–5
  see also foreign investment
isolationism policy 2, 84

J

Japan
  bureaucracy in 164
  democratic system in 139
  developmental legitimacy in 144
  developmental state as obstacle 43
  financial policies 214, 215, 218, 219–20,
    223, 224
  industrial policies 170–2, 175
    business actors 200–1, 203
    learning and innovating 181–2, 187
    targeting 189, 190, 191, 197, 199
  nationalism in 130, 134
  political systems in 24, 231
  relational aspect of state in 146, 148,
    149, 150
  relationship with Korea and Taiwan 30
  rural reform in 176–9
  security and US support for 29–30
  state interventionism in 160
  strength of state in 140
  trade policies 203–4, 210
Jefferson, J.H. 107
Jeon, J.-G. 11
Jiang Zemin 98
Johanssen, L. 178
Johnson, Ch.A. 9, 25, 26, 170–1

K

Kagami, M. 171–2
Kazakhstan 112
keiretsu conglomerates 200–1
Kim, K.S. 172
knowledge-intensive industries 190, 192,
  196–7
Kohli, A. 30, 188, 201
Kolodko, G.W. xi, 1, 55, 58, 63, 67, 106
Korea
  bureaucracy in 151–2, 164–5
  corruption in 153
  developmental legitimacy in 144
  financial crisis in 44
  financial policies 213, 214–15, 217–18,
    220, 224
  industrial policies 172, 175
    business actors 201
    learning and innovating 182–3, 187
    targeting 189, 190, 191, 197, 199, 200
  nationalism in 130
  relational aspect of state in 15, 146, 148,
    149, 150
  relationship with Japan and Taiwan 30
  rural reform in 176–9

socialist industry in 188
state interventionism in 160
strength of state in 140
trade policies 204–5, 210
US support for 29–30
Kornai, J. 64
Kyrgyzstan 112

L

labour see working class
labour-intensive industries 194
land ownership 89
  reforms 16, 176–8, 247
landlords see rural elites
Lange, Oskar 34
Latin America
  developmental state in 10
  industrial policies in 169–70
  post-socialist transformation in 60–1
  and Washington Consensus 65
Latvia 112
leadership
  and strength of state 141–2
  see also ruling elite
learning phase of industrial development
  180–8
Leftwich, A. 15, 24, 26, 118–19, 124, 145
legislation and regulations 85, 141, 142–3,
  185, 186
legitimacy of power 26, 143–5
Levi-Faur, D. 20–1
light industry 189–90, 191–2, 194, 198,
  237
Limongi, F. 23
Lin, Ch. 68, 74, 94, 131
Lin J.Y. 2, 73
List, Friedrich 2–3, 4, 20
Lithuania 113
Liu Shucheng 97
Loriaux, M. 36
Lu, X. 155, 156

M

machinery industry 192, 193–4
marginalisation see societal marginalisation
market economy
  and post-socialist transformation 58
  in China 159–60
  compared with state-command system
    59–60
  nature of 32–4
  and state-business alliance 17
market institutionalisation 59, 85–7
market socialism 33–5, 72–3
marketisation 58
Marxist theory 56
  and China 96–101
mercantilism 2

microeconomic restructuring 59, 87–91
migrant workers 159, 179
Ministry of Commerce (MOFCOM) (China) 163
Ministry of International Trade and Industry (MITI) (Japan) 164, 181
Moldova 113
monetary policy 213–14, 238
Mongolia 113
Montenegro 114
Monterey Consensus 67

N

National Development and Reform Commission, (NDRC) 162–3, 164, 165
nationalism 20–1, 129–38, 235
Naughton, B. 94, 191, 192, 208, 237
neo-authoritarianism 93, 139, 140, 231
neo-liberalism 5, 36–7, 41
  and financial crisis 44–5
  limitations of 249, 250
  rejection of 252–3
'New Left' 132
North East Asia, interdependencies 30

O

OECD (Organisation for Economic Co-operation and Development) 86–7, 206
Oi, J.C. 52
opening up 44, 84–5, 93–7
  see also economic liberalisation; trade policies
ownership reforms
  in China 58–9, 87–90, 201–2
  land ownership 16, 89, 176–8, 247
  in Russia and Poland 239–40

P

partial reform equilibrium 81
partnership, EU and China 186–7
People's Bank of China (PBC) 71, 213–14
pilot agencies 39, 162–5, 233
plan-rational system 31, 73
Poland
  GDP compared with Spain 59, 60
  industrial policy in 173
  institutionalisation in 234
  privatisation in 239–40
  radical reform in 63
  rural policy in 178, 235–6
  transition indicators 114
policies
  future in China 248–9
  in post-socialist developmental states 235–9

see also financial policies; industrial policies; rural policies; trade policies
policy loans 217–18
political arrangements
  of developmental state 22–30, 139–45
  regional differences before transformation 102–3
political economy 2–3, 21, 160
political elite see ruling elite
political liberalisation 80–1, 249
political reforms
  categorising 108, 118
  in China 78–81, 96, 231–2
political repression 145
political systems, and development 22–6
politics, relationship with economics 2–3
popular nationalism 133
post-communist transformation 55–7
post-socialism, Dirlik's concept of 76–7
post-socialist developmental state (PSDS)
  and China 6, 243–4
    business actors 239–42
    development policies 235–9
    economic ideology 234–5
    economic reform 232–4
    inequalities 242
    political reform 231–2
    state interventionism 234
  compared with historical developmental state 123–6, 228–9
  effectiveness of 249–51
  future growth within 247, 248–9
  nature of 227–30
  transferable lessons of 253–4
post-socialist transformation (PST)
  in China
    Chinese perspective 95–100
    chronology 91–5
    developmental exceptionality of 120–7
    and developmental state 5–6, 242–3
    economic reforms 83–91
    GDP and HDI data 120–1, 125
    influence of initial conditions on 101, 102–3
    influence of policy choices on 103–4
    political reforms and gradualism 78–83
    process of 72–7
    state-command period 68–72
  debates on process of 62–8
  and developmental state comparisons 123–6
  geographical dimension 60–2
  and industrial policy 173, 198
  measurement of 107–8
  national comparisons 108, 109–17
    categorisation 105–6

GDP and HDI data 120–6
  influence of initial conditions 101–3
  influence of policy choices 101,
    103–4
  and neoliberalism 5
  overview 55–62
Post-Washington Consensus 67
power, legitimacy to 26, 143–5
predatory states 13–14
price control policy 86, 223
private sector 201–2, 239
privatisation 58–9, 87–90
  in Poland and Russia 239–40
procurement practices 136–8
Programme for Science and Technology
  Development 185–6
property rights 247
  see also intellectual property rights; land
    ownership
protectionism 2, 36, 42, 46, 102, 206
protectionist policies 42, 46
  see also import discrimination policies
Przeworski, A. 23
public consultations 149

Q

quota systems (imports) 204, 205

R

R&D (research and development) 181–6,
  187
radical reform 63–4, 105
Ramo, J.C. 67–8
Rawski, T.G. 107
re-centralisation 90, 221
readjustment period in China 92, 93
reforms
  radical versus gradual 63–4, 105
  see also economic reform; political
    reform
relational aspects of developmental state
  13–18, 146–57
renewable energy 184, 191
rent seeking 154–5
Richet, X. 201–2
Robinson, M. 22, 23
Romania 114
ruling elite
  and legitimacy of power 26
  and predatory states 13–14
  relationship with bureaucracy 146–8,
    152
  relationship with business 148
  relationship with society 149–50
  see also rural elites
rural cooperative foundations (RCFs) 216
rural credit cooperatives (RCCs) 216
rural economy

Chinese state-command of 70–1
  and establishment of developmental state
    177–8
  role of banking sector 216
  see also agricultural sector; rural
    policies
rural elites 16, 176–7
rural governance, democratisation of 81
rural policies 87–8, 93, 176–9, 224,
  235–6, 247
rural reforms, in China 93, 247
Russia
  industrial policy in 173
  influences on post-socialist
    transformation in 103–4
  institutionalisation in 233–4
  privatisation in 239–40
  radical reform in 63
  transition indicators 115

S

Sachs, Jeffrey 63, 64, 66, 67, 233
scientific concept of development 97, 99,
  100, 101
Scott, B.R. 252
security issues
  and development 29–30, 42
  and nationalisation 132–3
Serbia 115
Shirk, S.L. 141–2
Singapore 11
Slovakia 115
Slovenia 116
Smith, Adam 1, 2, 66–7
socialism
  in China 51, 68–9, 72–7, 96–8, 131, 188
  defining communism and 55–7
  emergence of 3
  industrial development under 187–8
  market socialism 33–5, 72–3
  relationship with developmental state
    31–2, 35, 51
  restructuring industry after 91, 229
  see also central planning
socialist developmental state 31–2, 35, 51
socialist market economy 75, 98
societal marginalisation 75, 126–7, 150–1,
  159
societal mobilisation 130
society, relationship with state 13–16, 38,
  149–51
SOEs (state owned enterprises)
  continued role of 248
  and corruption 155–6
  and economic reform 87, 89–90
  and industrial development 202
  in post-socialist developmental state
    239, 240–2

privileged position of 137
and state-business relations 148
subsidies for 218–19
soft state 28, 139–42
Soviet Union see USSR
Spain, GDP compared with Poland 59, 60
special economic zones (SEZs) 208–9,
 221, 222, 225
standardisation policies 206–7
state
 and globalisation 44, 45–6
 importance of role 251–2
 predatory and developmental types
  13–14
 role in Chinese banking 216–17
 role in development 3–4, 41
 role redefined in post-socialist
  developmental state 228
 strength and capacity of 28, 36, 139–42,
  232
 see also bureaucracy; ruling elite
state capitalism 33–4
state interventionism 35–6, 37–9, 46,
 160–2, 234, 252–3
 see also policies
state owned enterprises see SOEs
state-business alliance 16–18, 39, 148,
 228–9, 239, 241–2, 248
state-business relations 31, 141, 148
state-command system 34, 59–60, 68–72,
 249–50
state-society relations 13–16, 38, 149–51
Stiglitz, J.E. 167–8, 252
strong state 22, 28, 36, 140
Stubbs, R. 8, 12, 15, 28
subsidies 217–23

T

Taiwan
 relationship with Japan and Korea 30
 rural reform in 176–7
 socialism and industry in 188
 US support of 29–30
Tajikistan 116
targeting, of industry for development
 189–200, 237–8
tariffs on imports 204–6, 210
tax policies 219–23
technological development see R&D;
 technology transfer
technology transfer 181–2, 183, 184–5,
 186–7, 197
textile industry 191
time frame, for developmental state
 11–13, 175
totalitarianisation 105–6
township-and-village enterprises (TVEs)
 88, 179

trade policies
 in China's post-socialist developmental
  state 238–9
 in developmental states 174, 203–12
 emergence of trade liberalisation 2
 financial support for exports 213–14,
  219–20, 221–3, 225
 future in China 248
 relationship with industrial policies 172,
  173–5
transformational vulnerability 228
transformative state, Weiss' concept of 12
transitional depression 119–20, 124
Turkmenistan 116

U

Ukraine 117
ul Haque, I. 168
Unger, J. 52
urbanisation 176, 245
USA
 state intervention and protection 2, 46
 support of capitalist East Asia 29–30, 42
USSR
 and post-socialist transformation 101,
  103, 105
 see also FSU
Uzbekistan 117

W

Wade, R. 17, 31
Walder, A.G. 87
Waldner, D. 15, 16, 27
Washington Consensus 64–7, 232, 250
Wedeman, A. 155
Weiss, L. 8, 12, 44–6
Wen Jiabao 84, 99, 141–2, 196, 211
White, G. 22, 23, 24, 31, 153, 154, 155
Winckler, E.A. 105–6
working class 16, 73, 150–1
 see also inequalities
World Bank 36, 75, 245
World Trade Organisation (WTO) 84, 94,
 161, 205

X

Xi Jinping 85, 106, 247

Y

Yao, Y. 89
Young, A. 83

Z

Zhang, W.-W. 78
Zhao Ziyang 92, 93–4
Zheng, Y. 80